Markets

THE ECONOMICS OF
Labour Markets

PETER FALLON & DONALD VERRY

Philip Allan
OXFORD AND NEW JERSEY

First published 1988 by

PHILIP ALLAN PUBLISHERS LIMITED
MARKET PLACE
DEDDINGTON
OXFORD OX5 4SE (UK)

and

171 FIRST AVENUE
ATLANTIC HIGHLANDS
NEW JERSEY 07716 (USA)

© Peter Fallon and Donald Verry, 1988

British Library Cataloguing in Publication Data
Fallon, Peter
  The economics of labour markets.
  1. Labour market
  I. Title II. Verry, Donald
  331.12

  ISBN 0-86003-068-7
  ISBN 0-86003-173-X Pbk

Library of Congress Cataloging in Publication Data
Fallon, Peter, 1946–
  The economics of labour markets/Peter Fallon and Donald Verry.
  p. cm.
  Bibliography: p.
  Includes index.
  ISBN 0-86003-068-7. ISBN 0-86003-173-X (pbk.)
  1. Labor economics. 2. Labor supply. I. Verry, Donald.
II. Title.
HD4901.F27 1988   88-22221
331—dc19   CIP

Typeset by MHL Typesetting Ltd, Coventry
Printed and bound in Great Britain at the Alden Press, Oxford

Contents

Preface

Labour economics today is almost unrecognisable as the subject that we studied as undergraduates twenty years ago. While it is true that most branches of economics have undergone substantial change over the same period, in few cases has the transformation been quite as dramatic as in labour economics. There are two main reasons for this. Firstly, what used to be a largely descriptive and institutional subject, often virtually synonymous with industrial relations, has become more analytical. Secondly, the subject has become more quantitative. Some very advanced econometric techniques are now commonly used in labour economics research.

It is perhaps debatable whether such changes have been for the better. We believe that, on balance, they have been. This book aims to give an overall view of how the subject looks today, with respect both to its analytical foundations and some recent applied empirical research.

Readers may be interested to know more precisely where we stand, and therefore what line this book takes, with respect to the trends mentioned above. We would be disturbed to see the subject becoming unduly abstract. We do not believe that labour economics can be studied in a historical or institutional vacuum. Nevertheless pure description is rarely very enlightening. The best of current research in labour economics, whether theoretical or empirical, does not ignore institutions, custom or convention but attempts to analyse what constraints they impose on more traditional economic motivations such as cost minimisation, profit maximisation and utility maximisation. Thus, for example, topics such as labour market discrimination, labour contracts, the wage and employment effects of trade unions clearly have customary and institutional aspects which cannot be ignored, but their treatment today is markedly different from what it would have been twenty years ago. In particular, each of these subjects is now treated much more rigorously so as to spell out more clearly why such institutions and conventions may have arisen in the first place and what their implications may be for the operation of labour markets.

With respect to the increasing 'quantification' of the subject, we do not believe that the application of state-of-the-art empirical techniques is mere academic exhibitionism, although of course that is a danger one must recognise. One of the messages of our book is that technique can be crucial in resolving empirical questions. If simple and conventional techniques produced similar results to newer and more sophisticated empirical approaches, there would be no justification for bothering with the added complexity — we certainly do not believe that there is any virtue in novelty or complexity for their own sakes. However, sometimes the simplest approach is *not* the best so we attempt to introduce the reader to the essence of some more complex empirical techniques. To do this we have chosen to forgo comprehensiveness, enabling us to describe in more detail the approach used in a selection of studies which we consider to be important and influential both in terms of their methodology and results. In addition, as this is a labour economics and not an econometrics text, we aim to provide the non-specialist with an intuitive understanding of what is going on even if some rigour is sacrificed in the process.

The extent to which we incorporate both the methodology and the results of recent empirical research is one of the ways in which this book differs from other labour economics texts. Another is that we provide extensive background material on each of the subjects we consider. In our teaching experience we have found that we cannot take for granted that students are well informed about the current characteristics of the labour market or about historical trends (in activity rates, employment patterns, union membership, unemployment and the like). Thus in each major section of the book we provide at least the essential facts, and sometimes attempt to go beyond an elementary outline. Furthermore, we attempt to provide this information for more than one country in order to set each country's experience in context. In some cases statistical trends prove to be pervasive — the secular increase in married women's participation rates and the rapid growth of unemployment following the 'oil shocks' of the 1970s are good examples. In other cases the differences between countries, in the degree of centralisation of wage setting mechanisms, for example, are revealing.

Our teaching experience has impressed upon us that, no matter how good in other respects, a text in which all (or the vast majority) of the applications and empirical illustrations refer to the USA will not be popular with British students. By the same token a British text would be unsatisfactory to American students. In writing this book we have tried hard not to be parochial. We hope the book will appeal to an international audience. We mostly compare the United Kingdom and the United States, but where space and data availability permit we provide information on other countries as well; mostly those belonging to the OECD.[1]

While the greatest care has been taken to ensure that the data we present for different countries are based on consistent definitions and measurement procedures, it is well known that international comparisons are fraught with difficulties and can be subject to substantial error. We do not repeat this caveat every time we present such comparisons, but it should be borne in mind throughout. We believe that the possibility of some inaccuracy in this respect is an acceptable price to pay in order to avoid the excessive concentration on a single country's labour market.

Although no previous knowledge of labour economics is required in order to read this book it is somewhat more advanced than some labour economics texts on the market. The reason for this is that we believe a gap exists between what students encounter in a basic text and what they are expected to read in specialist journals. Sometimes textbooks will present some of the results of recent empirical research, but the student has little idea how such results are arrived at. This book attempts to bridge, or at least to narrow, this gap. Of course it is not possible, or even desirable, to eliminate it entirely. Frontier research will always utilise theory and empirical methods whose detail and technical sophistication are beyond undergraduates. However, we do believe that simplification and clear exposition can make some of the methods and problems of empirical research accessible to a wider audience. This is what we have tried to do. In doing so we have chosen to explain the empirical methodology and results of a few selected studies, used as examples, rather than attempt comprehensive surveys of the empirical research in each topic. The sheer volume of such research makes a comprehensive survey of any one area, let alone the whole subject, quite impossible within the confines of a single text.

Most of the material in the book should be easily accessible to undergraduates (or first-year graduate students) who have already acquired a good background in intermediate economic theory (especially microeconomics). A basic knowledge of quantitative methods in economics would also be helpful, although there are substantial portions of the book which are quite accessible to readers without this background. To preserve the flow of the main text some of the more technically demanding material has been relegated to appendices. These will appeal more to graduate students and those undergraduates with some quantitative background.

However, the book is not intended exclusively for a student audience. We believe that it contains some sections which will be of interest to applied economists in government or industry, or even to the interested lay reader. Probably of greatest interest to these groups are the sections dealing with the factual background to the various topics covered, and the discussions about policy. Much of the pure theory is in separate sections and can be avoided by the reader with more applied interests. However, the complete separation of theoretical and applied analysis is not possible or desirable. So, while we aim broadly to keep them separate, we have not been slavish in the pursuit of this objective. Where small amounts of extra theory are required to explain some empirical research we have included it at the appropriate place in the largely empirical chapters. Wage differentials and trade unions are topics which each have a single chapter devoted to them in which theoretical and empirical material is integrated.

To enable us to treat the topics we have included in the depth we believe to be appropriate, we had to exclude several topics which are sometimes found in labour economics textbooks. While no formal exclusion criteria were adopted, the objective was to write a microeconomic text on labour markets in developed economies. Thus macroeconomic topics such as the theory and empirical estimation of the Phillips curve (in either its original or expectations-augmented form) are not discussed in any detail. However, we have tried to be flexible. The chapters on unemployment are a case in point. In writing these we found it was unrealistic to limit ourselves to a purely microeconomic treatment, so, although the focus remains microeconomic, some macroeconomic aspects are included. By the same token there is little here on labour markets in less developed countries. Some of the general principles we discuss apply to such economies, but an adequate treatment would require a book of its own. This is also true of labour in planned socialist economies. Our book is limited to the analysis of labour markets in the mixed economies of North America, Europe and Scandanavia, and Australasia — broadly speaking to the OECD countries.[1] (Of course there is also great diversity *within* this group of countries and we would not claim that a single approach will be equally relevant to them all.)

The extent of our coverage of unemployment reflects the fact that the book was conceived and written during the deepest recession since the Great Depression of the 1930s. At the time of going to press, unemployment is falling slightly in all OECD countries, although still extremely high by historical standards. We would be delighted if unemployment were to fall to substantially lower levels during the working lifetime of this book. However, the recessions of the early 1970s and 1980s have shattered the illusions, fostered during the 1950s and the first half of the 1960s, that rapid economic growth could be sustained indefinitely with only minor fluctuations around a long-run trend, and that growth combined with the tools of Keynesian aggregate demand management had made modern economies proof against mass unemployment.

Many people have helped with this book. Students and colleagues at the University of Sussex and at University College, London, bore the brunt of much trial and some error. We would especially like to thank Nick Rau and an anonymous reader for reading and commenting on draft chapters. Barbara Fallon and Camilla Loewe, apart from providing valuable typing assistance, have had to live with this project for much longer than they (or we) could have imagined — they did so cheerfully and supportively.

July 1988   Peter Fallon
                                                                                   Donald Verry

---

1. The OECD countries are: Australia, Austria, Belgium, Canada, Denmark, Finland, France, the Federal Republic of Germany, Greece, Iceland, Ireland, Italy, Japan, Luxembourg, the Netherlands, New Zealand, Norway, Portugal, Spain, Sweden, Switzerland, Turkey, the United Kingdom and the United States.

1

The Theory of Labour Supply

1.1 Introduction

Labour supply decisions affect the well-being of individuals and, when aggregated, the welfare of the whole economy, in two ways. Firstly, because labour is a factor of production, labour supply decisions, in conjunction with the demand side of the labour market, affect the amounts of goods and services available for consumption at any given time. Secondly, labour time itself, or its complement, leisure, directly affects an individual's well-being. Thus it is reasonable to assume that an individual or an economy that can consume a given amount of goods and services at a lower cost in terms of labour time (i.e. can combine given amounts of goods and services with greater leisure) is better off than an individual or economy producing and consuming the same quantities of goods and services with more labour (less leisure).

A succinct analytical way of putting this point is to write the individual's utility function[1] as

$$U = U(X, L)$$

where U is the individual's utility

         X is a composite of all consumer goods and services consumed by the individual

         L is the individual's leisure time

and where we assume

$$\frac{\partial U}{\partial X} > 0$$

and $\dfrac{\partial U}{\partial L} > 0$

1

If we call H hours of work and T total time available, then $T - L = H$. Thus

$$\frac{\partial U}{\partial H} < 0$$

for a given T. But as, *ceteris paribus*, more labour supply leads to more goods and services ($\partial X/\partial H > 0$), the basic problem faced both by individuals and economies is to trade off the added utility gained from greater consumption against the reduced utility resulting from the greater work effort required to produce such consumption.[2] Although many modifications to this simple characterisation of the labour supply decision are required, some of which are considered below, it does convey the essence of the problem. For example we can see straight away that in spite of the widespread concern with the possible disincentive effects of various policies (e.g. progressive income taxation) it is not possible to say a priori that a policy which results in people working less (we are not saying that progressive income tax always *does* have this effect, see below) is necessarily an undesirable policy. Whether less work (more leisure) is 'good' or 'bad' depends on the relative importance individuals and society attach to consumption and leisure.

In other words, it is important to separate the positive aspects of labour supply (how will labour supply be affected by a given change in, say, tax rates?) from the normative aspects (how is social welfare affected by the labour supply consequences of a change in tax rates?). The remainder of this chapter concentrates primarily on positive analysis.

To talk of 'labour supply' begs many questions because there are many dimensions of labour supply. Some of the more important of these are:

(i)   the decision to participate or not participate in the labour force (including the age distribution of such participation as affected by educational decisions, retirement decisions, etc.);
(ii) the number of hours worked per week and weeks worked per year;
(iii) the allocation of non-leisure time between paid and unpaid work (market work and work in the home);
(iv) the intensity of effort brought to each given hour of labour supplied;
(v)   the amount and type of skill that participants bring to the labour market.

There exists little theoretical or empirical analysis of (iv), work intensity,[3] while the analysis of (v), the supply of skills, properly belongs to the analysis of human capital formation and is covered in Chapter 5. The remainder of this chapter deals with topics (i) and (iii): the labour force participation decision and the supply and allocation of work hours. We begin with the neoclassical model of an individual's labour supply at a given point in time and then discuss various modifications and developments of that model.

1.2 The Supply of Hours

The Basic Model

Consider an individual with a utility function represented by the equation above, i.e.:

$$U = U(X, L) \tag{1.1}$$

The individual is assumed to maximise utility subject to the budget constraint, which can be written as

$$PX \leq WH + Y \tag{1.2a}$$

or

$$X \leq \frac{W}{P} H + \frac{Y}{P} \tag{1.2b}$$

where P is the price of the composite commodity X, W is the nominal (money) wage rate and Y is nominal non-labour income.

The maximisation of equation (1.1) subject to (1.2b) yields the labour supply function[4]

$$H = f\left(\frac{W}{P}, \frac{Y}{P}\right) \tag{1.3a}$$

The number of hours of labour supplied by an individual depends on the *real* wage he faces, and on his endowment of (real) non-labour income.[5] Without any loss of generality we now set $P = 1$ and rewrite the labour supply function as

$$H = f(w, y) \tag{1.3b}$$

in which w and y are henceforth to be understood as real wage and real non-labour income.

The analysis is amenable to a simple diagrammatic treatment. In Figure 1.1 total time available (T) is shown on the horizontal axis and is divided between leisure (L) and work (H). The left-hand vertical axis measures the sum of labour and non-labour income (and, therefore, consumption possibilities). The right-hand axis measures real non-labour income only. The individual's budget constraint is a straight line with slope[6] w (showing the rate of transformation of working hours into labour income), intersecting the right-hand axis at his non-labour income y. The vertical height of this budget constraint for any given H is the equivalent of the right-hand side of the budget constraint (equation (1.2b)). The individual has an indifference map which is the diagrammatic equivalent of equation (1.1), and is assumed to choose his hours of work in such a way as to reach the highest indifference curve attainable with his particular budget constraint. In our diagram

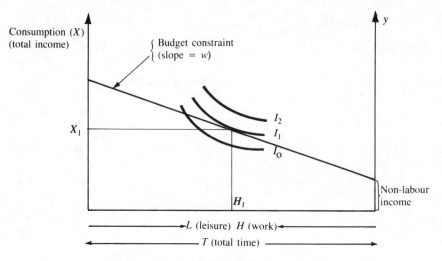

Figure 1.1   The Individual's Labour Supply

he works H_1 hours (per week) and secures a total income of $wH_1 + y$. This is a useful diagrammatic device which we use again in this and subsequent chapters.

The Effect of Tax Changes in the Basic Model

Having derived the labour supply function, it is of interest to use it to analyse how hours of work vary with the arguments in the supply function w, y.[7] The effects of wage changes are especially important for estimating the labour supply response to changes in tax rates (which change the net wage). Consider a wage increase. We are interested in evaluating $\partial H/\partial w$, the 'uncompensated' or 'total' wage effect. As in the standard analysis of consumer demand (of which labour supply analysis is a special case) there will be a substitution effect $(\partial H/\partial w)_S$ whose sign, given the usual assumptions about indifference curves, is unambiguously positive (the increase in the price of leisure reduces the demand for leisure and H increases)[8] and an income effect (provided that leisure is a normal good the increase in the budget increases the demand for it, and H increases). The sign of $\partial H/\partial w$, depends on which effect predominates. The Slutsky decomposition of $\partial H/\partial w$ is[9]

$$\frac{\partial H}{\partial w} = \left(\frac{\partial H}{\partial w}\right)_s + H\left(\frac{\partial H}{\partial y}\right) \tag{1.4}$$

or, multiplying throughout by w/H,

Wage elasticity   = substitution + $\dfrac{wH}{y}$ × income elasticity
(uncompensated)   elasticity

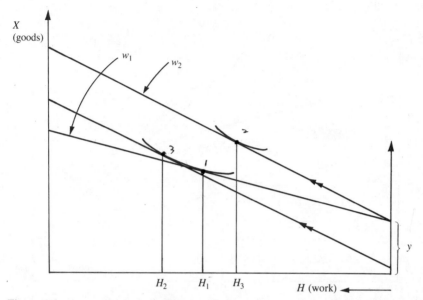

Figure 1.2   The Individual's Labour Supply Response to an Increase in the Net Wage

The above analysis of the effect of a change in the wage can be illustrated using the diagrammatic apparatus of Figure 1.1. In Figure 1.2 the increase in the wage from w_1 to w_2 is represented by the increase in the slope of the budget constraint. The substitution effect causes hours worked to increase from H_1 to H_2. The income effect causes H to fall from H_2 to H_3 and the net effect, H_1 to H_3, shows that in this case the increase in the wage has caused hours worked to *fall*; we are on the backward bending portion of the labour supply curve. Supposing now that we wish to examine the labour supply response to a change in *both* w and y. Differentiating equation (1.3b) totally, and substituting equation (1.4) (the Slutsky equation) yields[10]

$$\mathrm{d}H = \left(\frac{\partial H}{\partial w} \right)_{\mathrm{s}} \mathrm{d}w + \frac{\partial H}{\partial y} (H\mathrm{d}w + \mathrm{d}y) \qquad (1.5)$$

To conclude this section we explain why it is not always sufficient simply to know the net effect of changes in the wage rate on hours worked — there are circumstances in which we need to evaluate the income and substitution effects separately. In Figure 1.3, *abc* is a pre-tax budget constraint.

Suppose that a tax on earnings is introduced with no exceptions. The new budget constraint is *ad*, with a new net wage of w_2. In this case the effect of the tax is measured by the uncompensated wage effect, $\partial H / \partial w$, from equation (1.3b). If this is zero the individual's equilibrium will shift from A to B — the income and substitution effects are exactly offsetting and taxation has no effect on hours worked.

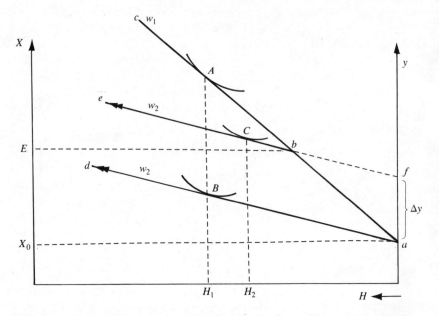

Figure 1.3   The Effect of a Tax Change Allowing for an Exemption Level (B)

Now allow the first $£(E - X_0)$ of earnings to be tax exempt. The budget constraint is now *abe* and the new equilibrium is at point C. The uncompensated wage effect, $\partial H/\partial w$, measured at point A no longer captures the effect of the tax on labour supply. Taxation has reduced hours worked from H_1 to H_2. This is due to the income effect created by the tax exemption (the higher the tax rate, the more it is worth). It is as if non-labour income increased by ΔY and the new budget constraint were *fbe*. Thus, in the presence of non-linear budget constraints, the evaluation of the effects of tax changes requires evaluation of the full labour supply function before and after the change rather than simply looking at the net (uncompensated) wage effect.

Although this basic model remains the foundation of most theoretical and empirical analysis of labour supply it is unsatisfactory in a number of ways. We now discuss some extensions of the model which remedy some of these shortcomings. Inevitably greater realism is purchased at the price of greater complexity, and in what follows we aim to present only the essence of the methods in which the basic model has been adapted, rather than to set out alternative models in full detail.

Family Labour Supply

What we have done so far is attempt to model the labour supply behaviour of a 'representative individual'. This simplification causes a number of problems. An obvious objection is that labour supply decisions are often taken not on a purely individual basis but within a context where there is interdependence between individuals' decisions; in particular labour supply is often determined by family decision making.

There is no consensus as to how best to model family decision making. The basic problem is to decide what it is that is being maximised in the family context. Differences in family or joint decision-making models can usually be traced to differences in the assumed maximand. One approach[11] is to assume that the family maximises a common or joint utility function:

$$U = (X, L_h, L_w) \qquad (1.6)$$

where L_h and L_w are the husband's and wife's leisure time respectively. X is the family's consumption of composite commodity. This utility function is maximised subject to the constraint

$$X \leq w_h H_h + w_w H_w + y \qquad (1.7)$$

which is analogous to equation (1.2a). y is now interpreted as the family's non-labour income. The maximisation yields the labour supply functions

$$H_h = H_h(w_h, w_w, y) \qquad (1.8a)$$

$$H_w = H_w(w_h, w_w, y) \qquad (1.8b)$$

and the Slutsky decompositions

$$\frac{\partial H_h}{\partial w_h} = \left(\frac{\partial H_h}{\partial w_h}\right)_S + H_h \frac{\partial H_h}{\partial y} \qquad (1.9a)$$

$$\frac{\partial H_h}{\partial w_w} = \left(\frac{\partial H_h}{\partial w_w}\right)_S + H_w \frac{\partial H_h}{\partial y} \qquad (1.9b)$$

$$\frac{\partial H_w}{\partial w_w} = \left(\frac{\partial H_w}{\partial w_w}\right)_S + H_w \frac{\partial H_w}{\partial y} \qquad (1.9c)$$

$$\frac{\partial H_w}{\partial w_h} = \left(\frac{\partial H_w}{\partial w_h}\right)_S + H_h \frac{\partial H_w}{\partial y} \qquad (1.9d)$$

Note that, because a single utility function is being maximised, the income compensated cross-substitution effects are restricted to be equal, i.e.:

$$\left(\frac{\partial H_h}{\partial w_w}\right)_S = \left(\frac{\partial H_w}{\partial w_h}\right)_S$$

It is also possible, and useful for estimation purposes, to write down the total differentials corresponding to equation (1.5):

$$dH_h = \left(\frac{\partial H_h}{\partial w_h}\right)_S dw_h + \left(\frac{\partial H_h}{\partial w_w}\right) dw_w + \frac{\partial H_h}{\partial y}[H_h dw_h + H_w dw_w + dy] \qquad (1.10a)$$

$$dH_w = \left(\frac{\partial H_w}{\partial w_w}\right)_s dw_w + \left(\frac{\partial H_w}{\partial w_h}\right) dw_h + \frac{\partial H_w}{\partial y} [H_w dw_w + H_h dw_h + dy] \qquad (1.10b)$$

In this model, apart from the 'own' income and substitution effects of a change in the 'own' wage, each family member's labour supply is potentially affected by cross-substitution and income effects arising from a change in the spouse's wage.

An alternative model of family decision making, for which the labour supply implications were first explored by Leuthold (1968), specifies separate utility functions for the husband and wife (in the two-worker household) each function being defined over common or joint consumption and own leisure time:

$$U_h = U_h(X, L_h) \qquad (1.11a)$$

$$U_w = U_w(X, L_w) \qquad (1.11b)$$

A simple extension is to introduce the spouse's leisure time into the utility function. This could be done to allow for the possibility of the two individuals' leisure activities being complementary, or as a way of introducing non-selfish behaviour, in which each individual cares about (and derives) utility from the leisure of the spouse.[12] Thus

$$U_h = U_h(X, L_h, L_w) \qquad (1.12a)$$

$$U_w = U_w(X, L_h, L_w) \qquad (1.12b)$$

The husband maximises the first of these utility functions subject to the common budget constraint equation (1.7), taking L_w as given, while the wife maximises U_w subject to equation (1.7) again, taking L_h as constant. These separate maximisations yield the short-run labour supply functions:

$$H_h = H_h(w_h, w_w, L_w, y) \qquad (1.13a)$$

$$H_w = H_w(w_h, w_w, L_h, y) \qquad (1.13b)$$

which are similar to equations (1.8), with the important exception that the presence of the spouse's leisure time means that as well as having cross-price effects, as in equation (1.9) above, we have the cross-quantity effects, $\partial H_h/\partial L_w$, $\partial H_w/\partial L_h$, which in turn are composed of substitution (or preference) effects and indirect income effects. For example, an increase or decrease in the wife's leisure affects the husband's labour supply both via his preference structure (remember that L_w was an argument in the husband's utility function) and also by changing his non-labour income ($y + w_w H_w$).

The problem with equations (1.13) is that there is no guarantee that the $L_w(L_h)$ which enters as an independent variable in the first (second) equation is equal to T minus the $H_w(H_h)$ that is the dependent variable in the second (first) equation. Household *equilibrium* requires such consistency, i.e.:

$$\overset{*}{H}_h = H_h(w_h, w_w, (T - \overset{*}{H}_w), y) \tag{1.14a}$$

$$\overset{*}{H}_w = H_w(w_h, w_w, (T - \overset{*}{H}_h), y) \tag{1.14b}$$

which are solved for the equilibrium values $\overset{*}{H}_h$ and $\overset{*}{H}_w$ as functions of w_h, w_w and y, i.e.:

$$\overset{*}{H}_h = H_h(w_h, w_w, y) \tag{1.15a}$$

$$\overset{*}{H}_h = \overset{*}{H}_w(w_h, w_w, y) \tag{1.15b}$$

These may be thought of as the long-run family labour supply functions specifying, for given wages and prices and non-labour incomes, the husband's and wife's hours of work, when the household is in equilibrium.[13] Note that equations (1.15) have the same general form as equations (1.8). Does this mean that the separate utility function approach is essentially identical to the more standard approach where the husband and wife's labour supply are derived from a common family utility function? No it does not, but what it *does* mean is that we cannot say anything interesting about the different labour supply implications of the two approaches without adopting some specific functional form for the utility functions and testing the implications of such specification to see whether the joint or the separate utility function approach best fits a given body of data.[14] At the empirical level one would expect different labour supply elasticities under the two approaches, so testing to see which better describes the real world can be important where the assessment of policy requires estimates of labour supply response.

Note that, in both the models of family decision making we have examined, consumption is analogous to a public good: more X implies more X for both — individual consumption is ruled out. An obvious extension of the model would be to allow, in addition to common consumption, some private or individualistic consumption financed by own labour plus non-labour income. When combined with a utility function of the type referred to in note 12, a general specification of the family decision-making problem may have family member i maximising

$$U_i = U_i[X_c, X_i, L_i, g_i(U_j)] \tag{1.16}$$

(where X_c is common consumption, X_i is own consumption, L_i is own leisure and U_j is spouse's utility), subject to the common budget constraint

$$\sum_i P_i X_i + P_c X_c \leq \sum_i W_i H_i + \sum_i Y_i \tag{1.17}$$

and the individual budget constraint

$$P_i X_i \leq W_i H_i + Y_i \tag{1.18}$$

Needless to say such generality is only purchased at the price of greatly increased complexity in terms of solving the model.

The Allocation of Time — More Complex Models

The basic model we have been considering allows for time to be used in only two ways: for market work or for leisure. In practice such a dichotomous treatment of time is not tenable. Many activities fit into neither category (housework, commuting, eating, etc.)

A first step towards a more realistic model involves retaining the basic utility function given by equation (1.1) but allowing the goods represented by X to be secured either by home production or by exchange, the latter implying market work.[15] Thus we have

$$U = U(X, L)$$

where $X = X_D + X_M$
    X_D = domestically produced goods and services
    X_M = market produced goods and services

Domestically produced goods and services are produced subject to the household production function

$$X_D = f(H_D) \quad \frac{df}{dH_D} > 0, \quad \frac{d^2f}{dH_D^2} < 0$$

where H_D = hours of home work. Market produced goods are, as before, subject to the budget constraint (in which P, the market price of goods, has been set equal to 1):

$$X_M \leq wH_M + y$$

In addition there is a total time constraint

$$T = H_D + H_M + L$$

where T = total time available
    H_D = home work
    H_M = market work
    L = leisure

Rewriting the utility function as

$$U = U\{[X_M + f(H_D)], L\}$$

and maximising subject to the budget and time constraints yields the following first-order conditions:

$$\frac{\text{marginal utility leisure time}}{\text{marginal utility (real) income}} = \frac{U_L}{U_X} = \frac{df}{dH_D}$$

and, where $H_M > 0$,

$$\frac{U_L}{U_X} = \frac{df}{dH_D} = w$$

The first of these conditions states that the shadow price of time must equal the marginal product of time spent on home production, while the second states that if the individual works in the market he will do so up to the point where the shadow price of time is equal both to the marginal product of home production and the real wage.[16] This analysis is illustrated diagrammatically in Figure 1.4. The curved line ABC is the home production function $[X_H = f(H_D)]$ and BD, whose slope is equal to the real wage, is the market budget constraint. Note that, up to point B, marginal hours spent in home production have a higher marginal product than do hours spent doing market work. To the left of B the opposite is true. Therefore ABD is the opportunity set, showing the maximum amount of goods attainable for given work hours. But the analysis goes further and enables equilibrium work hours to be divided between H_D and H_M, home and market work. The individual maximises his utility when he reaches the highest possible indifference curve (I_1) permitted by his opportunity set. In our diagram the individual takes OL hours of leisure and consumes OX_1 goods, which he produces with H_D hours of home work and H_DL hours of market work. In terms of the first-order conditions, the slope of the indifference curve at Q is equal to the slope of the market budget constraint $(U_L/U_X = w)$ and both are equal to

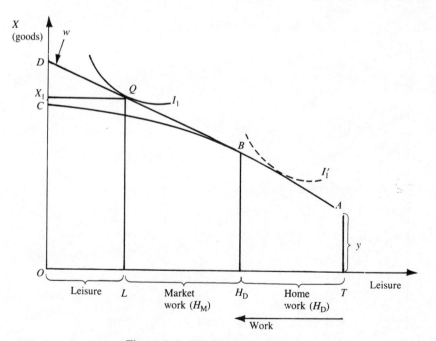

Figure 1.4 The Allocation of Time

the slope of the home production function at B. Note that if the individual had preferences indicated by the broken indifference curve I_1' then the equilibrium solution would have involved home work only ($U_L/U_X = \mathrm{d}f/\mathrm{d}H_D > w$).

This diagrammatic analysis can be used to analyse the effects of changes in y and w. A change in non-labour income, y, will shift the whole opportunity set, ABD, upwards. The point H_D, where market hours become more productive than home hours, will not change and therefore home hours will not normally change. If leisure is a normal good it will increase so market hours will fall. Consider now an increase in the real wage (Figure 1.5). The wage increases from w_1 to w_2. Consider the individual whose indifference curves are labelled I_1 and I_2. He increases his leisure from L_1 to L_2, reducing his home work from TH_{D_1} to TH_{D_2}. The effect on market work depends on which of these two effects predominates. In the diagram the reduction in home work exceeds the increase in leisure, and market work increases, but in general the effect is indeterminate. Consider now the individual with the broken indifference curves I_1' and I_2'. Before the wage increase this individual did no market work, consuming L_3 hours of leisure and putting in L_3T hours of home work. The wage increase induces this individual to enter the labour force, doing $L_4H_{D_2}$ hours of market work, working TH_{D_2} hours at home and consuming L_4 hours of leisure.

Is this approach an advance on the more traditional labour–leisure analysis? The answer would appear to be a qualified yes. The essence of the approach lies

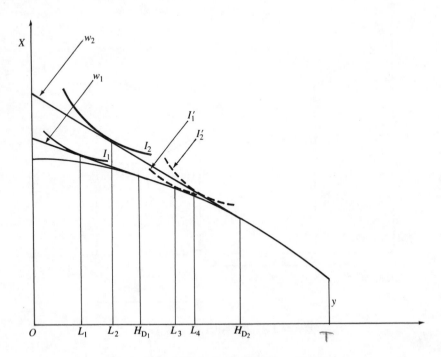

Figure 1.5 An Increase in the Wage Rate

in the distinction between work in the home and leisure, and this distinction does have implications not present in the simpler model. For example it may help to explain why married women have a more elastic labour supply function than do men (because their marginal product in the home is likely to be less sensitive to hours spent in domestic work than is the case with men). Similarly it is clear that, although we observe that men's hours of market work have negative wage elasticities (backward bending labour supply curves) and women's have positive elasticities, men and women could, at least in principle, still have very similar income elasticities of demand for leisure if, for example, their increase in market work due to a wage increase were more than offset by a fall in work in the home. Further implications of the approach are discussed by Gronau (1977) whose paper also shows that the model can be successfully estimated with existing time budget data. However, the analysis does not achieve full generality at the theoretical level. Only three uses of time are considered and, as in the traditional analysis, one of these, leisure, is without real justification, singled out as having some special attributes which require it to be entered separately into the utility function. In a stimulating article Becker (1965) has demonstrated that many additional insights can be obtained from a more general treatment. We concentrate only on the essentials of his analysis and their labour supply implications.

The essence of the approach lies in the specification of the utility function. Leisure is no longer treated as a separate utility-yielding good. Instead utility, in Becker's analysis, is derived from *basic commodities*, or activities, all of which are treated symmetrically (differing only, as we see below, in their time and earnings intensities). Thus

$$U = U(Z_1, \ldots, Z_m) \tag{1.19}$$

where Z_j is commodity/activity j.

These basic commodities are produced by households using combinations of different market goods and time.

$$Z_j = Z_j(X_j, T_j) \qquad (j = 1, \ldots, M) \tag{1.20}$$

where X_j is the bundle of market goods used in the production of Z_j, and T_j is the amount of time (or a vector of time inputs). Equation (1.20) can be thought of as a household production function; in this approach the consumption/production distinction disappears. If, for example, Z_j is the activity of eating a meal, the activity is produced by combining the market ingredients X_j (e.g. food, cooker depreciation, electricity, gas, etc.) with preparation and eating time. To keep the analysis simple it is convenient to assume initially that the production functions (1.20) are of the fixed proportions type with

$$t_j = \frac{T_j}{Z_j}$$

$$b_j = \frac{X_j}{Z_j}$$

i.e. t_j is the fixed time input per unit of j, and b_j the fixed goods input. (Both t_j and b_j can be interpreted as vectors of input coefficients.) The household's maximisation is subject to a time constraint

$$H \leq (T - \sum_j t_j Z_j) \tag{1.21}$$

and a budget constraint:

$$\frac{\sum_j p_j b_j Z_j - Y}{W} \leq H \tag{1.22}$$

where p_j is the market price per unit of X_j
$\qquad W$ is the market wage[17]
$\qquad T$ is total time
$\qquad Y$ is non-labour income

However, a moment's thought reveals that inequalities (1.21) and (1.22) are not independent constraints. We can collapse them into the single constraint

$$\frac{\sum_j p_j b_j Z_j - Y}{W} \leq T - \sum_j t_j Z_j \tag{1.23}$$

Because market work can always be increased (decreased) by using less (more) time in household production, if inequality (1.23) is satisfied then a value of H can always be found which satisfies both (1.21) and (1.22). Note, however, that we have the freedom to do this only because leisure time, L, does not enter directly into the utility function or, equivalently, because we have assumed that there are no Zs which can be produced with time only, not requiring any market inputs (this is sometimes referred to as the 'no nude sunbathing' assumption). Where leisure time on its own gives utility then the welfare function would have to be maximised with respect to it and subject to the separate constraints of inequalities (1.21) and (1.23).

Note that the term in brackets on the right-hand side of (1.23) represents hours of market work, H,[18] and that $b_j Z_j$ is equal to x_j so that (1.23) is in fact equivalent to our earlier budget constraint, equation (1.2). For our current purposes (1.23) is more usefully expressed in the form

$$\sum_j (p_j b_j + W t_j) Z_j \leq WT + Y \tag{1.24}$$

where the right-hand side is 'full income', the money income available if all time were devoted to work (or the value of the sum of the individual's time and non-labour income endowments). The term in brackets on the left-hand side of (1.24) is the full unit price of Z_j[19] which has two components: the direct component $p_j b_j$ which is the money value of the market goods inputs per unit of Z_j, and the indirect component $W t_j$ which measures the earnings forgone by using time to produce a unit of Z_j.[20]

Maximisation of the utility function (1.19) subject to the constraint (1.24) yields solutions for the Z_j ($j = 1, \ldots; m$) which enable us to solve for hours of work residually from

$$H = T - \sum_j t_j Z_j$$

Consider the case of two goods only, Z_1 and Z_2, which we assume differ in their indirect costs as follows:

$$\frac{Wt_1}{p_1 b_1 + Wt_1} > \frac{Wt_2}{p_2 b_2 + Wt_2} \tag{1.25}$$

that is to say Z_1 is more (forgone) earnings intensive than Z_2 and also more time intensive,[21] i.e.:

$$\frac{t_1}{p_1 b_1 + Wt_1} > \frac{t_2}{p_2 b_2 + Wt_2}$$

The utility function is $U = U(Z_1, Z_2)$, the budget constraint is $(p_1 b_1 + Wt_1)Z_1 + (p_2 b_2 + Wt_2)Z_2 \leq WT + Y$ and the constrained maximisation problem is illustrated in Figure 1.6. We are interested in the labour supply implications of changes in: 1. non-labour incomes, 2. the wage rate, and 3. market prices.

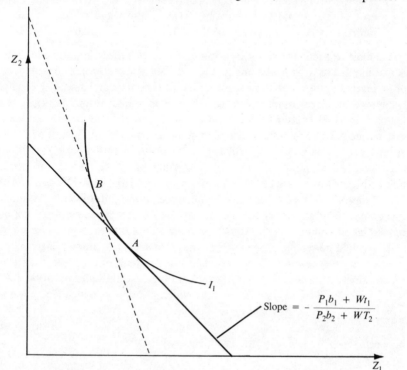

Figure 1.6 The Effect of a Change in the Wage Rate on the Consumption of Basic Commodities

1. When non-labour income, Y, increases, the budget constraint is shifted outwards, its slope remaining unchanged. Normally the consumption of both
   Z_1 and Z_2 would increase, more time would be spent on consumption, i.e.
   producing Z_1 and Z_2, and therefore less time would be available for market
   work. Labour supply would fall. A possible exception occurs when the time
   intensive commodity Z_1 is inferior. If it is sufficiently so, labour supply
   could increase. A similar analysis applies when Y falls.
2. When the wage rate rises our assumption that Z_1 is the activity, that is,
   intensive in earnings forgone ensures that the budget constraint becomes
   steeper. The compensated effect of this wage increase therefore is to reduce
   the consumption of Z_1 and increase that of Z_2 (the individual moves from
   A to point B in Figure 1.6), i.e. consumption is shifted to the less time
   intensive commodity, consumption time falls and labour supply increases.[22] A compensated wage decrease has the opposite effect, while the
   labour supply effects of uncompensated wage changes depend on the relative
   strengths of income and substitution effects in the normal way.
3. A compensated increase in p_1, the price of the market goods input to Z_1
   causes substitution towards Z_2 and an increase in hours of work. A compensated general (equal percentage) increase in the price of all market goods,
   however, would lead to substitution away from Z_2, the goods intensive
   activity, with a consequent reduction in hours worked. In this case the direct
   cost of Z_1 has fallen (relatively) whereas the wage increase raises the
   indirect costs. The analysis of the two cases is symmetrical.

The most restrictive simplifying assumption we have made in the above analysis
is that the Zs are produced using goods and time in fixed proportions. Once we
drop this assumption and allow substitution between time and goods, the analysis
becomes a bit more complex, because changes in W and/or market prices result
not only in a substitution between commodities (the Zs), but in substitution between time and goods in the production of *each* commodity. Thus, for example,
an increase in the wage rate will lead to a substitution of Z_2 for Z_1 as before
(increasing labour supply), but it will also mean that the minimum cost production of both Z_1 and Z_2 will be less time intensive. This, in itself, will increase
labour supply, reinforcing the substitution effect of the shift towards Z_2. Similarly a compensated equal percentage increase in all market prices would not only
reduce labour supply via the substitution towards Z_1, but also because both Z_1
and Z_2 would now be produced more time intensively. A compensated increase
in p_1 alone, on the other hand, now has a less certain effect. Again there is a
substitution effect away from Z_1 causing an increase in hours of work, but Z_1
will be produced more time intensively which has the opposite effect on hours
worked. The net effect would depend upon the relative sizes of the elasticity of
substitution between Z_1 and Z_2 in consumption and the elasticity of substitution
between goods and time in the production of Z_1.[23]

1.3 Labour Force Participation

The analysis in this chapter has for the most part examined the supply of hours to the market conditional on labour force participation.[24] But the labour supply decision can be regarded as a two-part decision: firstly, whether or not to participate in the labour market, and secondly, given a decision to participate, how many hours to supply. We have looked at the second part of this decision at length, but how is the first part analysed? The answer is that although participation is empirically an important determinant of the overall supply of labour, and one which has been subject to some interesting trends when broken down by age and sex, it does not pose any particularly serious analytical problems.[25] Basically non-participation is just the limiting case of the supply of hours as H gets very small.

The similarity of the analysis to that of the supply of hours can be seen in Figure 1.7. This differs from Figure 1.1 only in that when the wage is w_1 the individual reaches the highest possible indifference curve (I_2) when $H = 0$. In analytical terms what is happening to this individual (facing given w) is that the constraint, T, on the total time available to be allocated between work and leisure becomes binding before the equality

$$\frac{\partial U/\partial L}{\partial U/\partial X} = \frac{U_L}{U_X} = w$$

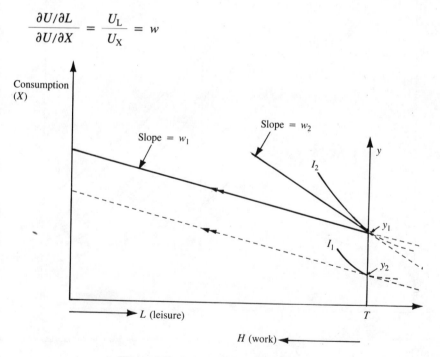

Figure 1.7 Labour Force Participation

required by the first-order conditions for utility maximisation can be satisfied. The corner solution is the best that the individual can achieve, but at this point ($H = 0$, $L = T$) $U_L/U_X > w$ (unless tangency between the indifference curve and the budget constraint just happens to occur at this point), and if T could somehow be increased the individual would consume even more leisure and fewer goods. In Figure 1.7 the individual could be induced into the labour market by a fall in non-labour income below y_2 (leisure assumed to be a normal good) or an increase in the wage rate above w_2,[26] the reservation wage, i.e. the value of w as the individual is on the margin between working and not working.[27] This analysis can be used to examine the case where the individual, contrary to what we have assumed up to this point, is not free to vary his hours of work at will. Consider the case where the individual must work at least 35 hours per week in order to secure employment. Thus in Figure 1.8 with non-labour income y_1

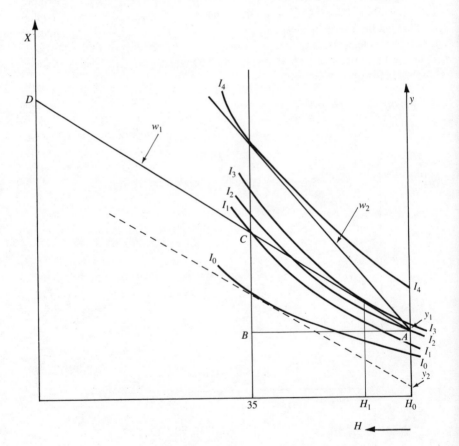

Figure 1.8   The Participation Decision with Constrained Hours

and wage rate w_1 his effective budget constraint is *ABCD*. Without the 35 hour constraint it would be *ACD* and the individual would maximise utility on indifference curve I_3 supplying H_1 hours of work (about 10 hours). However, as this solution is ruled out by the 35 hour minimum the best the individual can do is at point *A* on I_2. Non-participation (labour supply is H_0) yields higher utility than working the required 35 hour minimum which would place the individual on indifference curve I_1. An increase in the wage to w_2 or a decrease in non-labour income to y_2 would induce the individual to supply the 35 work hours necessary to secure employment.

1.4 The Effects of Fixed Costs of Working

The existence of fixed costs of work can affect both participation and hours worked. Such fixed costs can be either money costs (commuting, uniforms or other job-related dress, etc.) or time costs (commuting is again the main example). The effects of such costs are illustrated in Figure 1.9. In Figure 1.9(a), the fixed money costs can be thought of as reducing the non-labour income of workers. In the diagram, a wage of w_R — the reservation wage — leaves the individual indifferent between working H_0 hours and zero hours. In this case the reservation wage is not, as in the simple participation model of the previous section, the MRS evaluated at Y_1 and $H = 0$. Similarly in Figure 1.9(b), in which the time costs of work are represented by the horizontal section of the budget constraint, or in money terms by F_T, w_R is again the reservation wage, i.e. the wage which leaves the individual indifferent between working and not working.[28] In both cases, if the individual decides to work, then working hours must be at least sufficient to pay the fixed costs. The implications for the labour supply function are illustrated in Figure 1.9(c) (which is drawn for a given value of non-labour income). With fixed costs the labour supply function S_F is discontinuous. Once the wage reaches w_R the individual 'jumps in' to the labour market supplying a minimum of H_0 hours. Thus the effects of small changes in the wage in the neighbourhood of w_R can be substantially greater than in the absence of such costs. If both supply functions are linear, an increase in the wage from just below w_R to w_1 results in an increase of H_1 hours in the absence of fixed costs but of H_{1_F} in their presence (although $\partial H / \partial w$ is the same for both functions for $w > w_R$).

Recent developments in econometric estimation techniques are well suited to dealing with discontinuities in the supply function caused by fixed costs. These costs are especially important for married women, who may be attracted by the possibility of part-time working, and several studies have attempted to estimate H_0 'reservation hours', for this group. Heckman (1980) and Cogan (1981) estimate that H_0 lies between 20 and 30 hours. They also find that actual (desired) hours are only about 20 per cent greater than reservation hours.

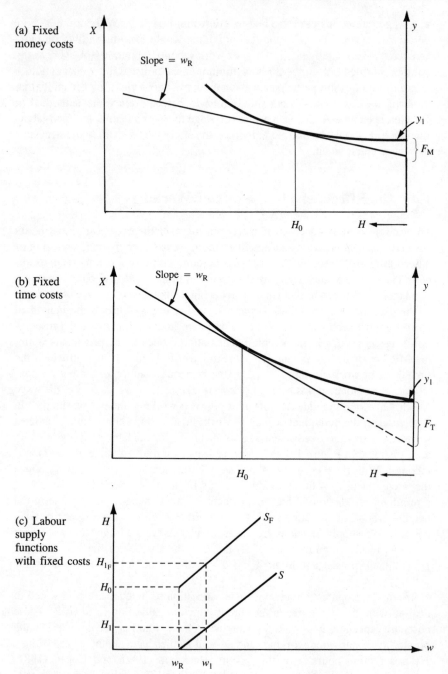

Figure 1.9 Labour Supply with Fixed Costs

1.5 Labour Supply over the Life Cycle

The analysis so far has treated the labour supply decision as referring to a single time period. The effects of such factors as age and the variation in the wage rate facing an individual over his or her lifetime have been ignored. Clearly there is much to be said for considering life-cycle factors. For example life-cycle models are useful not only for analysing how the supply of hours varies with wages over an individual's working life, but also for analysing the determinants of the optimal pattern of investment in human capital and of the retirement decision.[29] Unfortunately, however, life-cycle models tend to become complicated quite rapidly when basic simplifying assumptions are relaxed. In this section we show how our basic problem of the individual's choice of H is analysed in a life-cycle context where wages vary exogenously over time. We ignore both human capital investment (which would make wage variation over the life cycle endogenous) and retirement, limiting ourselves to showing how the problem is set up, and to highlighting the factors that affect the solution. Some simple results are stated and discussed intuitively, but not proved.

In a life-cycle context the utility function to be maximised can be written as:

$$\overset{*}{U} = \int_0^N e^{-it} U_t(X_t,\, L_t)\,dt \tag{1.26}$$

where $\overset{*}{U}$ = lifetime utility
      U_t = utility at time t
      X_t = consumption at time t
      L_t = leisure at time t
      N = the time horizon (length of life)
      i = the individual's pure time preference rate

Thus lifetime utility is the sum of the present value of utility at each age, t, discounted at the rate of pure time preference over the lifetime N. In order to make the analysis tractable, we assume that the utility function U_t is the same at each age (i.e. for all t) and that the lifetime utility function is 'strongly', or 'additively' separable between periods. This assumption of additive separability, although commonly made, is by no means innocuous. It implies not only that the marginal rate of substitution between leisure and consumption in period t is independent of the amounts of leisure and consumption enjoyed in all other periods (weak separability) but also that the marginal rate of substitution between leisure (consumption) in period t and leisure (consumption) in period $t+1$ is independent of the amounts of leisure and consumption enjoyed in all periods other than t and $t+1$ (strong separability). These assumptions are clearly unrealistic; the more so the shorter the period of unit length used in the analysis. It is possible, although unlikely, that the MRS between leisure at age 41 and leisure at age 42 is independent of leisure and consumption at ages 40 and 43, but it is extremely unlikely that the MRS between leisure on Tuesday and leisure on Wednesday is independent of consumption and leisure on Monday and Thursday.[30] However, accepting the assumption of additive separability in order to facilitate the analysis, we proceed to write the lifetime budget constraint as

$$\int_0^N e^{-rt}(P_t X_t) \, dt \leq Y + \int_0^N e^{-rt}[W_t(T - L_t)]dt \tag{1.27}$$

where r is the market rate of interest and all non-labour income, Y, is assumed to be an initial endowment, i.e. it is available at time $t = 0$, so that no discounting is necessary. The budget constraint is an exact analogy, in present value terms, of equation (1.2).[31]

The method of solving for labour supply is also analogous. The consumer-worker is assumed to maximise (1.26) subject to (1.27). From the first-order conditions and the budget constraint, one can solve for X_t and L_t (and hence H_t):

$$X_t = X_t(W_t, P_t, Y, i, r) \tag{1.28}$$

$$H_t = H_t(W_t, P_t, Y, i, r) \tag{1.29}$$

where, taken over all ages, these equations give the equilibrium consumption and work *paths* over the life cycle. One question of interest is whether the consumption path will be independent of the wage path (and vice versa). It turns out that these paths will be independent if and only if the utility function is separable in leisure and consumption, i.e. leisure and consumption are neither substitutes nor complements for each other.[32]

Clearly, if we assume that wages and prices do not vary over the life cycle and that the subjective discount rate is equal to the market rate of interest, then both X_t and H_t will be constant over the life cycle. Introducing exogenous wage growth (say at an exponential rate), but keeping $i = r$, it can be shown (see Heckman, 1974; Weiss, 1972) that the individual works most at ages when wages are highest[33] (i.e. consumes least leisure when it is most expensive). The effect of wage growth on consumption depends on whether leisure and goods are complements ($U_{LX} > 0$) or substitutes ($U_{LX} < 0$). If they are complements, periods of high earnings will coincide with periods of low consumption, while if they are substitutes, periods of high wages and earnings will also be periods of high consumption. These results are not surprising. If this model is correct then empirical evidence that wages and consumption both follow similar patterns (peaking on average between 45 and 55 years of age for white males in the US) implies that goods and leisure are substitutes in utility.

Any divergence between r and i introduces an additional reason for variation in H and X over the life cycle. Hold W_t and p_t constant for all t but assume $r > i$, i.e. the market rate of interest exceeds the time preference rate. This creates an incentive to postpone both consumption and leisure to later ages.[34] If $r > i$ is combined with exogenous monotonic wage growth then the outcome with respect to labour supply depends on the relative strengths of the two effects: $r > i$ creates an incentive to work harder at early ages, wage growth to work harder when wage rates are higher. Hours of work could peak at an interior age in the life cycle but corner solutions are also possible. Clearly the analysis becomes more complex when patterns other than monotonic growth are assumed for the exogenous wage change.

1.6 Summary

This chapter has been concerned with providing a reasonably comprehensive treatment of the neoclassical analysis of labour supply. Beginning with the individual's choice between labour and leisure, the analysis showed how the conditions required for this choice to be made in such a way as to maximise utility can be used to derive a labour supply function in which the individual's hours of work depend on the wage rate he faces, his non-labour income and on product prices. Particular attention was paid to decomposing the effects of a change in the net wage on hours worked into an income and a substitution effect. The basic model was extended (and thus made more realistic) in three separate directions. Firstly, labour supply was considered in the context of family decision making. Here the specification of the utility function to be maximised was shown to be a crucial factor in determing the analytical results. Secondly, the model was extended by dropping the assumption that time is used either for market work or leisure. When other time uses and different time intensities of different basic utility-yielding activities are allowed for, one can draw a richer set of implications than is possible from the basic model. In particular, the relative productivities of home and market time become an important determinant of labour supply, and the interdependence between labour supply and commodity demand can be more fruitfully analysed. Thirdly, we considered how the supply of labour and demand for goods could be analysed over the life cycle when wages were assumed to change exogenously. The outcome was shown to depend crucially on whether leisure and consumption were substitutes or complements in utility and on the relationship between the subjective discount rate and the market rate of interest. Finally we showed how labour force participation could be analysed as a special case of the theory of the supply of hours.

Notes

1. Throughout the chapter the utility function is assumed to be twice continuously differentiable and strictly quasi-concave.
2. To put it another way, the problem is to compare, and at the margin equate, the benefits of extra work (additional consumption) with the costs (reduced leisure).
3. Hall (1980), using data on output per hour over the business cycle, shows that workers tend to put in extra effort during booms and take it easy during slumps.
4. The Lagrangian method of solving the maximisation problem yields:

$$\mathcal{L} = U(X, L) - \lambda \left[X - \frac{W}{P} (T - L) - \frac{Y}{P} \right]$$

With one consumption good only we have

$$\frac{\partial \mathcal{L}}{\partial X} = U_X - \lambda = 0 \qquad \left(\frac{\partial U}{\partial X} = U_X \right)$$

$$\frac{\partial \mathcal{L}}{\partial L} = U_L - \lambda \frac{W}{P} = 0 \qquad \left(\frac{\partial U}{\partial L} = U_L \right)$$

i.e. $U_X = \lambda$

$$U_L = \lambda \frac{W}{P}$$

These, together with the budget constraint (equation (1.2b), written as an equality), yield, for given values of W/P, Y/P, three equations in three unknowns: X, L, λ. From this we get

$$L = L \left(\frac{W}{P}, \frac{Y}{P} \right)$$

and thus

$$H = T - L$$

$$= T - L \left(\frac{W}{P}, \frac{Y}{P} \right)$$

$$= f' \left(\frac{W}{P}, \frac{Y}{P} \right)$$

Also, from the conditions $U_X = \lambda$ and $U_L = \lambda(W/P)$ we can write

$$\frac{U_L}{U_X} = \frac{W}{P}$$

The term U_L/U_X, i.e. the marginal utility of leisure divided by the marginal utility of consumption, is called the marginal rate of substitution (MRS) between leisure and consumption. In equilibrium, MRS is equated to the real wage — leisure and consumption are chosen such that their substitutability in terms of preferences (MRS) is equal to their substitutability in terms of relative market prices (W/P). In Figure 1.1, U_L/U_X, the MRS, is the slope (absolute value) of the indifference curve and W/P is the slope (absolute value) of the budget constraint. Therefore $U_L/U_X = W/P$ describes the tangency solution.

5. We have of course implicitly assumed that the individual is free to choose his hours of work. In practice this is not always the case. We return to this problem later.
6. We express the slope in absolute value throughout, i.e. we ignore the minus sign.
7. If T were variable we could also examine the response of H to changes in T. The reader may find it useful to confirm that if both X and L are normal goods, an increase in T will unambiguously increase H, but by less than the increase in T.
8. The magnitude of the substitution effect will of course depend on the elasticity of substitution between goods (X) and leisure (L); when the elasticity is large — goods

and leisure are close substitutes — then the substitution effect of a change in the wage rate will be large; when goods and leisure are poor substitutes, a compensated change in the wage will induce a smaller labour supply response. We do not prove this result rigorously but the reader can easily confirm it using the diagrams; ease of substitution between X and L will be illustrated by 'flat' indifference curves, more limited substitution possibilities by more 'curved' indifference curves.

9. The first term is simply the substitution effect (i.e. a movement along a given indifference curve in any diagram). An intuitive derivation of the income effect is as follows. We want $\Delta H/\Delta w$ caused by a change in income. Call this

$$\left[\frac{\Delta H}{\Delta w} \right]_{\mathrm{M}}$$

If the wage increases by Δw and H hours are being worked, then it is possible to continue consuming the same leisure and purchase extra goods to the value of $\Delta w \times H$. As this extra income is achieved with no change in work effort, it can be thought of as an increase in non-labour income:

$$\Delta y = \Delta w \times H$$

or

$$\Delta w = \frac{\Delta y}{H}$$

Substituting into $[\Delta H/\Delta w]_{\mathrm{M}}$ yields:

$$\left[\frac{\Delta H}{\Delta w} \right]_{\mathrm{M}} = \frac{H \times \Delta H}{\Delta y}$$

or, in the limit,

$$\frac{H \times \partial H}{\partial y}$$

10. We have concentrated on the labour supply responses to changes in w and y. It is also possible to analyse the response to changes in commodity prices in the same way. Consider the effect of an increase in p_j, the price of x_j, one of the goods in X. It is convenient to write the income and substitution terms in the Slutsky equation in terms of L rather than H:

$$\frac{\partial H}{\partial p_j} = - \left(\frac{\partial L}{\partial p_j} \right)_{\mathrm{s}} + x_j \left(\frac{\partial L}{\partial Y} \right)$$

where $(\partial L/\partial p_j)_{\mathrm{s}}$ is the income compensated effect of a change in the price of x_j on the demand for leisure. When this term is positive, $(\partial L/\partial p_j)_{\mathrm{s}} > 0$ and leisure and commodity x_j are substitutes; when it is negative they are complements. Assume leisure is a normal good $((\partial L/\partial y) > 0)$. The sign of $\partial H/\partial p_j$ can now be seen to depend on $(\partial L/\partial p_j)_{\mathrm{s}}$. If leisure and x_j are substitutes, the effect of an increase in p_j on hours worked depends on the relative strengths of the income and substitution effects; the price rise reduces real income and thus increases work effort, but it also leads to an offsetting substitution away from x_j towards leisure (reducing work effort). If x_j and leisure are complements, the increase in p_j will increase labour supply; the income and substitution effects reinforce each other.

11. Kosters (1966), Ashenfelter and Heckman (1974).

12. For fuller discussion of family utility functions which allow for caring, see Becker
    (1974) One possible form of such utility functions is

$$U_h = U_h[X_h, g_h(U_w)]$$

$$U_w = U_w[X_w, g_w(U_h)]$$

Becker discusses the restrictions required to ensure the stability of such a mutually
interacting system.

13. We consider in the text only the static solution to the interdependent maximisation
    problem. The dynamic adjustment process by which the equilibrium is reached is
    also of interest; what one has in mind is an iterative process by which H_h and H_w
    converge to $\hat{H}_h$ and $\hat{H}_w$. However, the actual adjustment mechanism and the condi-
    tions ensuring convergence are beyond the scope of this chapter.

14. See Ashworth and Ulph (1981) for an empirical test of which of the two models best
    fits UK data.

15. For a fuller treatment of this approach, including empirical testing, see Gronau (1977).

16. $U_L/U_Y = w$ is of course the first-order condition that applies in the traditional
    labour−leisure analysis. See note 4 above.

17. Note that because prices appear on the left-hand side of (1.22), wages and non-labour
    incomes are specified in nominal terms.

18. As we are no longer distinguishing market work from home work, we label the former
    H, not H_M as earlier.

19. When the relative shares of direct and indirect components in full price vary across
    products and/or individuals, concentrating only on the direct component, as is com-
    mon in empirical studies, can lead to biased results. For example cross-sectional studies
    of income elasticities do not hold full price constant where higher income is the result
    of higher wages. Higher wage earners face higher indirect costs. Hence studies based
    only on market prices will underestimate true income elasticities.

20. The time costs may not always be accurately measured by using the wage rate. For
    those Z_js which use weekend or evening time, the wage W may not represent the
    true opportunity cost of the time input per unit of Z_j. Similarly, as suggested in note
    19, the unit cost of the given Z_j will differ across individuals with different wage
    rates. Becker discusses some implications of these points.

21. Where W is not constant and independent of the Z_j, the earnings intensity and time
    intensity of different Zs need not be positively correlated (although Becker argues
    that they are likely to be so in practice).

22. When the wage, or more generally the opportunity cost of time, varies across the
    Zs a possible exception arises if earnings and time intensiveness are negatively cor-
    related. In that case the fall in the consumption of the earnings intensive commodity
    actually requires more time for the production/consumption of the time intensive com-
    modity and the increase in W could cause labour supply to fall.

23. Second-round effects may also lead to changes in factor proportions used in the
    production of Z_2.

24. The exception was our discussion of the three-way allocation of time between market
    work, home work and leisure which touched on the question of participation in the
    labour market.

25. Participation *does* present special estimation problems, however. Some of these are
    discussed in the next chapter.

26. Which is the same principle as the wage-induced increase in participation illustrated
    in equation (1.5).

27. Formally the reservation wage is found by solving the first-order condition $U_L = \lambda w$ at $H = 0$, i.e. the value of U_L/λ at $L = T$ is the reservation wage. (This calcula-
    tion is conditional on the value of X or, equivalently, y at $H = 0$.)

28. Increases in either type of fixed cost (at wages above the initial w_R) could cause a working individual to cease work. If the individual continues working, however, an increase in fixed money costs will increase hours worked (if leisure is a normal good) while an increase in fixed *time* costs will reduce hours. We leave it to the reader to verify this.

29. Schooling and retirement are sometimes viewed as corner solutions to an optimal lifetime labour supply model, i.e. solutions which give $H = 0$ at either end of the working life. However, as there is evidence that many students work part-time and that labour supply tends to taper off rather than end abruptly on a given retirement date, it may be preferable not to treat schooling and retirement as special cases but simply as periods when fewer hours are devoted to market work. Some of the models which incorporate schooling into life-cycle models are given by Ben-Porath (1967, 1970), Becker (1964) and Heckman (1976). Retirement is analysed by Boskin and Hurd (1978).

30. For more on intertemporal utility functions and separability assumptions, see Morishima (1969, Ch. XII).

31. $(T - L_t)$ is of course equal to H_t. The model implicitly assumes the individual knows the time pattern of wages and prices over the life cycle. Alternatively W_t and p_t could be interpreted as expected values. The budget constraint also assumes perfect capital markets, i.e. unlimited borrowing or lending at the market rate of interest r is possible so long as all loans are repaid.

32. i.e. $U_{XL} = U_{LX} = 0$.

33. Some economists, especially those of the 'rational expectations' school, believe that this intertemporal substitution is the explanation of unemployment, i.e. individuals, expecting future real wages to exceed present wages, take more leisure today — making themselves voluntarily unemployed (see Lucas and Rapping, 1969). Of course similar considerations affect labour *demand* decisions. Hiring will depend on employers' expectations about future wages and prices.

34. This is easy to see intuitively when consumption and leisure are complements, but it can also be shown to hold when they are substitutes (see Heckman (1974)).

2

Empirical Aspects of Labour Supply

2.1 Introduction

This chapter examines some important characteristics and trends in labour supply. The methodologies, problems and results of selected empirical studies are surveyed and assessed to see how far applied economists have progressed in explaining labour supply behaviour, past and present, and in providing methods for predicting future changes.

If we think of the annual labour supply in an economy as being the annual hours worked by members of the labour force (and we argued in Chapter 1 that this does not capture all the dimensions of labour supply in which we are likely to be interested, in particular the *intensity* of effort per hour is missing from this definition), and if we subdivide the population into n demographic groups[1] then we can write the identity

$$\text{LS} = \sum_{i=1}^{n} P_i p_i H_i \omega_i \tag{2.1}$$

where LS = annual labour supply measured in hours per year
P_i = number of persons in group i
p_i = measured labour force participation rate (activity rate) for persons in group i
H_i = average weekly hours worked per person in group i
ω_i = average number of weeks worked per year per person in group i[2]

28

Equation (2.1) does not, of course, offer any fresh insight into the workings of the labour market. It is an identity, and only one amongst several ways of defining the labour input. Nevertheless it does provide a simple way of focusing on some major elements whose variation causes the labour input to vary between countries (or regions) at a point in time or within countries (regions) over time. Thus if one were interested in the percentage change over time in the annual hours of labour supplied per head of working age population, our formula implies that, to a first approximation, this is given by the sum of the percentage changes in (i) the overall participation rate, (ii) the average number of hours worked per week by participants and (iii) the average number of weeks worked per year by participants. The relative importance of (i), (ii) and (iii) in contributing to changes in labour supplies will of course change over time, and will also vary by demographic group. It would be interesting to compare the relative contributions made by changes in these three components to the overall change in annual hours over a long period of time, say 100 years, but unfortunately the data required to make such a systematic comparison simply do not exist. Below we make more piecemeal calculations which tell us something about the changes in each of these three factors.

We shall not spend much time on the population element P. Briefly, variation in labour supply due to this factor can come about because of the following:

1. Changes in birth rates in any particular period will, with appropriate time lags, affect the population of potential workers in given age groups. Labour force projections must combine these birth rates with the relevant participation rates, weekly hours and weeks worked to trace through the effects of such changes.
2. Changes in the average age of marriage affect the number of single women of working age in the population. If married and single women have different participation rates then this will, *ceteris paribus*, change labour supply.
3. Institutional changes such as raising of the school leaving age or raising or lowering of compulsory retirement ages in the civil service.

The other three factors on which we shall concentrate, i.e. participation rates, weekly hours and annual weeks worked, are, to a greater or lesser extent, all the consequence of the labour—leisure choices made at the individual level which we analysed in detail in the previous chapter. We say 'to a greater or lesser extent' because it is obvious that, especially in the short run, such choices are constrained by insititutional factors which limit the amount by which individuals can vary their weekly hours or annual weeks worked. In the longer run, however, such variation may be attainable by job switching, trade union activity and the like. In addition, weekly hours and annual weeks may sometimes be constrained by macroeconomic conditions leading to short-time working, redundancies, etc.

Finally, before turning to a fuller discussion of the empirical background, note that the individual elements on the right-hand side of equation (2.1) need to be independent of each other. Thus, for example, falling birth rates could be both a cause and effect of increases in the participation rate of married women while the availability of part-time jobs (affecting average H_i) could again affect participation rates.

2.2 Empirical Background

Activity Rates

The 'activity rate' or 'participation rate' for any particular group is the proportion of that group which is working or seeking work, i.e. the proportion that is 'economically active' or 'participating' in the labour force. Thus apart from those actually working, participation includes those waiting to take up a job, those seeking work and, in most definitions, those who would normally be seeking work but are prevented from doing so by temporary illness. Full-time students are not usually considered to be economically active in defining the labour force. Table 2.1 shows activity rates for selected European countries, USA, Japan and Australia, in 1985. For males the variation in these rates is not very large (as measured by the coefficient of variation, CV, the standard deviation divided by the mean) but for females the variation is much greater.

While it is interesting to speculate on some of the marked differences between countries revealed in the table — such as why the female activity rate in Sweden is nearly twice that in Italy (social customs and the greater availability of part-time work in Sweden probably contribute to the explanation) we will learn more

Table 2.1 Participation Rates (per cent), Selected OECD Countries, 1985

	Males	Females	Males & females
Australia	85.4	54.3	70.1
Canada	84.8	62.4	73.6
France	76.3	55.0	65.7
Germany	79.8	50.4	65.1
Italy	79.2	41.3	60.0
Japan	87.6	57.1	72.3
The Netherlands	78.8	40.8	60.1
Sweden	85.7	78.0	81.9
United Kingdom	87.7	59.8	73.8
United States	84.9	64.0	74.3
Mean	83.0	56.3	69.7
CV	0.05	0.19	0.09

Source: OECD (1986).
Notes: The figures for The Netherlands refer to 1984.
Activity based on the population aged 15–64.

Table 2.2 Participation Rates (per cent), Great Britain, All Ages, 1891–1986

	Males and females	Males	All females	Married females	Other females
1891	57.8	83.2	34.4	n/a	n/a
1901	56.6	83.7	31.6	n/a	n/a
1911	56.7	87.2	32.2	9.6	n/a
1921	58.1	87.1	32.3	8.7	53.8
1931	60.7	90.5	34.2	10.0	60.2
1951	59.6	87.6	34.7	21.7	55.0
1961	60.5	8.60	37.4	29.7	50.6
1971	61.3	82.5	43.0	42.3	44.4
1981	61.4	76.5	47.6	49.5	43.6
1974	61.6	79.2	45.6	47.7	41.4
1975	61.5	78.7	45.7	47.9	41.8
1976	62.1	78.9	46.8	49.0	43.1
1977	62.2	78.3	47.5	50.4	42.6
1978	62.0	77.9	47.5	50.0	42.8
1979	61.8	77.5	47.0	49.6	42.8
1980	61.8	77.0	47.7	49.3	42.9
1981	61.4	76.5	47.6	49.5	43.6
1982	60.7	75.3	47.3	n/a	n/a
1983	60.0	74.2	47.0	49.4	43.6
1984	60.8	74.2	48.4	51.5	44.2
1985	60.9	74.0	48.8	52.2	44.3
1986	60.8	73.4	49.2	53.0	44.2

Sources: Department of Employment and Productivity (1971)
Department of Employment, *Employment Gazette*, various issues.
Note: Full-time students (above the minimum school leaving age) excluded from the
   economically active.

by concentrating on one or two countries in more detail. We begin with Great Britain. Table 2.2 shows how activity rates have changed between 1891 (1911 for married women) and 1986; over this period the overall participation rate has shown a slight increase, from just under to just over 60 per cent, while that for males has fallen.

The really interesting part of the story relates to female participation rates. While these are still substantially lower than the male rates, they have increased rapidly over the period, especially over the last 25 years. Looking at the final two columns we see that this increase in the female activity rate is entirely due to the increased participation of married women. This has more than *doubled* since 1951; the activity rate for unmarried women has *declined* substantially over the period, falling below the rate for married women from the early 1970s onwards. In fact in absolute terms the labour force in GB grew by 3.7 million (from 22.6m to 26.3m) between 1951 and 1981 while the number of married women participating grew by 4.0 million (from 2.7m to 6.7m), married women being the only category showing an absolute increase. For males the declining activity rate almost exactly

Table 2.3   The Distribution of the Labour Force by Sex and Marital Status, GB, 1951
            and 1986 (%)

	Males	Married females	Other females	Total
1951	69.2	11.8	19.0	100
1986	58.3	27.6	14.1	100

Source: Department of Employment, *Employment Gazette*.

offset population growth, keeping virtually constant the number of economically
active males. The effect of these changes is clearly reflected in the change in
the demographic distribution of the total labour force, as shown in Table 2.3.
    Thus the increased participation of married females has been the only source
of growth in the aggregate labour force. We examine below the extent to which
cross-section analysis can explain differences at a point in time in the participation of married women by variation in wages and non-labour income. To the extent
that the results from such studies can be used to explain changes over time, the
basic conclusion is that increased real wages available to women are probably
the main reason for increased participation rates. But cross-sectional studies do
not provide a full explanation of the fivefold increase in the married women's
activity rate shown in Table 2.2. Historical changes, which cannot be satisfactorily simulated in a cross-section, also contribute to the explanation. Amongst
these are changes in the social attitude of and to women in the labour force, the
increasing availability and decline in the relative price of substitutes for labour
in the home (washing machines, etc.), improved child care facilities offered by
the state (nursery schools), reductions in average family size, etc. Of course it
is difficult to know the extent to which these are genuinely independent explanatory
variables, as opposed to being themselves, at least in part, the result of the growing attachment of married women to the labour force.
    The second part of Table 2.2 showing annual data for 1974—86 reveals that
the increase in female participation rates came to an end in 1977—8. Given the
hint of an upturn in 1984—6 we might conclude that female participation is procyclical, that is to say the 'discouraged worker effect' of increased unemployment outweighs the 'added-worker effect'.
    Age-specific activity rates for 'prime-aged males' (ages 25—55) have declined
slightly from over 98 per cent early in the century to just under 95 per cent in
1986 — participation is still almost universal for this group. For unmarried women,
the prime-aged rate, at about 75 per cent, is lower than the male rate. Like the
male rate it has also declined slightly over the last half century. For all demographic
groups, substantially lower participation rates are observed at either end of the
working lifespan; for males under 20 in Britain in 1985 the participation rate was
72.3 per cent, for males aged 60—64 it was 54.5 per cent and for males over

65 only 8.4 per cent. Furthermore, activity rates for these age groups show a steady decline over time.

Increases in the minimum school leaving age and increased enrolments in post-compulsory education are largely responsible for the reductions in labour force participation by young people. In turn these educational trends reflect sustained high rates of return to educational investment and increased demand for the consumption components of education resulting from real income growth.

The low participation rates of the elderly may, as in the case of the young, be in part explicable by the lower wages (reflecting lower productivity) available to this group. Such an explanation depends on the dominance of the substitution effect in the demand for leisure (dominance of the income effect would imply the taking of extra leisure during the high-wage, prime-aged, years). Pension schemes, especially those where the benefit payable is inversely related to labour earnings, also reduce participation of the elderly, as do the longer unemployment durations they face if they become unemployed (inducing them to give up job search and move into full retirement). Changes in these factors also contribute to the declining participation of the elderly over time (married women are again the exception — the strong trend to increasing participation is evident at all ages). For example there is no doubt that the coverage and 'generosity' of pension schemes has improved over time. Secular increases and improvements in education, along with the increased educational 'requirements' of production, have put older groups at an increasing disadvantage relative to younger groups of workers, further lowering their relative wages. Another factor that has been operative over time in reducing the labour force activity rates of the elderly is the relative decline of those sectors and occupations employing disproportionate numbers of the elderly and/or allowing the gradual tapering off of employment rather than an abrupt transition to complete retirement — the secular decline of agriculture is a case in point.

Changes over time in participation rates for married women have been more dramatic than for any other labour force group. Table 2.4 shows this for Britain. While the increases are greatest for the prime-aged groups, increased participation has been sufficient to prevent declining activity rates for younger married women — in marked contrast to the trends for males and unmarried women.

The above discussion has assumed that the cross-sectional pattern and time trends in participation result from voluntary supply decisions. This is not always true of course. Institutional and demand-side constraints may also be part of the explanation. Compulsory schooling and compulsory retirement (and their time trends) are examples of the former while employers' preferences for younger workers may severely constrain the employment opportunities of the elderly, although it would be more difficult to argue that the reductions over time in the participation of the elderly result from *increased* employer discrimination against this group.

Patterns and trends in the United States bear many similarities to those in Britain.[3] However, in the US the trend towards increased female participation began

Table 2.4 Activity Rates by Age, Married Women, GB, 1911−1986

	Under 20[a]	20−24	25−34	35−44	45−54	55−59	60−64	65+
1911	12.6	20.4	9.9[b]		9.3[c]			4.9
1921	14.6	12.5	9.1[b]		8.0[c]			4.2
1931	18.7	18.5[d]	11.7[b]		7.7[c]			2.9
1951	38.1	36.6	24.4	25.7	23.7	15.6	7.2	2.7
1961	41.1	41.4	29.5	36.4	35.3	26.0	12.7	3.4
1971	42.4	46.7	38.4	54.5	57.0	45.5	25.2	6.5
1981	48.9	56.8	51.3	66.6	66.8	51.9	23.3	4.7
1985	38.4	58.4	57.9		71.5[e]	58.4[f]	19.4	3.9
1986	40.7	59.4	59.6		72.1[e]	59.1[f]	18.7	3.4

Sources: Department of Employment and Productivity (1971).
Department of Employment *Employment Gazette*, various issues.
Notes: (a) 1921 = ages 12−19, 1931 = ages 14−20, 1951 = ages 15−19, 1971 and 1985 = ages 16−19.
    (b) Ages 25−44.
    (c) Ages 45−64.
    (d) Ages 21−24.
    (e) Ages 35−49.
    (f) Ages 50−59.

around the turn of the century (in GB the trend is really only discernible since World War II). In 1890 the overall female labour force participation rate in the US was 18.2 per cent, in 1940, 25.8 per cent and by 1981, 52.1 per cent. The growth in female participation by age has been far from uniform in the US. Prior to 1940 female participation grew most strongly in the age groups 20−24 and 25−34. Between 1940 and 1960, however, the main increases came in the older age groups with participation in the 20−24 group actually declining and growing only very slowly for the age group 25−34. This tilt in the age structure of increases in female participation is a reflection of the effects of the 'baby boom'. After 1960 the pattern of participation growth tilted back to the pre-war age pattern with most rapid growth for young and middle-aged women.

Hours Worked per Week

As with activity rates, variations in hours worked, across a given population or over time, reflect not only labour supply decisions but also employers' preferences, legislation, trade union activity and short-term fluctuations in the economy. We return to this mixed causality issue below but for the time being we treat hours worked in a labour supply context.

Table 2.5 shows actual average hours worked per week by male and female workers in selected European countries and in the United States. The variation in hours worked illustrated in the table reflects two main features. The first is

Table 2.5 Average Actual Hours Worked per Week in Selected European Countries (1985) and in the USA (1986)

	Denmark	France	Germany	Italy	The Netherlands	UK	USA
Male	39.4	43.1	43.3	40.6	41.6	42.3	41.9
Female	30.6	36.3	36.0	36.0	28.5	28.6	35.3
Total	35.5	40.3	40.5	39.1	37.2	36.6	39.0

Sources: Europe: *Eurostat* (1987)
         US: US Department of Labor (1985).
Note: European figures use national definitions of full and part-time. For the USA full-time is defined as 35 hours or more per week.

Table 2.6 Distribution of Hours Worked by Part-time and Full-time Workers in Selected European Countries (1985) and in the USA (1986)

	Denmark	France	Germany	Italy	The Netherlands	UK	USA
Part-time Percentage working 20 hrs or less	64.4	59.8	61.1	52.1	67.8	73.5	n/a[a]
Full-time Percentage working 40 hours or more	19.6	29.3	23.0	26.1	28.3	37.0	34.2

Sources: As for Table 2.5.
Note: (a) Average hours for non-full-time workers (including those on short-time) were 20.1.

differences across countries in the hours worked both by part-timers and full-timers.

Table 2.6 illustrates one aspect of these differences, showing the percentages in each country of part-timers working 20 hours or less, and of full-timers working more than 40 hours. The UK has the highest percentages in each of these categories.

The second factor causing average hours worked to differ across countries is differences in the proportion of workers who are part-time. Table 2.7 presents information on these differences. (In most countries this proportion has increased during the post-war period. This increase is associated with the growth of employment in services and the growth in female employment.)

Obviously, part-time working is relatively more common for females than for males. In all countries, as the final column of Table 2.7 shows, women make up the majority of the part-time labour force, but again the proportion varies considerably across countries. Comparison of Table 2.7 with Table 2.1 also reveals a correlation across countries between female participation and the proportion

Table 2.7 Part-time Employment in Selected OECD Countries, 1986

	Percentage of male employees who are part-time	Percentage of female employees who are part-time	Percentage of all employees who are part-time	Female share of part-time employment
Australia	6.6	37.9	18.9	78.7
Canada	7.8	25.9	15.6	71.2
Denmark[b]	8.4	43.9	23.8	80.9
France	3.5	23.1	11.7	83.0
Germany[a]	2.1	28.4	12.3	89.8
Italy[b]	3.0	10.1	5.3	61.6
Japan	5.5	22.8	11.7	70.0
Netherlands[b]	8.7	54.2	24.0	76.1
Sweden	6.0	42.8	23.5	86.6
UK[b]	4.2	44.9	21.2	88.5
USA	10.2	26.4	17.4	66.5

Source: OECD (1987).
Note: (a) 1984.
   (b) 1985.

of women working part-time (compare Italy and the UK for example). Of course the direction of causation is not revealed by such a comparison. Part-time jobs may both induce and respond to female participation.

Table 2.8 provides more information, for 1983, of the differences in hours worked both as between men and women and between full-time and part-time workers. While it is no surprise to learn that manual workers work longer hours than non-manual workers, the extent of this difference, for full-time male workers in particular, is remarkable. This point is spelled out in more detail by looking at the hours *distribution* which shows that while 50 per cent of full-time manual males work 40 hours or less per week, the comparable figure for full-time non-manual males is 82 per cent. At the upper end of the distribution, while one-fifth of all manual males work more than 48 hours per week, less than 5 per cent of non-manual males do so.

Table 2.8 teaches us another lesson, however. It shows that considerable variation of hours of work exists for both sexes and for both manual and non-manual workers. This has some bearing on the frequently made claim that the traditional labour—leisure analysis of labour supply is irrelevant to the real world, in which workers are alleged not to be able to vary their hours of work as that analysis generally assumes. This table suggests that the scope for variation may be considerable. Of course it may be the case that the table gives an exaggerated picture of the real choices confronting an individual, at least in the short run, because the hours distribution within that individual's occupation and region may be much less dispersed. We do not have the space to examine this in detail. In general, however, it is true to say that hours also show considerable variance within

Table 2.8   Distribution of Total Weekly Hours, GB, April 1983 (percentage of employees)

A.   Full-time

	36 hours or less	36—40	40—48	48+	Average
Males					
Manual	1.8	48.4	29.6	20.2	43.8
Non-manual	23.9	58.4	13.3	4.4	38.4
All	11.5	52.8	22.4	13.3	41.4
Females					
Manual	17.8	64.3	14.1	3.8	39.3
Non-manual	35.3	59.5	4.5	0.7	36.5
All	31.1	60.6	6.9	1.4	37.2

B.   Part-time

	8 hours or less	8—16	16—21	21—26	26+	Average
Males (21 and over)	17.5	26.6	22.8	17.2	15.9	17.7
Females (18 and over)						
Manual	8.9	27.6	26.4	20.0	17.1	19.1
Non-manual	6.3	19.4	35.5	20.7	18.1	20.1
All	7.6	23.5	30.9	20.3	17.7	19.6

Source: Department of Employment, *New Earnings Survey* (1983).
Note: Full-time: Employees with normal basic hours above 30; part-time: employees with normal basic hours of 30 or less.

occupation and region, so even in the short run there is a choice of hours available, while over the longer run, for which Table 2.8 has greater relevance, that choice is considerable.

Comprehensive data on time trends in hours worked are not plentiful, at least if one requires comprehensive coverage over a long period. However, for selected sectors and occupations we can go back quite a long way. In Britain adult males in agriculture worked approximately 58½ *normal* hours (i.e. exclusive of any overtime) per week in 1914, a figure which fell to 51 hours by 1924 and 44 hours by 1967/8. Not only in agriculture were long normal hours required, as the following figures for fitters and turners (working in London) show:

	1850	1900	1924	1950	1968
Fitters & turners	59	54	47	44	40

Source: British Labour Statistics Historical Abstract, 1896—1968.

Of course, these figures, being for *normal* hours, may overstate the downward trend in *actual* hours worked if overtime hours have been increasing. Evidence that this is exactly what has been happening, at least for full-time manual workers, is presented in Table 2.9. Actual hours have fallen, but by less than normal hours. It is worth noting the different forms in which increased leisure has been taken; whereas in the late nineteenth and early twentieth centuries the main effect was due to a shortening of the working day, more recent reductions have come through

Table 2.9   Normal and Actual Weekly Hours of Manual Workers, UK, 1924–1983

	Men		Women		All workers	
	Normal	*Actual*	*Normal*	*Actual*	*Normal*	*Actual*
1924	—	—	—	—	47.0	45.8
1935	—	—	—	—	47.3	47.8
1945	—	49.6	—	43.2	47.1	47.2
1950	44.4	47.3	45.1	41.7	44.6	45.9
1955	44.4	48.9	45.1	41.7	44.6	47.0
1960	43.4	48.0	44.4	40.7	43.7	46.2
1965	41.2	47.3	42.1	38.9	41.4	45.3
1970	40.1	45.7	40.8	37.9	40.3	43.9
1975	39.9	43.6	40.1	37.0	39.9	42.2
1983	39.8	43.8	38.2	39.3	39.1	42.2

Sources: Department of Employment and Productivity (1971).
        BLS Year Book (1976).
        New Earnings Survey (1983).
Note: The figures refer to full-time workers only. Agriculture and mining are excluded.

Table 2.10   The Average Work Week in the US, 1900–1960

	Average weekly hours	
	All non-agricultural wage and salary workers[a]	*Manufacturing workers*[b]
1900	58.5	55.0
1910	55.6	52.2
1920	50.6	50.4
1930	47.1	43.6
1940	42.5	37.6
1950	41.1	38.7
1960	41.0	38.1

Sources: Kniesner (1976); Hamermesh and Rees (1984).
Notes: (a) Average hours paid for.
        (b) Hours actually worked.

the spread of the five-day as opposed to six-day working week. Other ways in which increased leisure is taken are earlier retirement and longer holidays (see the following section).

In the United States the average work week fell by about 9–10 per cent per decade between 1900 and 1940 as shown in Table 2.10. The column referring to all non-agricultural workers reflects not only shorter hours for a labour force with a given structure but also changes in that structure — in particular the growth of female participation. These structural changes are less important in manufacturing. This secular decline in the average work week seemed to come to an end in the US in the 1940s; the post-war period has seen relative stability in the average work week. Whether *annual* hours worked have continued to decline due to growth in paid holiday time is a matter of debate (Kniesner, 1976).

Paid Holidays

The trend towards increased leisure which is evident in the time series of hours worked per week is also reflected in an increase in annual holiday entitlements. Unfortunately it is not easy to document this trend with great precision as most of the available data refer to the *paid* holiday entitlements of manual workers. Thus, although holidays with pay are a relatively recent phenomenon, it is undoubtedly the case that the growth of paid holidays has been accompanied by reductions in unpaid holidays.[4] However, even if for this reason the growth of paid holidays somewhat exaggerates the true increase of leisure taken in the form of holidays, the story of this growth is an interesting one (for Britain see Cameron (1965) for an excellent history up to the mid-1960s). Today it seems almost incredible that, except in a few cases where firms used paid holidays as a reward and incentive for punctuality and regular attendance, most manual workers[5] had no paid holiday entitlements at all prior to World War I, and that the first collective agreements giving paid holidays in engineering, coalmining, shipbuilding and the steel industry were not struck until 1937/8.[6] It was not really until this time that the principle of paid holidays was universally accepted (for manual workers). By the end of World War II the vast majority of manual workers were entitled to at least one week's holiday with pay. Subsequent improvements have been in the duration of paid holidays. Table 2.11 picks up the story for manual workers. Holidays have more than doubled since 1951, with the fourth week of paid holiday becoming virtually universal with the average currently being about 4.5 weeks. The table refers to basic paid holidays and the trend in actual holidays may be rising even faster due to the growing practice of providing additional days of paid holidays depending on length of service. Similarly any secular shift in employment from manual to non-manual occupations will result in an increase in the average paid holiday for the labour force as a whole because non-manual workers have longer paid holiday entitlements (about 25 per cent longer on average) than manual workers.

THE ECONOMICS OF LABOUR MARKETS

Table 2.11 Holidays with Pay — Manual Workers, UK, 1951—1985

Percentage of full-time manual workers entitled to annual paid holidays (duration in weeks)

	1	1–2	2	2–3	3	3–4	4	4–5	5+	Average
1951	28	3	66	2	1					1.73
1955		1	96	2	1					2.02
1960			97	1	2					2.03
1962			97	2	1					2.02
1964			92	7	1					2.05
1966			63	33	4					2.21
1968			56	34	10					2.27
1971			28	5	63	4				2.72
1972			8	16	39	33	4			3.05
1974			1	1	30	40	28			3.47
1976				1	18	47	34			3.57
1978				1	17	47	35			3.58
1980					2	24	19	55		4.14
1982						5	21	53	19	4.35
1985						1	16	63	20	4.51

Sources: Department of Employment and Productivity (1971).
           Department of Employment, *Employment Gazette*, various issues.
Notes: Averages: Take mid-points of columns which give a range. The column '5 weeks and
         over' is counted as 5 weeks for averaging purposes. This assumption is probably less
         realistic the greater the percentage of workers in this category, i.e. the final column may
         slightly understate the trend to longer holidays.
         Excludes paid public and statutory holidays.

Relative Impact of Components of Labour Supply over Time

While data are not available to enable us to assess the relative impact, over a long period, of the various factors examined above, comparisons are possible over a more limited period. Table 2.12 compares the annualized growth rates of the supply of labour in the UK and Germany and the components of that growth rate. Labour supply is measured as the annual hours of work per member of the potential labour force, i.e. the 15—64-year-old population. This can be defined as

$$\frac{LS}{P} = peH\omega \tag{2.2}$$

where e is the employment (proportion of the labour force in employment) and other variables are defined as in equation (2.1).

Table 2.12 shows that, over the 18 years covered by the data, the trend towards greater leisure was strongly in evidence in both countries with annual hours falling twice as fast in Germany as in the UK. (In absolute terms the 1960 annual hours per member of the 15—64-year-old population were 1355 in the UK and 1441 in Germany, while the 1978 figures are 1143 and 1094 respectively.) Looking

Table 2.12   Annual Compound Growth Rates (% p.a.) of Labour Supply Components, Germany and the UK, 1960–1978

		UK	Germany
1. Annual hours worked per member of 15–64 aged population	(LS/P)	– 1.21	–2.83
2. Activity rate	(p)	+0.46	–0.82
3. Employment rate	(e)	– 0.41	–0.48
4. Hours per week	(H)	– 0.62	–1.19
5. Weeks per year	(ω)	– 0.54	–0.97
Σ(2–5)		– 1.11	–3.46

Source: Derived from tables in Maddison (1980).
Notes: Annual growth rates are calculated as b in the regression $\ln Y = a + bt$, where Y is the labour supply variable and t is time.
The 'component growth rates' in rows 2–5 do not, of course, add up to the overall growth rates of row 1 of the table, the latter being determined by the interactions between the various components as well as by each one separately. Nevertheless the component growth rates do show the major forces at work in producing the overall growth rate of labour supply.

at the annual growth rates of the components of labour supply we see that a major difference between the two countries is that while labour force participation in the UK was increasing, due to the rapid increase in female participation, the overall participation rate in Germany was actually falling, ending up in 1978 at 65.6 compared to 74.8 for the UK.[7] Germany has not experienced the growth in female labour force participation so evident in other countries, falling participation resulting from virtually constant female activity rates and declining male rates. Of the other factors, while Germany experienced lower unemployment rates than the UK, German unemployment increased slightly faster on average. Similarly, while German workers work more hours per week (and per year) than their British counterparts, and did so throughout the period, their hours fell more rapidly — from 46.26 to 41.25 compared to a decline from 42.28 to 38.61 in the UK; paid holidays, while longer in Germany, increased at roughly the same rate in the two countries. Other factors which potentially affect weeks worked, such as days lost through industrial disputes, are in fact of negligible quantitative significance.

2.3   Econometric Research — Methods

The Importance of Estimation Methods

Having examined some of the main features of labour supply that can be observed directly from published statistics, we devote the remainder of the chapter to a discussion of econometric research on labour supply. This research has concentrated primarily on the response of participation (including voluntary retirement), and of hours worked, to changes in the net wage and non-labour income. Real net wages and non-labour incomes can change for a variety of reasons, but econometric research has paid special attention to estimating directly or indirectly the effects on labour supply of changes in these variables which are brought about by changes in various types of taxes and benefits. Because both the effectiveness and the costs to the government of various types of tax—benefit policies, such as the introduction of negative income tax, depend on the labour supply response of those affected by the policy change, policy makers require knowledge of these responses. We consider below whether econometric studies have provided any clear guidelines for policy.

The discussion covers both methods (technique) and results. While the importance of results is fairly obvious, it might be asked why we need concern ourselves with methods. Why not leave the technical problems to the econometricians and concentrate on their findings? To some extent, of course, we are forced to do this. Econometric problems and techniques are discussed in Appendix 2.1, and even there the exposition is intuitive rather than rigorous. However, the text retains some discussion of these topics, which we feel is required on two counts. Firstly, in order to evaluate the results, we need some understanding of how they are arrived at. For example some widely used estimation procedures are now known to be flawed and likely to produce inaccurate and, in all likelihood, biased results. Secondly, because econometric estimation of labour supply models has been something of a testing ground for new and more sophisticated model specifications and estimation techniques, it seems only natural to attempt to give something of the flavour of the advances that have been made. This is not a concern with technique for its own sake; one of the lessons that emerges from surveying empirical labour supply studies over the last decade or so is that the results (labour supply elasticities with respect to wages, non-labour income) are quite sensitive to the econometrics used to produce them. It is not possible to argue that results are little affected by the techniques used to derive them. This is not the case. The same data are capable of yielding different estimates of the crucial elasticities depending on how they are analysed. Having said that, it is always necessary to evaluate the costs and benefits of increased econometric sophistication. The benefits are to be found in more accurate and reliable estimates, but there are also costs in terms of the resources required to produce them and the inaccessibility of the studies to all but highly trained econometricians.

The obvious approach to estimation of labour supply parameters is to use ordinary least squares (henceforth OLS) to estimate labour supply functions whose functional form is chosen arbitrarily or to conform with certain common-sense restrictions. Thus $H = f(w,y)$, the basic labour supply function of the previous chapter, could be specified for estimation purposes as

$$H = \alpha_0 + \alpha_1 w + \alpha_2 y + e \qquad\qquad (2.3)$$

From the Slutsky equation (see previous chapter) we can then write

$$\text{wage elasticity} = \hat{\alpha}_1 \left(\frac{\bar{w}}{\bar{H}}\right)$$

$$\text{substitution elasticity} = (\hat{\alpha}_1 - \hat{\alpha}_2 H) \left(\frac{\bar{w}}{\bar{H}}\right)$$

and

$$\text{income elasticity} = \hat{\alpha}_2 \left(\frac{\bar{y}}{\bar{H}}\right)$$

where $\hat{\alpha}_1$, $\hat{\alpha}_2$ are the OLS estimates of α_1, α_2 and $\bar{H}$, $\bar{w}$, $\bar{y}$ are mean values of the previously defined variables. Most estimation of labour supply parameters in the late 1960s and early 1970s used this approach or some variation of it. Some of the best of these studies are to be found in Cain and Watts (1973).

Many of the early econometric labour supply studies implicitly assume that equation (2.3), or something similar, can be applied interchangeably to different dimensions of labour supply and in particular to participation and hours worked. This is not generally correct, and we shall see below, and in Appendix 2.1, that explicitly modelling participation and hours as different aspects of the individual's labour supply decision has important implications for estimation techniques. First, however, we examine the consequences of not paying explicit attention to how the participation decision is made when using equation (2.3) to estimate the determinants of the supply of hours. The question then arises of how to treat non-workers for estimation purposes. Two 'solutions' were used in the early studies:

1. Non-workers were included in the sample used for estimation, with values of H set at zero. Apart from the question of what value of w should then be used for these non-workers this procedure implies that equation (2.3) holds for all values of w, whereas theory tells us that this is not the case. As we showed in the previous chapter, participation is determined by the value of wage an individual can earn in the labour market relative to his or her (endogenous) reservation wage. Hours are then determined by equating the MRS with the wage. This latter procedure lies behind equation (2.3). For the vast majority of non-participants the MRS exceeds the real wage (a very few by pure chance may have a tangency at $H = 0$). Thus it is a misspecification to have non-workers choosing $H = 0$ in the same way that workers choose their positive values of H.
2. The alternative treatment of non-workers in early econometric analysis was simply to exclude them from samples used to analyse the supply of hours. Unfortunately this procedure also has major disadvantages. In particular it is one source of what has come to be known as 'sample selection bias'. Selection bias is a pervasive problem in econometric analysis of labour supply. Appendix 2.1 explains how it arises and what can be done to avoid it.

Implications of Complex Budget Constraints

In explaining the analysis of labour—leisure choice in Chapter 1, we restricted ourselves for the most part[8] to linear budget constraints. While linearity is quite adequate in the context of elementary theory, it is not a good description of budget constraints actually confronting individuals whose labour supply may be affected by complex tax and benefit systems, overtime premia and the like. It follows that estimation procedures must use more complex budget constraints to allow for such factors. Only where there is a single tax rate which applies only to earned income, and with no exemptions, can labour supply implications be analysed as in Figure 1.2 of Chapter 1 (which illustrates a reduction of the tax rate). Should the tax fall on non-labour income as well as on earnings the budget constraint is still linear for strictly positive hours of work. However, there is now an extra income effect to be considered when the tax rate changes. Thus, in Figure 2.1, we need to consider the effect of the increase in non-labour income, Δy, as well as the effect of the changed slope when the tax rate is reduced.

In practice, however, taxation is unlikely to produce budget constraints as simple as this. A more realistic picture is represented by the progressive tax schedule in Figure 2.2 where earnings are tax exempt up to $(X_1 - y_1)$ (w_1 is the pre-tax market wage), are taxed at rate t_1 between X_1 and X_2 ($w_2 = w_1(1 - t_1)$), and at a higher rate, t_2, beyond X_2 ($w_3 = w_1(1 - t_2)$). If we assume that beyond H_1 (say 40 hours per week) an overtime premium, π, is payable, the individual's budget constraint may become non-convex as in the diagram [$w_4 = w_1(1 + \pi)$ $(1 - t_2)$]. Of course, Figure 2.2 is still an over-simplification, but it illustrates the type of complex budget constraint likely to arise in practice.

Complex budget constraints have important implications for the estimation of labour supply functions. The individual's choice set can no longer be described

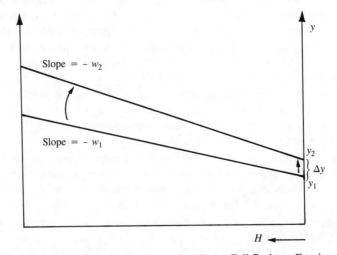

Figure 2.1   Reduction of Income Tax Rate when Taxes Fall Both on Earnings and on Non-Labour Income

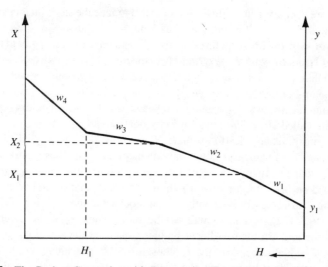

Figure 2.2   The Budget Constraint with Progressive Taxes and an Overtime Premium

by two simple exogenous variables y and single net wage w. Thus a single equation like $H_i = \alpha_0 + \alpha_2 w_i + \alpha_2 y_i$, using for each individual, i, observed net wage w_i and non-labour income y_i (as explanatory variables representing the budget constraint), is inappropriate. Some of the early labour supply research (see, for example, Hall, 1973) attempted to preserve the simplicity of the linear budget constraint by using the concept of 'virtual income', which is illustrated in Figure 2.3.

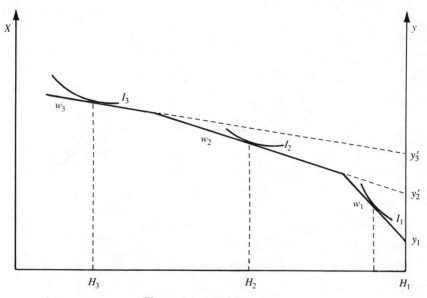

Figure 2.3   Virtual Income

In Figure 2.3, three individuals are assumed to face the same budget constraint, represented by y_1, w_1 (no tax), w_2 (tax rate $= t_1$) and w_3 (tax rate $= t_2$), but because of their different preferences they locate on different segments and have observed hours of work H_1, H_2 and H_3 respectively. Now individual 2's choice of H_2 could equally well have been produced by a linear budget constraint with slope w_2, and non-labour income y_2'. Similarly, individual 3 acts as if his/her non-labour income was y_3' and the net wage was w_3 for all hours worked. y_2' and y_3' are called *virtual incomes* for individuals 2 and 3. Why not therefore proceed as before, using OLS to estimate $H_i = \alpha_0 + \alpha_{1w_i} + \alpha_2 y_i$ substituting virtual income, y', for measured non-labour income, y, for those individuals (like 2 and 3 in our example) where the two are different? In a non-stochastic model this would be fine, but a moment's thought tells us that w_i and y_i' are not true exogenous variables. Equivalently in the stochastic specification, $H_i = \alpha_0 + \alpha_1 w_i + \alpha_{2y_i} + e_i$, w_i and y_i' will not be independent of e_i as is required for OLS estimation. On the non-linear budget constraint the actual w_i and y_i' faced by any individual depend on the H_i chosen by the individual. While the whole budget constraint is exogenous the *segment* on which the individual locates is not. In econometric terms because e_i partially determines H_i and H_i determines w_i and y_i', w_i and y_i' are not independent of e_i (e_i represent preferences in our example). Thus OLS would produce biased estimates of the coefficients. Alternative estimation procedures are required. These are discussed in Appendix 2.1.

A further problem with complex budget constraints (again with implications for econometric estimation) is that they can give rise to multiple tangencies unless

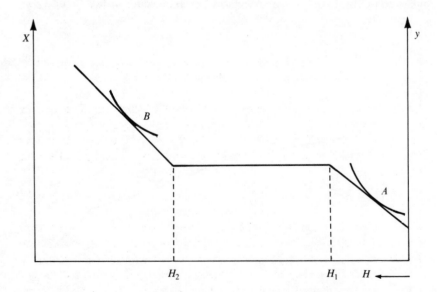

Figure 2.4 Multiple Tangencies on a Non-Convex Budget Constraint

the budget constraint is convex (ensuring a unique optimum). Where it is not, due to overtime premia, fixed costs of work, poverty traps, etc., then more than one feasible optimum may occur, as in Figure 2.4, where the individual faces a marginal tax rate of 100 per cent over the range H_1 to H_2 and has two local optima at A and B. In this case estimation proceeds (see Appendix 2.1 for details) by specifying a functional form for the utility function (direct or indirect) and estimating its parameters. This enables one to compare points such as A and B and to derive the labour supply parameters. Alternatively, specify a functional form for the labour supply function and recover the utility function.[9]

2.4 Econometric Research — Results

The number of studies of labour supply is now so great that a comprehensive survey requires a specialised monograph (Killingsworth, 1983). Here we make some general comments on what has been learned from such studies and focus in slightly more detail on some selected studies whose results illustrate general principles.

Hours Worked

Early studies The results produced by early, 'first generation', studies (up to and including the early 1970s) do enable us to draw some general conclusions, in particular with respect to differences between male and female labour supply response to changes in own wage rates and non-labour income:

1. For prime-aged males estimates of the gross own-wage elasticity are often negative, i.e. the income effect dominates and the supply curve is backward bending.
2. The female gross own wage elasticity is generally positive. The substitution effect dominates, resulting in a forward sloping supply curve.
3. Negative elasticities of labour supply with respect to non-labour income (including spouse's wage) are found for both sexes, with magnitudes being greater for women.

Together, 1−3 imply a much stronger compensated own wage elasticity for females.

While the above qualitative findings are of some interest, closer examination of the actual estimates reveals some disturbing features. In models where parameter values are not restricted in sign or size the estimates are sometimes inconsistent with the underlying labour supply model on which they are based; for example negative compensated own wage elasticities have been found, and, in family labour supply models, symmetry of compensated cross-substitution effects (see Chapter

1, Section 1.2) is not supported by empirical estimates. More seriously, the range of estimates of labour supply elasticities is very substantial. For example, in Killingsworth's tabulation of first generation labour supply elasticities the uncompensated wage elasticity for men varies betwen -1.0 and $+0.34$ (although positive elasticities are very much the exception), while for women the corresponding elasticity is estimated to lie between -4.46 and $+4.46$ (with *negative* elasticities here being the exception).

While it may be possible to narrow these ranges by excluding some studies whose estimation methods are now known to be suspect, and/or by focusing on certain homogeneous subgroups (e.g. white prime-aged male workers), the general conclusion must be that labour supply estimates from these studies are too imprecise to be of much use to policy makers. For example Cain and Watts (1973) note that the estimates contained in their volume imply that the working poor would reduce their labour supply by anything between 4 and 46 per cent in response to the introduction of a negative income tax scheme.

Of course, with studies conducted at different dates, in different regions (or even countries) and using differently selected samples, one would expect some variability of results: convergence to a single 'best' elasticity estimate is not a realistic or even desirable objective. However, what is desirable is to eliminate variability which results from model misspecification or use of less than best-practice estimation technique, and many of these early studies are now regarded as being deficient in one or both of these ways.

More recent studies   Has the greater econometric sophistication of 'second generation' studies (see Appendix 2.1) paid dividends in terms of the accuracy and usefulness of the resulting estimates? 'Modest dividends only' must be the simple answer. The range of available estimates from second generation studies is as bewildering as was that from more *ad hoc* first generation work. Of course, as in the case of first generation results, this is to be partly expected. Nevertheless uncompensated wage elasticities quoted by Killingsworth for males varying from -0.23 to $+0.14$ and for (white) wives from -0.32 to close to $+15.0$ can hardly be said to indicate that this elasticity is one of nature's constants; policy makers wishing to use such estimates to evaluate, say, the consequences of tax and/or benefit changes are unlikely to be impressed.

However, simply quoting the range of available estimates does not do justice to what we can learn from labour supply studies. The range can be reduced by limiting comparisons to specific groups within one country (comparing like with like), and by eliminating results which violate the underlying model by estimating negative compensated elasticities. Doing this would, for example, provide uncompensated elasticities for US males within the range -0.03 to $+0.14$, and for US white wives between $+0.13$ to over $+15.0$, (averaging at about 3.0). We can conclude that female labour supply is more sensitive to changes in the net wage than is male labour supply;[10] this is primarily due to the much larger compensated wage elasticities of females who, if anything, appear to have somewhat smaller (absolute value) non-labour income elasticities.

Another lesson to be learned from second generation studies is that the estimation techniques used in such studies produce results which differ significantly from those of first generation studies. In general, elasticities are greater in absolute value. For example, Heckman (1976a), using the same data set, finds an uncompensated own wage elasticity for US females (married) of 1.46 when the labour supply function is estimated by OLS and of 4.31 when estimated by maximum likelihood in a second generation specification. So one cannot say that, while second generation techniques are superior in principle, one might just as well, for practical purposes, use OLS or an *ad hoc* specification of the labour supply function.

Labour Force Participation

One of the characteristics of recent econometric estimation of labour supply is the emphasis placed on the participation decision (see Appendix 2.1). One might expect, therefore, to find explicit results relating participation to net wages, non-labour income and to personal characteristics. In fact, such results are not widely reported, major attention still being given to hours worked by participants. Some studies, however, do incorporate participation results. This can be done either indirectly by reporting parameters of the total supply function, showing how total hours respond to a change in the net wage, where the response includes any change in participation induced by the wage change, and/or directly by calculation of the elasticities of participation with respect to wages, non-labour income, etc. A study which does both is by Arrufat and Zabalza (1983). Their analysis is based on the 1974 General Household Survey (UK), using data on approximately 3500 married women aged less than 60 who were neither unemployed nor self-employed and who had working husbands. The study uses what were at the time the best available econometric estimation technqiues. It is based on a CES utility function and allows for (i) non-linear budget constraints (due to taxation), (ii) heterogeneous tastes, and (iii) optimisation errors which prevent the complete adjustment of actual to desired behaviour. The elasticities in Table 2.13 are calculated by simulating in turn the effect of a 10 per cent change in wife's own wage, husband's wage and non-labour income and are evaluated at sample means. Thus the total labour supply response of wives to changes in own wage, husband's wage or non-labour income comprises a participation response and an hours response conditional on participation, the former predominating in each case. The final column shows the effect of an equiproportional rise in all wages and in non-labour income. Arrufat and Zabalza also show how the participation probability is affected by age, and by the number and ages of children. Dependent children, not surprisingly, have a major impact. Thus a married woman between the ages of 25 and 34 (with average values of own wage, husband's earnings and non-labour income) has a 73 per cent probability of being a participant if she has no children. With one child aged 0−2 this probability falls to 24 per cent, with 2 children aged 0−2, 3−5, to 13 per cent.[11]

Table 2.13 Wage and Income Elasticities for Wives, UK, 1977

| | Elasticity with respect to: | | | |
	Own wage	Husband's wage	Non-labour income	Total
Overall elasticity	2.03	−1.27	−0.20	0.56
Participation elasticity	1.41	−0.93	−0.14	0.34
Hours elasticity conditional on participation	0.62	−0.34	−0.06	0.22

Source: Arrufat and Zabaiza (1983).

Cross-section studies of this type can offer at least a preliminary explanation of the secular trend in women's labour force participation chronicled at the beginning of this chapter. In most countries real wages for both women and men have been rising.[12] Even if they had been rising at the same rate, the higher absolute value of the elasticity of female participation with respect to own wage (compared to husband's wage) implies increasing female participation. In fact real wage growth has generally been greater for women than men, at least over the last 30 years or so.[13]

Of course there have been, apart from real wage growth, a number of social and economic changes which have occurred over long time periods which may well have affected women's labour supply, and which it is difficult to imagine being adequately accounted for in cross-sectional data relating to a single year (or even in pooled data covering several years). Amongst such potential determinants of female labour supply one might include:

(i) declines in fertility and postponement of childbearing;

(ii) declining marriage rates and later marriage;

(iii) increasing divorce and separation rates;

(iv) increases in the amount and changes in the quality and type of women's education;

(v) urbanisation and decline of the family farm (of less importance in explaining more recent trends);

(vi) growth in the availability of part-time work;

(vii) institutional and legal changes in relation to taxation, equal pay, maternity leave, availability of day care facilities, etc.;

(viii) increased availability, and falling prices, of labour-saving devices for the home.

A number of points need to be made about a list like this. Firstly, it is clearly unrealistic to regard all these factors as exogenous determinants of female labour force participation. It is almost certain that the causation runs both ways; increased labour force participation may cause or accentuate the above trends as well as responding to them.[14]

Secondly, not all of the above factors have clear, monotonic, secular trends. Fertility for example is almost untrended for most of the century, although it is subject to large variation (falling from the beginning of the century or earlier, and rising after World War II with minor interuptions until the late 1950s to mid-1960s). So, with female participation showing a much smoother increase, it is obvious that fertility changes on their own are far from a complete explanation. Also it must be borne in mind that many of these changes are not themselves independent of changes in real wages. For example, although it may act independently as well, education can lead to higher real wages due to human capital accumulation, and higher real wages (for women) can in turn lead to increased participation. Another example is the relation between women's real wages and fertility. Higher real wages lead to fertility reductions which facilitate increased participation. In both cases the real wage variable will pick up these effects or, conversely, conditioning on education and fertility in a participation equation will reduce the estimated impact of real wage growth.

Time series studies are, in principle, capable of exploring these issues. Such studies are relatively scarce due to the difficulty of securing data of comparable scope and quality to that found in cross-sectional data sources.[15] Nevertheless, some time series studies do exist. We comment briefly on two such, relating in turn to women's labour force participation in the USA and GB. The studies use disaggregated time series data which provide observations of average values, by age, of labour force participation (or female employment), real wages, education, fertility, etc. In other words the data describe life-cycle histories of individual birth cohorts. The econometric technique used in both studies enables the authors to separate out the factors that cause participation to vary over the life cycle for women within a given cohort from those which cause participation to vary from cohort to cohort, abstracting from life-cycle effects.[16]

Applying the approach of note 16 to American data covering the 31-year time span 1950–81, Smith and Ward (1985) estimate both within-cohort and across-cohort wage elasticities of women's labour supply (measured by employment rates rather than activity rates for reasons of data availability). Having established in a separate analysis that fertility depends negatively on the female real wage, these elasticities are calculated, both conditional and unconditional, on fertility. Table 2.14 presents a selection of the findings. Thus, for example, a 1 per cent increase across cohorts in both male and female wages induces a 0.158 per cent growth in female employment holding fertility constant. Allowing for the fertility reduction due to the wage growth almost doubles the labour supply response (to 0.304 per cent). Applying the unconditional elasticities 0.823, –0.519 to actual growth of men's and women's wages explains 60 per cent of the actual post-war increase in female labour supply.[17]

Table 2.14 Wage Elasticities of Women's Employment Rate, US, 1950–1981

	Equiproportional change in:		
	Female wage	Male wage	Both wage rates
A Fixed effects			
Fertility conditioned	−0.082	−0.259	−0.341
Not fertility conditioned	−0.809	0.095	−0.714
B Life-cycle effects			
Fertility conditioned	0.433	0.066	0.499
Not fertility conditioned	1.632	−0.614	1.018
C Total effects			
Fertility conditioned	0.351	−0.193	0.158
Not fertility conditioned	0.823	−0.519	0.304

Source: Smith and Ward (1985, Tables 17, 19).

In the British time series study (Joshi *et al.*, 1985), the estimates of wage elasticities are less satisfactory, attracting the 'wrong' sign in the life-cycle equation but yielding an elasticity of 0.36 per cent for 1 per cent growth in wages of both men and women in the across-cohort equation.

On the time series effects of real wage growth a final issue deserves brief mention. Given the increase in female participation, which is at least in part a response to real wage increases, why has male participation decreased rather than increased in response to increases in male real wage rates? In other words why is male leisure demand a positive function of real wages, while female leisure demand appears to respond negatively to real wage increases? Firstly we have to be careful to make sure we are comparing like with like. Reductions in male participation occur largely at early and late ages in the potential working life, while participation for prime-aged males has not changed much. For older women, participation has also begun to decline, while, for prime-aged women, once participation reaches something approximating male levels it may also behave similarly because at these levels there is simply not the scope for the large increases induced by wage rises at lower levels of participation (the participation–wage relation is likely to be non-linear). Additionally the alleged difference in male and female leisure demand could be a spurious phenomenon arising from the simplistic division of total time into market work and leisure. Thus if a larger proportion of the non-market time of women is spent on non-market *work* (housework) as opposed to pure leisure, then it is possible that women's increased market participation has been accompanied by a more than offsetting reduction in non-market work (perhaps due to labour-saving devices in the home), resulting in a net increase in leisure. In this case women's demand for leisure is as positive a function of the real wage as it is for males. Testing of this hypothesis requires detailed longitudinal time budget data.

Evaluating Reforms — Simulation

One of the main purposes of empirical labour supply analysis is to use the results to evaluate the effects of reforms of the tax−benefit system. In this section we discuss how such evaluation can be conducted, firstly, using labour supply functions estimated from cross-sectional survey data and, secondly, by examining the impacts of experiments especially designed to study a particular reform.

If we were dealing with the effects of a tax on earnings only, if the budget constraint were linear and if the population were homogeneous with respect to preferences, needs, etc., then we could evaluate the effects of the change in the tax rate on labour supply by looking at the estimated uncompensated own wage effect, $\delta H/\delta w$, i.e. the wage coefficient in the labour supply function. We would multiply this by the actual change in the net wage caused by the change in the tax rate. This would typically be done at mean levels of w, H, y, etc. Unfortunately this procedure is quite inadequate because none of the required assumptions are likely to be even approximated in practice. At the very least taxation is likely to apply to non-labour income, y, so that we would need an estimate of $\delta H/\delta y$ to evaluate the effect of the tax change. More fundamental problems are raised by non-linearities in the budget constraint and by heterogeneity in the sample. To consider the effect of the former, assume a very simple tax schedule with a single tax rate, t, but an exemption level of income, E, below which the individual's tax liability is zero. This is illustrated in Figure 2.5. Thus the introduction of this tax changes the labour supply function from

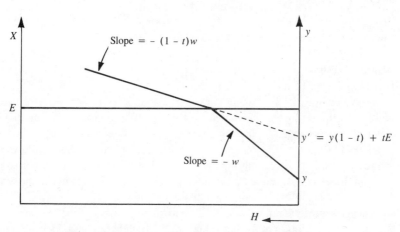

Figure 2.5 Income Tax with an Exemption Level

$$H = H(w,y)$$

to

$$H = H[(1 - t)w, \ (1 - t)y + tE]$$

Thus a change in t will have the effect

$$\frac{\partial H}{\partial t} = -H_1 w + H_2 (E - y)$$

where

$$H_1 = \frac{\partial H}{\partial[(1 - t)w]}$$

$$H_2 = \frac{\partial H}{\partial[(1 - t)y + tE]}$$

Substituting in the Slutsky equation ($H_1 = [H_1]_s + H_2$) gives

$$\frac{\partial H}{\partial t} = -[H_1]_s w + H_2[E - (wH + y)]$$

Thus knowledge of the uncompensated own wage effect H_1 is insufficient to evaluate the labour supply effects of changing the tax rate, t. For an individual we require knowledge of the substitution effect, the income effect, the wage and how close the individual is to the exemption level, i.e. $[E - (wH + y)]$. Note that if this is very small, i.e. if taxpayers are very close to the exemption level, the effect of changing t is almost a pure substitution effect because $H_2[E - (wH + y)]$ is very small. Thus even if the labour supply is backward bending ($H_1 < 0$), an increase in the tax rate could still reduce hours of work. Whether this will be true in the aggregate will depend not only on the estimated parameters of the labour supply function but also on the distribution of individuals around their tax threshold (i.e. on the distribution of $[E - (wH + y)]$ in the population). This is also true of the effect of a change in E ($\partial H/\partial E$).

Non-convexities in the budget constraint are another reason why we cannot simply use the estimated uncompensated wage effect (elasticity) to predict the effect of a tax change.[18] The point here is that the tax change might cause an individual to shift to a different segment of the budget constraint. Such shifts cannot be predicted simply by examining the estimated parameters of the labour supply function. Indeed the latter could even predict a labour supply change in the wrong direction, not just of the wrong magnitude. To know whether a given individual will change segments, not only do we need to know the utility function parameters but an exact description of the budget constraint both before and after the change to be evaluated. To estimate the expected change in *aggregate* labour supply we need to know the population distribution of all these factors (tastes, slope of each segment, virtual income associated with each segment). In short, we can only accurately predict the effects of a given tax and/or benefit change by respecifying each individual's budget constraint after the change and then recomputing equilibrium hours of work using the utility function (or related) parameters that were estimated with pre-change budget constraints. Clearly this is a much more complex exercise than simply applying those parameters to some hypothetical 'representative individual'.[19]

Simulation of the effects of a tax–benefit change on a large sample of individuals, carefully modelling the new budget constraint of each, is clearly a complex and difficult task, but not an impossible one with the aid of modern computers. A pioneering attempt in the UK is documented in Brown (1981). Using a sample of 333 weekly-paid married male workers in the UK in 1971 Glaister *et al.* (1981) simulate the effects of changes in the standard rate of tax, changes in the tax allowance (exemption level) and changes in taxes and allowances simultaneously so as to leave total tax revenue unchanged. Table 2.15 shows, in part A, the results of 2 per cent and 5 per cent changes in the standard rate of income tax (the benchmark tax rate is 30 per cent) leaving allowances (tax-exempt income) unchanged, while part B shows the effect of the same changes when allowances are simultaneously adjusted to make the total change revenue neutral.

Because the sample is unrepresentative of the whole labour force these results are best thought of as being illustrative. Nevertheless a number of interesting points do emerge. Firstly, although the authors estimate the uncompensated wage elasticity (evaluated at sample means) to be –0.16, the simulation shows hours worked change in the opposite direction from that implied by the negative elasticity, i.e. reductions (increases) in the net wage brought about by increases (decreases) in the tax rate *decrease* (increase) hours worked rather than increasing (decreasing) them as a backward bending labour supply schedule would imply. This is

Table 2.15 Simulation of Tax Changes, UK Males, 1971

	Tax rate			
Percentage change in:	*25%*	*28%*	*32%*	*35%*
A.				
Mean hours	0.83	0.37	–0.55	–1.35
Mean gross income (GNP)	0.60	0.27	–0.40	–0.99
Mean tax revenue	–15.32	–6.04	5.76	13.94
B.				
Mean hours	1.65	0.62	[a]0.84	[a]2.04
Mean gross income (GNP)	1.39	0.50	[a]0.69	[a]1.72

Source: Brown (1981, Ch. 12, Tables 12.2, 12.8).

because, for many in the sample, income is close to the exemption level, $[E - (wH + y)]$ is small, so that the effect of the tax change is primarily a substitution effect. Note secondly, that the percentage change in GNP is less than the percentage change in hours. This implies that the marginal wage is less than the average wage (marginal product less than average product). Thirdly, contrary to the claims of advocates of the 'Laffer curve', increases (decreases) in tax rates do not reduce (increase) tax revenue, at least not close to the standard rate of tax.[20] Finally, note that the magnitudes in part B of Table 2.15 are larger than the corresponding figures in part A; this is because the income effects of changes in the exemption level required to maintain revenue neutrality reinforce the substitution effects of the tax rate changes.

Hausman (1981), using 1975 data from the University of Michigan Panel Survey on Income Dynamics, simulates the effects of replacing the then current US income tax with an equal-yield proportional tax on all income above an exemption level. Table 2.16 shows the results of four such schemes in relation to the actual tax system in 1975 (all five schemes yielding equal revenue). The simulation is done on a sample of approximately 1000 husbands. All the alternative schemes have less disincentive effect and impose lower deadweight loss (see Appendix 2.2) than the current tax system.

While the results we have quoted from the UK and US studies deal in averages, the simulation technique lends itself well to the examination of the distributional effects of tax−benefit changes; overall inequality indices (the Gini coefficient, the Atkinson measure, etc.; Sen, 1973) can be computed before and after the proposed reform and/or the distributions of gainers and losers (classified, for example, by pre-reform disposable income) can be analysed.

One shortcoming of both the above studies is that estimation is based on a single, and possibly restrictive, functional form. Thus Glaister et al. use a CES direct utility function, while Hausman uses a linear labour supply schedule. The work of Blundell et al. (1984) simulates reforms using much more flexible functional forms. Their work also has the advantage of being embedded in a life-cycle analytical framework; although the estimation is based on cross-section data, the model is specified in such a way as to be consistent with life-cycle decision making.

Table 2.16 Simulation of Effects of Proportional Tax with Initial Exemption

Exemption level ($)	Tax rate (%)	Effect (%) on annual desired hours of work	Deadweight loss as percentage of taxes
0	14.6	− 27.5	7.1
1000	15.4	− 28.2	8.3
2000	16.9	− 29.9	9.8
4000	20.7	− 34.5	14.5
Current tax system	IR code	−197.5	28.7

Source: Hausman (1981, Table 7).

Evaluating Reforms — Experiments

As an alternative to simulating the effects of tax/transfer programs by using the coefficients of a labour supply function estimated from cross-section data, it is possible to introduce the reform on an experimental basis and observe its effects directly. This can be done either by comparing the behaviour of those receiving and paying the experimental transfers and taxes with their own behaviour prior to the experiment, and/or by comparing the behaviour of those in the experiment with the behaviour of a control group outside it.

The use of experimental data to estimate labour supply effects of a reform has both advantages and disadvantages. On the positive side it may be that changes in w and y do not have the same effect irrespective of how they arise; for example if the stigma attached to state benefits affects the responses to a new transfer program then we might be led astray trying to predict program effects from existing differences in non-labour incomes, which do *not* arise solely from state transfers. A direct experiment will, in principle, avoid this problem. Furthermore differences in w and y between the experimental and control groups should be truly exogenous, determined only by eligibility, whereas, as we argued above, there are often strong grounds for believing that observed w and y are endogenous in non-experimental data. On the other hand, the results of an experiment may be difficult to generalise to the population as a whole, the experiment generally being conducted within a limited geographical area. Similarly, the experimental group will tend to be selected by some specific criterion (e.g. workers with household income below some cut-off level), which can introduce selection bias.

A more fundamental objection arises from the fact that experiments only run for a limited duration (known to its subjects). This makes it unlikely that the predictions of the effects of the *permanent* introduction of the same tax/transfer reform are unbiased. For example if an experimental scheme offers a generous guaranteed income (irrespective of work hours) this will be an inducement to bring forward planned leisure (or education or retraining) from the future to the present. In a similar way, changes in wage rates during the experimental period can lead to life-cycle induced substitution effects not present in a permanent program. On the other hand, while a permanent scheme may induce job changes (e.g. to a lower paid but more pleasant job), a temporary one may not, because it is known that at the end of the experiment income support will be reduced. Similarly long-term availability of benefits will have a much more pronounced wealth effect on labour supply than short-term availability during an experiment. It is extraordinarily difficult to predict the net effect of these different biases (but see Metcalf, 1974). It would be convenient if they simply cancelled out, so that the limited duration experiment accurately predicted the effects of a permanent reform. Unfortunately there is no good reason for believing this to be the case.

Experimental data on labour supply come primarily from the four government-funded negative income tax[21] experiments in the US: the New Jersey—Pennsylvania experiment, the Gary, Indiana experiment, the rural experiment in

Iowa and North Carolina and finally the Seattle—Denver income maintenance experiment. These experiments have been extensively described and analysed.[22]

When such studies are used to estimate structural labour supply elasticities (uncompensated and compensated wage elasticities, non-labour income elasticity) a range of estimates is produced which is not inconsistent with, but at least as wide as, the results of estimation using non-experimental data.

A more direct way of examining the labour supply effects of the NIT is simply to estimate its effect on hours (or earnings) of the experimental group relative to the control group. Regression analysis can be used to standardise for any differences in personal characteristics (age, education, job experience, etc.) between the two groups.[23] Using this approach some general conclusions emerge (Killingsworth, 1983):

(i)   for whites hours are reduced by the introduction of the NIT;
(ii) this reduction is substantially greater for wives (about 20 per cent for wives and 8 per cent for husbands);
(iii) black husbands on the other hand increase hours of work (about 5 per cent on average); evidence for black wives is mixed;
(iv) white husbands' earnings are also reduced but there appears to be a problem of differential underreporting of earnings (experimentals underreporting by more than controls) so this result may be biased.

These results display less variability than do estimates of substitution and income elasticities, and may therefore be of greater immediate use to policy makers who wish to know how labour supply response would effect the cost of introducing an NIT. However, simple comparisons of (regression adjusted) group means describe but do not explain behaviour, and are thus no substitute for structural estimates of the underlying behavioural model.

2.5 Summary

The first objective of this chapter has been to provide a statistical sketch of some of the more important trends and current features of labour supply. Secondly, we explained the essence of some econometric techniques used to analyse labour supply. Finally, we have attempted to give at least a flavour of the results of applied econometric work.

We have not attempted to make this survey fully comprehensive. On the statistical/descriptive front we have not been able to discuss in any great depth the inter-country diversity of experience in the evolution of the labour force; for example while growth in female labour force participation is a near universal trend it has not been uniform in extent or speed.[24] With regard to empirical studies we have ignored both the questionnaire approach[25] and life cycle studies; the first of these is becoming outdated, while the second is still too new. It is likely that the interview approach has now been permanently supplanted by the econometric and experimental approaches described in this chapter.

Even within our chosen compass there are areas we have been forced to pass over. For example, while we have discussed the estimation of participation responses to changes in net wages and property incomes, we have not surveyed models which focus on participation at specific points in the life cycle; in particular we have not surveyed the literature on how retirement is affected by social security. A number of studies suggest that state pension schemes have reduced aggregate labour supply by increasing the incidence of early retirement.[26] The retirement decision is best modelled within a life-cycle framework. Although the analytic specification of such models is achieving considerable maturity (Heckman and MaCurdy, 1980), it seems fair to say that estimation of the parameters of life-cycle models is, relatively speaking, in its infancy (this applies in particular to life-cycle models in which wages are endogenously determined by human capital investments). Heckman (1976b) has made a start in this direction. Even single-year cross-section studies are increasingly attempting to ensure that the models estimated allow life-cycle interpretation (see for example Blundell and Walker, 1984b; Blundell et al., 1987). It seems a safe bet to predict that much of the action in empirical labour supply research over the next decade or so will be concerned with estimating life-cycle models, possibly including uncertainty and job-search aspects intrinsic to life-cycle decision making.

Another area likely to command research attention is the incorporation of unemployment into empirical models, thus relaxing the assumption (not always stated explicitly) in most current models that no non-participants have positive desired hours of work. If some individuals would work at existing wages but cannot find jobs, this assumption is obviously violated (see Ashenfelter (1978), Blundell et al. (1987) for some first steps down this road).

A further promising and important area to explore is the specification of the utility function. One interesting issue here is whether the government's tax and transfer activity directly enters the utility function. It could do so via externalities, public goods' provision and the like (what governments do with their tax revenue is important), or simply because individuals have feelings about government activity (for example the stigma associated with receiving welfare benefits, the resentment towards tax demands). Where the utility function *is* so affected one cannot predict the labour supply effects of changes in taxes and/or benefits simply by examining the relationship between wages, non-labour income and labour supply in a cross-section facing a given tax−benefit system.

Yet another aspect of the specification of utility functions meriting further attention relates to family decision making. In particular, the empirical finding of Ashworth and Ulph (1981) — that separate but interdependent utility functions for family members are more compatible with the data than is a single family utility function — is one which deserves further exploration, especially as the two approaches can imply very different labour supply elasticities.

Finally, it must be remembered that all the econometric studies discussed in this chapter use a partial equilibrium approach to estimating labour supply elasticities. That is to say, they do not attempt to pursue the possible consequences of individuals' responses to a change in the net wage, for example, beyond the possible labour supply (and, in some studies, commodity demand) responses of the group of individuals being studied. But, particularly when one is evaluating proposed tax and benefit reforms, this may be inadequate. Consider the simplest possible case, limiting ourselves to the labour market. Suppose a tax increase reduces labour supply in the aggregate. Assuming an upward sloping supply curve this will, in general, lead to an increase in the gross wage.[27] This in turn will further affect labour supply (the budget constraint will shift). To estimate the new equilibrium in this case one needs to know the parameters of the labour *demand* function as well as those of the supply function. In practice the indirect effects are likely to spread beyond the labour market — changes in gross wages could well, in their turn, affect commodity prices, non-labour incomes, interest rates, the exchange rate etc., all these changes feeding back again into the labour market. Of course the government's tax revenue will be affected by all these changes and tax rates may be altered again if the revenue effect of the initial tax rate is different from that initially predicted. Similar effects, of course, follow from the spending of tax revenue.

Most researchers, using the partial equilibrium approach, are of course fully aware of these general equilibrium, or 'knock-on', effects of labour supply changes. Unfortunately to fully account for them is virtually impossible given the current state of the art in econometric modelling (and given the data requirements of an estimable general equilibrium model).[28] Nevertheless, it would not be surprising if future research were to begin to account for indirect effects of taxes and transfers, perhaps initially restricting attention to supply—demand interactions within the labour market.

Appendix 2.1   Further Issues in the Econometrics of Labour Supply

Variables — Problems of Measurement and Definition

In the text, when considering labour supply models of the type $H = f(w,y,\mathbf{Z}) + e$, we did not worry unduly about how H, w and y were defined or measured in practice, nor about what other explanatory variables, if any, to include in the $\mathbf{Z}$ vector. We discuss these issues now.

The Dependent Variable

The dependent variable — desired labour supply — can refer either to the results of dichotomous decisions such as whether or not to work, or to results of decisions about the *amount* of work to supply (usually measured in hours per week or per year). Where participation and hours are estimated jointly, then H can be a continuous variable with $H = 0$ for non-participants.

In practice, the hours-of-work variable is often derived rather than measured directly. For example, if the dependent variable is annual hours, this will usually be derived using weekly hours in a survey week multiplied by weeks worked per year. But this latter component is a potential source of error where inadequate data exist on paid holidays, absenteeism, time not working due to illness, occasional moonlighting, etc. If these factors are not adequately allowed for then, at best, there will be a loss of efficiency in estimated labour supply parameters. If the measurement error is correlated with included variables, the parameter estimates will be biased.

Another source of error arises where observed hours (or weeks) do not correspond to *desired* hours, due to constraints on either the supply side of the market (for example health constraints) or the demand side (employers impose a minimum and/or maximum number of hours — unemployment is an extreme case where maximum available hours are zero). If the discrepancy is independent of included explanatory variables the estimated coefficients on the variables will not be biased, but again there is loss of efficiency in their estimation. This problem is usually best dealt with by explicitly modelling the source of the divergence between desired and actual hours or by adding independent variables to explain the divergence, but another possibility is to construct a desired hours variable by adding to actual hours some estimate of the discrepancy such as time spent on voluntary job search.

Independent Variables

The wage variable (w)   As in the case of H the object must be to measure w in such a way that it corresponds as closely as possible to the definition of w in our theoretical model. In other words w must correspond to the exogenous real net marginal wage that produces the observed hours for each individual in the sample (where estimation uses cross-sectional data on individuals). A number of problems can arise:

1. Where only the gross wage is observed, the net wage may have to be derived from official income tax schedules. In the absence of full information about the circumstances of the individual it may be difficult to ascertain the true marginal tax rate. In principle we should allow not only for explicit taxation but also for the implicit taxation caused by loss of means tested benefits on earned income increases. In addition, tax avoidance (or evasion) may make the official tax rate inappropriate for calculating the individual's true net wage.

2. Often the researcher may have information on the average wage (derived, say, by dividing annual earnings by annual hours worked). Average and marginal wages are not, in general, identical (the budget constraint is non-linear); so the measured wage does not correspond to the theoretical specification. In order to specify the marginal wage corresponding to given hours what is needed is knowledge of the full budget constraint confronting the individual. As explained in the text, non-linear budget constraints introduce a further problem in that the net marginal wage applying to the

individual is no longer exogenous. This makes OLS estimation inappropriate.

3. Not only does dividing annual (weekly) earnings by annual (weekly) hours produce a measure of average rather than marginal wages but it also means that H and w are definitionally related, so that errors in the measurement of H are transmitted to the measure of w. Clearly this spurious correlation between measured H and measured w can distort the true relationship between desired hours and w which we are trying to estimate.

4. Where non-workers are included in the sample there is obviously no observed wage, and yet we wish to explain their non-participation ($H = 0$) by the same variables as we explain hours worked by participants. A standard procedure is to impute the wage for non-participants from a regression explaining the wages of *participants;* $w_i = \mathbf{Z}\beta + u_i$, where the $\mathbf{Z}$ vector contains variables such as age, sex, education and work experience. Then using non-participants' observed $\mathbf{Z}$s and the estimated β coefficients, w is predicted for non-participants (sometimes predicted w is also used for participants in order to avoid simultaneity bias). Unfortunately this procedure may itself produce a sample selection bias (see below) because u_i, when the sample is restricted to workers, may not be a zero mean, random variable. In this case the imputed wages of non-participants will not be unbiased (on balance participants may be more motivated, ambitious, diligent, etc., causing non-participants' wages to be overestimated by the above procedure, leading in turn to underestimation of the estimated coefficient of w in the labour supply function). To avoid this problem one can use the wage equation $w_i = \mathbf{Z}\beta + u_i$ to substitute w out of the hours equation so that H depends only on y, $\mathbf{Z}$ and stochastic terms from the wage and hours equations. An example of this approach is to be found in Heckman (1974), in which an estimation technique treating w and H as being simultaneously determined is explained.

5. Finally, we note that different models of labour supply would imply conceptually different w variables. Our model has implicitly assumed away non-pecuniary differences between jobs. Should these be important, their imputed value should be added to the observed money wage. For example if jobs requiring longer hours have, as well as higher money wages, relatively greater non-pecuniary benefits, then the wage coefficient would be overestimated in a regression omitting non-pecuniary benefits. More fundamentally, if we move from a static model to a dynamic, life-cycle model, we would have to replace the current net wage by either a vector of perceived net marginal wages at different stages in the life cycle, or by some notion of a permanent wage, and distinguishing between the labour supply effects of changes in the permanent wage and the effects of changes in the transitory component of the observed wage.

The non-labour income variable (y)   One set of problems that arise with respect to this variable relate purely to measurement. They arise because of the necessity to impute an income stream to certain physical assets such as housing. But even if such measurement problems are overcome it is still the case that, like w, non-labour income may not be a true exogenous variable. In the case of non-linear budget constraints (see below) where we replace measured y with virtual income y' this is obvious, but three other possible sources of endogeny are worth mentioning:

1. Some components of y may be directly dependent on hours worked. Unemployment benefit is an extreme case, but other types of state benefit such as Family Income Supplement (in the UK), housing benefits, etc. may also be income contingent and therefore dependent on labour supply.
2. In family models of labour supply the earnings of other family members are taken to be exogenous non-labour income for the family member whose labour supply function we are estimating. This inevitably makes y endogenous. For example in the simple case of a two-member family where subscript h refers to husband and subscript w to wife:

$$H_w = \alpha_0 + \alpha_1 w_w + \alpha_2 y_w + e_w$$

can be written

$$H_w = \alpha_0 + \alpha_1 w_w + \alpha_2(y + w_h H_h) + e_w$$

but husband's hours H_h similarly depend on $w_w H_w$. Therefore y_w depends on H_w. In terms of the error, let e_w increase. This increases H_w, affecting H_h via the income effect. Thus y_w and e_w are not independent.
3. In a life-cycle model, individuals will seek to establish a particular pattern of non-labour income over time (Section 1.5 of Chapter 1 explains the general principles involved). If at a particular time y_t is not at its equilibrium value then H_t may change so as to enable the stock of assets generating non-labour income to be increased or decreased depending on whether actual y is less than or exceeds its desired level.[29] In each case the solution, in principle, is to model explicitly the simultaneous determination of H and y, although in practice few empirical studies do this (but see Blundell and Walker, 1984b).

Other variables   In terms of the elementary labour supply model of the previous chapter, w and y are the only independent variables required. In practice most empirical studies introduce further explanatory variables to allow for two major determinants not allowed for in the simple model — constraints on actual hours an individual can work and heterogeneous preferences.[30] With questionnaire data, dummy variables reflecting respondents' answers to questions about whether they were constrained (either by their own or family circumstances, by health considerations or by employers) in the number of hours they worked in the survey week are frequently used to model constraints (see Brown *et al.*, 1976). Ashenfelter (1980) adds measured unemployment as an explanatory variable to test whether unemployment is involuntary and acts as a constraint on labour supply (see

Heckman *et al.* (1981) for a critique of the Ashenfelter methodology). Variation of preferences and needs across individuals within the sample are generally allowed for by adding variables measuring age, education, family size and structure, region, job satisfaction, etc. Alternatively variation in preferences can be allowed for by imposing a distribution on one or more of the coefficients to be estimated (and simultaneously estimating the parameters of this distribution (see Hausman, 1981)).

Sample Selection Bias

For a population of working individuals, let the true supply of hours function be given by

$$H_i = \alpha_0 + \alpha_1 w_i + u_i = H_i^* + u_i \tag{2.4}$$

where $H_i^* = \alpha_0 + \alpha_1 w_i$ is the exact, or systematic, part of the relationship. Let u_i be a true random variable with mean zero and constant variance.

Now suppose that we want to estimate this relation using cross-sectional data on a sample of individuals taken from this population. Often the choice of the sample is made according to some criterion other than randomness. For example, in estimating equation (2.4) it is often convenient to use data relating to workers only or, when monitoring the effects of an experimental negative income tax (henceforth NIT), researchers are often interested in the effects of the experiment's income support on the labour supply of the 'working poor'. In this case the sample selection rule may be to include all those individuals whose earnings do not exceed a cut-off level y_1, i.e. for whom

$$w_i H_i \leq y_1 \tag{2.5}$$

or

$$H_i \leq \frac{y_1}{w_i}$$

On the sample so selected one could use ordinary least squares (OLS) to estimate the parameters of

$$H_i = \alpha_0 + \alpha_1 w_i + e_i \tag{2.6}$$

where e_i is the *sample* error term, not to be confused with u_i which refers to the *population*.

Had the regression been performed using the whole population, it would have produced estimates with the following property (where E is the expected value):

$$E(H_i) = E(H_i^* + u_i)$$
$$= H_i^* + E(u_i) \tag{2.7}$$
$$= H_i^* \quad (E(u_u) = 0 \text{ by assumption})$$

for all $i = 1, \ldots, n$ members of the population. This property can be expressed in terms of the estimated slope coefficient as

$$E(\hat{\alpha}_1) = \alpha_1 + E\left[\frac{\Sigma(w_i - \bar{w})(u_i - \bar{u})}{\Sigma(w_i - \bar{w})^2}\right] \qquad (2.8)$$

$$= \alpha_1$$

because the second term on the right-hand side of (2.8) disappears due to the assumption that, in the *population*, $E(u_i) = 0$. Equation (2.8) of course means that $\hat{\alpha}_1$, the estimate of α_1, is unbiased when data from the whole population are used for estimation purposes. However, using *sample* data selected according to the income criterion (2.5) the predicted value $\hat{H}_i$ is

$$\hat{H}_i = E(H_i) = E(H_i^* + e_i|_{H_i \leq y_1/w_i}) \qquad (2.9)$$

$$= H_i^* + E(e_i|_{H_i \leq (y_1/w_i)})$$

The question is whether the conditional expectation $E(e_i|_{H_i \leq (y_1/w_i)})$ in the sample is, like the unconditional expectation $E(u_i)$ in the population, equal to zero. Equivalently, in terms of the estimate of the slope coefficient, is the expectation

$$E\left[\frac{\Sigma(w_i - \bar{w})(e_i - \bar{e})}{\Sigma(w_i - \bar{w})^2}\right]$$

equal to zero?

Two simple diagrams (Figures 2.6 and 2.7), one relating to the *population*,

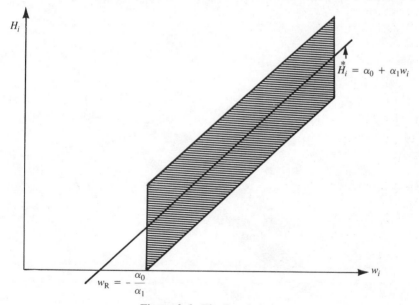

H_i

$\hat{H}_i^* = \alpha_0 + \alpha_1 w_i$

$w_R = -\dfrac{\alpha_0}{\alpha_1}$

w_i

Figure 2.6 The Population

the other to the *sample*, will help us to answer this. The population of observations is assumed to be evenly distributed throughout the shaded area of Fig. 2.6. If we conducted our regression analysis using these observations we would get unbiased parameters. The reservation wage would be $(-\hat{\alpha}_1/\hat{\alpha}_1)$, and equal to the true value $(-\alpha_0/\alpha_1)$. The slope coefficient $E(\hat{\alpha}_1)$ would equal true α_1. However, if we select from the available observations only those for which $w_i H_i \leq y_1$ we are left with observations evenly distributed throughout the shaded area in Fig. 2.7. Clearly the errors e_i, which lie about the true line, $H_i^* = \alpha_0 + \alpha_1 w_i$, no longer have a zero mean (the mean is negative) or a constant variance. The expected value of e_i is not independent of w_i because the selection rule has not removed observations randomly from the shaded band in Fig. 2.6. It has removed more observations representing positive u_i than negative u_i. At higher w_i (above w_{i_1}) there is a greater chance of observing H_i below the 'true' or 'expected' H_i^* than there is at lower w_i (i.e. the probability that observed H_i represents negative error increases with w_i). So the estimated OLS regression would look something like the dotted line in Figure 2.7 because it would have to pass through the new mean H_i and w_i (both lower than the population means because above average values have been removed) and because OLS requires that the *residuals*, $(H_i - \hat{\alpha}_0 - \hat{\alpha}_1 w_i)$, have a zero mean even though the e_i, $(H_i - \alpha_0 - \alpha_1 w_i)$, do not. Thus the reservation wage and the slope coefficient will be underestimated.

The above explanation is mechanical. To understand the underlying cause of the selection bias, note that for any given distribution of u_i in the *population* two factors determine the variation of H_i in the *sample*:

(i)   the variation in H_i, acting via the systematic relation $H_i^* = \alpha_0 + \alpha_1 w_i$

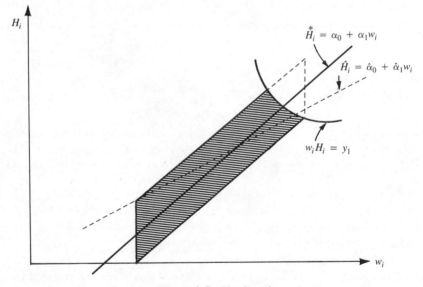

Figure 2.7 The Sample

and

(ii) The selection rule which causes the error distributon in the *sample* to differ
from that in the *population*.

If we use OLS to estimate the hours relation allowing for the first of these factors
only, then the second, the selection rule, can be thought of as a variable which
has been omitted from the estimating equation. Furthermore the omitted variable
is, as we have seen, related to the included variable w_i (wages are negatively
associated with 'taste for work', i.e. negative errors, within the sample, biasing
downward the estimated coefficient of w). Thus the sample selection bias can
be thought of as a special case of omitted variable bias.

Finally, consider two further sources of sample selection bias.

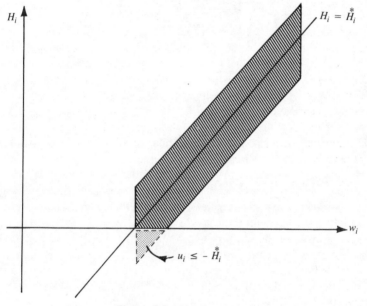

Figure 2.8 The Population

Omitting non-workers This may be done because the researcher has no information on the appropriate wage to apply to such individuals if they were to be
included when estimating an equation like (2.4). Remember that for the population ($H_i = H_i^* + u_i$), omitting non-workers is equivalent to omitting all observations for which $u_i \leq - H_i^*$. So if u_i in the population has a zero mean and
constant variance, the sample error e_i will *not* have these properties because
observations have been systematically rather than randomly excluded. This is
illustrated in Figures 2.8 and 2.9.

Stratified samples It is common practice to estimate separate labour supply functions for different demographic groups, such as teenagers, married workers, rural

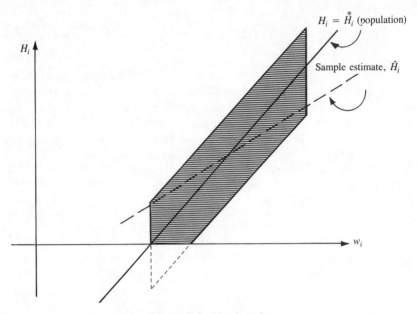

Figure 2.9 The Sample

workers, etc. It is possible that selection rules of this type may not be independent of taste factors incorporated into the error term. If this is the case, then even
though such factors are randomly distributed in the *population* (u_i random) they
will not be randomly distributed in the *sample* (e_i non-random). For example if
married workers have a stronger 'taste for work' than unmarried workers, then
an hours of work function estimated for married workers only will not be an
unbiased estimate of the function which applies to the population as a whole.

The general solution to the problem of sample selection bias is to use an
estimating technique which pays explicit attention to the selection rule, i.e. which
estimates hours conditional on both the included explanatory variables *and* the
selection rule.

One method of doing this is to add an extra variable to the potentially biased
regression equation which explicitly measures the non-random error term. Readers
wishing to fully understand this technique should see Heckman (1976a) and Melino
(1982).

Functional Form

In the main text we write the labour supply function to be estimated in the simple
linear form:

$$H_i = \alpha_0 + \alpha_1 w_i + \alpha_2 y_i$$

We do this partly for simplicity of exposition, although in fact many actual empirical studies use this form for empirical estimation of the labour supply function (for example Hausman, 1980). It has a number of advantages:

1. If $\hat{\alpha}_1 \geq 0$ and $\hat{\alpha}_2 \leq 0$ then (as long as $H \geq 0$) the equation is consistent with the requirement that the compensated wage effect, $\delta H / \delta w_{\text{iU constant}}$, i.e. the pure substitution effect, is not negative. In other words the labour supply function we estimate can be consistent with the theory of utility maximisation on which it is based.
2. The function is very convenient to estimate; it is linear in parameters, it is simple to add further explanatory variables (for instance variables indexing household characteristics), and stochastic variation in H can be incorporated in an additive error term.
3. The coefficients have straightforward interpretations. Compensated and uncompensated elasticities are easy to calculate.
4. It is relatively straightforward to write down the specific form of the direct utility function, $U = U(X,H)$, or the indirect utility function, $V = V(w,y)$, specifying the maximum utility available with given w,y, or cost (expenditure) function, $y = y(w,U)$, showing the minimum income (expenditure) required to achieve a given utility level when faced with given wage rates. These functions may be required in estimation (for example in the presence of a non-convex budget constraint where the utility of multiple tangencies has to be compared, or for evaluating the welfare effects of proposed tax reforms).
5. If necessary, aggregation across individuals to form an aggregate or average labour supply function is straightforward.

However, the linear supply function also has its disadvantages:

1. It is very inflexible in its permitted response of hours worked to changes in the net wage. If $\hat{\alpha}_1$ is positive, the labour supply function is upward sloping throughout, with an extra £1 of net wage inducing the same increase in hours worked at high wages as well as at low wages. There is nothing in economic theory which requires such uniformity of response, or even that the substitution effect dominates the income effect at all wage levels, as is implied by $\hat{\alpha}_1 > 0$. It is perfectly feasible for the substitution effect to dominate at lower wage levels and the income effect at higher levels (the reverse pattern, while intuitively less plausible, is also possible). The use of the linear supply function prejudges such variation in response to be inadmissible. The use of inflexible functional forms which, as in the linear case, rule out change in the slope and/or sign of the labour supply function could result in very misleading predictions about the effect of a tax change on labour supply if the true function is non-linear or non-monotonic in wages.
2. A related inflexibility occurs when $H = 0$. We may wish to allow for the possibility that some properties of the utility function may alter at low levels

of H. In particular we may wish to allow indifference curves in consumption—leisure space to slope upwards due to negative marginal disutility of work (less leisure and more work could be accompanied by less consumption without reducing utility).[31] Although this property is compatible with the linear supply schedule (it implies a negative intercept on the w axis), it then constrains α_1 to be positive if the function is to describe behaviour in the quadrant of positive wages and hours. Further restrictions are imposed on the parameters if the Slutsky condition is to be fulfilled in this quadrant.[32] Less stringently one may wish leisure to be an inferior good at $H = 0$ (implying income and substitution effects are reinforcing, and an increase in the net wage must increase participation). This simply requires α_2, i.e. $\partial H/\partial y$, to be positive at $H = 0$. The problem with the linear functional form is that if $\partial H/\partial y$ is positive at low levels of H it must be positive, i.e. leisure must be inferior, at *all* levels of H. Again this restriction is not required by theory and seems intuitively implausible.

The lesson to be learned from the above discussion is that while the linear functional form scores highly on some counts (tractability, ease of estimation, ease of interpretation of estimated coefficients, ease of calculation of utility functions), it also has some inbuilt disadvantages such as its implications for behaviour at low levels of H and the inflexibility of the permitted response of H to changes in the net wage. The point is a general one. *Any* functional form chosen for the labour supply function will confront the researcher with a trade-off; a preferred form when evaluated by one or more criteria (relative to an alternative functional form) will be less preferred than the alternative when different criteria are used for the comparison. For example we can overcome the built-in inflexibility of the linear form by using a quadratic labour supply function:

$$H = \alpha_0 + \alpha_1 w + \alpha_2 w^2 + \alpha_3 y + \alpha_4 y^2 + \alpha_5 wy$$

The response of H to changes in the net wage is no longer monotonic; labour supply can increase with w for low wages but decrease at higher wages. However, the direct and indirect utility are no longer simple to derive (although matters are simplified if $\alpha_4 = \alpha_5 = 0$). Other alternatives, such as the log-linear and semi-log form, while enabling easier calculations of indirect and/or direct utility functions, are again restrictive in the permitted response of H to w.

Similar conflicts between criteria exist when analysis or estimation begins with the utility function (direct or indirect), from which a labour supply function or labour supply responses are derived.

For detailed discussion of the pros and cons of various functional forms of labour supply and utility functions see Stern (1984) who counsels empirical researchers to check the robustness of their conclusions (about the effect of tax changes on labour supply, for example) by experimenting with a diversity of functional forms.

'Second Generation' Estimation Techniques

From the early 1970s onwards the degree of sophistication in estimation of labour supply parameters increased very dramatically. While the pay-off, in terms of unanimity and robustness of empirical estimates, may still be debatable, there is no question that estimation is now more soundly based analytically. Computational developments (both hardware and software) have enabled the *ad hoc* procedures used in early studies to be replaced by systematic procedures firmly rooted in utility maximising behaviour, with the constraints faced by individuals being carefully and realistically modelled. Sources of bias in earlier techniques have been recognised and allowed for. While many problems still remain to be solved, few labour economists would argue that the developments we summarise as 'second generation estimation techniques' do not represent significant progress.

Analytically, second generation models rely on using a specific utility function, or one of its related functions (for example the MRS between consumption and leisure), to model optimising responses to the full set of constraints faced by the individual. The totality of the labour supply decision is modelled, rather than one particular aspect of it. In particular the decision whether or not to participate and the supply of hours if participating are seen as interrelated rather than separate decisions, both being the result of maximising the same preferences subject to common constraints.

Econometrically, estimation utilises the assumed error structure embedded in the above process to estimate the labour supply parameters (and the parameters of the error distribution) most likely to have generated observed behaviour. Care is taken to distinguish between the error distribution in the underlying population and in the particular sample used for estimation. As we have seen above, failure to take account of this distinction introduces bias into the estimation procedure.

These general principles will be clarified by working through a specific case. Write the utility function in general form as

$$U = U(X, L, e) \tag{2.10}$$

where U, X, L are defined in the usual way (utility, consumption, leisure) and e is an unobservable error term representing taste differences which result in individuals deriving different utility from identical combinations of consumption and leisure. Next choose a specific functional form for the utility function. For ease of exposition we use the multiplicative form. Substituting the budget constraint ($X = wH + y$), setting T, total time available for allocation to work and leisure, also equal to 1 so that $H = 1 - L$, and assuming that the error operates additively on H we have

$$U = [w(H + e) + y]^{\alpha_1} [1 - (H + E)]^{\alpha_2} \tag{2.11}$$

The marginal rate of substitution (MRS) between consumption and leisure is thus

$$\text{MRS} = \frac{\partial U/\partial L}{\partial U/\partial X} = \frac{\alpha_2}{\alpha_1} \frac{w(H + e) + y}{1 - (H + e)} \qquad (2.12)$$

It will prove convenient to write (α_2/α_1) as $a/(1 - a)$ (i.e. $a = \alpha_2/(\alpha_1 + \alpha_2)$). As explained in Chapter 1 the reservation wage, w_R, is the MRS defined at zero hours of work $(L = 1)$, i.e.:

$$w_R = \frac{a}{1 - a} \frac{we + y}{1 - e} \qquad (2.13)$$

An individual will participate (work) when his/her wage exceeds the reservation wage, i.e. when $w > w_R$. Substituting for w_R and expressing the participation criterion as a condition on the error term implies

$$H > 0 \quad \text{if} \quad \epsilon > -\left[(1 - a) - a \frac{y}{w}\right]$$
$$H = 0 \quad \text{if} \quad \epsilon \le -\left[(1 - a) - a \frac{y}{w}\right] \qquad (2.14)$$

where $\epsilon = -e$

It is clear from (2.14) that whether an individual with given w, y works or not depends on the magnitude of ϵ (or e), the unobserved error (taste for work) term.

If a particular individual *does* work, then his/her hours are found by solving for H in the equation $w = $ MRS, which of course is the tangency of the indifference curve and budget constraint.

$$w = \frac{a}{1 - a} \frac{w(H + e) + y}{1 - (H + e)}$$

i.e.

$$H = (1 - a) - a \frac{y}{w} + \epsilon \qquad (2.15)$$

which is the labour supply function for workers, while $H = 0$ defines the labour supply of those for whom

$$\epsilon \le -\left[(1 - a) - a \frac{y}{w}\right]$$

Now, while the labour supply function (2.15) looks superficially like the more *ad hoc* specifications of much first generation work, we shall see that the crucial threshold conditions (2.14) are an integral part of the estimation procedure. This was not so in first generation work.

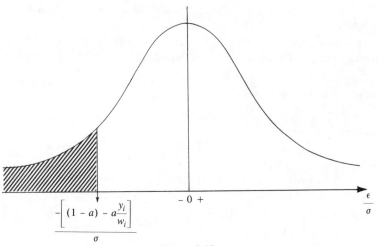

Figure 2.10

To proceed, we require assumptions about the distribution of ϵ in the population. Assume, therefore, that ϵ is normally distributed with mean zero and standard deviation σ. To work with the standard normal distribution we divide ϵ by σ, its standard deviation. We can now illustrate condition (2.14) diagramatically (Figure 2.10). Call the right-hand side of (2.14) $\hat{H}$ (i.e. $H = -[(1-a) - a(y/w)]$. Consider an individual i with a given H_i, corresponding to given w_i, y_i. Even if we knew the value of a, which we do not at this stage, we could not know if individual i would work or not, because we do not know the value of the unobservable ϵ_i. However, we are now in a position to specify the *probability* that the individual works:

$$\Pr\,[i \text{ works}] = \Pr\,(\epsilon_i > -\hat{H}_i]$$

$$= \Pr\left[\left(\frac{\epsilon_i}{\sigma}\right) > -\left(\frac{\hat{H}_i}{\sigma}\right)\right]$$

which, because the area under the standard normal curve $= 1$, can be written

$$\Pr\,[i \text{ works}] = 1 - F\left(\frac{-\hat{H}_i}{\sigma}\right) \qquad (2.16)$$

where F is the standard normal cumulative density function, i.e. $F(-\hat{H}_i/\sigma)$, is the shaded area in Figure 2.10. To express (2.16) differently we note that, if we had a large sample of individuals, all with the same $\hat{H}_i$, the proportion of those not working would be given by the shaded area in Figure 2.10 and, of course, the proportion working by the unshaded area.

We now turn to estimation. Suppose the researcher has a sample of N individuals of whom k are observed to be working. Assume further that we observe w_i and y_i for all individuals in the sample. We can write down the probability of observing the N individuals doing what they are observed to do as

$$\mathcal{L} = \prod_{i=1}^{k} \left[1 - F\left(\frac{-\hat{H}_i}{\sigma} \right) \right] \prod_{i=k+1}^{N} \left[F\left(\frac{-\hat{H}_i}{\sigma} \right) \right]$$

or, in full

$$\mathcal{L} = \prod_{i=1}^{k} \left[1 - F\left[-\frac{1-a}{\sigma} + \left(\frac{a}{\sigma} \right)\left(\frac{y_i}{w_i} \right) \right] \right]$$

$$\times \prod_{i=k+1}^{N} \left[F\left[-\frac{1-a}{\sigma} + \left(\frac{a}{\sigma} \right)\left(\frac{y_i}{w_i} \right) \right] \right] \qquad (2.17)$$

The first term gives the probability that the k individuals, with their given y and w values, will all work, while the second gives the probability that the $(N–k)$ individuals will all be non-workers, given their y, w. The product of the two terms is the probability of observing *both* the k participants and the $(N–k)$ non-participants. Equation (2.17) is known as a *probit* equation. A computer program is used to search for the values of a and σ which maximise $\mathcal{L}$. These are the estimates we require.

The above procedure utilised data on participation, wages and non-labour income only. Frequently the researcher will, in addition, have data on hours worked by participants. A simple modification of the estimation techniques just described enables this extra information to be utilised. Again suppose that we have a sample of N individuals with wage and non-labour income for all, as well as hours of work, data for the k participants. This enables us to write the likelihood function as

$$\mathcal{L} = \prod_{i=1}^{k} f\left(\frac{e_i/\sigma}{\sigma} \right) \prod_{i=k+1}^{N} \left[F\left(\frac{-\hat{H}_i}{\sigma} \right) \right] \qquad (2.18)$$

The second term is again the probability of observing the $N–k$ non-workers, while the first term is the probability of observing individual i working H_i hours. e_i is defined as $[H_i - (1 - a) + a(y_i/w_i)]$ using observed H_i, y_i, w_i for all working members of the sample. Maximising $\mathcal{L}$ will again yield estimates of a and σ. This is called *tobit* analysis; it models both discrete and quantitative choices. Probit dealt with discrete (work, not-work) choices only. Note that once this or a similar model has been estimated, it can be used to provide answers about conceptually different aspects of labour supply. For example suppose there is a change in the net wage due to a tax reform. We could examine the consequences with respect to:

(i) the hours of work supplied by a *given* (representative) *worker*, i.e. computed for a fixed value of ϵ_i, ((ii)–(iv) below all allow for the variation of ϵ_i across the population or the subsample of participants);
(ii) the participation ratio in the *population*;
(iii) the average of expected hours of work of all *workers*;
(iv) mean or expected hours of work of all *individuals*, participating or not (note if all individuals work (i) = (iii) = (iv)).

Many first generation studies failed to distinguish between these concepts. For example if: $H_i = \alpha_0 w_i + \alpha_2 y_i + e$ is estimated for participants *and* non-participants (with $H = 0$ and w imputed) then $\hat{\alpha}_1$ is not the same as (i) above, rather it approximates (iv).[33] Even if the equation is estimated for participants only, $\hat{\alpha}_1$ will still not be a good estimate of (i) because the model is misspecified unless participation and hours are jointly estimated.

The methodology described in this section, while it may seen complex to those unfamiliar with econometrics, provides only an intuitive outline of the basic principles of second generation estimation techniques. Many modifications, refinements and extensions are necessary to deal with the complex budget constraints resulting from taxes and benefits, to allow for fixed time and money costs of working, to incorporate rationing, etc. Some of these techniques extend basic probit analysis to what is called ordered probit in which not one but a series of threshold levels of e_i are examined to estimate the probability of individuals locating only one of a number of possible segments or kinks of a complex budget constraint. While the econometrics is more complex the basic principle is as above; use a specific form of the utility function (or some related function) including its assumed error distribution to explicitly evaluate the full range of labour supply choices open to an individual with given characteristics and opportunities and then determine the parameters of both the derived labour supply function and error distribution which are most likely to produce the observed labour supply decisions of all individuals in the sample.

Appendix 2.2   The Deadweight Loss of Taxation

Apart from any impact it may have on labour supply, the taxation of income also affects welfare due to its distortionary effect. This deadweight loss, or excess burden, is illustrated in Figure 2.11 which illustrates the effect of imposing a tax at rate t on earned income only. Initial pre-tax equilibrium is at A on indifference curve U_1. Post-tax equilibrium is at B on U_0. Clearly taxation has reduced utility. But utility will also be affected by how the government spends its tax revenue. This revenue is BC in the diagram (the difference between pre- and post-tax earnings at new hours of work H_0). Even if this is returned to the individual as a cash grant it is insufficient by an amount CD to return the individual to the initial utility level U_1.[34] This amount CD is the 'excess burden'

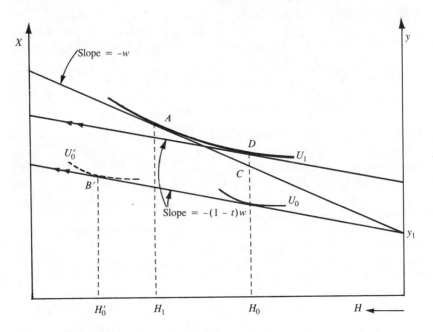

Figure 2.11 Excess Burden of a Tax on Earnings

or 'deadweight loss' of the earnings tax. Note that although in this case the substitution effect dominates (the income effect has been set at zero for expositional convenience) and labour supply is reduced, the existence of excess burden does not depend on this: if the post-tax indifference curve had been U_0', so that the income effect dominated, then restoring the individual to U_1 would again require a grant of BD which would reduce hours to H_0, producing BC tax revenue — insufficient to finance the grant.

Clearly in designing or reforming tax systems the government should attempt to minimise the excess burden. Because second generation estimation techniques (see Appendix 2.1) involve estimation of utility function parameters, they are well suited to calculation of excess burden. One study that does this explicitly is Hausman (1981).[35] For the average husband in his sample with an hourly wage of $6.18 (sample mean) he finds that the deadweight loss is $235 per annum (1975 prices) which is 2.4 per cent of net income and 22 per cent of his tax bill (federal taxes only). If this same individual earned $10 per hour the deadweight loss rises to $1883, which is 11.7 per cent of net income and 54 per cent of his tax payment. Clearly the progressivity of the tax system imposes substantial increases in welfare costs as income increases;[36] indeed Hausman calculates substantial reductions in excess burden arising from a revenue-neutral switch from progressive to proportional taxation. For a sceptical appraisal of Hausman's estimates see Browning (1985).

Notes

1. Age and sex are the subdivisions we will mostly concentrate on although regional, racial and educational subgroups are also frequently studied.
2. This term could incorporate the effects of unemployment. Alternatively a separate term measuring the proportion of the labour force employed could be introduced into the equation.
3. The source for the figures in this paragraph is Smith and Ward (1985).
4. For example in 1906, when paid holidays for manual wage earners were exceedingly rare, the Board of Trade estimated that manual workers on average took 11−12 days unpaid holidays per annum.
5. Non-manual salaried workers received between one and two weeks' paid holiday.
6. Possibly because employees were eager to pre-empt the Committee of Enquiry — the Alumree Committee — which was sitting at the time and which was expected to legislate more disadvantageous — from the employer's point of view — holiday entitlements for industries not already covered by voluntary collective agreements.
7. These activity rates are higher for both countries than those quoted in Table 2.1. This is mainly due to (a) the inclusion of students in the labour force and (b) the exclusion of those aged 64 and over who have low participation.
8. The exception was the curved budget constraint reflecting the decreasing marginal productivity of work in the home.
9. To move from the indirect utility function to the labour supply function or vice versa one invokes Roy's identity:

    Let $U = U(X, L)$
    then $V = (w, y)$

    is the indirect utility function, specifying the maximum utility available for given w, y. Roy's identity states

    $$\frac{\delta V/\delta w}{\delta V/\delta y} = H \quad \text{(desired hours of work)}$$

10. Note that small, or even zero, uncompensated wage elasticities do not imply negligible labour supply effects of taxation if tax applies to non-labour income as well as earnings, and if estimated income elasticities are large. Thus Hausman (1981), in spite of estimating an essentially zero wage coefficient for husbands, still finds the average husband in his sample works 8 per cent less than he would in the absence of taxes. This is due to the significant estimated income effect.
11. For more detailed results on the effects of children on female labour supply see papers by Hanoch (1980) and other papers in Smith (1980).
12. Note that observed growth in real wages for women may be subject to selectivity bias. The coreect variable is the growth in the average potential wage for all women, both participants and non-participants.
13. For the USA see Smith and Ward (1985, Table 16) and for UK Joshi et al. (1985, Table 6). Both of these studies provide rich analysis of the female labour supply effects of non-wage factors as well as real wage effects.
14. In technical terms this means that OLS regressions which regress women's labour force participation rates on some measures or indices of the above factors will be subject to simultaneous equation bias.
15. Very few time series studies have reliable series on *net* wages (*gross* real wage series can be obtained relatively easily). Changes in net real wages must carefully allow for tax changes, changes in non-pecuniary fringe benefits, changes in holiday entitlements (if per hour or per week wages derived from annual earnings), etc.

16. The first stage is to estimate an equation of the form

$$P_{ti} = f_i + X_{ti}\beta + Z_t\tau + e_{ti}$$

where subscript t refers to date and i to cohort,

P_{ti} = participation of cohort i individuals at date t

X_{ti} = vector of life cycle variables — they change from year to year and are also age specific, e.g. no. of children ages 0–4 per woman; the contemporaneous wage variables are also included in X_{ti}

Z_t = vector of purely calendar time variables, i.e. variables which change from year to year but have an approximately equal impact on all age groups; the level of aggregate demand in the economy is one such variable (although this could also be given a cohort subscript as different age groups are not equally affected by the state of the economy)

f_i = fixed (cohort) effects which do not change over the life cycle of members of a given cohort (estimated as coefficients on cohort dummy variables)

β, τ = vectors of coefficients to be estimated

The second stage of the estimation procedure is to use the estimated fixed (cohort) effects, $\hat{f}_i$, as the dependent variable in a second regression in which the explanatory variables are cohort specific, e.g. wages at specific ages, years of completed education, a summary fertility variable (e.g. completed family size), etc.

17. In estimating the fixed effect elasticities, Smith and Ward (1985) use as the wage variable five-year lags in wages (standardising for life-cycle point). This is intended as a summary proxy for the expected cohort wage profile; the negative signs in part A of Table 2.14 therefore represent the wealth effects of parametric shifts in the cohort wage profile.

18. The arguments in this paragraph are more easily understood against the background of the discussion in Appendix 2.1 of 'second generation' estimation methods.

19. For an analysis of the inadequacy of the 'representative individual' approach to reform in a related context see Atkinson et al. (1983).

20. More specifically the finding contradicts the claim of those who believe that economies like the US and UK are on the downward sloping part of the Laffer curve. This curve describes a relationship between tax rates and tax revenues in which increases in tax rates initially increase tax revenues but beyond a certain point further increases in tax rates actually reduce the tax take.

21. A negative income tax (NIT) is, at its simplest, an income maintenance program which replaces existing taxes and benefits and provides everyone in the labour force, whether working or not, with a guaranteed income G, and taxes all earnings at a rate t. Together G and t define y_B ($y_B = G/t$) the break-even level of income beyond which the individual stops receiving net benefits (A in Figure 2.12) and begins to pay positive (net) taxes (B). Working individuals below y_B are likely, prior to the introduction of the NIT, to have had non-labour income less than G and a net wage greater than $w(1 - t)$ (they may have been tax exempt). For such individuals the income and substitution effects of the change reinforce each other and hours of work must fall.

22. See, for example, for New Jersey: Cain and Watts (1973); for Gary: Burtless and Hausman (1978) and Kehrer et al. (1980); for Iowa and North Carolina: Palmer and Pechman (1978); for Seattle–Denver: Robins et al. (1980), Keeley et al. (1978) and Moffitt and Kehrer (1981) for a survey.

23. Using observations from both groups, one regresses hours (or earnings) on the vector of personal and job characteristics as well as on a dummy variable taking the value 1 if the individual is in the experimental group and zero otherwise.

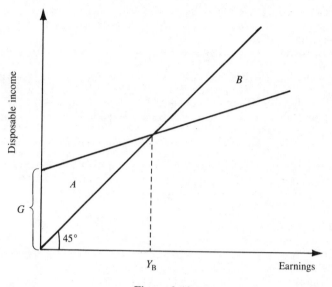

Figure 2.12

24. See *Journal of Labour Economics*, Vol. 3, No. 1, Part 2 (Jan. 1985) for separate country studies covering USA, Britain, France, Spain, Germany (Federal Republic), The Netherlands, Sweden, Italy, Australia, Israel, USSR and Japan.
25. Often quoted studies are Break (1957) and Fields and Stanbury (1971). A more carefully designed study is described in Brown and Levin (1974).
26. See Boskin and Hurd (1978), Gordon and Blinder (1980), Mitchell and Fields (1984) and Aaron and Burtless (1984).
27. The tax increase, by lowering the net wage, causes a movement along the labour supply curve which has net wages on the vertical and hours on the horizontal axis. This represents a shift of the labour supply curve denominated in terms of the gross wage.
28. At a different level of aggregation, some macroeconometric models *do* attempt to model both sides of the labour market, and real wage adjustment when the market is in disequilibrium. However, such models are often only loosely based on the utility and profit maximising behaviour of individuals and firms. Nevertheless some such models do concern themselves with similar questions to those addressed by microeconometric studies, e.g. the labour market response to changes in taxes and benefits (see Wallis, 1984, Ch. 4).
29. Blundell *et al.* (1984) go further than this and argue that life-cycle considerations make the inclusion of y in a single period model a misspecification. The correct variables to include are net benefits and net dissavings.
30. Constraints can alternatively be dealt with by omitting constrained individuals from the sample or by using discrete choice analysis to model labour supply decisions with restricted budget constraints (see Heckman *et al.*, 1981).
31. Note that this implies that the shadow wage required to induce participation is negative.
32. If $\alpha_2 > 0$ then the Slutsky condition for the compensated substitution effect, $(\alpha_1 - \alpha_2 H) \geq 0$ requires $(\alpha_1/\alpha_2 > H)$. If $\alpha_2 < 0$ then $H \geq 0$ is sufficient for Slutsky, but the requirement $(\alpha_0 + \alpha_2 y) > 0$ requires $(\alpha_0/-\alpha_2) > y$.

33. It is an approximation because strictly speaking the equation applies to participants only, as our discussion should have made clear. If non-participants are included, the model is misspecified.
34. *BD*, the size of the cash grant that *would* be sufficient is known as the compensating variation.
35. In essence Hausman (1981) uses the expenditure function (showing minimum expenditure for given *W, Y* and personal characteristics, *Z*, required to achieve a given level of utility) to calculate *BD* in Figure 2.11 from which taxes are subtracted to yield the welfare loss *CD*. However, taxes apply to income, not just earnings, in Hausman's study.
36. Of course these costs could be offset if there are distributional benefits associated with progressive taxation.

3

The Theory of Labour Demand

If we are to understand the workings of the labour market, it is clear that we will need a comprehensive understanding of the determinants of labour demand. In this chapter we will review the standard neoclassical theory of the firm's demand for inputs. We will then examine both the extensions of the theory and some of its limitations.

In the early parts of our discussion we will assume that all workers are identical and that labour input may be expressed in terms of a single unit. If, for example, labour input per worker does not vary with the length or timing of the working day, then man-hours may be taken as just such a unit. Later in the chapter we will relax these assumptions and consider the treatment of heterogeneous types of labour.

3.1 The Short-Run Demand for Labour

It is best to begin with the simplest case. Suppose we imagine that a firm is endowed with a given amount of machinery and equipment which is employed for a predetermined number of hours in a working day. The firm is free to employ any number of man-hours that it may choose, but is unable to vary its capital input. How will the firm determine the amount of labour that it should employ?

At this point we must make certain key assumptions which we shall retain until later in the chapter:

1. The firm is a price taker in both factor and product markets. Thus, for example, the firm is unable to influence the level of wages or rents paid elsewhere by its hiring decisions and cannot alter the market price that is paid for its output by its production decisions.
2. The firm can employ its inputs in any desired proportion. The use of driver only or driver plus conductor buses might serve as a rather crude example

81

here, particularly if we allow that buses may be built to different sizes. Although this assumption has led to much criticism in the literature, in fact it may be relaxed considerably without altering our main conclusions, although its retention considerably simplifies our exposition.

3. The firm wishes to maximise profits.

The firm's decision rule is very simple. It looks at its expected level of profits before employing an additional unit and again after employing that unit. If it expects profits to increase, then it employs the additional unit and moves on to consider whether it is worthwhile employing further units. It then carries on in this way until marginal profit is zero. The profit maximising condition is thus

Marginal cost of additional labour unit	=	Marginal revenue generated by employing extra unit
	=	Marginal product of labour $\times$ Marginal revenue from extra output unit

Now if the firm is a price taker in both factor and product market (assumption 1 above), then the marginal cost of employing an additional labour unit is simply the wage, W (i.e. gross of tax and employer's contributions), and the marginal revenue obtained from selling an additional unit is the product price, P. If we further assume the existence of a production function

$$Q = F(K,L) \tag{3.1}$$

where Q is output, K is some index of non-labour inputs and L is labour input, then the first derivative of the function with respect to labour $(\partial Q/\partial L = F_L)$ is the marginal product of labour.

Our profit maximising condition can now be rewritten as

$$W = F_L P \tag{3.2}$$

As we take the product price to be a constant, then the only way in which a firm can react to a change in the market wage is to alter F_L by changing the quantity of labour that it employs. Normally we impose the hypothesis of diminishing returns upon the production function, i.e. that as we increase the input of one factor, other factors being held constant, then after some point the marginal product of that factor will decrease. More formally this requires that the first derivatives of the production function be positive and the second own derivatives of the function be negative:

$$F_L > 0, \ F_K > 0, \ F_{LL} < 0, \ F_{KK} < 0$$

Thus, holding K constant, the marginal physical product of labour, F_L, and the marginal value product of labour, $F_L P$, will diminish as L is increased. This is illustrated by the MVP curve in Figure 3.1.

Let us suppose that the firm is initially in its profit maximising position and

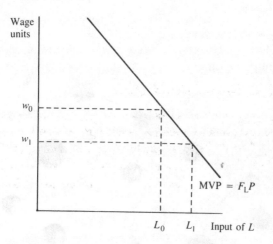

Figure 3.1 The Short-Run Demand Curve for Labour

it is currently employing L_0 units of labour input at wage W_0. If the wage should now fall to W_1, then according to equation (3.2) the firm will expand its employment to L_1. The marginal value product curve can therefore be regarded as a short-run demand curve for labour. The elasticity of this curve is greater the less readily the marginal product of labour diminishes with increased labour input, i.e. the smaller the absolute value of F_{LL}. It is also in general true that the elasticity is greater the more easily the firm can substitute between labour and non-labour inputs.

3.2 The Long-Run Demand for Labour

Obviously the demand curve above is conceptually different from the kind of demand curve that one normally meets in introductory economics textbooks. If we draw a demand curve for (say) butter, then we normally do this on the assumption, among others, that the prices of substitutes such as margarine and complements such as bread remain constant. Yet our demand curve above does not specify that the prices of non-labour inputs remain constant, but their quantities. What then happens to our analysis of labour demand if we alter this assumption?

Clearly, we can write a marginal productivity condition for non-labour inputs as

$$R = F_K P \tag{3.3}$$

where R is the rental paid per non-labour input unit. Let us suppose that equation (3.3) held at L_0. If we assume that increasing quantity of labour input would increase the marginal productivity of other inputs, i.e. $F_{KL} > 0$, then equation (3.3) would be violated when we expand employment to L_1. The rental paid per machine would be less than its marginal value product. The firm would then wish to increase both its machines and labour input further until both marginal productivity conditions were satisfied.

There are, however, two further complications that we must take on board. Firstly, if the firm expands its employment of inputs, then its output must also increase. Under the assumption of perfect competition, other firms in the industry will react in an identical manner to a given change in the market wage rate, which means that industry output will increase correspondingly and the product price, P, will tend to fall. Secondly, as each firm seeks to employ more non-labour inputs, the rental of the latter, R, may tend to rise. Both of these effects will influence the two marginal productivity conditions and hence the firm's optimal input combination.

Returning to Figure 3.1, the firm's increased use of machines will tend to shift out the MVP curve which means that the optimal labour employment level will now be greater than L_1. On the other hand, a fall in product price or a rise in the machine rental will have the opposite effect. We will now demonstrate these arguments more rigorously.

First let us assume that our firm is initially in equilibrium in the sense that labour and machines are being paid their respective marginal value products. We therefore have three equations which must be satisfied.

$$Q = F(K,L) \tag{3.1}$$
$$W = F_L P \tag{3.2}$$
$$R = F_K P \tag{3.3}$$

Suppose we now allow the wage rate of labour, W, to change by one unit holding the price per machine, R, constant but allowing the quantities K and L to change in response. For the moment we will hold Q constant.

The displacement from equilibrium for changing W is

$$0 = F_L \frac{\partial L}{\partial W} + F_K \frac{\partial K}{\partial W} \tag{3.4}$$

$$1 = F_L \frac{\partial P}{\partial W} + P\left(F_{LL} \frac{\partial L}{\partial W} + F_{LK} \frac{\partial K}{\partial W}\right) \tag{3.5}$$

$$0 = F_K \frac{\partial P}{\partial W} + P\left(F_{KL} \frac{\partial L}{\partial W} + F_{KK} \frac{\partial K}{\partial W}\right) \tag{3.6}$$

We therefore have three equations and three unknowns: $\partial P/\partial W$, $\partial L/\partial W$ and $\partial K/\partial W$. Now if output is constant then the only effect that a change in the wage rate can have on a firm's demand for factors is via its ability to substitute one factor for another. To capture this, we introduce the concept of the elasticity of substitution which may generally be defined for a world with only two factors of production as

$$\sigma_{KL} = \frac{\% \text{ change in } K/L}{\% \text{ change in } F_L/F_K} = \frac{d \log K/L}{d \log F_L/F_K} = \frac{d \log K/L}{d \log W/R}$$

The elasticity of substitution thus gives us a measure of how readily factor proportions change in response to changing relative factor prices. Knowing the value of σ_{KL} tells us something about the shape of the isoquants generated by the production function. This is illustrated in Figure 3.2 for three different cases. The left-hand panel shows an isoquant where $\sigma_{KL} = 0$. Clearly this implies that the ratio of K to L is constant. The right-hand panel ($\sigma_{KL} = \infty$) shows a very different case in which the slope of the isoquant is invariant to the factor proportions employed. This means that the ratio of marginal products is constant.[1] The middle isoquant shows an intermediate case.

Unfortunately the simple definition above is not usually the appropriate one when we move beyond two factors. The appropriate measure is the Allen partial elasticity of substitution which reflects the effect upon the quantity demanded of one factor of a change in the price of another, holding output and the prices of all other factors constant. For a more precise definition and a brief review of factor demand theory extended to n inputs, the reader is referred to the discussion in Chapter 4.

By solving equations (3.4) to (3.6) we find the following relationships[2]

$$E_{LL} = (v_L - 1)\sigma_{KL} \tag{3.7}$$

$$E_{KL} = v_L \sigma_{KL} \tag{3.8}$$

where v_L is the share of labour in total cost, i.e.

$$v_L = \frac{F_L L}{F_L L + F_K K}$$

E_{LL} is the wage elasticity of demand for labour and E_{KL} is the wage elasticity of demand for machines.[3] Equation (3.7) then tells us that the demand curve for labour will be the more elastic, the greater is labour's share and the greater is

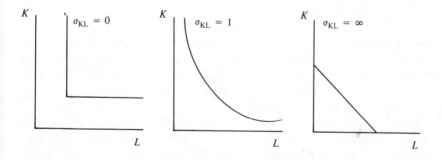

Figure 3.2   Two-Factor Isoquants

the elasticity of substitution. Equation (3.8) gives similar predictions regarding the cross-elasticity between machines and labour.

Now, so far, we have only included the substitution effect. If, for example, machines and labour could only be combined in fixed proportions, then σ_{KL}, F_{LL} and E_{KL} would all be zero. Clearly, however, as product price changes, then the demand for the industry's output will change accordingly and so, therefore, will the output of each firm. The simplest procedure is to make the demand for output a negative function of its price:

$$Q = Q(P) \qquad \frac{dQ}{dP} < 0 \qquad\qquad (3.9)$$

The right-hand side of this equation will be $1/N$ times the demand function for industry output, where N is the number of firms in the industry. However, the price elasticity of demand for output is the same for both firm and industry. We shall denote this as η.

Therefore we replace equation (3.1) by

$$Q(P) = F(K,L) \qquad\qquad (3.1')$$

and equation (3.4) by

$$\frac{dQ}{dP} \frac{\partial P}{\partial W} = F_L \frac{\partial L}{\partial W} + F_K \frac{\partial K}{\partial W}$$

or

$$0 = -Q\eta \frac{1}{P} \frac{\partial P}{\partial W} + F_L \frac{\partial L}{\partial W} + F_K \frac{\partial K}{\partial W} \qquad\qquad (3.4')$$

To obtain reasonably simple results, it is convenient to impose constant returns to scale at this point.[4]

Solving (3.4'), (3.5) and (3.6) then yields

$$E_{LL} = v_L (\sigma_{KL} + \eta) - \sigma_{KL} \qquad\qquad (3.7')$$
$$E_{KL} = v_L (\sigma_{KL} + \eta) \qquad\qquad (3.8')$$

The larger is the elasticity of substitution, then the more elastic will be the long-run demand curve for labour and the larger will be the cross-elasticity between the two factors. On the other hand, although demand for labour will be more elastic, the higher the (absolute value of) price elasticity of demand for output, the lower will be the cross-elasticity.

There remains one additional possibility that we might like to take into account. As the firm (or industry) expands its stock of machines, it may be that the supply price or rental per machine increases. This therefore means that we have an additional equation of the form

$$R = R(K) \qquad \frac{dR}{dK} > 0 \qquad\qquad (3.10)$$

We therefore replace equation (3.3) by

$$R(K) = F_K P \qquad\qquad (3.3')$$

and equation (3.6) by

$$\frac{dR}{dK} \frac{\partial K}{\partial W} = F_K \frac{\partial P}{\partial W} + P\left(F_{KL} \frac{\partial L}{\partial W} + F_{KK} \frac{\partial K}{\partial W} \right) \qquad\qquad (3.6')$$

where dR/dK refers to the supply function for machines.

If we define S_K as the supply elasticity of machines, we find

$$E_{LL} = \frac{v_L(\sigma_{KL} + \eta) - \sigma_{KL}}{1 - (1 - v_L)\eta/S_K} \qquad\qquad (3.7'')$$

$$E_{KL} = \frac{v_L(\sigma_{KL} + \eta)}{1 - (1 - v_L)\eta/S_K} \qquad\qquad (3.8'')$$

Both E_{LL} and E_{KL} then increase in absolute values with S_K. We should notice that as S_K approaches infinity, i.e. machines are in perfectly elastic supply, then equations (3.7″) and (3.8″) become identical with (3.7′) and (3.8′). Generally speaking, in micro-analysis we are usually content to assume that the supplies of other factors are perfectly elastic and we shall follow this procedure from now on.

One might wonder at this stage exactly how a demand function for labour is arrived at. After all, the various expressions for E_{LL} and E_{KL} derived above simply tell us the properties of the various demand elasticities but they do not specify the demand function itself. How is this accomplished?

Suppose we return to our original production function and marginal conditions, i.e. equations (3.1) to (3.3). We also know that we define the cost of producing any output as

$$C = WL + RK \qquad\qquad (3.11)$$

If we solve the resulting four equation systems, then we can eliminate P, K and L and we can write our cost function as

$$C = G(W,R,Q) \qquad\qquad (3.12)[5]$$

This function then describes the minimum cost at which any output Q can be produced given input prices W and R. We should first notice that if W rises by a single small unit, then the cost to the firm of maintaining output at Q is L units. Thus:

$$\frac{\partial G}{\partial W} = L$$

and

$$\frac{\partial G}{\partial R} = K$$

The own first derivatives of the cost function are therefore the demand functions for the inputs and are of the form $L = L(W/R,Q)$.[6] Likewise it follows that the various second derivatives of the cost function describe the properties of the demand functions given fixed output, for example

$$\frac{\partial^2 C}{\partial W^2} \frac{W}{L} = E_{LL}\Big|Q \text{ fixed}$$

and

$$\frac{\partial^2 C}{\partial R \partial W} \frac{W}{K} = E_{KL}\Big|Q \text{ fixed}$$

This brings us to the end of a rather long section. We have seen that our simple model predicts that the demand for labour will be inversely related to the wage, and normally positively related to the price of other inputs and output. The determinants of the elasticity of demand for labour may be neatly stated in four rules originally given by Marshall (1920) and partly modified by Hicks (1932). The demand for labour will be the more elastic, the bigger is:

(i)   the absolute value of the price elasticity of demand for output;
(ii) the elasticity of substitution between labour and other inputs;
(iii) the share of labour providing that the elasticity of substitution is less than the price elasticity of demand for output, i.e. $\sigma_{KL} < |\eta|$;
(iv) the elasticity of supply of other inputs.

Our analysis above has only explicitly considered the case of two factors, i.e. labour and capital. The general case of many factors is briefly dealt with in Chapter 4.

3.3   Some Extensions of the Model

The framework that we have presented can be easily extended to include a large number of complications. In this section we shall briefly examine a few of them.

Monopoly or Imperfect Competition in Product Markets

Let us now drop our assumption that the firm is a price taker in the product market and instead suppose that it faces a downward sloping demand curve for its output. We must carefully distinguish between this and our previous example in which the firm faced a downward sloping curve for its output because other firms in the industry reacted in an identical manner to a given wage change. If in this latter case the individual firm had been the only one to face the wage change, then we would have retained the assumption of perfectly elastic demand for output. However, we are now discussing in this section a situation in which the firm faces a downward sloping demand curve for its output even if no other firm changes it behaviour.

The basic profit maximising condition is as before

$$\text{Marginal cost of additional labour unit} = \text{Marginal product of labour} \times \text{Marginal revenue from extra output unit}$$

However, the marginal revenue from output is no longer the price. Marginal revenue is now defined as

$$\text{MR} = \frac{d(PQ)}{dQ} = P + Q\frac{dP}{dQ}$$

As dP/dQ is strictly negative, MR must be less than product price. Our marginal condition is then

$$W = \frac{\partial Q}{\partial L}\left(P + Q\frac{dP}{dQ}\right) \tag{3.13}$$

The right-hand side of this equation is known as the marginal revenue product of labour which is necessarily less than the marginal value product. We may rewrite this as

$$W = \frac{\partial Q}{\partial L}\lambda \tag{3.14}$$

where λ is marginal revenue. Similarly the marginal condition for machines is

$$R = \frac{\partial Q}{\partial K}\lambda \tag{3.15}$$

Equations (3.14) and (3.15) thus take the place in our system of (3.2) and (3.3).

Finally, we may note that

$$\lambda = P\left(1 + \frac{1}{\eta}\right)$$

Thus if output is some negative function of price, $Q(P)$, then we can also write output as a negative function of marginal revenue, $Q(\lambda)$. We therefore can repeat our previous systems of equations with λ replacing the product price, P. We then obtain exactly the same results as before (i.e. (3.7), (3.8), (3.7'), (3.8'), (3.7''") and (3.8''")) except that η, the price elasticity of demand for output, is replaced by E where E is the elasticity of the marginal revenue curve. Since the marginal revenue curve is generally less elastic than the demand (or average revenue) curve, it will normally be true that a monopolistic industry will have a more inelastic demand for labour than the same industry producing under conditions of perfect competition. We might also note in passing that the cost function specified in equation (3.12) is identical for both the monopolist and the competitive firm. Dropping our assumption of competitive product markets, therefore, does little to alter the general conclusions of our earlier analysis.

Labour Efficiency and Wages

It has sometimes been argued that if we pay a man more for doing his job, then he will contribute more labour input during his working hours. In poor countries this is ascribed to an improvement in nutritional levels; in developed countries it is usually associated with the psychological effects of a higher wage.

In Figure 3.3 we show an employment level N_0 corresponding to a wage per man of W_0. If the wage is raised to a new higher level such as W_1, the effect is to shift the marginal productivity schedule outwards. Thus instead of observing a new employment level at N_1, we find a higher level at N_1. Labour is still of course paid according to its marginal product, but even in the short run the individual marginal productivity schedules cannot be thought of as labour demand curves.

The easiest way of approaching this problem is to imagine that each worker (or man-hour) embodies a given number of labour efficiency units which we shall denote as E. We may further suppose that E is a positive function of the wage. Thus

$$L = NE(W) \qquad \frac{\mathrm{d}E}{\mathrm{d}W} > 0$$

where N is the number of workers. Now as we have seen this makes no difference

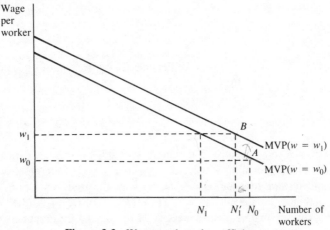

Figure 3.3   Wages and worker efficiency

to our profit maximising condition for employment; the firm will still take on
labour efficiency units until the wage per unit is equal to its marginal value product. However, there is a circumstance under which the firm may pay a wage
that is higher than is needed to attract sufficient labour. —*Skill, human kapital*

A necessary pre-condition for maximising profits is to first minimise the cost
of producing any given output. If we restrict ourselves to the short run, then this
is simply a matter of minimising labour cost. Our problem may then be written as

minimise $C = WN$
subject to $Q = F(K,L)$
where $L = NE(W)$

The first order condition with respect to the wage is then

$$N = \lambda \frac{\partial Q}{\partial L} N \frac{dE}{dW}$$

or   (3.16)

$$1 = \lambda \frac{\partial Q}{\partial L} \frac{dE}{dW}$$

where λ is marginal cost.[7] If the firm maximises profit, then this will equal
marginal revenue and under perfect competition it will also equal product price.

The interpretation of equation (3.16) is straightforward. Obviously if a firm
were able to reduce wages, it would save in terms of the wage bill. On the other
hand, it would also lose out in terms of efficiency units per worker. The balance
occurs when the firm has reduced wages to such a point that a further reduction
of one monetary unit (e.g. 1 penny) in the wage is exactly compensated by a
loss of a penny's worth of a worker's marginal product. Thus if the wage per
man is greater than the current supply price of labour, then we will observe excess labour supply and unemployment in the labour market as a whole.

What, in effect, our firm is doing is to juggle with the wage per man so as
to find the minimum wage payable per efficiency unit. But what happens if the
supply price per man in the market is above the desired minimum? Essentially
our analysis is identical to that earlier in this chapter. From the $E(W)$ relation
the firm finds the number of efficiency units per man that it can expect at the
going market wage, and hence the wage per efficiency unit. The firm then decides
upon the number of efficiency units that it wishes to employ (and thus the number
of men) according to the usual marginal conditions. Thus, although the 'economy
of high wages' is an interesting explanation of why labour markets might be
characterised by excess supply, it is essentially an extension of, rather than an
alternative to, our earlier analysis.

Wages and Labour Turnover

We have been implicitly assuming so far that wages are the only element in labour
cost. This is not as unrealistic as it may seem, since wages are normally taken

to include fringe benefits and payments in kind. There are, however, two additional forms of payment which an employer may have to make.

In the first place there may be fixed costs of employment, e.g. UK employers' contributions to National Insurance which do not necessarily increase with hours worked or total wages. Clearly, our marginal conditions, and therefore optimal choice of input mix, are unaffected. The firm's profit will, of course, be lower and the firm would, in the absence of higher overtime rates, have an incentive to employ fewer men for more hours.

The second type of additional cost is more interesting. If a worker leaves his job, then the firm will necessarily incur some cost in recruiting a replacement and in providing any necessary training. Even if no formal tuition is required, there may still be a period during which the new employee is finding his feet and getting the 'feel' of his new place of work. Consequently his productivity will be below the norm during this time. Now it seems reasonable to suppose that the quit rate, q, is negatively related to the wage rate paid by the firm relative to elsewhere, and one is therefore tempted to apply a similar analysis to that of wages and labour efficiency and to argue that the firm will raise the wage rate so as to offset turnover costs. In fact this line of reasoning is probably faulty, as other firms in the economy would have exactly the same incentive to raise wages so that wage differentials between firms would be unchanged. Thus, providing that individual employers set wages according to an assumption that other employers will react in a similar manner, there is no incentive to raise wages in this fashion in the first place since at the end of the day quit rates, and therefore turnover costs, would be restored to their original levels.

The optimal wage from the firm's viewpoint will, however, be influenced by the ratio of the wage rate to non-wage incomes. It is sometimes argued, for example, that in less-developed countries firms deliberately set wages substantially above alternative agricultural incomes so as to discourage migrant workers from quitting their jobs to return home to the countryside. The decision rule in this case is simple — firms will set wages so that the costs of raising the wage by one unit are offset by the gains in terms of reduced hiring and training costs via reduced quits. The higher is average agricultural income (or the value placed by workers on non-employment activities), then the greater is the quit rate at any given wage rate and thus the higher the equilibrium wage.

Clearly, the greater are the hiring and training costs, the higher the wage that employers will be willing to pay to offset labour turnover. Since it is generally believed that turnover costs rise according to skill levels,[8] this must tend to raise wage differentials. Higher turnover costs are also usually cited as the reason why employers are less willing to lay off skilled workers during depressions. If a skilled worker finds alternative employment prior to his recall during the upswing, then the cost of replacing him is greater. To summarise then, our model is that firms seek to minimise the sum of wage and turnover costs for a given level of output:

$$\text{min} \qquad C = WN + C_t qN$$
$$\text{subject to} \quad Q = F(K,N)\,[9]$$
$$\text{where} \qquad q = q(W)\,[10]$$

$$\frac{dq}{dW} < 0$$

C_t is training and hiring cost per replacement per period, and q is the quit rate (i.e. proportion who quit per period). The first-order conditions are then

$$W + C_t q = \lambda \frac{\partial Q}{\partial N} \qquad\qquad (3.17)$$

$$N = -C_t N \frac{dq}{dW} \qquad\qquad (3.18)$$

or

$$1 = -C_t \frac{dq}{dW}$$

Equation (3.17) tells us that labour cost per worker (wage plus expected turnover cost per worker) equals marginal cost times marginal physical product. Thus although the wage rate is less than marginal revenue product, this is only because of the existence of non-wage costs. Equation (3.18) defines the optimal trade-off between wage and turnover costs.

In Chapter 5 we take this topic much further when we investigate the implications for labour market theory if firms and workers alike put a sufficiently high valuation on reduced turnover and security of employment.

3.4 Many Types of Labour

In the real world, of course, hours of work supplied by different people are by no means equivalent. Normally, for example, we would expect hours supplied by skilled workers to embody more input than hours supplied by the less skilled.

Clearly we can easily rewrite our production functions as

$$Q = F(K,L_1,L_2, \ldots, L_n)$$

where L_i is the ith type of labour input. Labour types could, for example, be distinguished by education, occupation, experience, sex or by some combination of these. If we repeat our earlier analysis of the demand for a given type of labour, then we find similar (although more complicated) results to those we obtained previously.

There is, however, one further issue that is of some interest. Can we somehow aggregate all of our different labour inputs together into a single measure[11] and, if so, what assumptions are we making? This implies that we can rewrite the production function as

$$Q = F(K, L^*)$$

where

$$L^* = g(L_1, L_2, \ldots, L_n)$$

It should first be noted that this means that labour and non-labour inputs are assumed to be separable in the sense that the ratio of the marginal physical products of any two labour types is independent of the quantity of K. This is sometimes called homothetic separability. If this condition is not met, then our measure of aggregate labour input would depend not only upon the numbers in different labour categories but also upon the quantity of non-labour input. Thus a rise in K might for example raise the marginal product of skilled labour more than that of unskilled labour and thus change the aggregate labour input measure, even though the number of workers has not changed.

The first and simplest way to aggregate is to add up the number of man-hours contributed by each kind of labour, for example:

$$L^* = L_1 + L_2 + \ldots + L_n$$

This, of course, is inappropriate as it denies that there can be any difference between the Ls in the first place. Such a measure (total man-hours) would be useful, however, if the various Ls happen to change in such a fashion that they always stand in fixed proportion to one another. This does not usually happen in practice.

A second commonly used approach is to weight the Ls by either base year wages or alternatively, in the case of a cross-section, by the sample average of wages. In either case let the wage (weight) corresponding to L_i be $\bar{W}_i$. Our aggregate is

$$L^* = \bar{W}_1 L_1 + \bar{W}_2 L_2 + \ldots + \bar{W}_n L_n$$

To obtain a clearer idea of what this means, suppose we divide through by $\bar{W}_1$

$$\frac{L^*}{\bar{W}_1} = L_1 + \frac{\bar{W}_2}{\bar{W}_1} L_2 + \ldots + \frac{\bar{W}_n}{\bar{W}_1} L_n$$

As $\bar{W}_1$ is a constant, then $L^*/\bar{W}_1$ can itself be thought of as a labour input index. This has a very simple interpretation. Since each of L_2 down to L_n has been multiplied by the ratio of its base wage to $\bar{W}_1$, we can think of this as converting each type of labour input into its equivalent in terms of L_1. We obviously get similar results if we divide by any other of the $\bar{W}$s. Thus L^* is proportional to total labour input in terms of any of the Ls.

The special assumption that is being made here is of course that relative wages (assumed equal to relative marginal physical products) are in fact constant. This in turn implies that all of the Ls are perfect substitutes for one another.

THE THEORY OF LABOUR DEMAND

We can relax this last assumption by introducing the constant elasticity of substitution function (CES). We now have

$$L^* = [a_1L_1^\theta + a_2L_2^\theta + \ldots + a_nL_n^\theta]^{1/\theta}$$

where

$$\sum_{i=1}^{n} a_i = 1$$

and the direct elasticity of substitution between any pair of Ls is $1/(1-\theta)$. In the special case where the elasticity of substitution is one, the function takes on the Cobb–Douglas form

$$L^* = L_1^{a_1} L_2^{a_2} \ldots L_n^{a_n}$$

where the as (*only* in the Cobb–Douglas case) are the shares of the Ls in total wages.

Sato (1967) has further extended the CES framework so that it is possible to at least partially relax the assumption of an identical elasticity of substitution between inputs. The reader is referred to Sato (1967) for further details.

3.5 Some Limitations of the Model

The traditional theory of demand for inputs has been criticised on many different grounds. Some writers have taken offence at what they believed were the ethical implications of the theory. However, it is unclear that any particular outcome in terms of factor rewards need have any special normative significance.[12] We therefore concentrate only upon those criticisms of the theory that are directed towards the underlying assumptions — profit maximisation, input substitutability and price taking in the labour market.

Profit Maximisation

There are two charges that are sometimes levelled against this assumption. The first is that firms may have many objectives other than the acquisition of profit. Baumol (1958) has argued that firms wish to maximise sales or sales revenue subject to a profit constraint, while Williamson (1966) and Marris (1964) see the firm as attempting to maximise its rate of growth subject to constraints placed upon the value of its equity by the wishes of its shareholders. Other writers such as Cyert and March (1963) have gone even further and have argued that even if profit is the main objective of the firm, then it still may not be legitimate to regard the firm as a maximiser but rather as a 'satisficer', i.e. an institution achieving a satisfactory level for each of its goals and for those of its various departments.

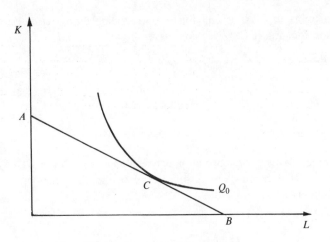

Figure 3.4 Cost Minimisation

Now the proposition that wages will be proportional to marginal products arises from the assumption of cost minimisation. Taking the standard problem as

minimise $C = WN + RK$
subject to $Q = f(K,L)$

then we find as first-order conditions

$$W = \lambda \frac{\partial Q}{\partial L} \quad \text{and} \quad R = \lambda \frac{\partial Q}{\partial K}$$

where λ is marginal cost. This is illustrated in Figure 3.4. The isocost line AB shows all possible combinations of machines and labour that can be purchased from a fixed budget. Now minimising the costs of producing a fixed output is equivalent to maximising the output that one can get from a given level of costs. The biggest output that can be achieved with isocost line AB is that relating to the isoquant tangential at point C. Likewise the process could be repeated in reverse. First fix the level of output at Q_0 and then find the lowest isocost line consistent with isoquant Q_0 which would of course be AB tangential with Q_0 at C.

The slope of AB is the ratio of factor prices, in this case W/R. The slope of Q_0 is the ratio of the marginal physical products. Since at a point of tangency such as C the two slopes must be equal, the proportionality between wages and marginal products is thus established. Furthermore, since

$$\lambda = \frac{R}{\partial Q/\partial K} = \frac{W}{\partial Q/\partial L}$$

the marginal cost of producing an extra unit of output will be the same if achieved by either input.

Why then do we use profit maximisation as opposed to cost minimisation? The answer is simple. Cost minimisation only refers to the supply side of the goods market; it cannot by itself tell us what level of output is going to be produced. Profit maximisation, on the other hand, requires us to consider both the supply and the demand sides of the market simultaneously and we find the profit maximising output where marginal cost is equated to marginal revenue. Thus knowledge of the output of a producer allows us to solve for the absolute quantities of factors that he will employ from the first derivatives of a cost function such as equation (3.12). But is profit maximisation the only way in which we can construct

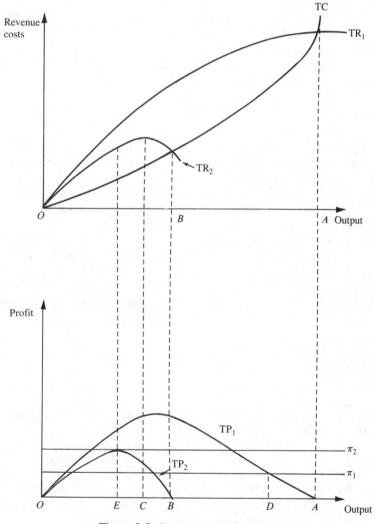

Figure 3.5 Revenue Maximisation

a theory of absolute demand for factors? Clearly the answer is no. Providing the firm minimises cost, then non-profit motives are still admissible providing we can solve for the firm's output.

There may of course be cases in which the firm may maximise its objectives without minimising costs. Under such circumstances we would have little faith in our theory of factor demand. Suppose that we compare two firms which are revenue maximisers. Firm 1 faces a downward sloping curve which is elastic over the entire range, while firm 2 faces a demand curve which becomes inelastic after some point. The associated total revenue curves are shown in Figure 3.5 as TR_1 and TR_2 respectively;[13] TC is the total cost curve while TP_1 and TP_2 are the total profit curves.

Now suppose both firms are asked to at least break even. Firm 1 will maximise revenue where $TR_1 = TC$ at a level of sales equal to OA. Firm 2, on the other hand, will *not* produce where $TR_2 = TC$, i.e. OB, but will produce instead at its revenue maximising level of sales OC. Firm 1 has therefore a clear incentive to minimise costs and operate along TC, while firm 2 has no such clear incentive. Likewise, if we consider both firms as facing a profit constraint, π_1, firm 1 will produce at OD where the constraint is binding, while firm 2 will continue to produce at OC.

Is there any circumstance under which firm 2 will be required to minimise costs so as to maximise revenue? Consider a profit constraint such as π_2 which is just compatible with the highest level of profits that firm 2 can attain. In this case firm 2 will produce OE and will be forced to minimise costs. In fact firm 2 will cost minimise if the profit constraint intersects TP_2 at any point between the profit maximising output OE and the revenue maximising output OC.

We might note in passing that both firms will always cost minimise if their objective is output or sales maximisation subject to a feasible profit constraint, as they will always produce at a point where the profit constraint is binding.

Another case in which a firm may maximise its objective without minimising costs is as the firm (or more realistically the firm's manager) obtains satisfaction from employment *per se*. Thus the manager's utility function may be written as

$$U = U(\pi, L)$$

where π is profit

$$\pi = pQ - WL - RK$$

Assuming for simplicity that the firm is a price taker in all markets, then the first-order condition for employment of labour becomes

$$\frac{\partial U}{\partial \pi}\left(p\,\frac{\partial Q}{\partial L} - W\right) + \frac{\partial U}{\partial L} = 0$$

Thus $p(\partial Q/\partial L) < W$, i.e. employment will be expanded beyond the point at which the marginal value product is equal to the wage.

The first-order condition for employment of capital becomes

$$p \, \frac{\partial Q}{\partial K} = R$$

Thus the ratio $(\partial Q/\partial L)/(\partial Q/\partial K)$ is not equated to W/R. The firm cannot therefore be a cost minimiser in the sense discussed earlier.

Yet at the same time it is intuitively clear that providing the utility function is well behaved, then we will still obtain a downward sloping demand curve for labour. A fall in the wage rate allows the firm to have both a higher level of profit and a higher level of employment. The trick is of course that optimising behaviour does require the firm to minimise costs, except that it is not the costs of output that are being minimised but rather the costs of a given level of utility.

If, however, we ignore this latter possibility, then the neoclassical economist may take much comfort from the preceding discussion. Although it is obvious, for example, that most of the nationalised industries in the UK are not profit maximisers, it is not so obvious that they are not cost minimisers. Budgetary constraints imposed by restrictions on the availability of public funds and borrowing limits may indeed make public enterprises very cost conscious. This will depend, of course, as discussed above, on what the objectives of the enterprises actually are. There are unfortunately special difficulties when one considers areas of government employment such as the Civil Service where it is presumably difficult for the executives of such agencies to decide upon what their output actually is. [14]

The other criticism which is sometimes made against profit maximisation is that firms are unable to make the decisions necessary to bring it about. It is often argued that firms do not know the shape of their own production functions and cannot therefore calculate marginal products. Firms do not in practice use concepts such as marginal cost, marginal revenue and marginal products and so, it is argued, the theory is inapplicable.

One can, of course, point out that firms do in practice make marginal decisions even if they do not employ marginal terminology as such. Investment appraisal as carried out in a large firm is clearly a marginal analysis, as are decisions regarding lay-offs and hires. The more important point, however, is that economists do not judge a theory by its descriptive content but rather by its ability to predict. The strength of the neoclassical theory is that it yields a number of testable predictions regarding the demand for factors of production. It is on the empirical performance of these predictions that the theory should be judged. [15]

Limited Factor Substitution

If the production function is of the fixed proportions type

$$Q = \min \, (aK, bL)$$

where a and b are constant parameters equal to the output–capital and output–labour ratios respectively, then we obtain the L-shaped isoquant given in the left-hand panel of Figure 3.2 in which the elasticity of substitution $\sigma_{KL} = 0$. An intuitive explanation of this situation would be that it takes, say, five men to operate a given machine. With less than five men the machine could not be operated, while with more than five men the additional men would stand idle. Clearly this indivisibility of men and machines renders the notion of separate marginal products inappropriate. But does this in any way contradict the basic model outlined earlier in this chapter? The answer is no. The elasticity of demand for labour in the long run is still negative, providing there is a downward sloping demand curve for industry output. Thus if we substitute in equation (3.8′) we get

$$E_{LL} = V_L \eta$$

One less severe possibility is that, in the short run, firms cannot alter factor proportions but that, in the long run, they can choose between different labour intensities of new machines that they install. 'Putty-clay' models of this kind have been extensively analysed in the literature on growth economics.[16]

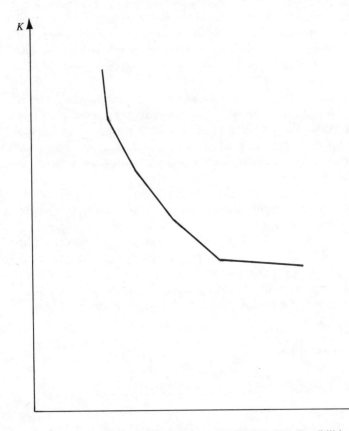

Figure 3.6 Discontinuous Substitution Possibilities

Another possibility is that at any point of time there are a finite number of techniques available to the firm which leads in turn to a kinked type of isoquant as shown in Figure 3.6. Limited substitution possibilities of this sort will cause the demand curve for labour to descend in a series of 'steps' rather than as a smooth continuous curve.[17]

The Price Taking Assumption

So far we have assumed that the firm is unable to influence the supply price of its inputs by its hiring and production decisions. There are, however, a number of circumstances in which this assumption is violated.

The classic case is that of monopsony, i.e. a monopoly buyer, in which the firm is the sole employer of a given type of labour. A famous example of this is the market for professional baseball players in the United States.[18] For our purposes, however, it is unnecessary to specify that the firm be a total monopsonist in the appropriate factor market but simply that the firm faces an upward sloping supply curve for the input in question. This might be the case, for example, if a firm is a major employer in an isolated area, so that it has to raise wages in order to attract workers from further afield.

This is illustrated in Figure 3.7. The upward sloping supply curve S faced by the firm is also its average cost of employing labour curve, AC. However, the marginal cost of employing an additional unit of labour is necessarily above the average cost since the marginal cost comprises not only the higher wage paid to the additional worker, but also the increase in the wage bill which must be paid to all other workers previously employed. The profit maximising level of

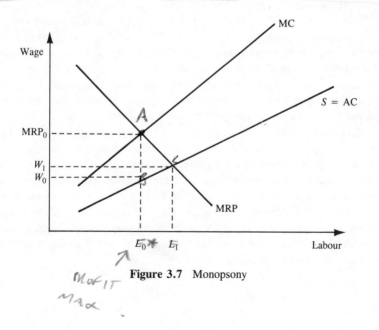

Figure 3.7   Monopsony

employment occurs at L_0 where MC = MRP. The employer then pays the minimum wage capable of attracting and holding L_0, workers which one can read off from the supply curve as W_0. Clearly W_0 is less than the marginal revenue product (or marginal value product if the firm is a price taker in the product market), MRP_0.

This can be illustrated very simply if we consider the case of a cost minimising monopsonist. Mathematically the problem is

minimise　$C = WL + RK$
subject to　$Q = f(K,L)$

where　　$W = W(L)$ [19]　　$\dfrac{dW}{dL} > 0$

The first-order conditions are then

$$W + \frac{dW}{dL} L = \frac{\partial Q}{\partial L} \lambda$$

$$R = \frac{\partial Q}{\partial K} \lambda$$

where λ is marginal cost (equal to marginal revenue if the firm maximises profit). Clearly

$$W < \frac{\partial Q}{\partial L} \lambda$$

and the ratio of factor prices is not equal to the ratio of their marginal products.

The standard result, that a monopsonist will pay less than the marginal revenue or value product, depends critically upon whether the firm can pay different wages to different workers. If the firm could somehow pay each worker his or her individual supply price (the case of a perfectly discriminating monopsonist) without paying the same wage to other workers, then the marginal cost of employing an additional worker would simply be the wage of that worker. In Figure 3.7 this would mean that the MC curve faced by the firm would coincide with the supply and the firm would employ L_1 workers with the wage of the last worker employed just equal to the marginal revenue product.

The fact that the firm will normally no longer equate the ratio of marginal products to the ratio of factor prices is not the only consequence of relaxing the assumption that factor supplies are perfectly elastic. Since the firm can choose *either* the wage *or* the number of workers employed, there is no longer a unique demand curve for labour. In terms of Figure 3.7, the quantity of labour employed depends not upon the value of the wage rate, but rather that *both* the quantity employed and the wage rate depend upon the position of the labour supply curve. Thus shifting the supply curve or changing its shape will yield a new combination of quantity employed and wage rate.

or or negotiated union contracts.

The model does generate an interesting policy implication, however. Normally we would predict that, if a government set a statutory minimum wage above that currently being paid, this would reduce the level of employment. This is not necessarily true for a monopsonistic firm. From the standpoint of the firm, the effect of the minimum wage is to effectively impose a perfectly elastic supply curve at that wage. Thus, in Figure 3.7, with a minimum wage greater than W_0 but less than W_1, it is actually possible to raise both the wage and employment simultaneously, while from W_1 to MRP_0, raising the wage will lower employment but nevertheless maintain it at a level higher than L_0.

The size of an employer relative to the local labour market is not the only reason why he might possess monopsony power. In a world in which both workers and employers are imperfectly informed about existing work opportunities, a given worker will face a distribution of possible wage offers across different firms. Each job seeker will then set for himself a reservation wage at or above which he will accept any given offer.[20] Now if all job seekers had identical characteristics, then they would all set the same reservation wage so that individual employers would be price takers in the labour market. If, on the other hand, job seekers set different reservation wages, then any given employer will find that he can attract more workers who are willing to accept his job offers providing he raises the wage. Imperfect information may therefore convey some monopsony power to the individual firm. However, a formal analysis along these lines would require us to consider not only the wage and quantity of labour employed but also the length of time required to fill the corresponding number of vacancies.[21]

3.6 Summary

In this chapter we have examined at length the standard neoclassical theory of demand for labour. We have developed the theory from the simple short-run case to the long-run in which other factors of production are assumed variable. Although the marginal value product curve may be taken as the demand curve for labour under competitive conditions in the short run, other influences arising from the variability of other factor quantities must be taken into account when determining the long-run demand curve. In particular one would note the relationship between the elasticity of demand for labour and the ease of substitution between labour and other inputs, the labour share and the price elasticity of demand for output.

We examined a number of extensions of the basic model, including a treatment of monopoly and imperfect competition in product markets, wages and labour efficiency and wages and labour turnover. We also briefly investigated a few ways in which different categories of labour input might be aggregated into a single input measure.

The assumptions of the theory were also explored at some length. Cost minimisation is a weaker and therefore more satisfactory assumption than profit maximisation, and is generally sufficient to derive a downward sloping demand curve for labour. Limited substitution possibilities would suggest that input prices may have little effect upon quantities employed, while the concept of a unique demand curve for labour has no meaning if the firm is not a price taker in the labour market.

In the next chapter we leave our discussion of pure theory and examine the main empirical facts and evidence.

Notes

1. From the production function we obtain $dQ = F_K dK + F_L dL$. For any given isoquant, output is fixed and therefore $dQ = 0$. Thus the slope of the isoquant dK/dL is equal to $-F_L/F_K$. For a further introductory exposition, see Brown (1966).

2. To obtain these results one must note that

$$\sigma_{KL} = \frac{F_K F_L (K F_K + L F_L)}{KL(-F_{KK}F_L^2 + 2F_{KL}F_K F_L - F_{LL}F_K^2)}$$

(see Allen, 1938).

3. Thus $E_{LL} = \dfrac{L}{W}\dfrac{\partial W}{\partial L} = \dfrac{\partial \log L}{\partial \log W}$

$$E_{KL} = \frac{K}{W}\frac{\partial W}{\partial K} = \frac{\partial \log K}{\partial \log W}$$

4. The problem is that if we do not impose constant returns, then marginal cost and hence the product price will vary with the scale of output. We would therefore have to take this explicitly into account in our analysis. In the textual discussion no such problem arc se as output was taken as fixed. A convenient mathematical property of constant returns is that of Euler's theorem: $Q = F_L L + F_K K$.

5. Notice that constant returns is not required in this equation. If we do impose constant returns, then equation (3.12) may be rewritten as $C = QG(W,R)$, i.e. total cost is proportional to output, given fixed input prices.

6. One should note that these demand functions are analogous to the compensated demand function of consumer theory, as introduced by Milton Friedman (see Friedman, 1949). To obtain a factor demand function analogous to the uncompensated demand function of consumer theory, we would hold cost constant rather than output.

7. These results are derived using the well-known method of Lagrange multipliers. If the problem is of the form

   min $F(x_1, x_2, \ldots, x_n)$

   subject to

   $g(x_1, x_2, \ldots, x_n) = b$

   we form the Lagrangian function

   $\mathcal{L} = F(x_1, x_2, \ldots, x_n) + \lambda [b - g(x_1, x_2, \ldots, x_n)]$

where λ is the 'Lagrange multiplier' and may be interpreted as the marginal impact of relaxing the constraint by a small unit upon the objective. Our example represents the impact of an additional unit of output on cost, i.e. marginal cost. The first-order conditions are found by setting the first derivatives of $\mathcal{L}$ (with respect to x, etc.) equal to zero. For a full treatment see Intriligator (1971).

8. This is usually justified by arguing that training periods of skilled workers are both longer and more intensive than those of less-skilled workers. It is therefore most expensive to replace a skilled worker.

9. Since L (labour input) is assumed proportional to N (number of workers), it is convenient to replace L by N in the production function.

10. Strictly speaking, W should be the ratio of wages to non-wage incomes. However, we assume the latter to be constant.

11. Aggregating labour inputs has clear advantages if one is assessing productivity changes or sources of economic growth as it considerably simplifies the analysis. See for example the aggregation procedures followed in Denison (1967).

12. Payments in accordance with marginal productivity are among the first-order conditions required for Pareto optimality. However, these first-order conditions do not yield a unique solution but rather a solution for each factor endowment. The problem of finding an optimal income distribution is not conventionally considered. Although it is true that perfect competition in the absence of externalities and satiation of consumers will yield a Pareto optimal allocation, there is no theoretical reason why the same result may not be deliberately achieved in a centrally planned economy.

13. Baumol (1958) argues that by the use of advertising, the firm can alter the shape of the demand curve and thus the total revenue curve from TR_2 to a monotonically upward sloping shape such as TR_1.

14. See Lindsay (1976).

15. For a further discussion see Friedman (1953).

16. See for example Solow (1962).

17. For a detailed discussion of production functions displaying discontinuous substitution possibilities, see Johansen (1972).

18. See the enjoyable discussion in Rottenberg (1956).

19. This is the 'inverse' of the labour supply curve facing the firm, i.e. the relationship showing the minimum wage required to attract a given amount of labour.

20. See the more detailed analysis of job search models in Chapter 7.

21. A complete analysis is given in Pissarides (1976, Chs. 2 and 3).

4

Empirical Aspects of Labour Demand

4.1 Introduction

In Chapter 3, we examined the standard theory of demand for labour and considered a few extensions. In this chapter we will try to use this as far as possible to explain both the allocation of labour across sectors and the changing pattern of employment over time. In particular, there are three especially interesting questions that we will try to answer:

1. Why has the distribution of employment across different sectors changed in a relatively similar fashion in most developed countries since the war? Why, for example, has the share of agricultural employment generally fallen while that of services has risen?
2. How does employment vary, given fluctuations in economic conditions?
3. What do empirically estimated labour demand functions look like? In particular, how wage elastic is the demand for labour?

The first question is presumably of largely historical interest although it does have practical implications. Manpower planners commonly project forward the existing sectoral employment distribution when trying to assess future manpower needs. Likewise, since industries sometimes have a tendency to be concentrated regionally, an understanding is needed of what determines the employment levels of different industries in order to forecast future regional employment levels.

The cyclical nature of employment has for many years been of great concern to economists. Most macroeconomic theories concentrate upon explaining the deviation of output from its 'full employment' or natural level, and arrive at their implications for employment by assuming some simple relationship between the two. In fact, as we shall see, recent econometric evidence suggests that the relationship between output and employment is much more complex than originally supposed. However, to evaluate the likely effects of macroeconomic stabilisation policy upon the labour market, it is vital that employers' reactions to, say, a sudden fall in demand for their products, are understood as fully as possible. Economists have put forward a number of theories that try to explain the firm's choice of utilisation rate and the mix between workers and hours. In most cases the predictions of the theory in question have been confronted with empirical data. We will therefore examine the available evidence as fully as possible and pay careful attention to the assumptions and methodology of the various studies concerned.

Finally, although labour economists assume that the demand curve for labour slopes downwards, it is only comparatively recently that economists were able to examine this relationship in a scientific manner. In fact, as should be clear from the discussion in Chapter 3, there exists a whole range of different wage elasticities of demand for labour depending on what is held constant when the elasticity is measured, e.g. other factor prices, other factor quantities, output, etc. Which measure is appropriate depends upon the context in which it is used. Nevertheless, knowledge of the parameters of the labour demand function could be immensely valuable when assessing, for example, the likely effects of a wage subsidy or an employment tax. Similarly, the impact of a trade union-induced real wage increase upon the level of unemployment must depend in part upon the ease with which firms can substitute other inputs for labour.

4.2 Post-War Trends in the Demand for Labour by Industry and Occupation

Table 4.1 gives a breakdown of the civilian working population, i.e. total labour force less armed forces and unemployed, by broad industrial sector for five

Table 4.1 Percentage Distribution of Civilian Working Population by Sector in 1985

	France	*Germany*	*Japan*	*UK*	*USA*
Agriculture, forestry, etc.	7.6	5.5	8.8	2.6	3.1
Mining and quarrying	0.6	1.3	0.2	1.2	0.9
Manufacturing	23.2	32.0	25.0	23.8	19.5
Electricity, gas and water	1.0	0.9	0.6	1.3	1.2
Construction	7.3	6.8	9.1	6.0	6.5
Wholesale and retail trade	16.7	15.2	22.7	21.2	22.2
Transport and communication	6.6	6.1	5.9	5.8	5.7
Services[a]	37.2	32.2	27.4	38.0	41.1
Total (millions)	20.9	25.0	58.1	24.1	107.2

Source: OECD (1986).
Note: (a) Includes financial services, real estate, banking, etc., public administration, other personal and community services.

industrialised countries. The data thus include employers, the self-employed[1] and, in countries other than the UK, paid and unpaid family household workers. Although countries like the UK and USA are often associated in terms of popular image with manufacturing, it is clear from the table that employment in advanced countries is nowadays more concentrated in the trading and service sectors. In fact, ever since the United States became the first economy, shortly after World War II, with over one-half of its labour force in activities other than industry or agriculture, a similar pattern has been repeated elsewhere. In all five countries, wholesale and retail trade, transport and communication, and services now account for over 50 per cent of the civilian working population.

The sectoral breakdowns are roughly similar in all five countries. The UK has

Table 4.2 Average Annual Percentage Rate of Change in Civilian Working Population (Employment), Output and Output/Employment by Sector, 1962–85

	France	Germany	Japan	UK	USA[c]
Agriculture, etc.					
Employment	–3.8	–3.8	–3.0	–1.7	–1.7
Output	1.5	1.6	0.7	2.7	1.9
Output/employment	5.3	5.4	3.7	4.4	3.6
Industry[a]					
Employment	–0.4	–1.0	0.9	–1.8	1.3
Output	3.9	3.2	8.2	1.5	2.8
Output/employment	4.3	4.2	7.3	3.3	1.5
Wholesale and retail trade					
Employment	1.1	–0.0	1.4	1.8	
Output	3.2	3.0	7.5	1.2	
Output/employment	2.1	3.0	6.1	–0.6	
Transport and communications					
Employment	1.0	0.1	0.7	–1.0	
Output	4.3	3.8	6.6	2.4	
Output/employment	3.3	3.7	5.9	3.4	
Services[b]					
Employment	3.0	2.4	2.1	1.8	2.9
Output	3.9	4.6	6.2		3.8
Output/employment	0.9	2.1	4.1		0.9
Total					
Employment	0.5	–0.2	0.7	–0.1	2.1
Output	3.6	3.3	6.6	1.9	3.2
Output/employment	3.1	3.5	5.9	2.0	1.1

Source: Employment: OECD, *Labour Force Statistics*, various issues (*op. cit.*)
         Output: *National Accounts of OECD Countries*, OECD, Paris.
Notes: (a) Mining, manufacturing, electricity, gas and water, and construction.
         (b) See note (a) in Table 4.1.
         (c) Services data for the USA include wholesale and retail trade, and transport.

a particularly low share of its workers in agriculture, while employment in this sector is most significant in Japan — the most recently industrialised of the countries shown. West Germany has the largest manufacturing sector and the smallest share of employment in the wholesale and retail trade, while the USA is the most service oriented country, followed by the UK in second place.

It is much more interesting, however, to see how sectoral employment has changed over time. Table 4.2 shows the percentage change in employment in each country between 1962 and 1985. To facilitate comparison, the mining, manufacturing, construction and electricity, gas and water sectors are aggregated together into a single 'industry' category.

In all advanced countries, employment in agriculture has fallen quite rapidly. Given the growth in total employment in the countries shown, this means that there has been a significant fall in agriculture's share of employment. In general, this movement out of agriculture has meant that additional labour became available to other sectors, although to some extent this has been limited by a tendency among women and children, who previously worked as unpaid farm workers, to withdraw from the labour force on moving to town. In Japan, for example, this effect was large enough to reduce the female participation rate between 1960 and 1980.

Industrial employment fell in all five advanced countries except Japan and the USA over the period, its share in total employment only increasing in Japan. This can be seen by comparing the rates of growth of employment in industry with those of employment as a whole. It should be emphasised that this decline in industrial employment is almost entirely due to its fall since around 1979 or 1980. This has been particularly pronounced in the UK, where industrial employment fell by 21 per cent between 1980 and 1985; the decline was even more severe in manufacturing. Smaller declines over the same period have also occurred in France and Germany, of around 13 per cent and 10 per cent respectively. In the USA, industrial employment was more or less static over the same five-year period, and only in Japan did industrial employment actually rise. If we consider only the earlier period, 1962−80, then employment rose in all five countries except Germany and the UK. In every country it is the services sector that shows the highest rate of growth in employment.

The central proposition of the theory, as presented in Chapter 3, is that the quantity demanded of labour will vary positively with the level of output and negatively with the ratio of the wage rate to other factor prices. There is little doubt that real wages have risen considerably relative to real interest rates in the past 30 years, so if we assume that, in a given country, factor mobility is sufficient to ensure that relative factor prices change in a similar way in each sector, then we can argue that the percentage change in employment will be greater:

(i) the greater the percentage change in output;
(ii) the less the elasticity of substitution between labour and other inputs.

There is, however, a further problem that we must consider. Previously, we assumed the state of technology to be fixed, but obviously this cannot have been true over the post-war years. We must therefore add a third condition to our list as follows:

(iii) the slower the rate of technical change[2] and the more labour-using its direction or bias.

The rate of change of employment is equal to the difference between the rate of change of output and of output per person. This last measure will be the greater, the more substitutable are non-labour for labour inputs in the face of real wage growth and the more capital-biased is technical change. The rates of change of both output and output per person are shown where available in Table 4.2.

The growth of any sector depends essentially upon what happens to domestic and foreign demand for the products of that sector. Higher than average output growth may indicate income elasticities of demand greater than unity, falling relative prices and/or increased trade competitiveness or trade restrictions in the sector concerned. It is not surprising, therefore, given low income elasticities for food and other primary products, that the agricultural sector experienced the lowest growth rate over the period. This, combined with a higher than average rate of increase in labour productivity, explains the significant reduction in agricultural employment discussed earlier. Non-agricultural output growth has generally been higher in France, Germany and Japan than in the UK or USA, although this has largely been offset by a faster improvement in productivity. The striking fall in UK manufacturing employment since the end of the 1970s was to some extent matched by falling output in the first couple of years. Since then output has increased with a corresponding rise in the output per worker. However, output of the services[3] sector has been growing faster than that of other sectors in every country.

The similarity in changes in employment distribution between countries seems, then, to be a falling share of employment in agriculture, and a rising share in the non-industrial sectors. This may be explained partly in terms of differences in the relevant income elasticities (low for agricultural products and relatively high for services) and partly in terms of the considerable growth, experienced in all countries, of central and local government employment. Although industrial output growth has been quite high in France and Germany and very high in Japan, it has also been accompanied by high productivity growth. In all countries except Japan, the share of industrial employment has fallen.

Does a changing production structure have implications for the occupational composition of the working population? By way of an example, the distribution of workers by occupation in the UK is compared for 1961 and 1981 in Table 4.3. The chief difficulty in moving from an industrial to an occupational classification is that a given occupational group may be represented in more than one industrial sector and vice versa. Thus the biggest white-collar group, clerical and related workers, is found in every sector of the economy, while the services sector will employ workers from all except agricultural occupations. Rapid growth of employment in, for example, the services sector will not therefore lead to rapid

Table 4.3 Percentage Distribution of Civilian Employment by Occupation in the UK for 1961 and 1985

	1961	1981	Average annual percentage change
Professional, technical and related workers	8.7	17.3	3.4
Administrative and managerial workers	2.7	9.6	6.5
Clerical and related workers	13.0	16.5	1.1
Sales workers	9.7	5.9	−2.5
Service workers	10.5	15.0	1.7
Agricultural, animal husbandry and factory workers	4.3	1.5	−5.3
Production and related workers	49.6	33.4	−2.0
Not classified	1.6	0.9	
Total (000s)	23 440	24 260	0.1

Source: *Yearbook of Labour Statistics*, 1981 and 1969, International Labour Office, Geneva.

growth in employment of service workers alone, but rather to an above-average rate of growth of those occupations which the service sector uses relatively intensively. The observed change in occupational employment composition over time thus reflects (i) different rates of employment growth in the various sectors; (ii) different occupational compositions within sectors; and (iii) changes in occupational compositions within sectors.

The largest occupational group in any industrialised economy is production and related workers. This group is used much more intensively in industry than in any other production sector. The decline in the share of industry in total employment in the UK is thus reflected in slower than average growth of blue-collar workers. Similarly, clerical and service workers are used most intensively in the service sector. As the service sector has grown faster than any other in recent years, it is not surprising that these two occupational groups have also been growing faster than the average.

The other reason why clerical workers have grown relatively quickly is that white-collar workers have tended to increase as a proportion of the labour force in all sectors of the economy. Growth in higher education is a major reason why the two high-level manpower groups, professional, etc., and administrative workers, display above-average growth. To put this another way, since the average educational qualifications of members of the labour force have increased significantly between 1961 and 1981, one would expect to find education-intensive occupations growing faster than less education-intensive ones. This last effect is, however, partly masked by a tendency for average educational qualifications within each occupational group to increase over time.

The overall pattern is similar in all other industrialised economies, although somewhat higher relative growth rates are found for blue-collar workers in other countries as their industrial sectors have been expanding more quickly.

4.3   Employment and Economic Fluctuations

Ever since the early 1930s, economists have been concerned with short-run fluctuations in employment. An understanding of the latter is vital to the study of cyclical unemployment and short-run income distribution and indeed, until comparatively recently, virtually the whole of macroeconomics was directed towards the problem of removing such fluctuations. However, whereas the orthodox body of macroeconomics has restricted itself to explaining the level of output in the short run, labour economics has the task of disentangling the rather complicated relationship that exists between output and employment. In this section we will review available evidence regarding the cyclical nature of employment in an industrialised economy.

In any free enterprise or even mixed economy, firms face significant variation in the demand for their products. They can react to this in a number of ways: by raising or lowering their prices, by accumulating or decumulating inventories of unsold output or by varying output itself. If they adopt the latter approach, and we take their plant and equipment as fixed, then they will have to vary either hours worked per employee or the number of employees itself. Price adjustment is not an option available to firms if they are price takers in the product market, as, for example, under perfect competition; but it may be a feature under other forms of market structure. Price adjustment may be costly in itself and a firm may lose some of its market if price uncertainty imposes costs on consumers.

Inventories take up physical storage space and represent an opportunity cost in terms of interest foregone. Employment and hours of work adjustment also impose other costs upon the firm, as we will see later in this section. If fluctuations are of short duration, as with, for example, seasonal variations in demand, the firm is more likely to meet discrepancies between sales and output by accumulating or decumulating inventories, as inventories are only held for short periods. Many industries, however, face cyclical fluctuations of one- to five-years' duration and here one would not expect inventory change to be a significant source of adjustment. Likewise in sectors such as agriculture and transport where storage is either expensive or, as in the latter case, impossible, one would expect both prices and output to vary seasonally. Thus although inventory change is a significant way of adjusting to very temporary or unanticipated changes in product demand in some industries, we shall leave it to one side in our discussion below.

To study fluctuations in a data series, it is convenient to first dispense with its trend. There are several ways of accomplishing this, but one of the most effective is to estimate the relationship between the variable in question and time itself and then to subtract the predicted values from the original series. Thus if the variable has a value Y_t at time period t, we first estimate by ordinary least squares (OLS) the equation

$$Y_t = a + bt + e_t$$

where a and b are estimated coefficients. The estimated residuals from the equation, e_t, then give a detrended series for Y_t. (Quite often for presentational purposes one prefers to use $Y + e_t$ where Y is the sample mean as this gives a series with the same mean as the original.) We have calculated detrended series by this method using annual data for output, employment and output per employee in UK manufacturing over the years 1950–79. For the period 1950–85 as a whole, we have, however, employed an extension of this method in which we allow for a change in trend after 1979. Further details are given in the footnote to Table 4.4.

All three series display clear signs of being subject to cyclical activity with a wavelength of roughly five years. For example, output is at a peak in 1955, 1960, 1965, 1969 and 1973 (1950 was also a peak year). We can roughly then divide the period into five cycles: I, 1950–5; II, 1955–60; III, 1960–5; IV, 1965–9; and V, 1969–73. The anticipated peak of 1978 turned out as far as output is concerned to be something of a damp squib, although a short peak does

Table 4.4 Summary Statistics on Cyclical Variation in Relevant Variables (Detrended Series), UK Manufacturing 1950–79 and 1950–85

	Coefficient of variation		Correlation coefficient with output	
	50/79	50/85	50/79	50/85
Output	0.047	0.042	1.00	1.00
Employment	0.041	0.041	0.57	0.59
Output/employment	0.039	0.033	0.34	0.29
Weekly hours (male manual worker)	0.017	0.016	−0.23	−0.16

Source: Computed from various series: Output: *Economic Trends* (various issues), HMSO;
Employment and hours: Department of Employment,
Employment Gazette (various issues).

Note: For the period 1950/79 the series were detrended around a single linear trend. However, noting the marked fall in manufacturing since 1979, the series were detrended around the equation

$$Y_t = a_1 + a_2 t + a_3 D_{80} + a_4 D_{80} t$$

where D_{80} is a dummy variable equal to unity for years subsequent to 1979. The coefficients a_3 and a_4 are significant when employment and output/employment are used as Y_t.

reappear in 1980 in all three series. We must remember, however, that manufacturing employment fell very sharply by around 23 per cent between June 1979 and June 1985. In effect, the downward shift observed in the trend in manufacturing employment after the late 1970s tends to dwarf any subsequent fluctuations around trend.

Labour productivity as measured by output per employee is clearly procyclical with output. The two series are largely synchronous, although output seems to have lagged a year behind productivity at the peaks of 1965 and 1969 and at the trough of 1971. Since output per employee tends to move in the same direction as output, one would expect employment to show less cyclical fluctuation than output. This is indeed the case, as the employment series reveals. The peaks and troughs in employment are generally more rounded and less well defined than those of the other two series, while the amplitude of its wave is less pronounced. There is also a time lag of somewhat uncertain duration between output and employment. As we shall see below, lagged employment response is allowed for in virtually all time series studies of employment behaviour.

We can also present information on the extent of fluctuations in various series in summary form. The coefficient of variation[4] for each variable is given in the left-hand column of Table 4.4. This is a unit free measure of dispersion and provides a useful indicator of the extent of fluctuations in a series. One can immediately see that output is a more volatile series about trend than employment or labour productivity, while variability in the latter two series is very similar. The procyclicality of employment and labour productivity with output is further illustrated by the two positive correlation coefficients between these two variables and output, as given in the right-hand column of Table 4.4.

One possibility is of course that higher output per employee during an upswing only reflects the fact that more hours are being worked by each worker. In fact the variation over time in hours worked in UK manufacturing over the post-war years has not been particularly great: the peak and trough for average weekly hours worked by male manual workers being 48.7 in 1955 and 43.5 in 1981 respectively. As Table 4.4 shows, the coefficient of variation for the detrended series is much lower than that of output. Surprisingly, the correlation coefficient with output is negative, which may at first glance suggest that hours and output move anticyclically to one another. This relationship is, however, statistically insignificant.

Whatever the explanation, changes in observed weekly hours cannot entirely explain the procyclicality of fluctuations in productivity. Kuh (1965) and Hultgren (1960) examined fluctuation in output per man-hour in US manufacturing and found well-defined procyclical behaviour. In particular, hours' productivity increased more rapidly in the early part of an upswing, although there was some evidence that the expansion tailed off near the end. Output per man-hour likewise fell quickly at the start of a recession but stabilised as the recession continued.

Clearly any further analysis of the effects of economic fluctuations requires us to specify a model of the underlying processes involved and to estimate and interpret its parameters. We report on some recent examples of such studies in the next section of this chapter. It is useful, however, to first consider some of the earlier attempts in this area which amount, in effect, to a statistical parameterisation of the processes described above.

Studies carried out in the 1960s were set very much in the short-run Keynesian mould, in which the emphasis was upon quantity adjustment rather than upon input and output price adjustment. The central assumptions were that

(i)   the stock of capital is fixed;
(ii) the product market operates under conditions of imperfect competition with administered prices.

The implications of these two assumptions can be seen in Figure 4.1. The administered price is set at a constant value, P, and the demand curve faced by the firm is D_1. The maximum quantity that the firm can sell is then Q_1. Now if the firm could sell as much as it liked under these conditions, it would choose the profit maximisation position at Q_{max}, where short-run marginal cost (SMC) equals the administered price. However, as it is constrained by its demand curve, its second-best alternative is to produce Q_1. Similarly if the demand curve shifts outwards to D_2, the optimal policy for the firm is to increase output to Q_2. The firm will therefore always satisfy market demand provided that the required level of output is less than Q_{max}. Sales, and in the absence of inventory change, output, are thus demand constrained in this model as long as the administered price is greater than short-run marginal cost.

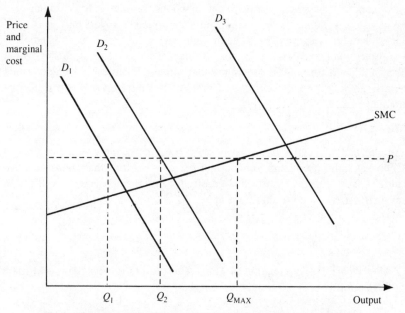

Figure 4.1   Imperfect Product Market with an Administered Price

If output is demand determined and the firm does not operate on its short-run marginal product condition, the latter is redundant and the only thing that matters is the production function to which we now add time subscripts:

$$Q_t = F(K_t, L_t, t)$$

Rearranging so as to give L on the left-hand side then gives us the *employment function*:

$$L_t^* = E(Q_t, K_t, t) \tag{4.1}$$

where L^* is desired labour input at time t.

A commonly used example is given by the Cobb–Douglas function:

$$Q_t = A e^{\lambda t} K_t^\alpha L_t^\beta$$

where λ is the (constant) rate of technical progress and A, α and β are parameters. If we rearrange this and take logarithms, we get

$$\log L_t^* = -\frac{1}{\beta} \log A + \frac{1}{\beta} \log Q_t - \frac{\alpha}{\beta} \log K_t - \frac{\lambda}{\beta} t \tag{4.2}$$

Although the earliest employment function studies[5] worked with equations of this kind, more recent studies have recognised that in practice there are adjustment costs involved in actually achieving the desired level of labour input. It is costly to take on new employees as vacancies often have to be advertised, applicants have to be interviewed and production losses may be incurred if successful candidates take time to settle into new jobs. Similarly, trade unions may take industrial action if workers are dismissed, while employers may be obliged to provide redundancy payments and may otherwise fall foul of existing employment protection legislation. A simple, although crude, way of capturing the net effect of adjustment costs is to assume that actual adjustment is some constant proportion, γ (the adjustment coefficient), of the difference between desired employment and its initial level:

$$L_t - L_{t-1} = \gamma(L_t^* - L_{t-1}) \tag{4.3}$$

An alternative specification, that is much more convenient in the context of a Cobb–Douglas production function, arises if we assume that adjustment difficulties arise according to the ratio of desired to initial employment levels rather than their difference. We therefore have

$$\frac{L_t}{L_{t-1}} = \left(\frac{L_t^*}{L_{t-1}} \right)^\gamma \tag{4.4}$$

Taking logarithms of equation (4.4) and substituting for $\log L_t$ in (4.2) (note that L_t^* is not directly observable) then gives us

$$\log L_t = (1 - \gamma)\log L_{t-1} - \frac{\gamma}{\beta} \log A + \frac{\gamma}{\beta} \log Q_t$$

$$- \frac{\gamma\alpha}{\beta} \log K_t - \frac{\gamma\lambda}{\beta} t \tag{4.5}$$

Given time series data on L, Q and K, equation (4.5) can be estimated directly and in fact many studies have used equations very similar to (4.5). There is, however, a snag. As things stand, the model is inconsistent. The production function tells us that we need L_t^* units of labour services to produce Q_t units of output. If, however, firms only employ L_t units as the adjustment process implies, then clearly they would be unable to produce Q_t in the first place. The trick employed by several writers (for example Brechling, 1965; Ball and St Cyr, 1966; Ireland and Smyth, 1970) is to assume that adjustment difficulties arise when firms try to change their employment of workers but not when they change hours per worker. Given fixed costs of employment per worker and the existence of overtime rates, it is possible to find a unique cost-minimising mix of hours and workers consistent with providing L^* units of labour services. It is quite plausible that this occurs at the point where no overtime or undertime is being worked, i.e. at standard hours per period, HS.[6] Thus, if labour services equals total hours worked, and N^* is desired employment of workers, we have

$$L_t^* = N_t^* \text{HS} \tag{4.6}$$

The adjustment process can be rewritten as

$$\frac{N_t}{N_{t-1}} = \left(\frac{N_t^*}{N_{t-1}} \right)^{\gamma}$$

If $N_t^* > N_{t-1}$ so that $N_t < N_t^*$ then this short-fall in workers will be compensated by more hours being worked per worker so as to supply the required total in manhours of L_t^*. Substituting into equation (4.2) as before yields an employment function similar to (4.5) except that N replaces L and there is an additional term in $\log$ HS,

$$\log N_t = (1 - \gamma)\log N_{t-1} - \frac{\gamma}{\beta} \log A - \frac{\gamma}{\beta} \log Q_t$$

$$- \frac{\gamma\alpha}{\beta} \log K_t - \frac{\gamma\lambda}{\beta} t - \gamma \log \text{HS}_t \tag{4.7}$$

We have now arrived at what might be described as the 'standard' employment function. There are of course variations from study to study: some researchers have preferred linear to log-linear equations, some have proxied K_t and/or HS_t with a time trend, while some have complicated the lag structure of the estimating equation by introducing demand forecasting mechanisms on the part of employers and more involved adjustment processes. However, these relatively minor complications need not detain us and we will concentrate instead upon the main results and related issues.

We have already noted the procyclical behaviour of labour productivity over time. It was originally hoped that the partial adjustment assumption incorporated in the employment function would explain this phenomenon, at least as far as output per worker is concerned, by its prediction that hours per worker rise during a boom and fall during a depression. This did not, however, turn out to be the case — perhaps the most striking conclusion that emerged from the early studies was that there appeared to be increasing returns to labour services alone. In terms of the Cobb—Douglas production function, values of β were obtained that for most industries were in excess of unity or, to put it in even simpler terms, a given percentage increase in the employment of labour services, with everything else held constant, seemed to lead to an even bigger percentage increase in output. Given the equivalence assumed between total man-hours and labour services in these studies, this result confirmed Kuh's earlier observation regarding the procyclicality of output per man-hour. This may of course indicate that the coefficient on log Q_t in the estimated employment function is downward biased. For example, if firms' expectations of Q_t were the relevant variable rather than Q_t itself, then the variable would be subject to measurement error and a downward bias in its coefficient could arise. Considerations of this kind have surfaced in much empirical work such as in Nickell (1984). It is now time to look at some other explanations.

The Productivity of Hours

The simplest explanation that one can offer is that if the marginal product of an additional hour is much higher than its average product, then we will observe the average product increasing as more hours are worked. There are two schools of thought on this: the first, which we can call the 'industrial relations' approach, rejects this proposition and argues that overtime reflects customary institutional arrangements in most developed countries and that much of it is wasteful and unproductive, while the second, the 'econometric' approach, argues in favour of the proposition largely on the grounds as discussed earlier, i.e. that the flow of capital services also increases with hours worked and that there may be fixed unproductive hours, i.e. setting-up time, lunch and tea breaks, etc. Evidence for the former view seems to be largely based on the personal experience of the writers concerned, although more direct evidence can be found in the UK National Board for Prices and Incomes Report (1970) on overtime and shiftworking. In a survey of over 2000 firms, 69.2 per cent of respondents thought that productivity of overtime and normal hours were about the same and 28 per cent thought that the productivity of overtime was lower. This result contrasts sharply with the econometric results obtained by both Craine (1973) and Feldstein (1967) who directly estimated a Cobb−Douglas function of the form

$$Q = AK^\alpha N^\beta H^\gamma \tag{4.8}$$

where H is hours worked per employee.

Craine fitted his equation to time series data on US manufacturing, while Feldstein used a cross-section of UK manufacturing industries repeated for three years. 'Hours' is not really a factor of production in itself, but is instead a variable representing utilisation of capital and labour.

Both studies found values for γ considerably in excess of unity: 1.89 (Craine) and 1.3 to 2.2 (Feldstein). A more recent study by Leslie and Wise (1980) gives a re-estimate of the equation for 28 UK manufacturing industries for each of the years 1948−68. The equation obtained is

$$\log Q = -3.85 + 0.78 \log N + 1.61 \log H + 0.24 \log K + 0.019t$$
$$(90.1) \qquad\qquad (8.90) \qquad\qquad (24.9) \qquad\qquad (13.0)$$

$$R^2 = 0.967$$

where t-statistics are given in parentheses.

Now an important property of a Cobb−Douglas production function is that if the exponents (i.e. α, β, etc.) add to unity then the underlying technology is one of constant returns to scale. If labour services could be approximated as assumed earlier by total man-hours, then we would expect β and γ to be the same and test for constant returns by examining the sum of α and β. In fact the latter do add to nearly one (1.02) but the estimate of γ is much greater than that of β. To put the equation into perspective, a doubling of hours per worker with the number of workers and machines held constant would apparently lead to a 161 per cent increase in output. This indeed appears to be very powerful evidence of increasing returns to hours worked per employee.

There are, however, three alternative interpretations of this result. The first, as proposed by Leslie and Wise, is that in a cross-industry study such as that of Feldstein, one must be careful to standardise for differences in production functions between different industries. In particular, firms that work long hours may be more efficient than others and the high value obtained for γ may simply reflect this. Leslie and Wise found that if they standardised for industry specific effects[7] then the coefficient on hours dropped dramatically and was almost identical to the coefficient on workers.

The second explanation is that hours worked per employee as measured in these various studies does not reflect hours actually worked at all, but instead measures hours paid for by employers. If we accept the existence of adjustment costs as before then, as we have seen, firms may prefer in the face of a recession to try and spread hours over the existing workforce rather than to lay workers off. Now one would naturally argue that if this were the case then surely we would pick it up in an hours worked measure. In practice, however, collective agreements usually specify a minimum number of hours for which a worker must be paid and, even in a recession, firms that paid workers for only part of a normal working week could well find workers quitting who would be hard to replace in the next upswing. Thus for either or both of these reasons, hours actually worked in periods of recessions are less than what is observed, namely, hours paid for. Now since we observe hours that are actually worked in periods of boom, the apparent variation in the hours series must be less than that actually occurring in reality. This proposition was suggested by Kuh and has been extensively investigated in a study of employment in US manufacturing by Fair (1969).[8] His approach differs from other studies in that he assumed a short-run fixed proportions production function rather than a Cobb—Douglas function and used it to directly estimate labour requirements during recessionary periods. The amount of excess labour is then defined as the difference between the actual number of workers employed and the required number, where the latter is assumed to be equal to total man-hours required divided by standard (i.e. non-overtime) hours per worker. Fair then developed an employment function in which the logarithm of the change in the number of workers employed per period was a negative function of the amount of excess labour in hand and a positive function of expected output. His model seemed to fit US data industry rather better than the standard employment function discussed earlier. However, Leslie and Wise found in their Cobb—Douglas production function study that, if an unemployment variable was added to the equation, the coefficient on hours remained unaltered.

Finally, there remains the possibility that the production function itself is wrongly specified. A Cobb—Douglas production function imposes the restriction that the elasticities of output with respect to each input are constant. Hazledine and others have criticised the use of a Cobb—Douglas function on the grounds that this is unsatisfactory and argue that productivity is, in part at least, a function of the vigour with which managers drive their workforce and that managerial input of this sort is a function of wage costs, i.e. overtime and demand pressure. Hazledine and Watts (1977) suggested that this idea could be incorporated by replacing the Cobb—Douglas function with a more flexible relationship between average labour productivity and employment, thus allowing an inverted U-shaped average product curve. In a time series investigation of 14 UK industries, they found what appears to be strong empirical support for this type of function, while in a more recent paper Hazledine (1978) demonstrated that an employment function based on the inverted 'U' function performed better than the standard model as derived from a Cobb—Douglas production function. This type of explanation would thus stress the unobserved variation in managerial input over the cycle as the main cause of procyclical movement in labour productivity.

What, then, do these studies imply about the relationship between the trade cycle and employment levels? Clearly the exact answer will depend upon the industry concerned. If the costs of holding inventories are relatively high and firms recognise that a depression is likely to be lengthy, then employment levels are certain to be varied. In industries facing high labour force adjustment costs, hours will be altered more than in industries with low adjustment costs. In a depression, hours reduction will take the form of both observed cuts in the working day, e.g. scrapping of overtime and unobserved cuts (e.g. reduced work intensity). Similarly, differences in technology will also play a role since industries with significant 'setting up' costs at the start of a shift, or with increasing returns to hours per worker, are more likely to reduce the size of their labour forces than to cut back on the length of the shift or working day.

4.4 Some Empirical Labour Demand Functions

It is important to recognise at the outset that the choice of specification of an individual empirical labour demand function essentially reflects the use to which the results are to be put. There have been, in fact, a bewildering array of empirical methodologies used, which differ not only in terms of their assumptions regarding the underlying technology, i.e. the mathematical form of the production function, but also in terms of the variables included in the function to be estimated and the implicit or explicit model in which the labour demand function is embedded. Rather than attempt the near-impossible task of reviewing this very complex literature on a model-by-model basis, we choose therefore to give a selective review under each of three main areas of application: the determinants of the aggregate demand for labour, the wage elasticity of demand for labour and the demand for different types of labour. There are, however, three basic specifications that we shall briefly consider before moving on.

The first is derived directly from the profit maximising position of a price taking firm employing labour, L, at a wage, W, a set of m other variable inputs with prices, $P_1, P_2, \ldots, P_m$ and k fixed inputs with quantities, $Z_1, Z_2, \ldots, Z_k$. The labour demand function may then be written as

$$L = L \left(\frac{W}{P}, \frac{P_1}{P}, \ldots, \frac{P_m}{P}, Z_1, \ldots, Z_k \right) \tag{4.9}$$

where P is the output price. This function then tells us how labour employed will vary given, for example, a rise in the wage rate where product price, other variable input prices and fixed input quantities are held constant. When, as discussed further below, imperfect adjustment is taken into account, this is an appropriate way of analysing the impact of changes in the relevant variables upon the demand for labour over various time periods.

The second approach concentrates upon the firm's cost-minimising decision where all inputs are variable. This version may be written as

$$L = L \left(\frac{W}{P_1}, \ldots, \frac{W}{P_m}, Q \right) \tag{4.10}$$

where Q is output. This function then tells us, for example, how labour employed will vary given a change in the wage rate where output and other input prices are given. This formulation therefore only reflects the substitution effects arising from a given input price change. At the micro level, it is thus most applicable to the case where output is demand constrained. If, however, this is not the case, then the effects of an industry specific input price change must take into account the effect upon Q of the induced change in the product price. If the input price change applies to all industries, then we move into a much more complicated general equilibrium analysis in which we would focus more upon relative price changes across different industries. At the macro level, this formulation may be appropriate if we assume that the output of the economy is, in the long run, determined by a full employment condition.

If capital is the only input included in the production function other than labour, then equation (4.10) may be rewritten as

$$L = L\left(\frac{W}{R}, Q\right) \tag{4.11}$$

where R is the capital rental. Note that here capital is treated as a variable input.

The third formulation concentrates upon the marginal productivity condition for labour. If we assume that the production function is separable between non-labour inputs and labour, and takes the CES form with constant returns to scale

$$Q = A[\alpha g(\mathbf{z})^{\theta} + (1 - \alpha)L^{\theta}]^{1/\theta} \tag{4.12}$$

where A is an efficiency parameter which may vary over time due to the effects of technical progress and $g(\mathbf{z})$ represents some function of a vector of non-labour inputs, $\mathbf{z}$, then the marginal productivity condition may be written as

$$\log \frac{Q}{L} = -\sigma\log(1 - \alpha) - \sigma\theta\log A + \sigma\log \frac{W}{P} \tag{4.13}$$

The elasticity of substitution, $\sigma\ (= 1/(1-\theta))$, may then be estimated by regressing log Q/L on log W/P with a further variable such as a time trend included to pick up the effects of variation in A. The elasticity of demand for labour can be found from the formula

$$E_{LL/Q} = (1 - v_L) \tag{4.14}$$

where $E_{LL/Q}$ is elasticity of demand for labour with respect to its own price (i.e. the wage) with output given and v_L is the share of labour. This approach is thus an alternative to estimating equation (4.10), except that it imposes the special assumption of a CES technology and does not require data on other input prices in its estimation. It is subject therefore to the same comments as those above.

Aggregate Labour Demand

Here the focus is very much upon how, in the short to medium run, employment responds to a given change in its determinants. By the short run we mean the more or less immediate impact of a change in, for example, the wage rate, such as over a one-year period, while by the medium run (e.g. three years) we refer to the final response by employers given a fixed capital stock. Note that the long run, as previously defined in Chapter 3, refers to the period over which all inputs including capital may be varied. Analyses of this kind may be used to examine the lagged response of employment to various stimuli and to therefore explain its cyclical behaviour, and have been addressed most recently to the question of why employment has fallen during the 1980s.

To link this back to our discussion in Chapter 3, we recall that the condition for profit maximisation, given a price-taking firm, was that the wage rate, W, should be equated to the marginal value product of labour. Noting that the latter is simply the product of the product price, P, and the marginal physical product of labour, which is in turn a function of labour input, L, and capital input, K, allows us, if we assume K to be given, to reshuffle the relationship so as to make the demand for labour some function of K and W/P:

$$L = L\left(\frac{W}{P}, K\right) \tag{4.15}$$

This equation is thus the simplest version of equation (4.9) where labour is the only variable input and there is only one fixed input. This equation does, in fact, provide the simplest basis for an empirical medium-run labour demand function, but there are a few extra modifications that are sometimes made. The first is that we need to make some assumption about the role played by intermediate inputs in the production process. If we assume that intermediate inputs are used in direct proportion to gross output (the Leontief assumption), then we can measure output by real value added and equation (4.9) is an adequate representation providing that we remember to use the value added deflator for P. If, however, we assume that the production function takes the form (e.g. Symons and Layard, 1984)

$$Q = F(K, L, M) \tag{4.16}$$

where Q is gross output and M is intermediate inputs, then we must solve separately for the marginal productivity conditions for both L and M, and then solve further for a function of the form

$$L = L\left(\frac{W}{P}, \frac{P_M}{P}, K\right) \tag{4.17}$$

where P_M is the price of intermediate inputs and P is this time the gross output deflator. Equation (4.15) is sometimes referred to as the *gross output* formulation, while (4.17) is the *value added* formulation.

A second modification as introduced by Layard and Nickell (1985b) is to drop the price-taking assumption at the level of the firm and instead assume that the economy consists of a number of identical imperfectly competitive firms. In this case the profit maximising condition is that the wage rate be equated to the marginal revenue product, i.e. marginal revenue times the marginal physical product of labour. The marginal revenue of the ith firm is related to its price, P_i, by the formula

$$MR_i = P_i(1 + 1/\eta) \tag{4.18}$$

where η is the price elasticity of demand facing the firm. If η is now allowed to vary with the level of aggregate demand in the economy, then Layard and Nickell show that an aggregate demand variable should be included in the aggregate demand function for labour. If, for example, η rises with aggregate demand, then the demand for labour should also similarly rise as the mark-up of price over marginal cost falls and the profit maximising level of output expands. Layard and Nickell chose, however, for reasons relating to the wider purposes of their general model, to measure aggregate demand not by its level *per se* but by its deviation from the full utilisation of resources.

The third modification brings us back to the lag structure. We have already seen earlier in this chapter that the simple partial adjustment model leads to the inclusion of employment lagged one period as an explanatory variable. Recent empirical specifications, applied to the UK at least, have tended to include employment lagged two periods as a further explanatory variable. One justification for this procedure is that if there are two different types of labour being aggregated where both are subject to a partial adjustment process but with different values for the adjustment coefficient, then a correctly aggregated labour demand function will include the dependent variable lagged in both one and two periods.[9] We may note, in passing, that if firms maximise the present value of future profits in the presence of input adjustment costs, then theoretically they will plan a complete future path for employment levels. Typically then, the labour demand function will include the future expected values of the various exogenous variables.[10] Recent studies have made some implicit allowance for this by including some lagged terms in exogenous variables such as the real product wage. The implication here is that future values are being predicted from those in the past.

One further modification may be dealt with briefly. If the effects of technical progress are not adequately picked up by either the functional form or the explanatory variables included, then a time trend may be added. This may also serve to allow for the effects of declining hours per worker.

Taking Layard and Nickell's formulation as an example, the labour demand function may be written as

$$\log N_t = a_0 + a_1\log N_{t-1} + a_2\log N_{t-2} + a_3\log \left(\frac{W}{P}\right)_t$$
$$+ a_4A_t + (1 - a_1 - a_2)\log K_t \tag{4.19}$$

where N_t is employment, $(W/P)_t$ is the real product wage, A_t is a measure of the level of technology and K_t is capital stock. Most studies use a logarithmic formulation and this is theoretically consistent with a Cobb–Douglas production function. The constrained coefficients on $\log K_t$ reflect an assumption of constant returns to scale, although this restriction is usually tested as part of the analysis.

As explained above, other studies differ in terms of their inclusion of variables, e.g. log $(P_M/P)_t$, as in Symons and Layard (1984), and in the imposition of further lags upon the exogenous variables.

Three results seem to stand out from these studies. The first is that there is a significant negative relationship between the aggregate demand for labour in the UK and the real product wage. Although both real product wages in UK manufacturing and real consumption wages in the economy as a whole have not grown faster between the mid-1970s and mid-1980s than those of other industrialised countries, it does seem that, in common with France and West Germany but in contrast to the USA, the gap between the level of actual real product wages and that at which there would be full employment widened over the period in the UK (Bruno and Sachs, 1985). In this context, trade union wage pressure and higher employment taxation may have played a role, although Layard and Nickell (1985b), in the context of their wider model, found that neither explained a major part of increased unemployment since the 1960s. A detailed discussion of wage-gap analysis is pursued in Chapter 8.

A second conclusion is that, in manufacturing at least, labour demand is negatively related to the real product price of raw materials. The positive substitution effects that one would anticipate in favour of employment if material prices increased are thus apparently outweighed by the negative output effects. This result was obtained by both Symons (1982) and Symons and Layard (1984). The oil price shocks of 1973 and 1979 presumably then had an adverse impact on UK employment.

The last conclusion is that the success reported by Layard and Nickell in finding a direct positive relationship between aggregate demand variables and labour demand, indicates that aggregate demand shocks have a direct influence on unemployment over and above their impact on prices. Demand shocks as anticipated or received by the British economy at the end of the 1970s and beginning of the 1980s thus played an important role in creating the sudden downturn in employment at around that time.

The Wage Elasticity of Demand for Labour

In Table 4.5 we show some selected estimates of the elasticity of labour demand with respect to the wage rate as measured by (per period) labour cost. Selected results are given from studies based upon versions of the three specifications discussed earlier, i.e. equations (4.15) or (4.17), (4.11) and (4.13). Starting with the results based on the first specification, we note first that Symons and Layard obtain a rather wide range of estimates across their sample of OECD countries, varying between –0.3 in France to –2.4 in Japan. Their estimate for the UK is twice that obtained by Layard and Nickell, the difference presumably arising from difference in specification and in the data base used: for example Layard and Symons include the price of materials in these estimated functions and employ

Table 4.5 Labour Demand Elasticities with Respect to the Wage Rate

		After 1 year	Long run
Capital stock constant			
Symons and Layard (1984)	France		−0.3
	Germany		−0.4
	Japan		−2.4
	UK		−1.8
	USA		−1.3
Layard and Nickell (1985b)	UK	−0.329	−0.9
Output constant			
Nadiri (1968)	USA	−0.19	−0.19
Coen and Hickman (1970)	USA	−0.14	−0.18
Clark and Freeman (1980)	USA	−0.48	−0.50
Estimate from elasticity of substitution			
Arrow et al. (1961)[a]	USA		−0.17
Rosen and Quandt (1978)[a]	USA		−0.3

Note: (a) Derived by multiplying estimated elasticity of substitution by share of non-labour
    inputs. This was assumed to be 0.3.

quarterly data for the manufacturing sector, while Layard and Nickell use annual
all economy-level data.

It is noticeable, however, that these results nevertheless indicate on the whole
a rather higher elasticity of demand for labour when equation (4.15) or (4.17)
is used as the estimating equation than when output is held constant as in equation (4.11). This result is nevertheless fully in accordance with economic theory
in that one would expect $E_{LL/K}$, the wage elasticity of demand for labour when
K is held constant to exceed $E_{LL/Q}$. Taking a Cobb−Douglas production function with constant returns to scale as an example, it may be shown that $E_{LL/K}$
$= -1/v_k$ while $E_{LL/Q} = -v_L$. Thus if $v_k = 0.3$ and $v_L = 0.7$ then we would have
$E_{LL/K}$ and $E_{LL/Q}$ equal to −3.3 and −0.7 respectively.

Differences in the form of the underlying labour demand function are not the
only important differences in the selected studies. All of the studies cited, with
the exceptions of Arrow et al. (1961) and Rosen and Quandt (1978) have specified
some form of lag mechanism in their empirical work. Coen and Hickman (1970)
provide perhaps the most comprehensive treatment in this respect, as they make
the speed with which employers adjust their employment of labour services depend
upon utilisation rates of capital inputs. They thus estimate a set of interdependent
input demand equations rather than a series of separate ones. Simultaneity feed-
backs of various kinds are allowed for in some of the studies, for example Symons
and Layard (1984) allow for the feedback effect of labour demand upon the wage
by the use of instrumental variables, while Layard and Nickell (1985b), Nadiri
(1968) and Rosen and Quandt (1978) estimate their labour demand functions in
the context of wider econometric models. Rosen and Quandt are particularly interesting in this context in that they employ a disequilibrium approach in which,
given slow wage adjustment, the level of employment observed is assumed to

be the minimum of labour supply and demand. Thus in some years the wage lies below its market clearing level, in which case we observe labour supply under conditions of excess demand for labour, while in other years the wage is above its clearing level, in which case we observe excess labour supply. Rosen and Quandt estimate separate labour demand and supply schedules in the context of this disequilibrium framework. Finally Clark and Freeman (1980) have criticised the restriction that W and R are included only as a ratio to one another in equation (4.11) and argue that they should be entered separately, given the presence of likely error in a capital rental series. They obtain a much higher wage elasticity under this second formulation.

We have observed that there are a number of different measures of the wage elasticity of demand for labour, each defined according to what else is being held constant when the wage elasticity is measured or estimated. We can, however, explore a little further the case in which a wage change is experienced by only a single industry, as in the case of an industry-specific wage tax or subsidy. We assume here that the supply of labour to the industry is perfectly elastic. Thus we can write a convenient expression for the overall wage elasticity of labour demand, E_{LL}, as

$$E_{LL} = E_{LL/Q} + E_{LQ}\eta v_L \qquad (4.20)$$

The right-hand side of equation (4.20) consists of two terms: $E_{LL/Q}$ which, as before, measures the substitution effect along a given isoquant, and a product of three measures which reflects the scale effect. The latter consists of the output elasticity of labour demand, E_{LQ}, which under constant returns to scale would simply be equal to unity, η, the price elasticity of demand for output, which obviously varies enormously from industry to industry and the elasticity of product price with respect to the wage rate, which under competitive conditions is simply equal to the share of labour in costs, v_L. To simplify the exposition below we will assume an imaginary but not atypical industry in which in the long run E_{LQ} equals 1, η equals -0.7 and v_L equals 0.7. In the real world, adjustment does not take place instantaneously and it is therefore also useful to know how much response in labour demand will occur after a given period. For the purposes of our calculations below we will assume that, after one year of adjustment, E_{LQ} equals 0.8, η equals -0.5 and that the elasticity of product price with respect to the wage rate equals 0.5. Our respective scale elasticities are then $1 \times -0.7 \times 0.7 = -0.49$ in the long run and $0.8 \times -0.5 \times 0.5 = -0.2$ after a single year of adjustment. Taking, for illustrative purposes, $E_{LL/Q}$ as -0.2 and -0.3, after one year of adjustment and in the long run respectively, would thus yield corresponding esimtates for E_L of -0.4 and 0.79.

Substitution Between Different Types of Labour

Clearly, the methodologies explored in the last two subsections of this chapter could easily be extended to cases with more than one type of labour. An additional consideration arises, however, when we move to many labour inputs, and that is how to deal with different degrees of substitutability and complementarity between other non-labour inputs included in the production function. The central point here is that dealing with substitution between a given pair of factors of production in a world with more than two factors of production means that one has to make an assumption about the remainder.

One measure that one might employ is a simple extension of the elasticity of substitution, σ, that we defined in Chapter 3. The *direct* elasticity of substitution, d_{ij}, between two inputs, L_i and L_j, is defined as the elasticity of relative input quantities with respect to the ratio of their respective prices, holding output and other input quantities constant. It is written as:

$$d_{ij} = \frac{\partial \log\,(L_i/L_j)}{\partial \log\,(W_j/W_i)} \tag{4.21}$$

The problem with this definition in a micro context is reasonably obvious. Even if we restrict ourselves to a fixed output case, changing W_j/W_i will not only affect L_i/L_j but is also likely to change other input quantities as well. In a macro context we might consider using the inverse of (4.21) and consider the effect of changing L_i/L_j on W_j/W_i. Here, however, we also run into a problem since, for example, changing the skill composition of the labour force will normally change in turn the full employment level of output. Thus, unless the production function is homothetic in these factors, i.e. the ratio of marginal products and hence factor prices associated with a given ratio of factor quantities is invariant with respect to the level of output, then the direct elasticity of substitution is of limited usefulness in a macro context.

For micro applications, an alternative measure is the Allen partial elasticity of substitution, a_{ij}, which is a symmetric measure of the effect of changing a factor price, e.g. W_j, upon the quantity demanded of another factor, L_{ij}, while holding output and other input prices constant. The cross elasticity of demand holding output constant, $E_{ij/Q}$ is then defined as

$$E_{ij/Q} = a_{ij}v_j \tag{4.22}$$

where v_j is the share of the jth factor. However, since the Allen elasticity is symmetric, i.e. $a_{ij} = a_{ji}$, it is clear from (4.22) that $E_{ij/Q}$ is not. The Allen partial elasticity is thus useful if we ask, for example, whether an increase in the wage of skilled workers will increase or decrease the demand for unskilled workers. The answer is in the affirmative if the relevant a_{ij} is positive.

A third measure that appears more appealing in the macro context is the partial elasticity of complementarity, c_{ij}, as introduced by Hicks (1970). This is the dual of the Allen measure and registers the effect of a change in the quantity of one factor upon the price of another when holding other input quantities and marginal cost constant, but allowing output to vary. An increase in the number of skilled workers will therefore raise or lower the number of unskilled workers according to whether the value for the relevant c_{ij} is positive or negative.[11] In the case where there are only two factors, $c_{ij} = 1/a_{ij}$. This is also true in the many-factor case, given homothetic forms of function such as the Cobb–Douglas or the CES. In general, however, this is a restriction that we do not wish to impose in the case of many inputs. Research in this area has therefore tended to concentrate on more flexible forms of function such as the multi-level CES, as introduced by Sato (1967), and the translog production and cost functions.

In its simplest two-level form the CES production function may be written as

$$Q = A[aZ^\rho + (1 - a) X_1^\rho]^{1/\rho} \qquad (4.23)$$

where $Z = [bX_2^\theta + (1 - b) X_3^\theta]^{1/\theta}$ \qquad (4.24)

This function is homothetic in the pair of inputs, X_2 and X_3 but not in the pairs X_1 and X_2, and X_1 and X_3. The function has the properties that

$$a_{12} = a_{13} = \frac{1}{1 - \rho} \neq a_{23}$$

and

$$c_{12} = c_{13} = 1 - \rho \neq c_{23}$$

The function allows us to test whether $a_{12} = a_{13} > a_{23}$, or whether $c_{12} = c_{13} < c_{23}$ by seeing whether $\rho > \theta$. The two-level framework can be extended almost indefinitely to many more inputs by including further nested groups of inputs such as Z above, and by extending the number of levels.

The translog cost function is written as

$$\log C = \log Q + a_0 + \sum_i a_i \log W_i$$

$$+ 0.5 \sum_i \sum_j b_{ij} \log W_i \log W_j \qquad (4.25)$$

where $\sum_i a_i = 1$

$$b_{ij} = b_{ji}$$

$$\sum_i b_{ij} = 0 \quad \text{for all } j$$

The Allen partial elasticities are then calculated as

$$a_{ij} = \frac{b_{ij} + v_i v_j}{v_i v_j}$$

The corresponding production function and the definitions of the partial elasticities of complementarity are written analogously as

$$\log Q = \alpha_0 + \sum_i \alpha_i \log X_i + 0.5 \sum_i \sum_j \beta_{ij} \log X_i \log X_j \qquad (4.26)$$

where $c_{ij} = \dfrac{\beta_{ij} + v_i v_j}{v_i v_j}$

Obviously one could directly estimate the above production and cost functions. The consensus is, however, that since all measures of substitution and complementarity ultimately depend upon the second derivatives of the production and cost functions, any reasonably unrestricted estimates are likely to be swamped by errors in measurement. By far the more popular approach is to estimate either the marginal product conditions as derived from the production function given profit maximisation, or the factor demand equations as derived from the cost function given cost minimisation. The translog functions yield factor demand equations and marginal productivity conditions of the form

$$v_i = a_i + \sum_j b_{ij} \log W_j \qquad (4.27)$$
and

$$v_i = \alpha_i + \sum_j \beta_{ij} \log X_j \qquad (4.28)$$

respectively.

Obviously, there is a vast array of applications to which these techniques could be put. Hamermesh (1986) surveys a wide range of studies concerned with substitution between blue-collar and white-collar workers. Here one finds consistently positive Allen partials between blue-collar workers and capital inputs generally in the range $0.5-2.0$, and between blue-collar and white-collar workers in the rather wide range of $0-6$. A number of the studies surveyed suggest, however, that the Allen partial between white-collar workers and capital is actually negative; thus suggesting that a rise in the white-collar wage leads to a fall in the demand for capital. In a further survey in the same article, Hamermesh shows that the Allen partials and the partial elasticities of complementarity between different age and sex groups are also generally positive, with the important exception of adult women and young workers, between which some studies have indicated that the partial elasticity of complementarity is negative. This result is important as it suggests that growing adult female supply may exert downward pressure on the wages of young workers.

Another area of application concerns the degree of substitutability between different types of educated labour. This is important for a number of reasons, including its relevance to the techniques employed by educational planners and its importance in evaluating the impact of educational expansion upon wage differentials and income distribution. Studies that impose separability between capital and non-labour inputs as in, for example, a two-level CES production function such as equation (4.23), where capital is X_2, and educated and less-educated labour are X_2 and X_3, have generally found a high degree of substitutability between labour inputs (for example Bowles, 1970; Dougherty, 1972). This would seem to fit in well with the empirical observation that wage differentials by education have remained relatively unchanged over long periods in spite of a substantial improvement in the educational composition of the labour force.

There is, however, an alternative hypothesis that has attracted much empirical attention which states that physical capital, K, is more complementary with skilled or educated labour, S, than with unskilled or uneducated labour, N. The capital—skill complementarity hypothesis (CSC) thus states that $c_{KS} > c_{KN}$ and may alternatively be tested by examining whether $a_{KS} < a_{KN}$. CSC would thus suggest that the tendency for wage differentials to fall in the face of educational expansion has been offset by an accompanying growth in the capital stock. This hypothesis also implies that wage differentials by education may be effected by capital subsidies or taxes on accounting profits. A number of studies have found evidence in favour of CSC (for example Rosen, 1968; Griliches, 1969; Fallon and Layard, 1975).

4.5 Summary

In this chapter, we have attempted to survey a very large and technical area of applied economic research. In doing so, we have moved through some fairly descriptive material regarding the main trends relating to the allocation of employment by sector and occupation and the behaviour of employment given fluctuations in economic activity. In this last context, we concentrated upon disturbances related to the trade cycle and other medium-term causes rather than upon short-run response such as generated by seasonal effects. The main empirical observation that labour productivity moves procyclically seems to be best explained by factors relating to changes in hours worked arising from employment adjustment costs. We must note, however, that theories stressing cyclical explanations have become less fashionable as cyclical regularities in employment, such as observed in the UK during the post-war years up to the mid-1970s, have largely been replaced by a more persistent downward trend during the 1980s.

Turning now to the literature on empirically estimated labour demand functions there are really three things that stand out. The first is that one simply cannot speak of *the* labour demand function, as one does, for example, with the production function. There are in fact a range of quite different such functions which differ, not only in terms of purely technical matters such as mathematical form, but more importantly in terms of the economic context, e.g. cost minimisation, profit maximisation, etc., in which the function is being estimated. One has to be careful therefore to ensure that the parameters estimated, such as wage elasticities, are interpreted correctly. Frequently such functions are estimated within the bounds of a much wider econometric model and the results are best used within the overall context of that model. The second point is that, in time series studies, increasing attention is being paid to the estimation of labour demand functions within a full dynamic optimisation framework as opposed to the rather *ad hoc* specifications such as the partial adjustment mechanism which have been used in the past. Whether this greater degree of sophistication in dynamic specification will yield a suitable pay-off remains to be seen, although the results so far are encouraging. Here one can expect more empirical insight into such areas as the effects of redundancy payments legislation and direct government controls upon firms' ability to fire workers. Finally, perhaps the most important conclusion is that empirical research on labour demand has, on the whole, supported the conclusions of economic theory in this area.

Notes

1. These would typically be found in agricultural households or in households owning a small business such as a shop. In the UK unpaid household members are excluded and paid members are included among the self-employed.
2. There are a number of ways in which economists try to characterise technical change. The simplest definition of neutral or unbiased technical change, as originally introduced by Hicks, is that a given change is neutral if the capital–labour ratio is unchanged, given the same ratio of marginal products. Graphically this means that as technical progress shifts an isoquant towards the origin, the slope of the isoquant will nevertheless remain constant at the point of intersection between the isoquant and a ray drawn from the origin. Capital-biased or capital-using technical change would thus imply a rise in the capital–labour ratio, given the same ratio of marginal products. Labour-using technical change is the exact opposite.
3. One should note in passing that the data for output and productivity growth in services have only a limited meaning, as much of the sector does not produce a marketable product, e.g. central and local government, public health and education, churches, charities, etc. National income accountants measure value added (contribution to GDP or GNP) of these activities as compensation of employees plus depreciation. Changes in real output measured in this way over time therefore reflect little more than changes in employment levels.
4. The coefficient of variation of a variable is its standard deviation divided by its arithmetic mean. It should be noted that the coefficients of variation and correlation coefficients given in Table 4.4 are calculated from the detrended series.
5. For a survey of the early literature see Nerlove (1967).
6. Let F be the fixed cost per worker, W the hourly non-overtime wage and r the overtime rate. Obviously costs per hour are always lower if the worker works HS than any number of hours less than HS, as the fixed costs are spread over more hours. In general HS will also represent a lower cost per hour than if the worker does overtime, providing that

$$rW\text{HS} > F$$

Thus if the basic wage is £5 an hour, standard hours are 40 hours per week and overtime is at time-and-a-half ($r = 0.5$) then HS is the cost minimising number of hours per worker if F is less than £100 per week. If F is greater than £100 then the employer would like the worker to work as many hours as possible.
7. This was accomplished by introducing industry-specific dummy variables.

8. A clear survey of labour hoarding theory can be found in Leslie and Laing (1978).
9. See Nickell (1986) for further details.
10. Two studies that directly address this problem in very different ways are those by Sargent (1978) and Pindyck and Rotemberg (1983).
11. If the production function is of the form

$$Q = F(X_1, X_2, \ldots, X_n)$$

with a corresponding cost function

$$C = G(Q, W_1, \ldots, W_n)$$

then convenient definitions of a_{ij} and c_{ij} are $a_{ij} = CG_{ij}/G_iG_j$ and $C_{ij} = QF_{ij}/F_iF_j$, where subscripts denote partial derivatives. For details of the interrelationships between the various measures, see Sato and Koizumi (1973).

5

Earnings and Earnings Differentials

5.1 Introduction

In past chapters we have looked at some of the most important approaches that economists have taken with respect to both the supply and demand for labour. Putting the two together and calling the resulting equilibrium price the market wage rate is of course a trivial exercise and needs no further discussion here. For a number of different reasons, such a procedure seems a rather odd one when we look at the real world. The first is that, given the enormous heterogeneity of the labour force, we would expect to observe a very wide array of different wage rates. We would naturally expect, for example, that a highly skilled labourer would earn more than a person with fewer skills. Similarly, we would expect workers whose skills are currently rather scarce (e.g. experienced energy economists) to command higher wages than those whose skills have recently been rendered less effective by technical change (e.g. hot metal printsetters). The term 'market wage rate' thus only really makes sense when we think of workers with identical characteristics from the viewpoint of employers. The second is that, contrary to the message of the supply and demand diagram, labour markets may not appear to work very well at all and we will observe apparently identical workers earning very different rates of pay. This may only indicate that, at a given point in time, a particular labour market is in disequilibrium, and that sooner or later a convergence towards wage equalisation will result. Some economists have, however, been extremely sceptical of this view and have pointed to various forms of market imperfection, including institutional factors, as the main determinant of earnings.

Before making any judgements about the anarchic state or otherwise of modern-day labour markets, we must first draw a picture based upon a number of inter-related theories regarding how wages are determined. We develop first the modern competitive labour market theory including the theory of human capital and consider what further role imperfections such as discrimination might play. We then review the empirical evidence in the second half of the chapter.

5.2   Under What Circumstances will Everyone Earn the Same?

To set things going, let us first make the following three rather extreme assumptions:

   (i)   identical workers;
   (ii) the wage is the only net benefit associated with employment;
   (iii) costless mobility between jobs.

A familiar argument can now be presented. Suppose that a particular industry paid lower wages than others. The result would be, of course, that workers in the badly paid industry would offer their services elsewhere, thus inducing advertised rates in that industry to rise. Equilibrium would only then exist when wages were equalised everywhere.

The first assumption need not, of course, refer to all members of the labour force, but only to a specific group of workers who fall under a given homogeneous skill category. Thus jobs with high skill requirements will pay higher wages than those requiring lower skill levels, although wages will be equalised within each skill category.

Solving through an appropriate set of n supply and demand equations, where n is the number of labour categories, would then yield the equilibrium values for the various wage rates. Changes in relative wage rates over time would thus be attributable to movements in the relative supplies and demands of the various categories.

It is important to distinguish between different sources of variation between workers. The first possibility is that workers differ according to innate characteristics such as physical strength, stamina and native intelligence. Here the supplies of different groups will, as a first approximation, be inelastic with respect to wages, and will only change relative to one another over time due to factors such as nutritional or genetic improvement. A second case is where workers are judged by innate factors such as their race and religion which, other things being equal, presumably do not affect worker productivity. Various theories of labour market discrimination are reviewed later in this chapter. The third, and even more discussed, case is where workers differ according to acquired characteristics such as education or training. In so far as the acquisition of such attributes is related to market incentives, the relative long-run supplies of different types of worker will depend positively upon wage differentials. This case is central to theories of human capital accumulation and, among their main critiques, to theories of screening, both of which are dealt with in the next section. Non-economic determinants of skill acquisition such as parental income and social class are also important and once again discriminatory factors have a role to play. Finally, workers may have different tastes. This, however, brings us to the last two of our assumptions.

The wage is not, of course, the only yardstick used by workers to evaluate the merits of different jobs. Workers are also concerned, amongst other things, with the unpleasantness or otherwise of working conditions, job safety and job security. The general principle that we apply here is that workers will assign a utility number to each job opening and will then try to occupy those vacancies associated with maximum utility. If individuals have identical tastes, then although observed rates of pay will differ between jobs, other unobserved job characteristics will exactly compensate. Unpleasant jobs will thus pay higher wages than those with better working conditions. This notion is often referred to in the literature as the principle of equal net advantage. For example, if the only differences between jobs are in promotion prospects and the length of required training periods, then although identical workers will face different starting salaries and salary scales, there will be much less variation in the expected present values of career earnings of different employments. Clearly jobs with low starting salaries will be associated with more rapid expected wage increase over future periods.

There are, of course, a number of reasons why it would be very naive to believe that the principle holds exactly in practice. Most of these derive from the fact that it is often costly or difficult for workers to move between different jobs. If mobility costs are of the fixed variety, such as physical moving costs or costs of breaching existing psychological inertia, then, although the equalisation principle is violated, it nevertheless remains true that improvements in the non-wage attributes of a given set of jobs should be associated with a deterioration in their wages relative to those elsewhere. If, however, certain sets of jobs are effectively rationed by, for example, trade unions, professional associations, labour market discrimination or strictly limited access to job information networks, then the labour market may become segmented. Market imperfections are thus a major reason why net advantages may not be equalised, and occupy the last section of this chapter.

5.3 Human Capital — Theory

The Basic Model

The essence of the human capital approach is the assumption that individuals make, or attempt to make, optimising decisions regarding the acquisition of further personal characteristics that yield net benefits in future periods. Such investments can, in principle, be taken to include virtually anything that generates individual self-improvement although most attention has been directed towards education, health and post-school investments in training. If one assumes, for the moment, that future benefits accruing to an individual can be adequately quantified in terms of increased income, then the value of a person's human capital can be defined as the present value of his future labour earnings. Optimal decisions regarding investment in further human capital are then those that maximise a person's total wealth. Since total wealth is made up of both human and non-human components, the individual must therefore always compare the returns from investments in self-improvement with those yielded by alternative investments.

There are two points to note here. The first is that it is conventional in the literature to distinguish between initial or *innate* human capital, such as the flow of services provided by intrinsic ability or physical strength, and human capital *acquired* through deliberate personal choice or through external imposition such as by compulsory school attendance. In fact the normal approach is to take the individual as possessing an initial range of characteristics often compressed into a single 'ability' term and to relate the concept of human capital only to additional investments. In empirical work there is usually some cloudiness introduced here, given the inevitable arbitrariness in defining what is innate and what is acquired. For example the amount and quality of child care undertaken by parents presumably adds to the human capital of their offspring. However, this will be treated as innate ability if one only considers investments made from school age onwards. The other point is that it is important to distinguish between the value of human capital or human wealth and the stock of human capital itself. One way to think about this is to imagine individuals buying a magic substance that improves their (per period) earning capacity by a fixed amount per unit purchased. The essential point about the substance, however, is that once it is acquired it cannot be removed and resold as such to anyone else.

The stock of human capital would then be simply the number of units of the substance (bottles?). The value of human capital would, in contrast, be the present value to the individual of the acquired substance over his remaining lifetime. Thus in the absence of physical depreciation of human capital, the stock of an individual's human capital would remain constant once accumulation had ceased, while its value must decline as the individual gets older. To illustrate this last point, suppose that an individual ceases accumulating human capital at age 25 and that he retires at age 65. At age 25, his human capital is valued according to the returns over the remaining 40 years to retirement. At age 45 only the last 20 years are relevant while at 65 the value of his human capital goes to zero. This is analogous to the fall in value of a machine as it ages, although its effectiveness as an input into production may remain unaffected.

To make things more concrete, suppose that an individual is contemplating whether or not to continue his education past the compulsory minimum schooling age. Let his annual earnings after receiving S years of schooling be W_S and his out-of-pocket costs, i.e. fees, expenditures on books, etc., of the Sth year of schooling be C_S. It will be profitable for him to undertake the Sth year of schooling if the discounted present value of the increment to his annual earnings arising from that additional year exceeds the cost. Thus if the individual considers a time horizon ending at age T and faces a discount rate, i, then he will undertake the Sth year of schooling if

$$\sum_{t=1}^{T-S} \frac{W_S - W_{S-1}}{(1 + i)^t} > W_{S-1} + C_S \tag{5.1}$$

The left-hand side of this expression is the present value of additional future earn-ings associated with the Sth year of schooling as evaluated at the end of that year. The right-hand side is the opportunity cost of the Sth year, i.e. his alternative earnings with $S - 1$ years of schooling, plus the direct costs of schooling, C_S. Another equivalent[1] way of describing this decision rule is to calculate the internal rate of return, r, to investing in the Sth year of schooling and to compare this with the interest rate, i. The individual thus finds a discount rate, r, such that

$$\sum_{t=1}^{T-S} \frac{W_S - W_{S-1}}{(1 + r)^t} = W_{S-1} + C_S \tag{5.2}$$

The additional year of education will then be undertaken if $r > i$.

This last expression may be approximated further if we assume that the individual considers an infinite time horizon, in which case we have

$$\frac{W_S - W_{S-1}}{r} = W_{S-1} + C_S \tag{5.3}$$

Thus if direct costs of schooling are small, as one would observe given a highly subsidised education system, then the internal rate of return is roughly given by

$$r = \frac{W_S - W_{S-1}}{W_{S-1}} \tag{5.4}$$

It is worthwhile at this stage to link this analysis of schooling investment deci-sions to our earlier discussion of human capital. The essential point here is that the human capital stock embodied in a given individual could then be found by summing the number of units conveyed by each year of schooling. Such a measure would, however, omit human capital derived from non-educational investments. Suppose the Sth year of schooling incorporated n units of human capital substance into the individual. The annual monetary return per unit of human capital would then be simply $(W_S - W_{S-1})/n$, but, as the cost of acquiring each additional unit is $(W_{S-1} + C)/n$, the internal rate of return to investing in additional human capital units via the Sth schooling year would be identical to the rate of return to education.

To maximise the present value of future earnings an individual should invest in education up to the point where the rate of return on the last year undertaken is equal to this rate of discount, i.e. where $r = i$. The existence of such a solu-tion is guaranteed if either the rate of return to successive years of schooling falls as the individual acquires more education, or if his rate of discount correspond-ingly rises. In Figure 5.1 this is shown for an individual facing a negative rela-tionship between years of schooling and the marginal rate of return to each year of schooling, i.e. schedule IRR_0, and a positive relationship between the marginal financing rate of cost of each year of schooling, i.e. MFC_0. The latter relationship may be rationalised by supposing that the individual or his family finances early post-compulsory schooling by dissaving from accumulated funds while later investments are financed by increasing expensive external borrow-ing. The rate of interest appropriate to each successive year of schooling, i.e. the marginal financing cost, thus rises with the level of acquired education. In practice one would imagine this relationship to be a somewhat discontinuous one, but for simplicity we approximate the MFC schedule as a continuous curve. The optimal years of schooling undertaken will then be where the IRR_0 and MFC_0 schedules intersect, i.e. S_0 years at a marginal rate of return, r_0.

If all individuals were identical, then everyone would choose to acquire the same number of years of education. The model may now be easily extended in two ways. Firstly, let us suppose that given the current equilibrium prevailing in the labour market, the earnings of the ith individual can be written as

$$W_i = W(S_i, A_i) \tag{5.5}$$

where W_i is earnings, S_i is years of schooling and A_i is his ability — presumably a vector of personal characteristics such as intelligence, motivation, etc., as possessed by the individual *prior to the acquisition of education*. This last qualifica-tion is particularly important as the use of current ability as opposed to pre-schooling ability would clearly be incorrect, as much of the earnings differential enjoyed by educated persons presumably reflects greater cognitive skills imparted by the educational process. We further assume here that earnings are positively

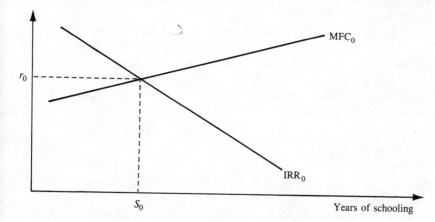

Figure 5.1 Choice of Years of Schooling

related to both schooling and ability and that the marginal increase in earnings arising from an additional year of schooling is positively related to pre-schooling ability. It thus follows that at any given level of education, the internal rate of return to a further year of schooling as defined above will be greater for a more able individual.

Individuals with higher ability endowments will then face IRR schedules to the right of those faced by those with less initial ability. In the presence of capital market imperfections, as reflected in an upward sloping MFC schedule, high ability individuals will both invest more in education and be observed to enjoy higher marginal rates of return to educational investments. In this case the observed rate of return should on average rise with the level of education.

The other obvious possibility is that individuals face different discount rates due to the wide variation that clearly exists in their personal and family circumstances. Essentially, people from poor households will either have to borrow to finance post-compulsory education or make considerable short-term sacrifices in terms of their consumption levels, while the wealthy are more likely to be able to finance education out of past accumulated savings. There will, therefore, be not one, but a whole range of MFC schedules with the poor investing less and receiving higher marginal returns than the rich. The observed rate of return should then fall with the level of education.

Human capital theory itself offers no guidance as to which of the two extreme cases outlined above is likely to dominate. Obviously even if individuals make decisions according to the assumptions of the theory and are not constrained by the availability of college places, then the world is likely to be some form of mixture. Though by no means conclusive, studies carried out over a number of different countries[2] seem to indicate that rates of return to education fall with educational level, which may indicate that differences in family background tend to be a more important source of educational, and hence earnings inequality, than innate differences in ability.

To move to a discussion of the market for educated and non-educated labour, it is useful to first make some simplifying assumptions. Suppose that there is only one educational qualification and that individuals are differentiated as above by innate ability and family wealth. Further assume that in the long run[3] the labour force can be divided into those both with and without education according to the relative supply function

$$\frac{L_E}{L_U} = S\left(\frac{W_E}{W_U}, \mathbf{Z}_S\right) \tag{5.6}$$

where L_E and L_U are the supplies of educated and uneducated labour respectively, W_E and W_U are the corresponding wage rates and $\mathbf{Z}_S$ is a vector of other relevant variables. Essentially what is happening here is that at any set of given values for W_E/W_U and $\mathbf{Z}_S$, there are some individuals amongst those of education age who face internal rates of return higher than or equal to their discount rates — the marginal individuals being those who just find such investments worthwhile

— while there are those who face inadequate rates of return. A higher ratio of W_E/W_U thus raises rates of return for all individuals and attracts some individuals into becoming educated who would previously have been uninterested in the investment. The vector Z_S includes a number of variables: the length of the educational process, the direct cost of education net of subsidies, the general level of interest rates and the average level of household wealth given the effects of capital market imperfections and any consumption benefits of education.

Suppose now that we may also assume a relative labour demand function in which the ratio demanded $(L_E/L_U)^D$ is some function of W_E/W_U and a vector of other variables, Z_D, which may include relevant technological parameters such as skill intensity and physical capital. We thus have

$$\left(\frac{L_E}{L_U}\right)^D = D\left(\frac{W_E}{W_U}, Z_D\right) \tag{5.7}$$

The initial long-run equilibrium is shown in Figure 5.2 at the wage ratio $(W_E/W_U)_0$ and a ratio of L_E to L_U of $(L_E/L_U)_0$. Suppose now that a technological change occurs such that the relative demand curve shifts outwards to $D^1 D^1$ as the skill intensity of production increases. Educated labour will now be in short supply and the relative wage will rise to $(W_E/W_U)_1$. Higher returns to education will, however, induce a larger proportion of the current education age cohort to obtain education thus shifting the short-run supply curve, S_S, to the right. This process will continue with future age cohorts until a new long-run

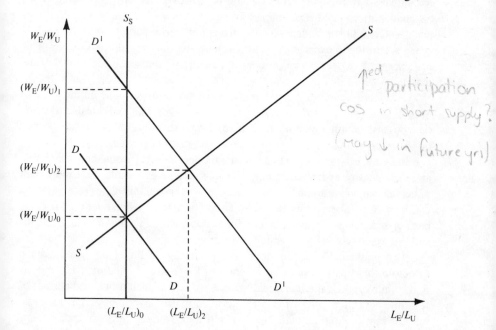

Figure 5.2 The Market for Educated and Non-Educated Labour

equilibrium is obtained with a relative wage of $(W_E/W_U)_2$ and a more educated labour force of $(L_E/L_U)_2$.

This simple model can be easily extended to encompass an unlimited range of educational levels and other forms of human capital investment. One can also easily substitute the word 'occupation' for education into the analysis, if one can clearly differentiate occupations by education and training requirements and if one ignores non-training occupational barriers. There are, however, a few other considerations that must be dealt with in order to complete the theory.

Experience and Training

In our analysis so far we have essentially pictured investment in human capital as either an essentially once-and-for-all lumpy investment or as a fixed series of investment possibilities in which the individual chooses when to stop investing and to enter full-time employment. In the case of education, this can perhaps be justified by supposing that the educational system itself tends to predetermine the ages at which various levels are taken so that the individual is faced effectively with a 'take it or leave it' situation. If, however, all human capital investments were made by taking formal qualifications then we would observe all individuals with similar educational and other qualifications earning similar wages at any moment in time. Similarly, in the absence of any general real wage growth, each individual's age earnings profile would be flat over his working lifetime once his qualifications had been obtained. In fact, this is not the case as age–earnings profiles derived from both cross-section and time series surveys show wages first rising according to experience and then flattening off later in one's career. This tendency is, however, more pronounced the higher the educational level of the individual.

This systematic curvature in the age–earnings profile would, in the absence of costless learning or improvement, therefore suggest that individuals make further post-education investments in human capital, presumably in the form of on-the-job training.

If individuals were free to make voluntary decisions regarding both the timing and the intensity of human capital decisions, then what would the chosen path of human capital accumulation look like and what would this tell us about lifetime earnings? A number of models of human capital accumulation over the life cycle have been developed in the literature (for example Heckman, 1976b; Rosen, 1976) and one relatively simple version is as follows.

Let an individual's maximum attainable earnings at time t be Y_t and assume as before that this is a positive function of his human capital at t, H_t, and his initial ability, A_0. If the individual has completed his institutionalised periods of full-time education and formal training, then it still nevertheless remains possible for him to continue with his own self-improvement through various part-time activities including informal or on-the-job training. Suppose that in any given period, t, he chooses to spend a proportion, h_t, of his potential working time in making further investments in human capital. His disposable earnings in this period are therefore $Y_t(1 - h_t)$. Clearly, however, the very action of allocating further time to human capital accumulation will increase his human capital stock and hence his potential income in the next period, i.e. $t+1$. The relationship between time invested and the additional number of units of human capital created is known as a *human capital production function*. Here we assume that this takes the rather simple form

$$H_{t+1} - H_t = h_t^b \qquad 0 < b < 1 \qquad (5.8)$$

The basic idea behind this formulation is that within any given period, the process of generating additional units of human capital is subject to diminishing returns to time invested. A unit of human capital is thus defined here as the amount produced when a person invests all of his available work time during the period.

The problem faced by the individual is to maximise his lifetime discounted earnings. If we work in continuous time then he chooses a time path for h_t and hence H_t and Y_t, so as to maximise

$$\int_0^T (1 - h_t) Y(H_t, A_0) e^{-rt} \, dt \qquad (5.9)$$

subject to the constraint imposed by the human capital production function

$$\dot{H_t} = h_t^b \qquad (5.10)$$

The diminishing returns property of the human capital production function is particularly important here, since if human capital production were directly proportional to time allocated, then the problem reduces to that discussed earlier in which the individual would invest full-time (i.e. $h_t = 1$) until he encountered a period in which further investment was no longer worthwhile. The fact that the individual encounters diminishing returns to investment within each period implies that it will be optimal to spread part-time investment over his working lifetime. The mathematical solution[4] to this problem yields the intuitive result that since additional human capital is more valuable to the individual in the earlier years, he will follow a declining path for h_t with $h_T = 0$ at the end of the time horizon. Human capital will thus be accumulated at an even slower rate over his working lifetime.

The corresponding time paths for potential and observed disposable earnings are shown in Figure 5.3 where the initial gap between the two at time $t = 0$ is progressively narrowed over the working lifetime until it vanishes entirely at time $t = T$. If the model were amended so as to take account of a fixed per period human capital depreciation rate, δ, then the constraint would become

$$\dot{H} = h_t^b - \delta H_t \qquad (5.11)$$

In this case the stock of human capital would reach a peak prior to the retirement

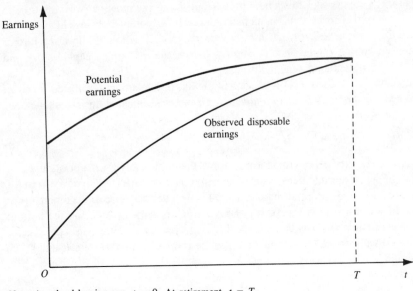

Note: At school-leaving age, $t = 0$. At retirement, $t = T$.

Figure 5.3   Potential and Observed Earnings by Age

age and this would be reflected in similarly shaped schedules for potential and disposable earnings. This then gives some theoretical rationale for the empirical observation that age—earnings profiles tend to display a peak among the more highly educated. Other extensions encountered in the literature include making $\dot{H}$ a positive function of the stock of human capital given h_t and introducing consumption/leisure trade-offs. These later modifications do not, however, change the results above. So far we have assumed throughout that acquisition of human capital will result in higher observed earnings. In general, this will be the case if additional human capital raises individual productivity over a reasonably wide range of prospective employments. But what happens if the productivity increase experienced by the individual from (say) a period of on-the-job training only applies within the company for whom he currently works? Firm *specific* human capital as in this example has rather different implications for the behaviour of individual earnings than human capital of the *general* type as assumed in the models discussed above.

Suppose that an untrained worker's wage and marginal product were equal to MP_A, which is constant over his working lifetime. If training of either type lasts for one period at a direct cost (e.g. trainers' fees, course expenses, etc.) of C_0 and the workers' marginal product is MP_0 while training is taking place, then the total cost of training C is given by

$$C = MP_A - MP_0 + C_0 \tag{5.12}$$

investment in training will take place until the discounted returns

$$\sum_{t=1}^{T-1} \frac{MP_t - MP_A}{(1 + r)^t}$$

are equal to C, where MP_t is the marginal product of a trained worker in the tth year, and T is either the remaining working lifetime where training is general, or the employment period with the current firm where training is specific. If training is entirely general, i.e. the entire productivity increase is applicable in other establishments, then the worker will be willing to bear the entire costs and receive all of the future benefits, as he knows that his newly acquired skills will be rewarded elsewhere if he leaves his current employer. Employers, in contrast, will be unwilling to bear any of the costs since, if they were to attempt to reap any of the returns by paying the worker less than the market wage for his skills he would simply quit and move elsewhere. He will thus receive a wage during training equal to $MP_0 - C_0$, thus sacrificing $MP_A - (MP_0 - C_0)$ and he will receive a wage equal to MP_t in all future years. If training is entirely specific, i.e. it is only useful within the current establishment, then it is obvious that workers will be unwilling to bear the entire costs since, in the event of future retrenchment, no further returns could be earned with other employers. In general we would suppose that the costs and benefits of specific training would be shared between workers and employers. If the worker's share is a then he would pay $a[MP_A - (MP_0 - C_0)]$ and receive a wage equal to $a(MP_t - MP_A) + MP_A$, i.e. $aMP_t + (1 - a)MP_A$ in the tth year.

What then determines the worker's share, a? Clearly the worker is concerned about the possibility that if his employment were terminated by the employer at some future date, he would lose the remaining returns to his investment, while the employer would have similar worries about the worker quitting. Suppose that the returns to training in any period, $MP_t - MP_A$, are shared out as before so that any fluctuations in the value of the worker's marginal product, both internal and external to the firm due to, for example, variations in product demand, are reflected in the rewards received by both parties. Provided then that the worker's marginal value product, MP_t, is greater than MP_A, the alternative marginal product and hence wage, then both the firm and worker gain from the continuation of his services. If MP_t should fall below MP_A then the employer will wish to lay off the worker and, to an equal extent, the worker will wish to quit. This will, however, be true independently of the size of a, and so it is clear that further considerations must be brought into the picture before the question can be answered.

One approach, as taken by Hashimoto (1979), is to suppose that bargaining costs and asymmetries of information regarding the true levels of both internal marginal productivity levels and external wages limit the responsiveness of wages to changing conditions. In this case, both suboptimal quits and lay-offs can arise. Suppose, for example, that the firm bears all the costs of specific training so that the employment contract simply specifies wages equal to existing alternative earnings. If the latter rise unexpectedly in the future, then an optimal contract would reflect this in terms of increased worker earnings and reduced returns to the firm. If, however, such conditional wage flexibility cannot be incorporated into workers' contracts, then quits will take place and the firm will lose the remaining future returns on its investments. Similarly, if the marginal product of a specifically trained worker falls relative to outside earnings then lay-offs will occur in the absence of downward wage flexibility and specifically trained workers will lose out. Hashimoto shows that a will be chosen so as to minimise such suboptimal quits and lay-offs.

In the model outlined above, workers will quit only when their wage falls below alternative earnings. In practice, however, workers quit for other reasons such as boredom and exogenous changes in personal circumstances. Thus if workers are differentiated by personal characteristics associated with the likelihood that they will quit, then we can write the quit rate per period, q, as a negative function of the wage rate, W, divided by alternative earnings, W_A, i.e.:

$$q = q\left(\frac{W}{W_A}\right) \qquad (5.13)$$

Thus quits may occur even when W and W_A are equal. The higher the quit rate for any given wage ratio, the less willing the firm will be to bear the specific training costs. However, as pointed out by Parsons (1972), the opposite is true if quit rates exhibit a high degree of negative response to increased wages. The central argument here is that by giving the worker a wage schedule in which the wage rises steeply from a point well below the marginal product at the beginning of his career to positions well above later on, then the firm can reduce the probability of experienced trained workers quitting. The truer that this is, then the more willing will be the employer to undertake specific training investments.

This general idea of some optimal wage schedule corresponding to a given present value has proved to have several further applications. Lazear (1979) uses this to explain why contracts usually specify mandatory retirement dates: the point here being that since wages exceed marginal products later in life, workers will not, in general, voluntarily retire at the optimal retirement age where present value of wages paid equals present value of lifetime marginal product. Retirement must therefore be imposed. Collier and Lal (1986) believe that quit-offsetting wage schedules are common in the modern sector of contemporary African countries such as Kenya, and argue that the imposition of a minimum wage in such countries will reduce specific training below its optimum level by giving employers less 'room' within which to offer an upward sloping wage schedule given a present value constraint. A recent explicit intertemporal analysis of an optimum wage schedule is given in Collier and Knight (1986).

Signalling and Sorting

Until now we have assumed that formal investments in human capital, such as in education, provide returns to an individual by increasing the quality of his embodied labour services and hence the wage that he can command. An alternative view, which has commanded, in various forms, a great deal of attention, is that rather than increase individual productivity, education is simply a screening device used to identify those individuals whose productivity would have been higher than that of others even if education had not taken place. Thus, the empirical observation that educated persons earn more on average than those with less education may simply mean that the former have innately higher productivity than others and have either been assigned to education on this basis or have self-selected themselves.

A rather extreme model based on this view has been developed by Spence (1973). Suppose that there are two sorts of people: those with high ability and those with low ability. Denote the number in each category as H and L respectively and their corresponding marginal products as W_H and W_L, where $W_H > W_L$. If employers cannot distinguish between the two groups then everyone will be paid the average marginal product

$$\bar{W} = \left(\frac{H}{H+L}\right)W_H + \left(\frac{L}{H+L}\right)W_L \tag{5.14}$$

Suppose now that employers have a belief that individuals with education have a marginal product, W_H, and that those without education have a marginal product, W_L. Clearly this belief will be justified if those with high productivity obtain education while those with low productivity do not. In this case education will be an accurate signal to employers regarding individual productivity. To obtain a 'separating' equilibrium of this sort, we assume that the net costs of obtaining education, i.e. direct and opportunity costs less consumption benefits, are less for those with high ability. The high ability person will therefore invest in education and those with low ability will fail to invest if

$$C_L < \sum_{t=1}^{T} \frac{W_H - W_L}{(1+r)^t} < C_H \tag{5.15}$$

where C_L and C_H are the net costs of education faced by those with low and high productivity respectively. Note that if the second of the above inequality signs is reversed, then we have an equilibrium in which no one obtains education. If the first equality sign is reversed then everyone obtains education, firms find their belief about the productivity of educated persons unjustified and the signalling function of education disappears with everyone earning the average marginal product.

A central feature of a *signalling* model of this type is that although it may be profitable for some individuals to invest in education, the gross social returns to education are necessarily zero as no gains are made in terms of increased output. This rather strong feature of the signalling model disappears once we introduce the idea that education may have some social value if it sorts people out according to their productivity. This idea may be clarified by considering a simple variant of the model developed by Arrow (1973). Suppose there are two kinds of jobs: type 1 and type 2 and that production is of the fixed proportions type requiring equal numbers of people in each type of job. Everyone can supply a unit of labour of type 1 but only one-half of the labour force has the innate ability to supply a unit of type 2. An optimal allocation would therefore be to allocate all of the talented labourers to type 2 and the rest to type 1. A random selection process would, however, assign only one-half of the talented labourers to type 2 which would, in turn, given the fixed proportions assumption, reduce national output by one-half. If the educational system efficiently identifies talented persons, then there can clearly be a positive social return to educational investment. The fixed proportions assumption is made here for simplicity of exposition. To illustrate this, further consider the case in which type 1 and type 2 jobs are perfect substitutes in the production of national output. If the marginal product of type 2 were twice that of type 1, then the optimal allocation would produce a national income equal to 1.5 times that if the allocation of jobs to workers were made randomly.[5]

5.4   Human Capital — Empirical Evidence

The obvious starting point to use as a base for an empirical investigation of human capital theory is to simply calculate the internal rates of return to observable investments in human capital such as in education. This was indeed the approach followed in a large number of studies produced in the 1960s, which between them provided estimates of both private and social[6] rates of return to education over a world-wide distribution of countries. The results of these studies, as surveyed by Psacharopoulos (1972) and (1981), indicate that wage differentials and the social rate of return tend to fall by educational level, the highest proportional differential observed being that in less-developed countries between those with primary education and those with no education. Psacharopoulos (1981) calculated that, on average, private rates were 29 per cent, 19 per cent and 24 per cent to primary, secondary and higher education respectively in less-developed countries, and 14 per cent and 12 per cent to secondary and higher education in developed countries.

Although typically rate of return studies have been restricted to individual or group cross-section data at a single point in time, evidence for both the USA (Psacharopoulos, 1981) and the UK (Pissarides, 1982) seems to suggest that the private rate of return to higher education has fallen in both of these countries during the 1970s. In both countries this was doubtless due in part to continued growth in the relative supply of well-educated persons, although higher education in the UK suffered something of a recession in the 1970s following rapid expansion in the 1960s.

Although many of these early studies made some attempt to isolate the portion of the earnings differential that could be attributed to education, these ranged from arbitrary assumptions about its magnitude, e.g. 0.5, 0.65, etc., to more sophisticated calculations based upon statistical estimation of sometimes rather *ad hoc* specifications of the relationship between earnings and its various determinants such as education. Such an *earnings function* may be written in general form as

$$W_i = W(S_i, \mathbf{Z}) \tag{5.16}$$

where W_i is the wage of the ith individual, S_i is either a continuous measure of education such as years of schooling or a vector of dummy variables denoting educational level completed, and $\mathbf{Z}$ is a vector of other relevant characteristics. Clearly there are a massive number of alternative ways in which such a function could be specified. The human capital version as developed by Mincer (1974) is as follows.

If we assume that the rate of return to investment in human capital, r, is constant, i.e. independent of the number of units invested by the individual, and we ignore the direct costs of schooling, then given a long enough time horizon the internal rate of return to any unit invested can be approximated by

$$r = \frac{\dot{Y}}{h_t Y_t} \tag{5.17}$$

where Y_t is potential earnings at t as before.

This is simply the continuous time analogue of equation (5.4) except that h_t, the proportion of the period spent in acquiring human capital, is also included. During the years of full-time education $h_t = 1$ so that after completing S years of schooling

$$Y_S = Y_0 \, e^{rs} \tag{5.18}$$

This is the solution to (5.17) when $t = S$ and $h_s = 1$. For the post-schooling years, Mincer assumes that the fraction of time devoted to human capital investment declines linearly with experience, i.e.

$$h_t = h_0 - \left(\frac{h_0}{T}\right)t \tag{5.19}$$

where T is working life as before. The solution to (5.17) for Y_x where x is the number of post-schooling years of experience is given by

$$Y_x = Y_s \exp\left(r \int_0^x h_t \mathrm{d}_t\right) \tag{5.20}$$

Now substituting (5.19) into (5.20) and noting that the integral expression

$$\int_0^x h_t dt$$

is given by

$$h_0 x - \left(\frac{h_0}{2T}\right)x^2$$

we find an expression for log Y_x by taking logs of (5.20),

$$\log Y_x = \log Y_0 + rS + rh_0 x - \left(\frac{rh_0}{2T}\right)x^2 \tag{5.21}$$

Actual observed earnings, W_x, are related to potential earnings, Y_x by

$$W_x = (1 - h_x)Y_x \tag{5.22}$$

Substituting this into (5.19) gives the earnings function as

$$\log W_x = \log Y_0 + rS + rh_0 x - \left(\frac{rh_0}{2T}\right)x^2 + \log(1 - hx) \tag{5.23}$$

The function actually used by Mincer and others in subsequent empirical work is identical to this except that the unobservable term in log $(1 - h_x)$ is omitted. Using cross-section data from the 1960 US Census, Mincer estimated this equation to be (t-statistics in parentheses)

$$\log W_i = 6.2 + 0.107S + 0.081x - 0.0012x^2$$
$$\quad\quad\quad (72.3) \quad\quad (73.5) \quad (-55.8)$$
$$R^2 = 0.285$$

The estimates of the model parameters are then $r = 0.107$, $h_0 = 0.76$ and $T = 34$ years. Psacharopoulos and Layard (1979) obtain similar results using 1972 household survey data for England and Wales with $r = 0.097$, $h_0 = 0.94$ and $T = 30$ and a comparable R^2 of 0.316. Although the estimates obtained for the rates of return seem plausible, one is struck by the very large proportionate gap between potential and actual earnings in the early post-schooling years as implied by the surprisingly high value obtained for h_0.

The model outlined above has been used as the basis for a large number of studies. Most of these have been restricted to cross-section data sets although some such as Lillard and Willis (1978), and Welch (1979) have used pooled cross-section/time series data. In general, the shape of the estimated earnings function is similar to that presented above, although the values of the estimated coefficients obviously vary across studies and particularly with the country source of the data set. Such studies have, however, understandably attracted a number of criticisms, although, to be fair to the original authors, their failure to address these problems arose more from deficiencies in their data sets than from ignorance of these problems.

The first, rather obvious, point is that the variables included in equation (5.21) may be measured incorrectly. Schooling, for example, may be little more than a proxy for acquired education if the quality of the latter varies. As is well known (e.g. Johnston, 1984, pp. 428–435) errors in independent variables lead to biased coefficients. More seriously, however, as pointed out by Lucas (1977), non-pecuniary rewards are necessarily excluded from conventional measures of earnings. Thus if, for example, individuals with higher earnings capacities tend to spend relatively more on psychic earnings by choosing enjoyable occupations, the coefficients on schooling will be biased downwards. Lucas' own results suggested that this underestimate of the rate of return to schooling was in the range of 15–30 per cent.

Inevitably, a number of criticisms have been directed at the specification of the earnings function itself. Willis (1986), for example, examines the implications for the earnings function of a whole series of models taking into account, among other things, heterogeneous human capital, non-competing groups, lifetime wealth maximisation, inequality of opportunity, etc. In general, he not surprisingly concludes that the function is unlikely to hold except under rather special circumstances. More specifically, even within Mincer's own framework, there is the problem of why different individuals obtain different levels of schooling in the first place. For if all individuals faced the same interest rate then, as things stand, they would all either choose no schooling at all, if the interest rate was greater than the rate of return to schooling, or their demand for schooling would be either indeterminate or unlimited. There are two obvious extreme ways out: either we assume that individuals face different MFC schedules as before but the same rate of return on schooling, or we assume that individuals have different innate ability levels but face the same interest rate. Note that any middle position will not help us here — if all individuals faced the same upward sloping MFC schedule and downward sloping IRR schedule then everyone would select the same level of schooling and we would have the same observation repeated *ad nauseam* apart from random errors in observed earnings. If, in contrast, individuals faced different upward sloping MFC schedules with a given downward sloping IRR schedule or vice versa or some combination, we would observe different rates of return to education across individuals which in turn violates a central assumption of the basic model.

Consider a model in which we leave experience to one side for the moment and assume that the logarithm of earnings is a linear function of schooling ability:

$$\log Y_i = a_1 + a_2 S_i + a_3 A_i \qquad (5.24)$$

If we were to estimate this equation by ordinary least squares without including a suitable ability measure, then the bias in our estimate of a_2 would be equal to $a_3 \text{cov}(AS)/\text{var } s$. Thus if higher ability persons self-select themselves for more years of schooling so that cov(AS) is positive, then our estimate of the rate of return to schooling will be upward biased. If we were now to include experience,

x and x^2 in the equation, then the bias would also include terms of $\mathrm{cov}(Ax)$, $\mathrm{cov}(Ax^2)$, $\mathrm{cov}(Sx)$, $\mathrm{cov}(Sx^2)$, and $\mathrm{cov}(x \cdot x^2)$, which makes it rather hard to think about. However, the direction of the bias on the schooling coefficient remains upward, although its size relative to that of the schooling coefficient itself seems sensitive to the measure of experience used.[7]

One question that immediately arises is 'How should ability be measured?' It is clear that whatever measure is used, it should refer to a point in time prior to the acquisition of schooling or further work experience, since any measure of *current* ability will pick up the ability raising effects of education and hence tend to obscure at least part of the returns to the latter. What is less clear is whether the use of IQ tests or other measures such as the AFQT test, as given to armed services' recruits in the USA, provide adequate proxies. Clearly the concept of ability as incorporated in the earnings function can only somewhat tautologically be defined as the ability to earn higher wages given schooling and experience. It may well be, however, that this is only loosely related to the kind of skills examined in IQ tests and that other unobserved attributes such as motivation, social acceptability and personality are also important. There seem to be two approaches taken in the literature.

The first is to simply use IQ tests, family background measures such as parental occupation dummies, etc. and to estimate with the best available econometric techniques. The approach in this case should be to first specify a model (for example Griliches and Mason, 1972; Bowles, 1973) and to estimate the earnings function by an appropriate econometric estimating procedure. Consider, for, example, the following very simple model:

$$
\begin{aligned}
\log Y_i &= a_1 + a_2 S_i + a_3 A_i + a_4 x_i + a_5 x_i^2 + v_{1i} \\
\mathrm{CIQ}_1 &= b_1 + b_2 \mathrm{FB}_i + b_3 A_i + v_{2i} \\
S_i &= c_1 + c_2 \mathrm{FB}_i + c_3 A_i + v_{3i} \\
A_i &= d_1 + d_2 \mathrm{FB}_i + d_3 \mathrm{PIQ}_i + d_4 \mathrm{UF}_i + v_{4i}
\end{aligned}
\tag{5.25}
$$

where A_i is 'unobserved' pre-schooling ability of the ith person, CIQ_i is childhood IQ, FB_i is a measure of family background, PIQ_i is parental IQ and UF_i is unmeasured family effects. The structure is then that measured and unmeasured family effects determine unobserved ability, A_i, which in turn along with FB_i determines CIQ_i and S_i. All four processes specified in (5.25) above include random error terms. If we now reshuffle the second equation above so as to express A_i in terms of the other variables and then substitute into the earnings function we obtain

$$
\log Y_i = a_1 - \left(\frac{a_3 b_1}{b_3}\right) + a_2 S_i + \left(\frac{a_3}{b_3}\right)\mathrm{CIQ}_i - \left(\frac{b_3}{b_3}\right)\mathrm{FB}_i
$$

$$
+ a_4 x_i + a_5 x_i^2 - \left(\frac{v_{21}}{b_3}\right) + v_{1i}
\tag{5.26}
$$

The problem with estimating this equation is that CIQ is not independent of the $-v_{21}/b_3$ portion of the error term. Consistent estimates can be obtained, however, by first regressing CIQ on the relevant background variables in the model, i.e. FB_i and PIQ_i, replacing CIQ_i in (5.26) by its predicted values from this regression and then, finally, by estimating this modified version of (5.26) by ordinary least squares. Although adjustment for ability effects in this fashion reduces US estimates of the schooling coefficient to the 0.05–0.07 range, the evidence does not seem to suggest that the instrumental variables procedure outlined above produces results very different from those obtained if unadjusted IQ test scores are used directly as the ability variable. Griliches (1977) does note, however, that the explanatory power of the ability variables themselves is sensitive to the measure used.

The alternative approach is to focus instead upon the relationship between differences in earnings and differences in schooling in circumstances in which pre-schooling ability can be reasonably assumed constant. One candidate is to examine the contribution of schooling to the earnings differences between identical twins. Taubman has carried out a number of studies of this kind (for example Taubman, 1976) and his results suggest that the schooling coefficient may be around the 0.03 mark. One problem with 'twins' studies is that the variance of schooling differences between twins is lower than that between randomly selected individuals. The impact of measurement error in schooling variables is therefore greater than in other studies and may lead to a substantial downward bias in the schooling coefficient. The other candidate is to compare the earnings of the same individual at different points in time. Longitudinal studies of this kind also seem to obtain lower schooling coefficients than their cross-section counterparts, although here once again a problem arises in that one can only observe the effects of schooling acquired subsequent to initial labour force entry, which obviously reduces the variance in observed schooling quite considerably.

It may be noted that there is nothing in these results which allows us to discriminate between the human capital and screening explanations for the higher earnings of better educated persons. In terms of the screening hypothesis, the schooling coefficient simply picks up the expected productivity differential associated with education after standardising for other observables. This does not tell us, however, whether this is due to the productivity raising effects of education itself, or to that of other variables associated with educational self-selection. It is in fact very difficult to devise a suitable discriminatory test given either existing data or, for that matter, any other data sets that are likely to become available in the conceivable future. In principle one can imagine an experiment in which the school-age population would be randomly divided into two halves, one half being forcibly educated and the other being systematically denied access to educational facilities. An appropriate test would then be to compare the post-schooling earnings behaviour of the two cohorts over time. Unfortunately (or perhaps fortunately) such an experiment has not been carried out. Layard and Psacharopoulos (1974) have argued in favour of the human capital interpretation of the role of education on the grounds that:

(i)   high school dropouts enjoy rates of return to education as high as those completing education;

(ii) private returns to education do not fail with work experience;

(iii) education seems a very costly way of screening workers.

However, as Riley (1979) points out, the first of these arguments implies a rather strong version of the screening model in which employers only take account of final qualifications, and breaks down if they instead consider overall educational attainment. The second argument is likewise false, as an assumption of the screening approach is that employers' expectations are fulfilled. If this is so, then there is no reason why, on average, rates of return to education should fall, even if, as Layard and Psacharopoulos argue, employers obtain more information about their workers over time. Finally, as Riley also points out, the existence of screening does not imply that this is education's only role. Riley further argues that screening is likely to be more important in some occupations than others and attempts to justify this on the basis of earnings functions fitted to cross-section data for different US occupational groups. The reader is referred to Riley's paper for further details of his own and other tests of screening hypotheses. It is clear, however, that the debate between human capital advocates and 'screeners' will continue into the indefinite future.

5.5   Discrimination and Wages — Theory

In the previous two sections we have concentrated upon individuals' decisions whether or not to acquire income-generating characteristics such as education and training. Innate characteristics such as strength, inherited intelligence, etc. have so far been simply compressed into a single background variable, namely innate ability. Earnings differentials arising from non-acquired characteristics were assumed to be strictly in accordance with related differences in individual productivity. This view is implicitly challenged, however, by the persistent income differentials observed in many countries between the different sexes, different ethnic groups and even different religions. Differentials of this type can be explained by

(i)   different work attitudes of different groups;

(ii) differences in productivity related characteristics, e.g. formal qualifications, between groups;

(iii) differences in wages given identical productivity related characteristics.

Of these, (i) is least obviously due to discriminatory causes, although the attitudes of, for example, minority groups are not unrelated to their acceptability or otherwise by other sections of society; (ii) is plausibly related to pre-market forms of discrimination such as prejudiced educational admissions procedures, but may also reflect historically rooted minority attitudes; while (iii) reflects pure labour market discrimination. In our survey below, we shall concentrate on (iii) as being more directly relevant to wage determination, although this does not imply any disregard for the more general importance of (i) and (ii). The theories are surveyed under three general headings: taste-based theories of discrimination, statistical discrimination and institutional based theories.

Taste-Based Theories

The central assumption in Becker's (1957) pioneering contribution to this area was that the utility levels of some or all of the relevant agents in the analysis are affected by transactions or association with members of other identifiable groups. Becker's examples are mostly confined to US black and white workers, although clearly there is no a priori reason why the analysis could not be extended beyond race to other areas of potential or realised prejudice such as sex, social class and religion.

As a first example, suppose that white employers dislike employing blacks. If the white wage is W_W and the black wage is W_B, where $W_W > W_B$, then the ith white employer, facing an implicit aversion cost to paying wages to blacks, perceives the corresponding wage costs as W_W and $W_B(1 + d_i)$ respectively. The term $W_B d_i$ is thus the aversion cost per black worker employed. If black and white workers are perfect substitutes, then the employer will employ all blacks if

$$W_W > W_B(1 + d_i)$$

and he will employ all whites if

$$W_W < W_B(1 + d_i)$$

For any given pair of wages, highly discriminatory employers, i.e. those with high values for d_i, will therefore tend to employ all whites, while less discriminatory employers will employ all blacks. If black and white workers are imperfect substitutes which would be the case if, for example, all whites possessed skills while blacks were unskilled, then firms will employ a mixture[8] of both worker types. However, except in the special case where blacks and whites are required in fixed proportions, discriminatory employers will employ higher ratios of white to black workers than non-discriminatory employers. These two cases are illustrated in panels (a) and (b) of Figure 5.4. In panel (a) we show the cost minimising positions for a pair of non-discriminatory and discriminatory employers where black and white workers are perfect substitutes in production. Given the same linear isoquant AB, the non-discriminatory employer will cost minimise at point A where his lowest budget line, AC, just touches this isoquant. In contrast, the discriminatory employer faces a higher perceived black/white wage ratio as given by the slope of DB and cost minimises at point B. Panel (b) correspondingly illustrates the imperfect substitutes case where the two employers cost minimise at points E and F respectively.

The final equilibrium will now depend upon the product market structure. The critical point here is that unit production costs will be larger the greater the value of the employer's discrimination coefficient, since discriminatory employers face

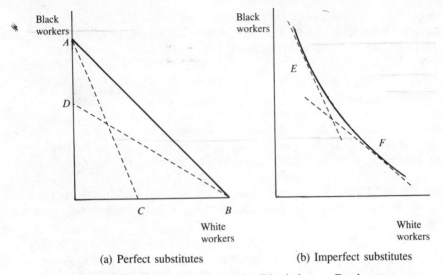

Figure 5.4 Discriminatory and Non-Discriminatory Employment

a higher perceived cost per unit of one of their inputs, namely black labour, than do less discriminatory employers. Given free entry in the product market, competition between firms will thus ensure that discriminatory firms are eventually driven out of the market, thus leaving only employers for whom, $d_i = 0$, or at least those with the minimum d_i existing among the entrepreneurial white population. An important corollary of the non-discriminatory equilibrium is that in the absence of monopoly labour power by either worker group, white and black workers with the same skills must also earn the same equilibrium wage rates. Suppose, for example, white wages are greater than those of blacks as assumed earlier. In the non-discriminatory equilibrium, employers will also prefer blacks to whites with the same skill levels. Competition in the labour market will thus ensure that black wages will increase until equality is achieved. Similarly, if blacks and whites have different skills then their equilibrium wage differentials will only reflect true differences in their marginal products. Finally, one should note that given this long-run equilibrium position, it makes no difference if both discriminatory white and black employers existed during the pre-equilibrium states, since both must ultimately be driven out of the market.

The situation is rather different if the market structure is one of monopoly or oligopoly, since excess profits can still be earned even if employers incur discrimination costs. Even here, however, discriminators may still disappear in the long run, as there remains an incentive for non-discriminators to buy out discriminatory firms and earn even higher future profits. Whether or not this actually happens, will depend upon the transferability of the franchise and the state of the capital market.

A central policy implication of Becker's analysis is that equal pay legislation will act as a brake on the processes outlined above, as discriminators can indulge their tastes by employing whites only without losing any competitive advantage to non-discriminators who are forced to pay the same wages to their black employees. A preferable approach would be to subsidise black employment, or perhaps to tax white employment, with the important proviso that such subsidies and taxes be removed once wage equality was approached. Another alternative would be to introduce employment quotas for minority workers.

Perhaps the most important empirical prediction of the analysis is that discrimination will be more prevalent in highly concentrated industries in so far as the latter possess a less competititve structure. If industries face perfectly elastic supply curves of labour of various types, the concentrated industries will tend to employ high wage favoured groups while less concentrated industries will employ more of the disfavoured groups. It is usually assumed by American and British writers that the latter are minorities, e.g. blacks, Hispanics, other non-whites and females, although there appears to be no reason why some minorities might not be in a favoured position. If industries possess some monopsony labour market power and therefore face upward sloping supply curves, then different majority/minority wage differentials may be observed across different industries.

Although a number of empirical studies have attempted to relate one measure or another of discrimination to some other measure of concentration by industry, the results are not entirely conclusive. For example, studies in the US have mostly found a positive relationship between the proportion of blacks in total employment and industrial employment (for example Comanor, 1973; Medoff, 1980), while Oster (1975) and Shepherd and Levin (1973) failed to find a similar relationship when the proportion of females is used as the dependent variable. Haessel and Palmer (1978) found significant positive relationships between relative wages by both race and sex and concentration across a number of occupational groups in the USA, although Fuji and Trapani (1978) failed to find a significant relationship using industrial aggregate relative wage data by race. For the UK, Chiplin and Sloane (1976) found no relationship between male/female wage differentials and concentration and obtained the unexpected result that the proportion of females appeared to be higher in the more concentrated industries. Clearly more work can be expected in this area, particularly in the USA, and one reason why no clear consensus has emerged is because past studies have differed in model specification.

The second type of discrimination considered by Becker is that of *employee* discrimination, i.e. where different groups of workers dislike working with each other. Suppose, for example, that white workers dislike working with blacks. The wage perceived by a white worker is then W_W if he works with other whites alone and $W_W(1 - d_i)$ if he works with blacks, where d_i is the discrimination coefficient of the ith worker. If the supply price of a white worker to white-only employment equals W_W, then the employer must therefore compensate him with a wage, $W_W/(1 - d_i)$, for mixed employment. One can similarly define a two-wage supply price regime for blacks if they also have aversion to working with whites. The market equilibrium in such a model is a fairly obvious one. If blacks and whites are identical as workers then completely segregated all-white and all-black establishments will arise with both sets of workers being paid identical wage rates. If black and white workers cannot be segregated because, for example, of complementarity of skills, then both will be paid at higher wages with a corresponding reduction in the employment levels of both groups.

A rather indirect test of the employee discrimination model is provided by Chiswick (1973). A brief outline of his argument runs as follows. Suppose that unskilled workers were segregated by race as in Becker's model, but that given the nature of the production process, skilled workers are needed in both black and white establishments. If skilled workers are predominantly white then we should observe white skilled workers in black factories earning higher wages than those in white factories. Thus observed mean earnings of skilled workers will be positively related to the proportion who work in black factories, which will in turn depend upon the proportion of blacks in the population as a whole. If we now stretch things a little further, we can argue that, since the inequality of earnings among white workers is positively related to the mean relative wage differential between skilled and unskilled white workers, then a suitable measure of white earnings inequality should in turn be positively related to the proportion of blacks in the working population. To test this, Chiswick examined the relationship between the variance of the logarithm of white earnings and the proportion of black workers over a cross-section of states in the US, white standardising for other relevant variables such as inequality in schooling, age and weeks worked. To further standardise for the degree of racial discrimination, he fitted his estimating equations across the Southern and non-Southern states separately and found a significant positive relationship within each group.

The rather aggregate and indirect nature of Chiswick's test limits its status as a validation of the employee discrimination model. Unfortunately, more direct evidence is currently unavailable, and there is no empirical indication of the relevance of the theory with respect to differentials by sex, except in so far as employee bias is reflected in the actions of trade unions. This is, however, examined in a later subsection.

Finally, we should note, following Becker, that taste discrimination may also be practised by *consumers* and by *governments*. In the first case, consumer discrimination against purchases from minority groups as expressed by lower demand prices will lead either to market and possibly residential segregation, or to reallocation of favoured groups towards jobs in public display such as sales representatives. Government discrimination is clearly extremely divergent between countries and is generally either opposed to group favouritism, or pro-disfavoured minority groups as in India where scheduled castes are allocated a fixed minimum quota of government jobs. Exceptions obviously exist as in modern-day USSR, the Republic of South Africa and in Southern Rhodesia during the 1970s.

Statistical Discrimination

In the signalling and sorting models discussed above, employers were unable to directly observe the productivity of job applicants, but instead used observed characteristics, such as education, as a signal or screen. If such characteristics include inherited or childhood acquired attributes, then a theory of discrimination arises based upon imperfect information as opposed to any inherent bias in the tastes of the parties concerned.

The basic model as developed by Phelps (1972) assumes that employers make hiring decisions on the basis of a performance test, y, which is an unbiased predictor of the worker's true productivity, q. Thus, for the ith job applicant,

$$y_i = q_i + u_i \tag{5.27}$$

where u_i is a random error term independent of q_i. The problem for the employer is to predict q_i given y_i. If he were, hypothetically, to regress q_i on y_i (imagine here that he tested a large random sample of workers for each of whom q_i was known), then the fitted equation would be

$$\hat{q}_i = (1 - b^*)\bar{q} + b^* y_i \tag{5.28}$$

where b^* would be a measure of the strength of association, theoretically equal to the square of the correlation coefficient between y and q in a sufficiently large sample,[9] and $\bar{q}$ is the known mean applicant quality. The coefficient, b^*, thus lies between 0 and 1.

Two extreme cases can be briefly illustrated. First suppose that $\bar{q}$ is identical between two groups of workers, but that the test is more reliable for the majority group, i.e. b^* is higher. An examination of equation (5.28) shows that for workers with the same test score, majority workers will be paid a higher wage than minority workers if $y_i > \bar{q}$, while the opposite will hold if $y_i < \bar{q}$. High quality minority workers will thus earn wages lower than their majority counterparts, while the opposite will be true for low quality workers. Majority worker wages will therefore be more dispersed around the mean than those of minority workers. Mean wages will, however, be the same for both groups.

The second case is where the test is equally reliable for both groups, except that mean productivity and therefore mean earnings differ. Note here, however, that providing $b^* < 1$ then it remains possible for a high productivity worker from the less productive group to earn less than a worker with lower productivity from the more productive group.

One may presume that in the real world, the most likely situations in which statistical labour market discrimination is likely to arise are

(i) with respect to recent immigrants whose different cultural and linguistic backgrounds are likely to render Western based ability tests inappropriate and whose work histories overseas are difficult to interpret by domestic employers;

(ii) with respect to female employees, and in particular married women, who may experience prolonged periods of future absence from work and a higher quit rate due to pregnancy.

In the US at least, however, the importance of female irregularity and instability may be less than once thought. For example, Viscusi (1980) indicates that, after the first few years at work, women are more stable than men, while Goldfarb and Hosek (1976) find that, although female absenteeism rates are higher than those of men, the difference is rather trivial.

Labour Market Monopsony and Monopoly

If firms possess monopsony power in the labour market and the supply of one group of workers is less elastic than that of another, then profit maximisation will imply that different wages will be paid in equilibrium. In Figure 5.5 we present a simplified version of this argument in which we assume, for the sake of an example, that the supply of males, S_m, is perfectly elastic, while the supply of females, S_F, is less elastic. A situation like this would arise if male workers enjoyed greater geographical mobility than females. Since the female supply curve is upward sloping, the marginal cost of female labour must be greater than the female supply price. If the firm can discriminate between the two groups, then it will employ a total number of workers such that marginal revenue product, MPR, is equated to the male wage, W_M. For females, however, MRP will be

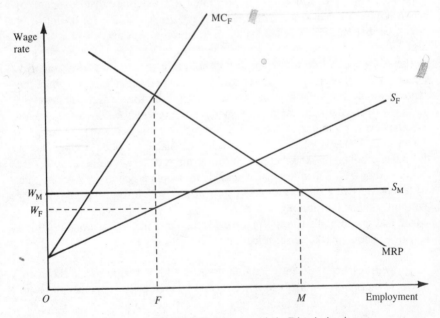

Figure 5.5 Monopsonistic Discrimination

equated to their marginal cost, MC_F. The female wage, W_F, will then be set equal to the supply price of female workers at this level of female employment and will be less than the male wage. Female and male employment will be equal to OF and FM respectively. Although Figure 5.5 incorporates the special assumption that male and female labour supply to the firm are perfectly elastic and less than perfectly elastic respectively, a similar argument holds as long as male labour supply is more elastic than that of females.

Although the theoretical case for monopsonistic discrimination is beyond dispute, the empirical status of the model is more questionable. On one side, there is the fact that although profit maximising monopsonists do exist — the baseball leagues in the USA providing one famous example — they are nevertheless unrepresentative of the labour market as a whole; while on the other side, it is not obvious that supply elasticities to those monopsonies that do exist differ in the systematic fashion assumed by the model.

The other possibility is that discriminatory power is exercised from the other side of the labour market, i.e. by trade unions. Clearly there is no obvious reason why unions should exercise discrimination in any one direction rather than another and this is reflected in the empirical literature. There *is* historical evidence of past discrimination by trade unions against women and against black workers in the USA. However, more recent evidence suggests that unions may act to reduce discrimination. For example, Ashenfelter (1972) calculated that the presence of unions raised black wages relative to those of whites by 3.4 per cent in the USA, although it also appeared to lower the female/male wage ratio by 1.9 per cent. Nickell (1977) found, however, that the wage mark-up attributable to trade unions in the UK was higher for women than for men.

The Measurement of Discrimination

Gross pay differentials between groups are quite large. The 1981 US Census showed that among full-time workers the ratio to annual white male earnings of those of white females, black males and black females was 0.58, 0.69 and 0.53 respectively. In the UK, female wages are currently at about 0.66 of male wages, while gross wage differentials by race seem to be much less than in the USA. For example Stewart (1983a) calculated that, in 1975, the average weekly earnings of non-white workers born outside the country were about 85 per cent of those of whites. The question is, however, 'What proportion of these differentials can be attributed to discrimination?'

The simplest approach, as often used in some of the earlier studies, was to start off with an earnings function such as the Mincer version discussed earlier, and to insert dummy variables for sex and/or ethnic group. This is, of course, only strictly valid if the coefficients of other variables such as education, experience, region, etc. are equal across the defined sexual or racial groups.

A preferable approach is to fit the specified earnings function for each group

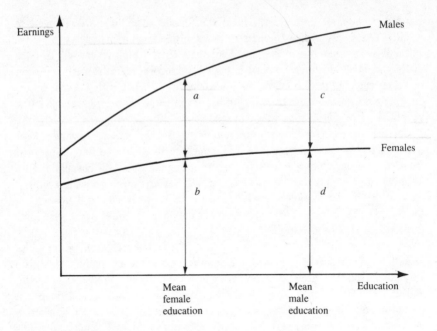

Figure 5.6 Measurement of Discrimination

separately. The extent of discrimination against (say) females could then be measured by inserting average female characteristics into the male earnings function, hence predicting what males would earn given average female characteristics, and then calculating the difference between this and actual average female earnings. This is illustrated in Figure 5.6 in which we plot the relationship between earnings and a single characteristic, in this case education, for males and females separately. The difference between predicted male and actual female earnings is given in the diagram by the distance a, while it is conventional to express this as a final measure of discrimination as the ratio of this difference to average female earnings, i.e. the ratio a/b. Alternatively, one could predict what females would earn given average male characteristics from the earnings function for females, and base the discrimination measure upon the difference between this and average male earnings. In Figure 5.6, this is given by the distance c, while the appropriate ratio is given by $c/(c + d)$. These two measures of discrimination, against females on the one hand and in favour of males on the other, are not normally the same and both have been used in past research. A further alternative is to take the average of the two as used by Greenhalgh (1980).

The results obtained from exercises of this kind vary from study to study. This is as one would expect, given the differing levels of data aggregation employed and different selections of other standardising variables used in the estimating equations. Cain (1986) surveys some twenty studies of male/female wage differentials and six studies of male white/black differentials, all of these using US data sets. It appears that the bulk of male/female studies indicates that only a minor part of the overall differential can be attributed to inferior observed female characteristics such as less education or work experience, although the results for white/black differentials appear less clear cut. Greenhalgh (1980) finds on the basis of UK data for 1975 that the unexplained differential between married men and single men, single men and single women, and single women over married women was of the order of 10 per cent, 10 per cent and 12 per cent respectively. The importance of marriage as a source of advantage to men and of disadvantage to women has also been observed in other studies.

5.6 Market Imperfections

There are essentially three sets of labour market imperfections: the systematic influence of government policies such as, for example, minimum wage legislation and job security regulation; monopoly or monopsony power as sometimes exercised by trade unions and large firms in local labour markets; and the malfunctioning of the allocative functions of the labour market arising from lack of information and various barriers to mobility. Although government labour market interventions may be of considerable importance, this obviously varies enormously between countries and over time, and therefore no discussion is attempted here. It may be noted, however, that even when such interventions are binding upon the labour market, as in the case of an effective legal minimum wage, market forces or the forces of custom may act so as to limit some of their effects. Thus, for example, employers may partly circumvent job security legislation by using temporary workers, while customary bargaining on the basis of relative wages may restore the differentials of better paid workers over and above the minimum wage. Trade unions are the most important source of monopoly power in labour markets and we attempt a short survey of empirical attempts to isolate their impact on wage levels in the next subsection. Finally, we round off with a look at the challenge to orthodox labour market models of some empirical evidence relating to the functioning of internal and local labour markets.

Trade Unions and Wages

The starting point for most studies in this area is as follows. Let W_n be the wage paid in a non-unionized occupation or industry, T be the proportion unionised and m be the proportional wage mark-up enjoyed by union members. The average wage, W, may then be written as

$$W = (1 - T)W_n + (1 + m)TW_n$$

or

$$W = W_n(1 + mT) \qquad (5.29)$$

Taking logs of equation (5.29) and noting that, for small values of mT, log $(1 + mT)$ is approximately equal to mT, we have

$$\log W = \log W_n + mT \tag{5.30}$$

The method used is therefore to insert T in a log-linear earnings function such as those discussed or referred to earlier and to estimate m as its coefficient. If the data are in the form of averages for groups of workers such as occupations, then T is the proportion unionised. If, however, as in many recent studies, each observation refers to an individual worker, then T takes the form of a dummy variable, with $T = 1$ for a member and $T = 0$ for a non-member.

Numerous studies of this form have been carried out using data from both the UK and the USA. Most of the UK based studies have taken the proportion covered by collective agreements as their measure of T, rather than the proportion of union members, as it is generally believed that the former is a better proxy for union strength; but they differ in terms of the measure of earnings used, the choice of other variables in the earnings function and the type of worker considered. Earlier studies employed data sets in which the union or coverage status of a given individual was unknown, and usually estimated T as the average proportion unionised or covered in his or her industry of employment. Individual specific information on union status has since become available in more recent data sets and has been used in more recent studies (for example Stewart, 1983b). More recent studies have also tended to estimate earnings separately for the two groups of workers and to estimate the mark-up by comparing the results.

Three main conclusions seem to emerge from the UK based studies:

1. The wages of workers covered by local agreements, i.e. establishment or area based agreements, as often negotiated by shop steward committees, are substantially above those of uncovered workers. Mulvey (1976), for example, found a zero mark-up on adult male hourly earnings in manufacturing industry associated with covereage by a national agreement only, which sharply contrasts with a mark-up in the 41–48 per cent range associated with other forms of agreement, i.e. supplementary, district, local and company agreements. These results, along with those of Pencavel (1974) and other studies, indicate that in the UK the impact of unions upon wage levels stems from the strength of local bargaining units and should therefore vary within industries across regions. Studies that fail to distinguish between national and other forms of bargaining have generally found average mark-ups in the 15–30 per cent range. All of these results are based, however, upon data sets which did not distinguish the coverage or union status of individual workers and which used a group proxy as a measure of T. Stewart (1983b) found a much lower estimate of the union markup of 7.7 per cent using a data set which identified individual union membership status. Unfortunately, his data did not permit a comparison of local and national agreement coverage.

2. Manual workers gain on average from coverage under a collective agree-

ment, while clerical workers seem, if anything, to lose out (Layard *et al.*, 1978). This last, slightly surprising, result may perhaps be explained by the fact that, in the UK, covered white-collar workers are disproportionately concentrated in public administration, education and health services, so that this negative mark-up may reflect the public/private sector differential existing at the time (1973).

3. The mark-up for women is greater than that for men (Nickell, 1977). This result has already been referred to earlier.

Studies based upon data for the USA have not in general yielded markedly different results. As in the UK, the union mark-up seems to vary considerably across both industries and occupation, although the overall impact of unions is less as union membership and collective agreements apply to a smaller proportion of the workforce. Lewis (1986) has surveyed a large number of studies based on US Current Population Survey Data which show union mark-ups during the period 1970−9 of between 10 per cent and 23 per cent. The result, noted above for the UK, that manual workers enjoy higher mark-ups than white-collar workers is also reflected in the American literature.

A number of problems arise when interpreting earnings function based estimates of the union mark-up. The more obvious of these include the question of what measure of earnings to use and the choice of standardising variables to include in the estimating equations. Another is that, by concentrating solely upon the union/non-union differential, these studies may implicitly underestimate the impact of unions upon average wages, as *spillover* effects from union to non-union sectors arising from the existence of customary interindustry differentials, and *threat* effects, where employers pay higher wages as a bribe to persuade workers not to join or form a union, may also be present. There are, however, two much more serious difficulties.

One difficulty arises from the interpretation of the union mark-up itself. As discussed in Chapter 6, there is some evidence that, in the USA at least, improved shop-floor−employer communications arising from unionisation may lead to increased productivity. In that case, it is also plausible that unions would be able to extract at least part of these gains in the form of higher wage rates. It would therefore be no longer obvious that unions were imposing the adverse welfare effects usually associated with the simple textbook monopoly model, since, although the wage per worker is increased, this may not be true of the wage per labour efficiency unit. In other words, it does not necessarily follow from this interpretation that the union mark-up is a 'bad thing'. An alternative possibility is that unions do increase wages per worker, but that employers then find it possible to attract better quality employees. Although to some extent this is taken care of by the inclusion of other quality standardising variables such as education and experience, important worker characteristics such as reliability and manual dexterity remain largely unobserved, and it is again difficult to adversely interpret the estimated mark-up.

The second problem is a particular example of selectivity bias in the estimating equation, in that workers are not assigned union or collective coverage status independently of their unobserved characteristics. Likewise, if workers choose union status according to going wage rates, given their individual characteristics, then the estimated coefficients of the earnings function will be similarly biased. This problem was first explored by Lee (1978) who developed an appropriate estimation technique and applied it to US based data. Lewis (1986) reports, however, that US studies using these techniques have produced a wider range of estimates of the union mark-up than less econometrically sophisticated studies.

An obvious limitation of cross-section studies such as those discussed above is that they can only estimate the union mark-up at one fixed point in time. Layard et al. (1978) have estimated the mark-up associated with collective agreement coverage for each year from 1961 to 1975 and found it to be positively related to the level of unemployment. This result echoes earlier findings by Lewis (1963) for the USA who concluded that unions had their maximum effect on wage levels at the lowest point of the Great Depression. There appear to be two explanations for this. One is that since collective agreements are in force for a pre-specified period — typically three years prior to the 1970s — wages determined by collective bargaining are less responsive to changing economic conditions than those determined by individual bargaining. This argument presumably loses force during periods of high inflation such as in the 1970s, as the collective bargaining period becomes shorter. The other explanation is that individual, as opposed to collective, bargaining power is increased when unemployment is low, as the cost of replacing a worker who quits is higher. The opposite would then be true when unemployment is high.

Compensating Differentials or Wage Anarchy?

There has always been a tradition in labour economics that, just as the mainstream pushes ahead along broad neoclassical lines and attempts to identify and quantify the parameters of more or less orthodox models, there is also another rather loosely knit group who deny that wages and wage differentials are determined as by standard theory, and who tend to view the labour market as a much untidier place altogether. Perhaps the earliest and most influential writings in this tradition were those of Cairnes (1874) and Taussig (1929) who developed the theory of non-competing groups as originally suggested by John Stuart Mill. To some extent, later work can be seen as a development of this theory.

The two main approaches that have surfaced in recent years are that of internal labour markets (ILM) and that of segmented labour markets (SLM). The concept of dual labour markets (DLM) is a popular special case of the latter approach. The theory of internal labour markets, as described by Doeringer and Piore (1971), assumes high turnover costs faced by large firms arising essentially from a high degree of firm specificity in the technology applied and hence a heavy specific component in training provided, while workers are assumed to place a heavy premium on job security. Under these circumstances, Doeringer and Piore argue that a labour market will develop within each firm which will tend to insulate itself from the external labour market by recruiting at low levels and then filling internal vacancies by promotion. Each internal labour market will then have its own set of rules governing the eligibility of candidates for internal posts. Such rules would include, for example, who is to be laid off first given a downturn and the circumstances under which external candidates may be hired. A major role of trade unions in this scenario is to see that the rules are enforced.

The determinants of the wage structure under such a system are far from clear. Since firms compete for new entrants at the lower level of the job spectrum, they must offer a career profile which gives workers a utility index comparable to those elsewhere. However, the emphasis placed by Doeringer and Piore upon the importance of custom and internal administrative procedures, such as job evaluation, as overriding factors in determining interval wage differentials, indicates that wages are unlikely to be equalised for comparable groups of workers across firms.

Empirical evidence in this area appears to be rather thin. MacKay (1970) examined the dispersion of weekly earnings within a few occupational groups in the engineering industry in Birmingham for 1959 and in Glasgow for 1959 and 1966. The dispersion did indeed seem considerable. For example, in Glasgow in 1966, the highest and lowest wages earned by turners were £22.5 and £14.6 respectively. MacKay also showed that the ranking of plants by the level of wages paid appeared stable over time. This last finding would therefore seem to cast doubt on the explanation that the initial wage dispersion was due to temporary non-equalisation. It is, nevertheless, difficult to draw strong conclusions from all this, as there would doubtless be significant quality variation among workers across plants, while working conditions may also have varied, although MacKay believed that conditions may have been better in the higher paid establishments. He did find, however, a significant negative relationship between the quit rate and the wage paid, a result which offers some support for the operation of a competitive labour market.

The other challenge to labour market orthodoxy comes from those who argue that the labour market is somehow broken up into high wage and low wage sectors. In the simplest dual labour market version, the primary sector pays high wages that are typically unresponsive to fluctuating economic conditions and, within which, workers receive substantial return to education and acquired skills. Unions will be concentrated in this sector and, in some versions of DLM theories, the sector consists of a series of internal labour markets. The secondary sector, in contrast, is a refuge for those who cannot obtain primary sector jobs, and wages then will respond in the usual way to the forces of supply and demand. The low skill content of secondary sector work also implies that there will be little or no wage differentials by education. The essential point about DLM theories is that there is a barrier between the two sectors preventing workers from moving between the two. Secondary sector participation is taken as an adverse signal by primary sector firms, presumably because the nature of secondary work may be inconsistent with primary sector requirements such as punctuality and reliability. Those displaced from the primary sector during a downturn will therefore prefer to remain unemployed and queue for primary positions rather than enter the secondary sector. This notion of secondary sector entrapment explains why some American versions of DLM theories are also theories of racial wage differentials, as it is argued that minorities are typically secondary sector workers. DLM theories are of course by no means peculiar in their application to developed countries. A substantial theoretical and empirical literature is devoted to this subject in the context of the urban areas in modern-day less-developed countries where labour market dualism seems much more conspicuous (for example Todaro, 1969).

Although some USA based studies, such as Osterman (1975) and Rumberger and Carnoy (1975), claim empirical support for the existence of a DLM on the grounds of structural breaks in the earnings function and lower returns to education in the secondary sector, these studies suffer from well-known[10] statistical deficiencies. Other studies in both the USA and the UK have failed to substantiate these findings.

The view that wage differentials are not determined as by conventional theory is not, of course, confined to the literature referred to above. Routh (1980), for example, has argued forcibly that the movement of occupational differentials over time cannot be explained by even the slow workings of market forces. Certainly the relative stability of occupational differentials over substantial periods of time could indicate the importance of non-economic forces such as status and custom, although they could be due to the shapes and/or shifts of the appropriate supply and demand curves. Similarly, it has sometimes been argued that industrial wage differentials are determined by the 'ability to pay' of individual employers, although no convincing empirical relationship has ever been demonstrated between the level of wage rates and profits.[11] At the end, all that one can safely conclude is that research and debate in this area will continue.

Notes

1. If the net benefits of a project were to oscillate back and forth between negative and positive values over the life of the project, then solving equation (7.2) for the internal rate of return may give multiple real values. However, in the case of human capital investments in which net benefits are negative early on and then positive in all later periods, there is only one value for the rate of return which always yields a decision rule entirely consistent with the present value criteria.
2. See Psacharopoulos (1972).
3. A rise in the relative wages of educated and uneducated persons will only change the educational composition of the labour force quite gradually as successive cohorts of young people become better educated. The long run thus refers to the period required for this process to be more or less completed.
4. See Intriligator (1971) for the mathematical details of dynamic optimisation.
5. For a full exposition see Arrow (1973).

6. The private rate of return is calculated from the wages and costs as actually faced by the individual. The social rate of return should, in contrast, be calculated from the social marginal products and costs of different levels of education. Thus given, for example, monopsonistic labour market conditions, the marginal product of labour should be calculated separately from the wage. Similarly, externalities from education should also be included when calculating social rates. In fact, however, in almost all studies, private rates of return were calculated with costs net of educational subsidy and wages net of tax, while social rates were calculated on the basis of gross educational costs and pre-tax wages. Although the social rate of return, when correctly calculated, is clearly the appropriate measure for social cost–benefit analysis, the private rate is the one more relevant to the discussion in this chapter.

7. For some illustrative results drawing on cross-section data see Griliches (1977).

8. A minor caveat here is that if the elasticity of substitution between black and white workers is greater than one, then it may still be the case that either all whites or all blacks are hired by sufficiently discriminatory and non-discriminatory employers respectively. If, however, the elasticity of substitution is less than one, then mixed employment is guaranteed.

9. More rigorously, the probability limit of $b*$ can be shown to be

$$\text{plim } b* = \frac{M_{qq}}{M_{qq} + M_{uu}}$$

where M_{qq} and M_{uu} are the asymptotic variances of q and u respectively. The right-hand expression is the population R^2 for relationship (5.27) and is therefore also equal to the square of the population correlation between y and q.

10. The problem here is that if the estimating equations are censored according to the value of the dependent variable, in this case earnings, the coefficients will be biased. See Cain (1976) for an exposition of this point.

11. For a survey of some of the best known work in this area, see Reder (1962).

6

The Economics of Trade Unions

6.1 Introduction

So far we have followed the normal practice in economics of first analysing the supply and demand decisions of individual economic agents such as workers and firms. If we followed the traditional approach further, then we would continue by telling the usual story that in equilibrium, prices (in this context wages) are determined such that overall supply and demand are equalised. Now, although there are some labour markets such as the market for casual labour in the towns and villages of less-developed countries and the market for part-time workers and 'moonlighters' in industrialised countries, which one could sensibly describe as approximating to the free market scenario, for most wage or salary earners there are important institutional influences at work when one looks at pay determination. The most important of the latter is undoubtedly the effects of trade union activity, although the impact of legislation and government policy and the exercise of monopsony power by large employers are also often extremely relevant. In this chapter we will concentrate for the most part upon the economic effects of trade unions, as this is perhaps the oldest and most widely discussed area of labour economics. Indeed, one may note in passing that many pre-war labour economists spent so much of their career writing about unions and the associated institutional framework, that a large proportion of their scholarship can be more accurately linked with the study of industrial relations than with economics.

The plan of this chapter is as follows. We start off with a brief factual review regarding the size and structure of unions in modern developed economies. We then set out a simple model in which the union fixes a wage rate and firms respond by dictating an employment level according to their demand curves for labour. This is the traditional textbook approach to union behaviour. This assumes, however, that firms are passive players in the drama while even a casual glance at the real world suggests that wages are often determined in a bargaining situation. The next section is accordingly concerned with extending the analysis to examine one or two solutions to the bargaining problem. (The empirical evidence regarding the impact of unions upon wage differentials is reviewed in Chapter 5.) Following this, we look at the determinants of union size and its behaviour over the trade cycle. This is one of the oldest areas of research in this field and makes an important contribution to an understanding of the ways in which union strength is itself at least partly determined by external economic circumstance. Historically it has usually been assumed that unions present an obstacle to higher levels of productivity. Recent empirical studies are divided as to whether this is in fact the case. The last section of the chapter reviews the evidence.

6.2   Union Power

Although it is true that the central feature of industrial relations is the same in most countries — employers on one side and workers on the other — there exist wide differences in the degree of organisation among workers and in the scope and structure of industrial bargaining. The concept of 'union power' is indeed a rather slippery one as the aims of unions vary as to their economic and political content, while the support of their members is much more reliable in some countries than in others.

The simplest indicator of union strength that one can use is the union density ratio, i.e. unionised workers as a proportion of the labour force. These are given for a number of industrialised countries in Table 6.1. The UK and Italy emerge as the most unionised countries with West Germany running in third place, while France and the USA are the least unionised. There are, in addition, a number of other developed countries in which the density ratio is higher than in any of those shown; for example in Sweden the corresponding figure is 80 per cent. Aggregate figures of this sort tend to hide the support that unions may have in

Table 6.1   Union Membership (% of Total Labour Force) and Days Lost Through Strikes (Est. % of Total Working Days), 1980

	Membership (%)	Days lost (%)
France	22	0.052
West Germany	40	0.016
Italy	50	0.378
Japan	31	0.035
UK	50	0.215
USA	20	0.049

Sources: Bratt (1982). ILO, *Yearbook of Labour Statistics*, 1983.
Note: It was assumed that there are 250 working days per year. Days lost were calculated as an annual average over the period 1980–82.

particular sectors of the economy. The density ratios in manufacturing and in strategic sectors such as electricity, gas and water are all generally higher than those quoted. Similarly, blue-collar workers are everywhere more highly unionised than their white-collar counterparts. It is also arguable that the proportion of workers covered by collective agreements is a better indicator of union strength than the density ratio, as in all countries there are some workers who receive wages determined by collective bargaining but who are not themselves union members. For example, in the UK about 78 per cent receive wages or salaries covered by some form of collective agreement or other, but only 50 per cent are actually card-carrying members. One can of course take the opposite view and argue that those who are not union members are unlikely to support union action. Finally, it is important to note that the figures themselves are not always reliable. In France and possibly in Italy, where there are rival union confederations, it is in these organisations' own interest to exaggerate their importance by inflating membership totals. The figure for France has been adjusted so as to allow for this effect.

A second approach that one can take is to consider, not so much the relative extent of unionisation, but rather how fragmented it is. Fragmentation can take many forms: rival confederations, a multiplicity of unions within a given industry and a range of different levels at which unions bargain with employers. We will consider each of these in turn.

The UK has only one confederation, the TUC, which, with 11.5 million members, is the largest union organisation in Western Europe. Although only 108 out of a total of 200 UK unions are affiliated to the TUC, the remainder are rather small, as can be seen by the fact that the TUC accounts for over 90 per cent of British union membership. Similarly, the USA also has only a single confederation, the AFL/CIO. By definition, competition between rival confederations does not arise in these countries. In West Germany and in Japan the situation is somewhat different as each country possesses more than one union confederation. However, it is fair to say that by and large this leads to few problems as the confederations tend to draw on different groups of workers. The DGB dominates West German unionism, with 79 per cent of all members, and organises both blue- and white-collar workers. The other two confederations, the DAG and the DBB, are exclusively white-collar, the former consisting mostly of private sector employees and the latter mostly of those in the public sector. The three Japanese confederations each comprise of different groupings of company unions. Direct rivalry between confederations is, however, a major feature of the industrial relations systems of both France and Italy. Of the six French confederations, the two largest, the communist dominated CGT (1.5 million workers) and the CFDT (0.8 million workers), both take a radical view of economic and political affairs. The often bitter wranglings between these two and other reformist confederations continue to act as a barrier to labour organisation in France. In Italy, the three main confederations also compete with each other although here there are some signs of greater unity in some sectors.

The UK has perhaps the messiest industrial relations set-up of any country in the world. There is a sizeable degree of multi-unionism at both the firm and the industrial level and many large factories have as many as 20 unions operating on their premises, a fact which has often led to industrial disputes regarding job demarcations. To a large extent this arises from the long industrial history of the UK. There are craft unions which exclusively organise workers in certain occupations, industrial unions, such as the National Union of Mineworkers, and general unions, such as the Transport and General Workers Union which has members from a wide range of industries and occupations. Recently the situation in the UK has changed somewhat as the overall number of unions has been steadily falling and there has been a shift towards company-level bargaining. To some extent this has been accompanied by a fall in membership but this can be entirely attributed to the sharp rise in unemployment in the late 1970s and early 1980s. The USA has about the same number of unions as the UK, and American unions are similarly divided along craft and industrial lines. Multi-unionism is, however, much less common than in the UK. Western European unions are almost entirely organised by industry or industrial sector. The DGB, for example, consists of only 17 industrial unions while in France there are 26 unions affiliated to the CGT. Japan has by far and away the most unions of any industrialised country: about 74 000 of them! However, this simply reflects the company or establishment base of individual Japanese unions.

There is no obvious way in which one can rank union bargaining strength according to different sets of union structure, although one would expect establishment unions to be weaker than more broadly based forms of union organisation. It has been argued that craft unions are more effective at pushing up wages than industrial unions, but, as discussed in the next section, this is not necessarily the case. What one can argue is that union influence will be weakened when different unions are in competition with each other and that the likelihood of industrial conflict is increased under multi-unionism.

The third type of fragmentation concerns the number of different levels and establishments at which bargaining occurs. Collective agreements can be made between a union and an employer or employer's federation at national, regional or plant level. In the UK, for example, agreements have proliferated at all levels and much attention has been paid to the existence of local agreements side by side with national and/or regional agreements. The Royal Commission on Industrial Relations (Donovan Commission) of 1968 observed that there appeared to be a two-tier structure in British industrial relations: the first tier consisting of negotiations taking place at industrial level between full-time officials of the union and employers or their representatives, while the second consisted of additional negotiations in local establishments between shop stewards and local management. The closed shop[1] is a common form of organisation at establishment level in the UK and it is known that about one-quarter of the labour force is covered by closed-shop agreements. Although these arrangements increase both local bargaining strength and overall membership, they can also loosen central union control. Unofficial or wildcat strikes are more frequent than official strikes in the UK and it is common practice for shop stewards to call a local strike and then seek central union blessing afterwards.

Bargaining structure in other countries is somewhat different. The USA and Japanese systems are both highly decentralised while those in Western Europe are much more cohesive, in that bargaining is normally conducted between the union and the appropriate employers' association. Plant bargaining is less common in Western Europe although company negotiations have recently become much more commonplace in Italy while works councils in West Germany negotiate some elements of the pay packet such as piece-rates.

The third way in which union strength is often assessed is in terms of the amount of trouble that they cause. Industrial unrest can of course take many forms, such as the go-slow, the overtime embargo and the work-to-rule, but it is the strike which has tended to dominate the literature on this subject. The reasons for this are fairly obvious in that the effects per period of strikes are greater than those of other forms of industrial action.

At first glance it would appear from Table 6.1 that strikes are of trivial importance in that the proportion of man-days lost through strikes is very low throughout the industrialised countries. It is even sometimes argued that strikes are of no economic relevance, as lost output can be made up after the dispute is resolved. This argument is, however, clearly fallacious as the recovery of lost output involves additional costs related to the working of overtime hours while plant and equipment can depreciate even when not in use. Strikes also impose social costs by increasing the uncertainty faced by consumers and firms. In addition, national output might fall if export orders are lost, while redistribution is likely among producers as strike-hit firms lose the goodwill of their customers. We must also remember that official statistics have only limited coverage of man-days lost through unofficial strikes, and, more importantly, secondary effects upon workers in other sectors of the economy are ignored. This latter point is particularly relevant with regard to strikes in the transport, raw materials and power industries as establishments elsewhere might have to close down if intermediate inputs cannot be obtained. The comparability of strike statistics is also open to question, although it is generally agreed that man-days lost is the most comparable measure, as large strikes are taken into account in all national statistical sources.

The incidence of strikes differs significantly across industries. Although individual industry rankings can fluctuate violently from year to year, one can broadly say that heavy industries such as iron and steel, engineering and vehicles are among the more strike prone, while agriculture and most service sectors are relatively strike free. As one would expect, the tedium of large establishments increases the proportion of working days lost as does the rate of technical change.[2]

The central question is, however, whether a measure of strike incidence can be taken as an indicator of union strength. To some extent it probably can: weak unions cannot count on the support of their members, and use the strike weapon very sparingly. The problem is that the relationship between union power and strike incidence is probably not a monotonic one: short of actually closing down, weak firms are going to give in to strong unions rather than incur the costs of industrial disputes that they are certain to lose.

6.3 Union Growth

In Section 6.2, we briefly compared the degree of unionisation in different countries. Although such comparisons are of interest in themselves, it is clear that no economic model can ever satisfactorily explain *levels* of unionisation given that the latter are essentially determined by historical experience, which in turn heavily influences the prevailing political ideology and the degree of pro- or anti-union bias in existing labour legislation. If, however, such non-economic influences can be taken as more or less fixed over time, then an economic model might still be of use in explaining *changes* in union membership. This latter approach is the one adopted in the existing economics literature on this subject.

Union density ratios are given in Table 6.2 for two countries with reasonably consistent data bases, i.e. the UK and the USA. While unionisation in the UK rose sharply since the war, although falling back sharply since 1980, American union density peaked during the 1950s and has continued to fall ever since. What sort of explanations can we put forward to account for changes of this sort?

The early literature concentrated upon the business cycle as the main determinant of fluctuations in union membership. There were several justifications put forward for this, the main ones being that:

(i)   unemployed workers tend to let their membership lapse, so that aggregate membership would fall during a recession;

(ii) firms are more willing to resist unions in a depression as the cost of a plant closure is less than in a boom thus reducing the benefits of union membership from the point of view of individual workers;

Table 6.2   Unionisation in the UK and the USA, 1950–1980

		1950	1960	1970	1980
UK:	% labour force	40.4	38.7	43.4	48.3
	% civilian employment: total	42.2	41.5	45.9	51.8
	men	51.3	50.7	54.3	—
	women	23.4	23.9	31.0	—
USA:	% labour force	23.2	25.1	24.2	18.6
	% civilian employment: total	32.8	33.4	22.3	21.9

Sources: UK: Department of Employment, *Employment Gazette* (various issues).
              USA: Neumann and Rissman (1984).

(iii) workers are less willing to antagonise employers during a depression by joining a union as their chances of re-employment elsewhere are less.

Nowadays we would probably take less notice of (iii), as victimisation seems to be less common than it used to be, and we would add the argument that unions will aim for lower wage differentials during a depression thus once again reducing the benefits of being a union member.

In terms of its empirical performance the cycle theory seems to give a reasonably satisfactory explanation of membership fluctuations up to the 1950s. However, it is clear that it cannot satisfactorily explain either the sustained downturn in US membership since 1954 or the steady rise in UK membership during the rather depressed 1970s. Explanations for the recent behaviour of union membership in these two countries must therefore be sought elsewhere.

One possible source of growth or decline in union membership could lie in the changing sectoral composition of output. If, for example, highly unionised sectors grew more slowly than others, then one would expect aggregate membership to fall. This is at first glance a plausible explanation of declining membership in the USA given the rise in the relative importance of the rather lowly unionised service sector. However, Neumann and Rissman have shown that between 1956 and 1980 only 40 per cent of the decline in US union membership can be attributed to industrial composition effects,[3] the remaining 60 per cent being explained by falling unionisation rates within sectors. In the UK, where union density was rising until 1980, one has to conclude that this must have been in spite of sectoral effects since, as in the USA, services grew faster than the industrial sectors. In any case, the sectoral hypothesis is not really a theory in itself as there remains the question of why, for example, the manufacturing sector should be more unionised than, say, the services sector. The intuitive reaction is to suggest that there are economies of scale in organising and recruiting within individual establishments so that manufacturing will naturally tend to be more heavily unionised, as its average establishment size is above average. If this is the case, however, then the sectoral hypothesis is really a smoke-screen obscuring the true mechanism relating to plant size and it seems clear that it is variables such as the latter that should be concentrated upon in empirical work.

The main addition to the business cycle theory has been to explicitly include changes in the price level as a positive determinant of unionisation on the grounds that a worker's real wage is likely to grow at a lower rate when prices are rising rapidly, and hence his incentive to seek the protection of a trade union is correspondingly greater. This was the justification, put forward by Ashenfelter and Pencavel (1969), for including the annual percentage change in the price level, ΔP_t, in their time series study of changes in union density in the USA between 1900 and 1960. Ordinary least squares becomes inappropriate when one includes ΔP_t or something similar as an explanatory variable, as the causality could well work the other way round, i.e. not only can price changes affect unionisation but also unionisation can help to push up prices. Ashenfelter and Pencavel thus used an instrumental variables technique rather than ordinary least squares. The following equation can be treated as a representative example of their results.

[handwritten: % Δin = unb]

$$\Delta T_t = -11.07 + 0.61\Delta P_t + 0.15\Delta E_t + 0.12\Delta E_{t-1} + 0.08\Delta E_{t-2}$$
$$(2.95) \qquad (1.46) \qquad (2.02) \qquad (1.79)$$

$$+0.04\Delta E_{t-3} + 0.22U_t^P - 0.06\left(\frac{T}{E}\right)_{t-1} + 0.23G_t$$
$$(1.29) \qquad (2.06) \qquad (1.96) \qquad (4.05)$$

[handwritten annotations: "% of Democrats in HoR (proxy for degree of pro-Labour sentiment)"; "Turnout as prop of emp in U sectors"; "unemp rate (proxy for worker discontent)"]

The left-hand variable, ΔT_t, is annual percentage change in US membership while the various current and lagged terms in employment change, $\Delta E_{t,t-1,\ldots}$, are intended to pick up both labour market (e.g. business cycle) effects and the trend effect upon union membership due to a growing labour force. The U_t^P variable is the unemployment rate in the preceding trough of the business cycle which Ashenfelter and Pencavel interpret as a proxy for worker discontent. This is very different from a current unemployment rate series, partly because of the lag effect but mainly because U_t^P takes only about one-quarter of the values taken by the current unemployment rate over the period. $(T/E)_t$ is trade union membership as a proportion of employment in the unionised sector and represents a rather crude attempt to take account of the fact that it must become increasingly difficult to recruit more union members once the membership rate has become sufficiently high. G_t is the percentage of Democrats in the USA House of Representatives and was used as a proxy for the degree of pro-labour sentiment in the USA. The t-statistics are given in parentheses.

The Ashenfelter and Pencavel model has been the subject of much criticism: some of it reasonable but much of it trivial. A number of attempts have also been made to fit and compare alternative models. The best known among the latter is probably that developed by Bain and Elsheikh (1976).[4] They included the change in the current money wage, ΔW_t as well as the lagged price change, ΔP_{t-1}, on the grounds that the former reflects the credit that workers attribute to unions while the latter represents the threat to workers' living standards. The simultaneity problem regarding ΔT and ΔW is ignored, presumably on the grounds that changes in union density affect wages only after a further time lag. Bain and Elsheikh felt too many different influences had been collapsed into the $\Delta E_{t,t-1}\ldots$ terms in the Ashenfelter and Pencavel model and used instead unemployment *changes* split into positive (ΔU_t^+) and negative (ΔU_t^-) components to allow for asymmetric effects. A density variable, $(T/L)_{t-1}$ where L is total labour force was included to proxy the saturation effect as in Ashenfelter−Pencavel, while a dummy variable, G_t, was introduced to catch the effects of the Wagner Act during the period 1937−47. One of their equations as estimated for the years 1897−1947 was as follows:

$$\Delta T = 12.00 + 0.74\Delta W_t + 0.48\Delta P_{t-1} - 0.10\Delta U_t^+ + 0.08\Delta U_t^-$$
$$\; (4.14)\qquad (2.65)\qquad (2.38)\qquad (4.04)$$
$$\; + 6.76G_t - 0.54D_{t-1}$$
$$\;(3.22)\quad (6.05)$$

Bain and Elsheikh applied similar empirical models to the UK, Australia and Sweden and found that a broadly similar story emerged for these other countries. However, for our purposes the main question should be whether models of this kind can throw light upon recent changes in union membership.

Essentially these results tell us that both employment and price changes have positive effects upon union membership while the other variables seem to perform more or less as expected. Although, by definition, G_t in both models is peculiar to the USA, the broad story does seem to fit the facts in the UK in which high rates of inflation in the 1970s could explain why union membership continued to rise in the face of generally rather slack labour market conditions. The fall-off in membership in the 1980s would then be explained by the much sharper fall in employment during this period and the lower rate of inflation.

The fact that union membership fell during the 1970s in the USA would be explained by the model in terms of the slower growth in employment in that decade and possibly by a revival in anti-labour attitudes, as ultimately reflected by the election of Ronald Reagan in November 1979. The extent to which the results presented above can be used as a guide to recent union growth behaviour has, for the USA at least, been questioned by Sheflin et al. (1981), who have shown that, contrary to assurances by both sets of authors, there are significant structural breaks in the fitted equations for both models at around 1937.

Neumann and Rissman (1984) have recently suggested that another force at work in the USA has been the substitution of government welfare services for those of unions. This hypothesis, as originally suggested by Reder (1951), would imply that as social programmes and legislation involving, for example, unemployment insurance, job insurance and workers' health and safety have been introduced, they have to some extent reduced workers' need for unions. Neumann and Rissman estimated a model similar to that of Ashenfelter and Pencavel and found evidence in favour of the substitution hypothesis.

6.4 Union Behaviour in the Absence of Bargaining

Let us suppose that a group of workers exist who can bid up their individual wage rates above competitive levels either by restricting entry to their industry or occupation or by some form of collective effort. We will also assume that this union of workers increases its happiness if wages are raised and/or if more of its members are employed. To keep the discussion simple, hours worked per worker will be kept fixed so that a union utility function can be defined as a function of only the real wage rate, W, and the number of workers employed, N. This utility function can then be written as:

$$V = V(W,N) \tag{6.1}$$

In the absence of bargaining, the problem for the union is to maximise (6.1) subject to the constraint provided by the demand function for employment

$$N = N(W) \tag{6.2}$$

As usual we will assume that the level of employment is a negative function of the real wage rate, W. The first-order condition for a maximum is then given by

$$\frac{V_W}{V_N} = -\frac{dN}{dW} \tag{6.3}$$

where V_W and V_N are the marginal utilities associated with small unit changes in the wage rate and the employment level respectively. This rather simple result — that the maximising position for the union occurs where the marginal rate of substitution between the employment level and the wage rate is equal to the amount by which employers will reduce employment, given a unit change in the wage — is illustrated in Figure 6.1. The constraint faced by the union is the downward sloping demand curve, $N(W)$, and the union maximises its utility at point A where it finds an indifference curve, $V(W,N)$, just tangential to the demand curve.

As it stands this analysis is not particularly illuminating and it is useful to probe more deeply into the origins of the union utility function. As a starting point let us suppose that in the absence of the union there would be a market wage, W_0, at which M workers would be employed. If all workers have identical tastes and the preferences of each can be represented by a single utility function, $U(W)$,

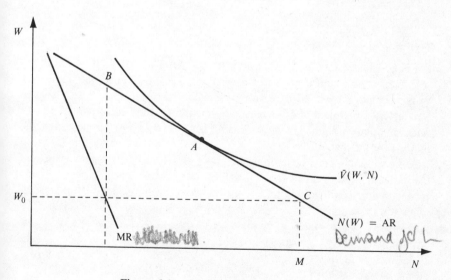

Figure 6.1 Alternative Union Objectives

then the task of the union would be to maximise this function for each of the M workers. The problem is of course that if the union obtains a wage above W_0, then less than M workers will remain employed in the union sector while the rest will have to seek employment elsewhere. The solution is for the union to maximise the expected utility of each given worker. The probability of being employed in the union sector is N/M and the wage rate in the non-union sector is W_0. The expected utility function can thus be written as

$$\frac{N}{M} U(W) + \left(1 - \frac{N}{M}\right) U(W_0)$$

or

$$\frac{N}{M} [U(W) - U(W_0)] + U(W_0) \tag{6.4}$$

The gain from unionisation can thus be neatly represented by the first term in (6.4) as the second term is simply the level of utility that would prevail in the absence of the union. If we multiply (6.4) through by M to obtain the 'total' utility function, then the union will seek to maximise

$$N[U(W) - U(W_0)] \tag{6.5}$$

subject to

$$N = N(W)$$

The first-order condition is then given by

$$\frac{N U_W}{U(W) - U(W_0)} = -\frac{dN}{dW} \tag{6.6}$$

this is best understood by comparing it with (6.3). The union's marginal utility with respect to a unit change in the wage (V_W) is $N U_W$ minus the number of workers employed multiplied by the corresponding marginal utility of each worker. Similarly the marginal utility received by the union when an additional worker finds employment in the union sector is $U(W) - U(W_0)$, i.e. the increase in the utility level of that worker.

The exact optimising position of the union clearly depends upon the form of the individual utility function, $U(W)$. It is well known that the latter is closely related to the individual's attitude towards risk. If the marginal utility of an additional wage unit diminishes as the level of the wage is increased, then the individual is said to be risk averse, i.e. he always prefers a sure outcome to a risky one with the same expected value, e.g. $50 for sure as opposed to an evens chance of $100. If the utility function is linear so that marginal utility is constant over all income levels, then the individual is said to be risk neutral, i.e. he is indifferent between a sure prospect and a risky one with the same expected value.

What happens if union members are risk neutral in the context of our model? The answer is very simple. If the utility function could be written as

$$U(W) = a + bW$$

where a and b are constants, then our maximand (6.5) becomes $bN(W - W_0)$ so that it is sufficient for the union to maximise the real value of monetary profit, $N(W - W_0)$. A union that is made up of risk neutral members can thus be treated analogously to a profit maximising firm. The optimising position is shown in Figure 6.1. The average revenue curve faced by the union is of course the demand curve, $N(W)$, and the marginal revenue curve is drawn correspondingly. The marginal cost to the union of supplying an additional worker is simply the non-union wage, W_0. The profit maximising condition that marginal cost equals marginal revenue thus yields the wage—employment combination at B.

In general, however, workers seem likely to be risk averse, in which case they will be willing to trade off some expected profit for a better chance of remaining employed in the union sector. We would therefore expect the union to set a lower wage than that at B such as, for example, at A. In the extreme case where workers are unwilling to accept any probability of displacement, the wage and the employment level will be at C as in the absence of union activity.

The above arguments assume that workers displaced from the union sector do not receive any compensation from colleagues who remain in employment at a higher wage. If full compensation were paid via redundancy payments or whatever, then workers displaced would be no worse off than those staying behind and it would then be optimal for the union to select the profit maximising position. It should be noted, however, that membership as defined above includes not only actual card-carrying members but also workers who would have been employed in the absence of union activity and for whom the union feels indirectly responsible. The latter are not in themselves in any sense an identifiable group of workers but merely a statistic that enters into union calculations. Workers who cannot be individually identified cannot by definition be compensated, thus an assumption of full compensation would seem to be unjustified in the present context and we will continue to assume that no compensation takes place.

So far we have assumed that all workers displaced from the union sector find employment at W_0. Obviously this is an oversimplification in that at any given point in time, some proportion of those displaced are likely to be unemployed. To get some insights into the effects of this, let us suppose that there is a probability, z, of individuals who are not employed in the union sector having a job in the non-union sector. If the particular union sector that we are looking at is small relative to the economy as a whole, then it is reasonable to suppose that z is negatively related to the unemployment rate and that unemployed workers are paid a state benefit, B, which is less than W_0. The expected utility function for a given worker is now

$$\frac{N}{M} U(W) + \left(1 - \frac{N}{M}\right) [(1 - z)U(W_0) + zU(B)]$$

The corresponding function for the union as a whole is once again obtained by multiplying through by M and can be written after suitable rearrangement as

$$N[U(W) - (1 - z)U(W_0) - zU(B)] + M[(1 - z)U(W_0) + zU(B)] \quad (6.7)$$

Maximising this expression subject to $N = N(W)$ yields a new first-order condition

$$\frac{NU_W}{U(W) - (1 - z)U(W_0) - zU(B)} = -\frac{dN}{dW} \quad (6.8)$$

The numerator and the denominator of the left-hand side of this expression can be interpreted as before: the numerator being the marginal utility to the union of a unit increase in the wage rate, and the denominator being the marginal utility associated with a unit increase in employment. To simplify the exposition we will assume that the demand curve faced by the union is linear so that $-dN/dW$ is a positive constant. The value of this parameter will of course vary across industries and occupations.

The interesting questions now relate to what happens when the parameters of the model are changed. For example, a rise in the level of unemployment benefit, B, will initially increase the left-hand side of (6.8). To restore equality the union wage must rise and the level of employment in the union sector must fall. By similar reasoning it can easily be shown that the equilibrium union wage will be higher and the corresponding level of unionised employment lower:

(i)   the higher the non-union wage, W_0;
(ii) the higher the level of unemployment benefit, B;
(iii) the lower the unemployment rate;
(iv) the more elastic the demand curve (Rau, 1985).

The last of these propositions is particularly interesting in that it is closely related to Milton Friedman's[5] famous contention that craft unions would be more successful in pushing wages above market levels than would industrial unions. The rationale for this was that, as the share of a particular occupation in an industry's costs is almost always less than that of labour costs as a whole, then the demand curve will, *ceteris paribus*, be more elastic for the former than for the latter. The generality of this argument depends, however, upon the other determinants[6] of the wage elasticities of demand for the two groups.

The other question that one may ask is what happens when the demand for union labour increases. To see the answer to this, let us imagine that the demand curve in Figure 6.1 shifted outwards in a parallel fashion so that the vertical intercept doubled in size. Effectively what we would now have is a twice blown-up version of the original diagram, except of course that the non-union wage, W_0, would be the same as before. It is easy therefore to see that both M and N would double in size while the union wage would be unchanged. In this model, the absolute size of the sector is irrelevant unless we were to bring in other considerations such as whether or not there are economies or diseconomies of scale in union organisation.

The last point to be considered is that labour displacement could of itself lead to a fall in the non-union wage, W_0. So far we have been implicitly assuming that each unionised sector was small relative to a general non-union sector in which all workers were paid the same wage. In a macroeconomic setting this is clearly unrealistic and we have to take into account the depressing impact of unions upon non-union wages when assessing the overall effect of unions on wage differentials. However, the problem remains even in a microeconomic context. Consider a union which controls the supply of workers of a given skill to a particular industry or group of industries, but not to the rest of the economy. Now it is reasonable to assume that the demand for workers with this particular skill will be less than perfectly elastic in the non-union sector. We would also expect that a low wage elasticity of demand for a particular skill group in the union sector would be associated with a relatively low value for the same elasticity in the non-union sector. It is therefore possible that there may be no simple relationship between the steepness of the demand curve faced by a union and the union-induced wage differential, as a steep demand curve in the union sector would be associated with a relatively steep demand curve in the non-union sector.[7] Thus although the union would find it easy to obtain a higher wage in the union sector by sacrificing workers, it would also find that wages would be severely depressed amongst those displaced as a result of its actions. The relationship between demand conditions and the union/non-union wage differential is therefore more complicated than originally supposed.[8]

One last feature of the material discussed in this section is that it attributes a very passive role to employers or employers' federations. This is because the union acts as a single utility maximiser so that the employer cannot exert monopsony power by taking advantage of differences in worker supply prices. The wage is never therefore below the marginal revenue product.

6.5 Unions and Bargaining

In the previous section we maintained the assumption that firms play no part in wage determination but simply set employment levels once wages are given. This would be consistent with a situation in which unions are monopoly suppliers to many firms. In practice, however, unions often negotiate with a single firm or with an employers' federation representing a group of firms; in both cases wages clearly arise from a bargaining process. What happens to our model under these circumstances?

As before, the union will seek to maximise its utility as, for example, given by expression (6.7). The difference in the analysis is that the firm must now be

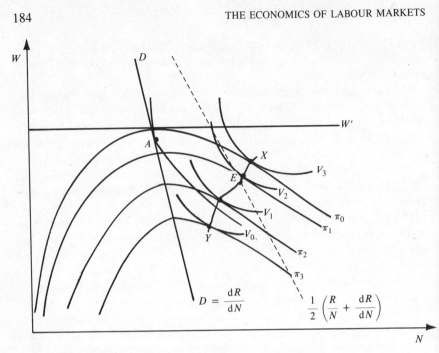

Figure 6.2 Union–Firm Bargaining

brought in as an active participant in the wage determination process. If for simplicity we leave the choice of labour inputs to one side, then a profit maximising firm can be represented as maximising

$$\pi = R(N) - WN$$

where π is profit, $R(N)$ gives total revenue as a positive function of employment and where the marginal revenue product of labour, dR/dN, is positive but diminishes as employment is increased. If profits are fixed at a constant level, e.g. π_0, then it is possible to draw a contour — the *isoprofit contour* — showing all combinations of the wage rate and employment level which yield that given level of profit. Isoprofit contours giving successively higher levels of profit, π_0, π_1, π_2 and π_3, are shown in Figure 6.2. As the firm is assumed to be interested only in profit, the isoprofit contours are the firm's equivalent of the consumer's indifference curves.

Efficient bargains can now be represented by points of tangency between the two sets of indifference curves. The justification for this is standard in microeconomic analysis: if one takes any given isoprofit contour such as π_0, then the optimal position for the union is the highest obtainable level of utility consistent with the firm remaining upon that isoprofit contour. This clearly occurs at point X. If we were to repeat this procedure for all feasible profit levels then we would end up with a contract curve such as XY showing the full set of efficient bargains.

What then determines the end-points of the contract curve? From the firm's point of view there is presumably a minimum level of profit, π_0, at which it can tell the union where to put its negotiators. This could be when the firm shuts down, where presumably $\pi_0 = 0$, or possibly where it breaks the union by bringing in scab labour and incurs the full costs of the associated industrial strife. The fall-back position for the union, V_0, presumably occurs when all its members receive their expected utility outside the union sector, so that in terms of our earlier model

$$V_0 = M[(1 - z)U(W_0) + zU(B)]$$

It is useful at this point to compare the bargaining model with our analysis in the previous section of this chapter. If the firm were a price taker in the labour market then it would seek the highest level of profit consistent with a given wage rate. Diagrammatically this means that if we draw in a horizontal line at, say, W', then the firm will operate on the geometrically lowest isoprofit contour (i.e. the highest level of profit) consistent with that wage. In Figure 6.2 this is illustrated by the point of tangency between the horizontal line, W' and the isoprofit contour π_0. This point necessarily occurs at the peak of the contour and the locus of all such points, defined for different wage rates, is the demand curve for labour, DD. As in Figure 6.1, point A is the utility maximising position for the union given that firms will operate along DD. Although there is no a priori way in which one can predict whether the bargaining model will lead to higher wages than the price taking model, we can see from Figure 6.2 that equilibrium in the bargaining model implies that the level of employment at the agreed wage will be higher than one would observe given the same wage in the price taking model. This last observation follows from the fact that all feasible efficient bargains as given along XY, lie to the right of DD.

So far, we have no single equilibrium position for the bargaining model but only a locus of points along which the solution must lie. To go further we require an explicit bargaining theory. The best known of the latter is the Nash Cooperative Solution[9] which deals with a non-constant (i.e. the cake to be divided is not of a fixed size) sum game in which the players can form coalitions and then divide the coalition pay-offs between themselves. Players make binding agreements regarding the strategies to be employed, subject to a situation in which failure to reach such agreements would lead to each player receiving a fixed payment known as the threat pay-off. The latter in our case are the fall-back levels V_0 and π_0 for the union and firm respectively. Using a number of axioms, Nash proved that the solution to this game is provided by the maximisation of the product of the differences between the individual pay-offs and their corresponding fall-back levels. In other words we should maximise

$$(V - V_0)(\pi - \pi_0)$$

or more explicitly

$$N\left\{\left[U(W) - \frac{V_0}{M}\right] [R(N) - WN - \pi_0]\right\}$$

The first-order condition with respect to the wage turns out to be simply the equation of the contract curve. This is hardly surprising as Nash used Pareto optimality as one of his axioms and so we know that equilibrium must occur at an efficient bargain. The first-order condition with respect to employment is that

$$W = \frac{1}{2}\left[\frac{R(N)}{N} + \frac{dR}{dN} - \frac{\pi_0}{N}\right] \qquad (6.9)$$

If for simplicity we set $\pi_0 = 0$, then we have the result that the wage should be equal to the arithmetic average of the marginal and average products of labour. This is illustrated in Figure 6.2. If $\pi_0 = 0$, then the isoprofit contour is identically the same as the average revenue schedule, R/N. The first-order condition above is shown by the dotted line and the point at which the latter intersects the contract curve (point E) represents the Nash solution.

What then are the predictions of this model? It is convenient to distinguish between labour market and product market disturbances while recognising that the two are likely to be empirically related. Labour market effects are essentially changes associated with the job alternatives of union members, i.e. the non-union wage, the unemployment rate, and the level of unemployment benefit. If non-union alternatives improve, then the indifference curve map of the union shifts in a roughly north-western direction thus leading to a corresponding movement in the contract curve. The other equilibrium condition is, however, unchanged and we can therefore predict unambiguously that an improvement in labour market conditions alone (e.g. a rise in unemployment benefit) will lead to higher wages and lower employment.

Product market effects are more difficult to sort out. If the firm faces an increased demand for its product, then the demand curve, the average revenue curve and the corresponding wage condition will all shift outwards. Meanwhile the isoprofit contour map will shift to the right thus leading to a southwesterly movement in the contract curve. An improvement in product market conditions thus leads unambiguously to a rise in employment but does not give any clear predictions regarding the direction of change of the wage rate.

Over the trade cycle as a whole one would of course expect to observe simultaneous changes in both labour market and product market conditions. The fact that in practice employment moves procyclically would seem to indicate that in this respect we must interpret our model in terms of product market effects dominating labour market effects. What is interesting, however, is that the model could easily predict wage stickiness over the cycle given the ambiguity of the effect of product market changes in this respect. As we will see in a later chapter, this is particularly relevant to the study of unemployment.

6.6 Unions and Efficiency

It is fair to say that traditionally economists have disliked trade unions. This dislike arose from a belief that unions imposed economic losses of two different kinds. These are

(i) *losses in allocative efficiency* arising from the fact that unions push wages and hence marginal products in the unionised sector above those in the rest of the economy;

(ii) *losses in productivity* arising from restrictive practices, feather-bedding, etc.

The first type of loss is best illustrated by a simple numerical example. Suppose that there are two sectors in the economy and that the marginal value product of labour is the same in both. A union now forms and pushes up the wage in one of the two sectors (the union sector) by 30 per cent. What is the overall economic loss expressed as a percentage of GNP? If we assume that the wage elasticity of demand for labour in the union sector is –0.3, that output changes are roughly 0.7 times those of employment and that the union sector accounts initially for one-half of GNP, then it follows that output in the union sector would fall as a percentage of GNP by $(30 \times 0.3 \times 0.7 \times 0.5) = 3.1$ per cent. The overall economic loss is, however, likely to be much smaller than this as some of those workers displaced from the union sector will be re-employed elsewhere in the economy. In fact, if full employment were re-established, then the only net loss arises from the fact that the marginal value product of labour in the non-union sector is now less than that in the union sector. If we assume for simplicity that the labour demand curves in the two sectors have the same slope, then this net loss can be computed as the induced initial union/non-union difference in marginal value products multiplied by the number of workers displaced expressed as a percentage of GNP. In our hypothetical example this loss turns out to be 30 per cent of that given above, or roughly 1 per cent of GNP. The point to be emphasised here is that allocative efficiency losses arising from union activities are likely to be relatively small. Two studies by Rees (1963) and Johnson and Mieszkowski (1970) found that in the USA there was an efficiency loss of around 0.15 per cent. Their results indicate a lower proportionate loss than the 1 per cent suggested above because they assume a smaller union wage effect (15 per cent as opposed to 30 per cent) and the union sector is smaller in the USA than is assumed above (20 per cent as opposed to 50 per cent). More recently DeFina (1983) has re-estimated the efficiency loss using a fuller general equilibrium model of the US economy and has found even lower proportionate losses than those previously calculated.

The second type of loss has attracted far more interest. Until fairly recently it was always assumed that unions reduced technical efficiency by imposing various forms of restrictive practices upon the production methods of firms. When this view is examined more closely, it becomes apparent that it was based heavily upon rather casual observation while hard empirical evidence was strangely lacking. Rees, for example, guessed that in the USA the losses from feather-bedding were at least as large as those stemming from union/non-union wage differentials. He appears, however, to have had no really solid empirical basis for his guesswork other than his years of distinguished experience as a labour economist. More recently the views of many labour economists have changed.

The central point of departure from the traditional approach stems from a recognition of the possibility that unions might act as a vehicle for the transmission of information between the shop floor and management. If, in the absence of such an information channel, workers are fed up with their present working conditions, then their only feasible option is to quit. Now although the quit rate does in itself convey some information to employers, it is nevertheless a rather unreliable and unsatisfactory indicator of shop-floor conditions. One problem is that from the employer's point of view there is a large random element in quit behaviour so that large samples of workers are required to detect a given change in the quit rate. Even if the employer can detect such a change, then there remains the problem of deciding whether the cause lies within his own establishment or in the outside labour market. It is also likely that quitters are a non-random sample of the workforce and may not be representative of general worker opinion. If 'exit' does not give the employer a good information channel then it is arguable that 'voice' does. The function of the union according to the 'exit–voice' approach is to give workers a collective voice, which in turn acts as an information channel between workers and management. If there were no union, workers would either be frightened of retaliation on the part of the employer if they expressed discontent or would simply find themselves ignored by the employer if they tried as individuals to bargain over establishment-wide matters. Thus, although an employer is unlikely to take much notice of a single employee who complained about the heating in his office or factory, it is in his interest to listen to the collective view as expressed by a trade union.

What then are the predictions of the exit–voice approach? The first and most obvious is that by substituting 'voice' for 'exit', unionisation reduces the quit rate. The second is that unions might actually improve the internal efficiency of firms by improving managerial information about the production process. The empirical evidence regarding these predictions is reviewed in the rest of this section.

The obvious way in which to try and find out whether the propensity to exit is affected by unions is to test whether joining a union or working in a unionised firm reduces the exit probability of a given individual. Let us first write down an equation such as

$$Q_{it} = Q(W_{it}, Z_{it}, O_{it}, T_{it}, M_{it}) \tag{6.10}$$

where Q_{it} is some measure of the propensity to exit of individual i during a given
 period t

W_{it} is his or her current wage

Z_{it} is a set of relevant individual characteristics such as age and education

T_{it} is time spent in the current job

O_{it} is a set of outside market variables relating to the individual at t, such
 as his expected wage and the relevant unemployment rate

M_{it} is a dichotomous variable usually referred to as a dummy variable
 (yes $= 1$, no $= 0$) denoting whether or not the individual is a trade
 union member

The exit–voice approach would predict that after standardising for everything
else, we should find a negative relationship between Q_{it} and M_{it}.

The overall effect of unions on quit rates is of course likely to be greater than
as implied by the direct impact of M_{it} upon Q_{it} in equation (6.10). It is reasonable
to suppose, and has indeed been consistently supported in a number of empirical
studies, that exit propensities are negatively related to wage rates. If one believes
that one of the effects of trade unions is to raise wage rates, then we have a
mechanism by which unions can lower exit propensities independently of exit–
voice considerations. In other words not only can joining a union lower Q_{it}
directly via M_{it}, but it can also lower Q_{it} indirectly by raising W_{it}. An evaluation of the overall effects of unions upon Q_{it} and the consequences in terms of
reducing firms' training and recruitment costs would thus require us to explore
both mechanisms. To do this we would require a further equation in which wage
rates were in turn related to relevant individual characteristics and M_{it}. However,
as the empirical determinants of earnings provide the discussion of a later chapter,
we will for the moment concentrate only upon empirical investigations of equations such as (6.10) above.

Many studies have been hampered by the fact that good labour turnover data
are available only as industry aggregates. This usually has led to some aggregate
form of (6.10) being applied to a single cross-section of industries. In most of
these studies the industry-wide quit rate is related to: the average wage rate; various
aggregates of workforce characteristics such as average years of education; the
proportions of professional workers, females and blacks amongst those employed;
regional variables; and various characteristics of the industries themselves such
as the concentration ratio, average firm size and, most importantly from our point
of view, union membership as a proportion of the workforce. Virtually all of
the studies which include the latter variable find a negative relationship between
union density and the quit rate.[10] Although these results are clearly consistent
with the exit–voice literature, the very aggregative nature of the data, and in
particular the danger of confusing union with industry specific effects, has meant
that the search for further evidence has continued more at the micro-level.

Freeman (1980) has examined the impact of union membership upon exit propensity with the aid of a number of different data sets giving information on the behaviour of *individuals* as opposed to 'average' behaviour across firms or industries. His basic estimating equation was a linear form of (6.10) with different alternative measures of exit propensity as the dependent variable, such as current job tenure and dummy variables denoting whether or not the individual had left his job during the period. If a dummy is used as a dependent variable, then least squares techniques are inappropriate and different techniques should be used such as *logit* analysis.[11] Apart from this technical difference, Freeman's analysis is more extensive than earlier studies in that he used three different relevant data sets. His results are on the whole remarkably consistent in showing that exit propensities are negatively related to union status.

It is always possible to argue, however, that no matter how carefully the researcher standardises for the effect of individual characteristics, many of the latter are unobservable and could therefore be reflected in the union variable. Thus if, for example, temperamentally unadventurous individuals are disproportionately likely to join unions, then we would observe lower quit rates amongst unionised workers even if the process of unionisation itself had no influence upon exit behaviour. In another paper Freeman (1978) avoided this problem by examining whether *changes* in the quit behaviour of an individual over time are negatively related to *changes* in union status. His conclusion was again strongly in support of the exit—voice hypothesis.

These various studies of exit behaviour seem to tell us that, in the USA at least, unions can offset some of their members' wage costs by reducing hiring and training costs. But do unions have any direct effects upon the efficiency of production establishments? Conventional wisdom tells us that unions, if anything, reduce the allocative efficiency of firms by introducing various restrictive practices which can potentially both knock the producer off his production frontier, i.e. reduce *technical* efficiency, and then further damage his ability to cost minimise with an appropriate factor mix, i.e. reduce *price* efficiency. This view seems very plausible in the UK, given the essentially defensive nature of the British industrial relations system, but the American evidence seems to indicate the opposite. Brown and Medoff (1978) fitted a suitably extended Cobb—Douglas production function to a cross-section of industries by US states and found that labour productivity seems to be positively related to the degree of unionisation. Clark (1980) and Allen (1984) have similarly analysed the US cement and construction industries respectively and likewise found evidence of positive union productivity effects. In contrast the only UK based study, Pencavel (1977), found that productivity in the British coal industry fell as the industry became more unionised.

In spite of these studies a consensus about union productivity effects is far from near. There is no reason to believe, for example, that because US unions seem to have a productivity-raising effect, then the same conclusion should apply elsewhere. The US studies themselves are certainly not above criticism given that the causation might very well work the other way round if unions find it easier to organise the more efficient plants. If true, this would in turn lend an upward bias to the union productivity effect as measured in these studies. Nor can such studies ever tell us the full story so long as they concentrate upon the production function as opposed to the cost function. It is perfectly possible, for example, that unions can raise productivity and reduce turnover costs and yet at the same time raise overall unit costs by impeding the choice of the lowest cost factor mix. This last possibility awaits further study.

6.7   Summary

In this chapter, we have looked at some aspects of union structure and strength; at some formal representations of the determinants of union growth; at an outline of two models of wage determination in the presence of a trade union; and at some views on the relationship between union activities and economic efficiency.

Of these areas, wage determination is probably the one being given the most attention in current research. For example Carruth and Oswald (1985) have applied the model developed in Section 6.4 in which the union maximises utility, given the employers' demand curve, to the case of miners' wages in post-war Britain, while MaCurdy and Pencavel (1986) have compared the empirical performance of this type of model with that of a bargaining model in the context of the American newspaper industry and found that the bargaining approach seems to perform better. Clearly empirical work in this area will continue.

Research on the efficiency effects of unions is likely to be hampered by an absence of suitable data. One suspects here, however, that rather different results would be obtained if comparable studies were carried out in different countries given differences in union objectives and in the industrial relations framework.

Notes

1. A closed shop is an establishment within which union membership is a necessary qualification for employment.
2. For an interesting study of the determinants of strike incidence by industry, see Shorey (1976).
3. See Neumann and Rissman (1984).
4. In particular, the terms in E and U presumably capture a number of different business cycle effects. For a discussion of various criticisms of the Ashenfelter and Pencavel model, and for an empirical investigation of alternative specifications, see Bain and Elsheikh (1976).
5. See Friedman (1951).
6. For a full discussion see Ulman (1955).
7. A model with this property is explored in Lazear (1983).
8. For further discussion of these issues, see Oswald (1982) and Rau (1985).
9. This was introduced in Nash (1950). The Nash solution (not to be confused with the concept of Nash equilibrium as used extensively in game theory) is formally identi-

cal to that provided by the Zeuthen bargaining model (Zeuthen, 1930). This latter approach is somewhat cumbersome in approach but gives a better descriptive feel for the bargaining process. For an exposition of the latter, see Addison and Siebert (1979). For further discussion of the present model and some alternatives, see McDonald and Solow (1981). Finally, for some discussion of a Nash-type bargaining model, in which bargaining occurs with respect to the wage rate only, see Nickell and Andrews (1983).

10. For a survey of many of these studies, see Parsons (1977). See also the study by Kahn (1977).

11. For a reasonably straightforward account of how logit and related techniques such as probit and tobit analysis work, see Maddala (1977, pp. 162–164).

7

The Theory of Unemployment

7.1 Introduction — Equilibrium and Disequilibrium Unemployment

Is unemployment an equilibrium or disequilibrium phenomenon? This question needs to be answered before we can usefully theorise about the causes of unemployment or hope to devise sensible policies to alleviate it. Note that even if actual unemployment corresponded to some notion of equilibrium it does not follow that it might not be desirable to do something to alleviate it; there may be an alternative equilibrium with lower unemployment that is generally preferred. It is for this reason that we prefer the equilibrium/disequilibrium distinction to that between voluntary and involuntary unemployment, although we sometimes use the latter. Where we do, it should be remembered that even those who are voluntarily unemployed may be better off if policies could be devised to put them to work; they may be voluntarily unemployed only because of the limited alternatives.

The distinction is illustrated in Figure 7.1. The diagram abstracts from the heterogeneity of labour, and the multiplicity of labour markets, to examine employment and unemployment of 'labour' in 'the' labour market. At the equilibrium real wage w_e, N_eN_1 persons are unemployed; they are seeking a first job, changing jobs, etc.[1] This is sometimes known as 'frictional' unemployment,[2] while in macroeconomics N_eN_1/ON_1 is sometimes called the 'natural' rate of unemployment — that rate of unemployment that exists even when the labour market clears. At the real wage w_1, on the other hand, equilibrium unemployment is reduced to N_3N_4 (note that as we have drawn the diagram the reduction in equilibrium unemployment is partially offset by the increase in labour force participation N_1N_4 induced by the higher wage). But we now have, in addition to equilibrium unemployment, disequilibrium unemployment N_2N_3 (excess supply of labour).[3] In practice it is not easy to tell the two types of unemployment apart. Official statistics do not distinguish equilibrium from disequilibrium unemployment. Indeed the question as to whether current unemployment is primarily of the equilibrium

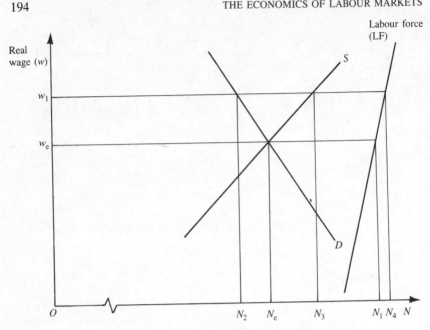

Figure 7.1 Equilibrium and Disequilibrium Unemployment

or disequilibrium variety is a source of empirical and, in some cases, ideological controversy.

The major task of this chapter is to provide some theoretical explanations of the failure of real wages to fall sufficiently to clear the market. At w_1 there appear to be unexploited opportunities for mutually advantageous trade. (The question is clearly irrelevant at w_e; to explain equilibrium unemployment we need to explain job turnover, average duration of job search, etc). Equally the equilibrium/disequilibrium distinction is crucial in devising appropriate policy. Policies aimed at reducing real wages (paid by employers, not necessarily those received by employees) will reduce or eliminate disequilibrium unemployment (increasing equilibrium unemployment) while real wage reductions starting from the market clearing wage only produce excess labour demand. Conversely policies aimed at reducing time spent between jobs, searching for a first job, etc. are largely inappropriate where unemployment is a disequilibrium caused by the persistence of real wages above their market clearing level.

As the distinction between equilibrium and disequilibrium is not directly observable we must rely on indirect evidence. This suggests strongly that observed unemployment is not primarily a friction associated with market clearing.[4]

Some of the theory discussed in the remainder of this chapter does in fact pertain to equilibrium unemployment (e.g. search theory). We also examine some possible explanations of wage stickiness in the face of mass unemployment. In some of these explanations the relative fixity of the wage is voluntarily agreed by both parties so that the resulting employment fluctuations are in a sense voluntary also (contract theory, bargaining theory). Nevertheless at such wage rates, excess supply of labour exists, so that we see such theories as contributing to an explanation of disequilibrium, or involuntary, unemployment. The equilibrium is involuntary in the sense that there are some individuals who cannot get jobs at the wages being paid to their employed counterparts with similar abilities and qualifications. While they could perhaps secure low-paid jobs (this is the sense in which their unemployment is voluntary) they may choose not to due to the loss of status involved, because they expect to return to or enter high-paid employment in the near future and are unwilling to incur the fixed costs of changing jobs, or because they fear that low-wage employment will signify low productivity to prospective employers in the future. The labour market is *segmented* and workers qualified for high-paid primary sector jobs are unwilling to become 'tainted' by secondary sector employment.

In the following discussion of the various classes of model which have recently been used to explain the growth and persistence of unemployment, we limit ourselves, where possible, to models of the labour market. We do not attempt a full macroeconomic treatment of unemployment which would require linking the labour market to the goods market, and in some models to the money market as well (such treatments are now found in most standard macroeconomic textbooks, e.g. Dornbusch and Fischer (1987)). Thus we do not broach such important topics as whether excess supply in the labour market is associated with rigidities in the goods market (Keynesian unemployment) or whether it is only a labour market rigidity (classical unemployment). Such issues are important, not least for the different policy prescriptions they imply (broadly speaking, while Keynesian unemployment requires expansion of aggregate demand, classical unemployment requires only a lower real wage), but they take us too far from our main focus, the labour market.

7.2 Job Search Theory

The first of the 'new'[5] labour market theories we examine is that of job search. If we explicitly allow both jobs and workers to be heterogeneous, then information about job and worker characteristics becomes valuable. Where such information is not fully and freely available, time spent acquiring it, although costly, can be productive — job searchers may for a time deliberately refrain from working because they can usually do better, in terms of maximising expected lifetime earnings, than simply accepting the first job offer that comes along. Similarly, when workers are not identically productive, search activities by employers which yield information on productivity can increase expected profits. We shall see that search models have implications which contribute to our understanding of unemployment although they do not, on their own, constitute a complete explanation of observed unemployment.

A Basic Job Search Model

We begin with an exposition of a basic job search model. Labour market information available to workers looking for jobs is incomplete. They do not know exactly where the best wage offers are to be found.[6] What they are assumed to know in this model is the *distribution* of wage offers in the market. Because we wish to concentrate on workers' search activities, and the contribution of search models to unemployment, we rule out on-the-job search, assuming in effect that search is most efficiently conducted as a full-time activity. We assume also that while workers search for jobs, employers do not need to search — an adequate supply of homogeneous workers of known productivity is available to the firm. Further simplifying assumptions are as follows.

1. Individuals maximise expected lifetime income, $E(y)$.
2. A job offer is an independent drawing from the known distribution of offers. We call a given offer w. This is to be interpreted as the value, at the time the job commences, of the wage and non-wage characteristics of the job. (Strictly speaking w refers to the lifetime value of the offer, but as we abstract from on-the-job training and other sources of wage growth, and as jobs last forever, we can think of the per-period and the lifetime value of the job offer interchangeably.) The terms of the offer hold indefinitely. The known probability distribution of such offers is $\phi(w)$.
3. A job commences at the beginning of the period after the offer is received.
4. Search activity generates one offer per period and simultaneously incurs a direct cost C.
5. While searching, unemployment benefit UB per period is received.
6. The searcher has an infinite time horizon, no intrinsic time preference,[7] and does not attach any utility to the 'leisure' aspect, if any, of job search. A job, once accepted, is expected to last indefinitely.

Clearly, these are rather restrictive assumptions, required to keep the model relatively simple. Much of the now extensive job search literature is concerned with examining the implications of relaxing one or more of these assumptions. For our purposes, however, such refinements are unnecessary.

In terms of notation we define w_R as the reservation wage (or acceptance wage) D^* as the expected duration of search required to receive a wage offer of w_R or above.

With the above assumptions the search model is solved by having the individual choose a reservation wage and accepting any offer at or above this level while rejecting offers below it.[8] w_R is chosen to maximise $E(y)$. This requires that it be set at a level which makes the expected gain from further search just equal to the expected cost.

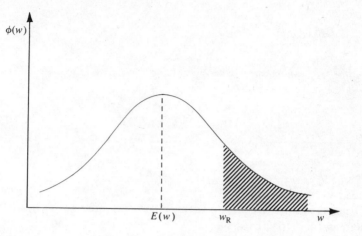

Figure 7.2 The Probability Distribution of Wage Offers

Call p the probability of receiving an offer $\geq w_R$. Then

$$p = \int_{w_R}^{\infty} \phi(w)dw \qquad (7.1)$$

which is shown as the shaded area in Figure 7.2 (the total area under the curve is equal to unity).

D^*, the expected search duration until an acceptable offer is received is given by[9]

$$D^* = \frac{1}{p} = \frac{1}{\displaystyle\int_{w_R}^{\infty} \phi(w)dw} \qquad (7.2)$$

The expected costs of continued search are given by[10]

$$\frac{C - UB}{p} = (C - UB)D^*$$

The expected benefits of continued search, given w_R, are

$$\frac{\displaystyle\int_{w_R}^{\infty} \phi(w)w\ dw}{\displaystyle\int_{w_R}^{\infty} \phi(w)\ dw} = E(w\,|\,w \geq w_R) \qquad (7.3)$$

which, by equation (7.1) is equal to

$$\int_{w_R}^{\infty} \phi(w)w \; dw \; D^*$$

Thus the reservation wage is set by solving for w_R in

$$w_R = \int_{w_R}^{\infty} \phi(w)w \; dw \; D^* - (C - UB)D^* \qquad (7.4)$$

| $E(y)$ if w_R accepted and search ends | = | $E(y)$ if search continued | − EPV of net direct costs of continued search |

In other words (7.4) simply tells us that w_R is chosen so as to equate the costs and benefits of continued search, having received an offer w_R. The costs are the opportunity costs (left-hand side of (7.4)) of forgoing w_R, while the right-hand side gives the expected net benefit of continued search.

A little rearrangement and substitution will enable us to provide a convenient diagrammatic illustration of the model. Thus

$$(C - UB) = \int_{w_R}^{\infty} \phi(w)w \; dw - pw_R \qquad (7.4')$$

Using (7.1) to substitute out p

$$(C - UB) = \int_{w_R}^{\infty} (w - w_R)\phi(w)dw \qquad (7.5)$$

or, for notational convenience

$$(C - UB) = A(w_R) \qquad (7.5')$$

Equation (7.5) has a straightforward interpretation: $(C - UB)$ is the marginal cost of searching an extra period (of generating another job offer) while the right-hand side is the expected marginal return. The reservation wage w_R is chosen so as to equate the costs and benefits of search at the margin.[11] $A(w_R)$ is strictly decreasing in w_R. We can thus show the determination of w_R diagrammatically. This is done in Figure 7.3. The figure enables us to do simple comparative statistics. For example:

1. An increase in UB (from UB to UB′) increases w_R, as shown in the figure, and, ceteris paribus, increases search duration. Unemployment insurance decreases the net cost of search and thus increases the optimal search duration.

   Not only does unemployment insurance increase the duration of search unemployment, but if such insurance (or other welfare benefits) is available on an indefinite basis there will be a critical level of UB which will make search unprofitable — the individual maximises expected lifetime income by living on benefits. Thus in Figure 7.3 with costs $(C - UB)$, if living

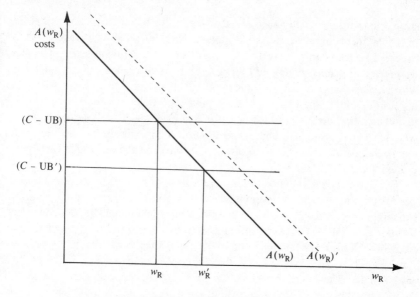

Figure 7.3 The Determination of the Reservation Wage

on benefits provides a level of income greater than w_R, not searching at
all becomes the individual's best strategy.

2. If the mean value of the searcher's wage distribution increases (due to training for example) while the dispersion relative to the mean remains unchanged
then, *ceteris paribus*, the net return function $A(w_R)$ will shift upwards
(shown by the dotted line in the diagram), increasing the reservation wage
and the duration of job search. An increase in dispersion will mean that
high wage offers are now encountered more frequently. So are low offers
but as these are rejected anyway, the expected returns to search increase
(the $A(w_R)$ schedule again shifts outwards) and so, therefore, does the
reservation wage. Should searchers be risk averse (i.e. if they dislike wage
variability) then this may partially offset the effect of a higher expected
wage gain from continued search, and the effect on w_R depends on which
effect, the increase in the conditional expected wage offer or the increase
in wage variability, dominates. This in turn, of course, depends for any
given increase in wage variability on how risk averse the searcher is.

3. Had our model incorporated explicit discounting, we would have seen that
an increase in r, the searcher's discount rate, would have reduced w_R and
hence search duration — the present value of the net future benefits of
additional search have been reduced.

While the model we have examined is a bare-bones version, it can be quite
readily adapted and extended to deal with a number of complications which make
it more realistic. For example, our assumption that jobs last forever (or searchers have an infinite time horizon) is clearly unrealistic, but it is a relatively

straightforward matter to attach to each wage offer sampled an expected period of employment (expected by the searcher). Now for any given wage offer the expected return is an increasing function of expected job tenure. Equivalently, for given marginal cost there will (in general) be some critical value of job tenure which makes marginal benefit equal to marginal cost for a given wage offer. One implication of this analysis is that one would expect older workers to search less than the young, *ceteris paribus*, because they have fewer working years during which to reap the benefit of high-wage jobs (the young may also have lower search costs). The parallel with the concentration of education and training in early years is obvious.

Our simple model assumed that search was such as to generate one job offer per period. This unrealistic assumption can be relaxed by allowing offers to arrive randomly (in which case the mean duration of unemployment will depend on the average time interval between offers as well as the probability of a wage offer exceeding the reservation wage) or, more interestingly, by allowing search *intensity* to be a choice variable for the searcher. Optimal search intensity, like w_R, will be determined by equating costs and benefits at the margin. An interesting implication of this version of the model is that search behaviour can be rational even in the absence of wage variability. If vacancies are scarce, then it is vacancies, not expected wage gains, that are sought, and unemployment duration will depend on search intensity, net search costs, etc.

The assumptions of the simple search model outlined above ensured that the reservation wage, once chosen, remained unchanged during search. In fact both theoretical models and empirical research (for example Kiefer and Neumann, 1977) suggest this is unlikely and that the reservation wage is likely to fall in the course of search. A number of factors make this a probable outcome. For example if search is non-random, the firms which are expected to make higher offers will be approached first; if they have no vacancies (or do not hire the searcher) the expected value of the remaining offers is now lower. This will lower the reservation wage. Another possibility is that the costs of search rise as search continues; less accessible firms have to be searched, savings run out and higher priced funds must be used to sustain search unemployment, the individual's marginal utility of leisure falls, etc. These are just some reasons why costs may increase. Figure 7.3 shows that an increase in C would lower the reservation wage. In our basic model, C is exogenous and does not alter during search. If it does, however, then w_R will vary from period to period during search. We have argued that it will fall. Finally a finite working life provides another reason why w_R is likely to fall as search is prolonged; there is less time to reap the benefits. In the extreme case, if a searcher has only one remaining period of working life, any wage offer will be accepted as long as it exceeds the benefit level.

Similarly, if we drop the assumption that the searcher knows the parameters of the wage distribution from the outset then the searcher's subjective estimate of the distribution is formed and revised during search itself. In this case, however, we cannot say that the reservation will fall during search unless we know that the searcher's initial subjective estimate of the wage offer distribution was over-optimistic. [12] Formal analysis of adaptive search is perhaps the least straightforward of the possible extensions of the basic model (Rothschild, 1974).

Before proceeding to examine the usefulness of the job search model as an explanation of unemployment, it should be noted that the assumption that there exists, for any searcher, or homogeneous category of searchers, a distribution of wage offers is far from being innocuous. Why should this be the case? Why is the 'law of one price' violated? That is, why is it that the combined effects of learning during search and subsequent competition do not eliminate any differences in the wages being offered to identical labour for identical work? (If this happened, of course, the fundamental rationale for job search is removed, although, as argued above, searchers may still vary search intensity in their pursuit of a job vacancy; in such a case, however, we would have to explain why some firms have vacancies while others do not.) If we wish to persist with the assumption of homogeneous workers and jobs we can appeal to the possibility of firm-specific stochastic product demand shocks to explain wage variability. However, for reasons which we examine more closely below, when we discuss contract theory and efficiency wages, it is unlikely that firms will readily change wages in response to temporary firm-specific demand variations (although wages may respond to *aggregate* shocks). That being the case the wage distribution may be the result of search strategy by firms when job matching is important, [13] i.e. where the productivity of workers is not intrinsic but depends on which firms they are employed in. Firm-specific variations in labour productivity can arise for a number of reasons — the quantity and quality of co-operating capital, the firm's recruitment and training policies, etc. Additionally, if due to different characteristics or tastes job seekers set different reservation wages then, as we argued in Chapter 3, firms will have monopsony power over the flow of applicants; by raising the wage offer they can increase the proportion of job seekers accepting their offers. Combining monopsony power and interfirm productivity differences can produce a wage distribution rather than a single market wage as Figure 7.4 shows.

Job Search and Unemployment

Consider job search as an explanation of voluntary frictional unemployment. Certainly our basic model provides a theoretical justification for delaying entry or re-entry into employment, thereby prolonging unemployment duration (relative to what it would be in a market where job seekers had full information on the location of vacancies and associated wage offers). It is sometimes objected that in a period of mass unemployment it is unrealistic to imagine unemployed job seekers balancing the costs and benefits of accepting job offers — vacancies are, it is argued, so scarce that they will be immediately accepted once located.

This argument can be countered on analytic grounds by pointing out that the

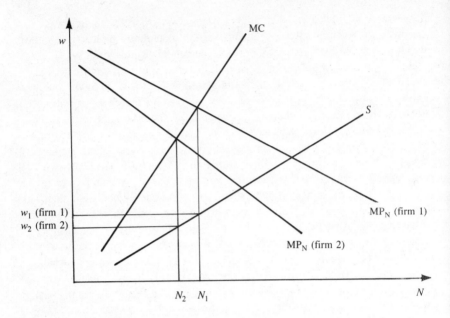

Figure 7.4 Monopsony and Interfirm Productivity Differences Generate Differences in Wages Across Firms

basic theory makes no claims about the frequency with which job offers arrive in practice and that the average time interval between offers can be included as a parameter in the job search framework (a reduction in the frequency of offers will lower the reservation wage while its effect on unemployment duration depends on whether this reduction in w_R is sufficient to offset the reduced frequency of offers). However, as we have seen, w_R is bounded from below by the level of benefits (and also in practice by the value of leisure). When the reservation wage is at this lower bound, unemployment duration depends *only* on the frequency of job offers because *any* offer will be accepted if we assume that the wage distribution is not supported below this minimum. Searchers are not holding out for higher wages — all market wages exceed the reservation wage. Under these circumstances unemployment can be said to be involuntary. Thus the search framework is not necessarily incompatible with involuntary unemployment (Hahn, 1987).

The claim that the job search model is a poor description of the behaviour of unemployed workers is also contestable on empirical grounds. Unemployed job seekers do turn down offers. For the US, Hamermesh and Rees (1984) report on a BLS survey showing that in 1976, when unemployment was high (between 7 per cent and 8 per cent of the labour force), the median number of contacts made per month by men who had been unemployed for at least a month was six. The median number of hours per month spent in job search by men was 20, although 16 per cent spent over 75 hours in job search. So at least at this very basic level the facts do not reject job search theory.

Before accepting job search as a determinant of unemployment duration we might ask ourselves why searchers have to be unemployed. Who do they not just accept the first job and then search on the job, quitting when they get an offer yielding a higher present value of lifetime earnings than the current job? Should the current wage be less than unemployment benefit the worker should then quit to search, setting a reservation wage to satisfy equation (7.4). In the first of these cases there should be no off-the-job search, so search theory could not explain frictional unemployment. That the second case is not of widespread relevance is shown by the fact that quits constitute only a small fraction of the flow into unemployment. For unemployed adult males the majority were made redundant (75 per cent in the USA in 1975);[14] only 8.7 per cent quit their last jobs. For unemployed adult females 50 per cent were made redundant, 32 per cent were re-entering the labour force and 14 per cent quit their previous job, while inflows into youth unemployment (both sexes) came from those who had never worked before (36 per cent), labour force re-entrants (30 per cent), job losers (26 per cent) and only 8.7 per cent from those quitting their previous job.

So it would seem that the main relevance of search theory to unemployment is to explain the behaviour of unemployed searchers rather than additions to unemployment due to quit behaviour. This could be explained by differential search costs, although it is by no means self-evident (although sometimes assumed) that off-the-job search is more efficient than on-the-job search. A more plausible reason for searchers looking for permanent jobs, rather than taking more or less any job and continuing to search on the job, is the existence of substantial costs involved in changing jobs (moving costs, worker financed on-the-job training, etc.). Of course, we are not arguing that all quitting is deterred by such costs; if workers are very disappointed in their jobs or perceive substantial gains to off-the-job search they *will* quit without having another job lined up. But this seems relatively unimportant quantitatively, being able at best to explain less than 10 per cent of the inflow into unemployment.

We have seen that job search theory may indeed be a partial explanation of frictional (equilibrium) unemployment. Does the theory have anything to offer by way of an explanation of cyclical unemployment as well? The job search view of the business cycle answers this question in the affirmative, but it requires relaxation of the fundamental assumption that workers are perfectly informed about the distribution of wage offers while not knowing where particular offers are located. Suppose that when the demand for firms' output falls, wages are fully flexible and fall to the level consistent with profit maximisation in the new demand climate. Searchers will start getting lower offers but, taking the extreme case, suppose this is simply regarded as bad luck and searchers still believe the previous distribution of wage offers prevails. The implications can be easily understood with the help of Figure 7.5.

Because they do not realise the distribution has shifted, searchers do not lower their reservation wage to w'_R but instead continue to accept only offers equal to or in excess of w_R. Thus the probability of an offer being accepted is cross-shaded in Figure 7.5, whereas before it was diagonally shaded. Unemployment

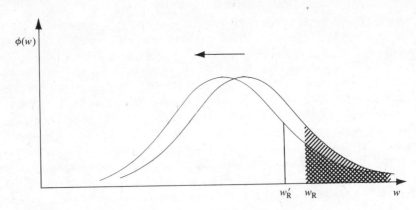

Figure 7.5 Searchers Fail to Perceive a Shift in the Wage Offer Distribution

rises due to increased job rejection. One empirical implication of this model is that vacancies should not vary procyclically — because they have reduced wages employers do not need to reduce vacancies. In fact vacancies *do* vary procyclically. The implication for observed wage rates reveals a nice paradox. Even though all firms have reduced wages, *observed* wages are still those equal to or greater than the prevailing (even if outdated) reservation wage w_R. Thus we observe wage stickiness and rising unemployment even though wages are fully flexible downwards. Searchers prevent observed wages from falling by remaining unemployed longer.

Most of the above argument follows through even if we make less extreme assumptions about searchers' misperceptions. Thus we can allow the arrival of lower wage offers to lead to some downward revision by searchers of their perception of the entire wage distribution, and hence of reservation wages, as long as the full shift of the distribution is not immediately taken into account in the setting of reservation wages. The essence of the argument is that searchers must to some extent be acting on the basis of an outdated reservation wage. Okun (1981) calls this the 'stale information' amendment (to the basic job search model) and forcefully argues for its validity:

> It is difficult to imagine how people could ever know (or even think they know) the distribution of wage offers without knowing anything about the location of particularly good offers. It strains credulity to suppose that, when some firms set higher wages, workers learn immediately just how much the distribution has shifted but get no clues whatsoever on which employers created the shift. (Okun, 1981, p. 37)

Nevertheless, although it might be perfectly reasonable to assume that today's decisions are based on yesterday's data, it is less reasonable to claim that misperceptions last for months or years. Searchers will learn from experience, and continued low (high) wage offers will eventually suggest that more than bad (good) luck is involved and that the whole distribution is shifting. The length of information lags cannot, of course, be determined by theory alone, but we can say they would have to be substantial to explain observed unemployment patterns. For the persistence of high unemployment during the recovery phase of the cycle to be explained by misperceptions about shifts in the wage distribution would require slow learning indeed. For example, at the time of writing, the UK economy has experienced approximately five years of economic growth (albeit slow growth starting from the depths of a severe depression) and yet unemployment has remained virtually unchanged. If initial increases in unemployment were indeed due to misperceptions about shifts in the wage distribution, it has taken an extraordinarily long time for such misperceptions to be modified. Okun makes the same point about the US labour market in 1936 and 1977, both years when the US economy had well and truly climbed out of the troughs of 1929–1932/3 and 1974–5 respectively:

> To account for an unemployment rate of 17 per cent in 1936 or even 7 per cent in 1977, one must invoke petrified — and not merely stale — information. (Okun, 1981, p. 41)

Surely no theory of how expectations are formed, be it by the suboptimal adaptive process or by making full and rational use of all available information, would generate such a stubbornly held view of the available wage distribution as to allow search unemployment based on misperceptions to persist for so long at such high levels.

Job Search — Evaluation

In the following chapter we shall examine the results of some empirical analysis based on job search models. But we do not need these results to take stock of the contribution of the job search model to our general understanding of unemployment. Firstly, in our view, the search model is essentially a supply-side model; in spite of attempts to model employer search along parallel lines, the model remains most successful as an explanation of why workers accept or reject jobs and, to a lesser extent, of their quit behaviour. Firms' demand for labour, and their wage-setting practices, are essential to a full explanation of unemployment. Job search theory has not provided a convincing model of these aspects of firms' behaviour. So while we must look elsewhere for a fuller understanding of inflows into unemployment, search theory does illuminate supply-side aspects of unemployment duration. Unemployment aside, search theory is an important building block in a model of the workings of a labour market in which information is incomplete and in which there is no auctioneer to call out wage rates to which both firms and workers react. The process by which wages are discovered and how labour supply responds is the solid achievement of search theory.

7.3 Contract Theory

If workers are inherently more risk averse than their employers[15] then they will wish to insure their consumption (or their income). Such insurance is provided by employers in exchange for a lower mean wage than they would otherwise be required to pay their workers. The insurance is a joint product with an employment contract (the full terms of which are usually implicit rather than explicit), which specifies real wages and employment for a range of possible states of the economic environment facing the firm. Such contracts usually imply more stable real wages and greater employment variability than would be observed in auction markets for labour.

  Viable contracts, whether implicit or explicit, require significant continuity of association between employers and workers; firms must be able to collect insurance 'premiums' from workers in good times if they are to make insurance payments in adverse circumstances. Indeed one stimulus to theoretical interest in contract theory has come from empirical evidence of worker—firm attachment. It is well known that such attachments are common in Japan with the nenko system of lifetime employment (see, for example, Hashimoto, 1979), but it is less commonly realized that long associations between workers and firms are also very common in countries like the UK and the USA. For example Hall (1982) finds that in 1978 the typical worker in the US labour force had a job lasting nearly eight years while nearly 50 per cent had jobs lasting 20 years or more. For men (whose jobs are typically longer than women's) once in their mid-thirties, i.e. once past the main years of 'job shopping', 50 per cent were in jobs lasting 20 years or more.[16] Continuity of association is partly explicable by older theories of fixed costs and firm specific training (Becker, 1964; Oi, 1962), which indeed are complementary rather than competitive with contract theory. In this chapter we concentrate on contract theory because of its implications for the behaviour of real wages under alternative 'states of nature', an aspect given less prominence in the earlier theories.

A Basic Contract Theory Model[17]

Assume workers have a utility function defined over consumption (Q) and leisure (L):

$$U = U(Q,L) \tag{7.6}$$

It is convenient (following Azariadis, 1975) to specify this initially in the form

$$U = U(Q + mL) \tag{7.7}$$

$$1 \geq L \geq 0$$

$$\frac{\partial U}{\partial (Q + mL)} > 0, \quad \frac{\partial^2 U}{\partial (Q + mL)^2} < 0 \text{ (risk aversion)}$$

Equation 7.7 of course describes linear indifference curves between goods and leisure which will produce corner solutions in which either $L = 1$ (all time spent on leisure — implying lay-offs) or $L = 0$; m is the constant marginal rate of substitution (consumption for leisure). In terms of our analysis in Chapter 2 it is the reservation price of time supplied to the market.

Firms are assumed to be risk neutral although this is not a necessary assumption to produce the basic contract theory results. They produce output subject to the production function

$$Q_i = \theta_i Q(N) \tag{7.8}$$

where N = employed workers

θ_i = a random variable which shifts the production function in each state of nature, i (in agricultural production changes in the weather are a commonly cited source of shifts in the production function)

Let p_i be the probability of state i occurring. We make the following informational assumptions:

1. The mean and probability distribution function of θ is known to all contracting parties.
2. Ex-post realisations of θ are costlessly observable by all parties (below we consider the implications of relaxing this assumption). We could, more generally, have allowed the MRP of labour rather than the MPP to have a known distribution function. That would have allowed for exogenous shocks to demand as well as supply conditions facing the firm. If we think of prices normalised at unity in our model the two types of shock are equivalent, but in general it would be better to allow independent variation in the price of the firm's product and the general price level. (Our model suppresses this covariation.)

The contract between workers and firms will specify Q and L contingent on θ. Because of equation (7.7), the contract will simply specify whether a worker works full-time or is laid off for any given θ. [18] If we let n be the number of workers the firm has under contract (which we do not explain in this version of the model) then

$$N = \rho n$$

where ρ (which obviously depends on θ) is the employment rate and $(1 - \rho)$ the lay-off rate for the firm. Which actual workers get laid off is decided as if by a random drawing from the pool n.

Let the firm pay Q_1 to retained workers and Q_2 to laid-off workers (below we consider what happens if $Q_2 = 0$). The expected utility of a worker is thus:

$$E(U) = \sum_i p_i \rho(\theta_i) U(Q_1) + \sum_i p_i [1 - \rho(\theta_i)] U(Q_2 + m) \tag{7.9}$$
$$\quad (L = 0) \qquad\qquad (L = 1)$$

The expected profits[19] of the firm (setting its product price = 1) are

$$E(\Pi) \;=\; \underbrace{\sum_i p_i\{\theta_i Q[\rho(\theta_i)n]\}}_{\text{value of output}} \;-\; \underbrace{\sum_i p_i \rho(\theta_i) n Q_1}_{\text{employee costs}}$$

$$-\; \underbrace{\sum_i p_i[1 - \rho(\theta_i)]nQ_2}_{\text{lay-off costs}} \tag{7.10}$$

If we assume that the workers can attain a level of utility U_0 outside the firm (i.e. U_0 is the utility value of contracts available from other firms) then the model is solved for Q_1, Q_2 and ρ by maximising (7.10) subject to $E(U) \geq U_0$.[20] If λ is the Lagrange multiplier[21] on the equality version of this constraint, the first-order conditions are

$$\partial U/\partial Q_1 \;=\; \frac{n}{\lambda} \tag{7.11}$$

$$\partial U/\partial (Q_2 + m) \;=\; \frac{n}{\lambda} \qquad (L = 1) \quad (7.12)$$

$$\theta_i Q_N(\rho n) - Q_1 + Q_2 + \frac{\lambda}{n}[U(Q_1) - U(Q_2 + m)] = 0 \tag{7.13}$$

where $Q_N = \partial Q/\partial N$. As (7.13) is used to solve for ρ, and as $1 \geq \rho \geq 0$, we can incorporate the latter constraint by multiplying (7.13) throughout by $\rho(1-\rho)$. From (7.11) and (7.12) we know (given our utility function (7.7) that $Q_1 = (Q_2 + m)$, therefore the term in square brackets in (7.13) disappears, and for $(Q_1 - Q_2)$ we can write $-m$. Making these substitutions and incorporating the constraint on ρ

$$\rho(1 - \rho)[\theta_i Q_N(\rho n) - m] = 0 \tag{7.14}$$

These results can be interpreted as follows: equations (7.11) and (7.12) imply that *ex-post* utility is the same whether an individual works or is laid off (a rather undesirable property of the model). The lay-offs are voluntary and Q_1 and Q_2 are invariant with respect to θ_i, given its mean value, μ ($E(\theta) = \mu$, is known before the contract is written). Thus for a given mean value of θ, real wages (Q_1) are independent of θ_i — this is the real wage rigidity result. Note, however, that Q_1 and Q_2 are *not* independent of μ, the mean value of θ_i, and, in a one-period model like the one we are using, it is only risks caused by fluctuations about μ that can be diversified — wages are not rigid with respect to changes in μ.

Equation (7.14) provides the solution to ρ. That equation shows that ρ is a function of θ_i; therefore there is a separate solution for ρ for each state of nature, i.

Consider first what happens when $1 > \rho > 0$. Then the term in the square bracket in (7.14) is equal to zero, i.e. $\theta_i Q_N(\rho n) = m$. The economic interpretation of this condition is straightforward; the marginal product of labour is equal to the reservation price of market time or, more simply, to the shadow wage. Equivalently, this condition is the standard one of MRS = MRT. As usual this condition does not apply to corner solutions. There will be some value of θ_i, call it $\underline{\theta}$, for and below which labour productivity is too low to make it worthwhile for the firm to employ any labour; $\rho = 0$ and, in general, $m > \theta_i Q_N(0)$ for $\theta_i < \underline{\theta}$. Similarly some value of θ_i, call it $\tilde{\theta}$, will imply $\rho = 1$ and, in general, $\theta_i Q_N(n) > m$ for $\theta_i \geq \tilde{\theta}$.[22]

Equation (7.14) clearly reveals the importance of the term mL in the utility function. If $m = 0$, i.e. if leisure were not valued, then $\rho = 1$, i.e. there would be no lay-offs. Full employment would then be ensured by having the firm pay the worker less than his/her marginal product in bad times and more in good times. Obviously workers will not accept voluntary redundancy unless there is some fall-back, but with $m = 0$ they would have to be paid the same whether working or not ($Q_2 = Q_1$). But the firm will not pay laid-off workers the same as employed workers — it might as well have them working if that were the case. So the lay-off result depends on workers having a fall-back — positive valuation of leisure is one possibility, government-provided unemployment insurance is another. Figure 7.6 illustrates the above interpretation of the contract model.

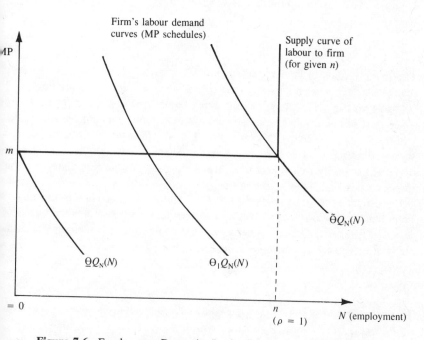

Figure 7.6 Employment Determination in the Contract Model

The Role of Unemployment Insurance in Contract Models

One feature of the above model which might surprise some non-American readers is the payment by the firm of unemployment compensation, Q_2, to temporarily laid-off workers.[23] This practice is by no means universal, being relatively rare outside the USA. We can see how this feature of the model affects the results by setting $Q_2 = 0$. Now as the firm is not choosing Q_2, equation (7.12) becomes irrelevant. Q_1, which must exceed m in order to induce market participation, is still constant for all the firm's employed workers and, more crucially, is invariant with respect to θ_i, i.e. for *employed* workers there is full consumption insurance. In this case, however, employed workers are clearly better off than laid-off workers in the same firm (because $Q_1 > m$) even though the latter voluntarily entered into the contract; unemployment is voluntary *ex ante* but involuntary *ex post*.

What about employment? Look again at the first-order condition described by equation (7.13). The term in square brackets is now not equal to zero. Setting $Q_2 = 0$ and substituting for λ/n gives

$$\theta_i Q_N(\rho n) - Q_1 + \frac{U(Q_1) - U(m)}{\partial U/\partial Q_1} = 0$$

(This can all be multiplied by $\rho(1 - \rho)$ to incorporate the constraint on ρ.) For $1 > \rho > 0$, therefore, employment is determined by

$$\theta_i Q_N(\rho n) = Q_1 - \frac{U(Q_1) - U(m)}{\partial U/\partial Q_1} \tag{7.15}$$

The shadow price of labour, the right-hand side of (7.15), is in this case less than m (this depends on $\partial^2 U/\partial(Q+mL)^2 < 0$, the risk-aversion assumption), call it Q_0. So, as Figure 7.7 shows, this generates more employment ($\rho(Q_0)n$), in any given state of nature, than when a firm pays unemployment compensation to its laid-off workers ($\rho(m)n$). (Of course, MPL $< m$, which this solution implies, is socially inefficient. There is excessive employment brought about by the individual's inability to adequately insure against the income loss of lay-off and thereby working at 'too low' a wage.)

If we reinterpret our model such that we think of m as including unemployment benefit provided by the state we can see that an increase in m will increase lay-offs; firms note and take advantage of externally financed unemployment insurance in writing contracts with their workers.

Interfirm Analysis

The analysis above has concentrated on a single firm and its work force. However, in a one-period model, concentrating on a single firm leaves unclear what kinds

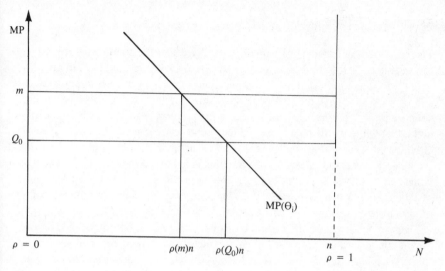

Figure 7.7   The Effect of Unemployment Insurance in a Contract Model

of risk workers are insuring themselves against. If θ_i was an economy-wide shock affecting all firms equally, then this risk cannot be diversified (in a one-period model) so that firms could not all guarantee their workers against adverse values of θ_i; feasible contracts are subject to a social budget constraint requiring, in the aggregate, all payments to workers to be met out of firms' output. Given that our model produces state-invariant payments Q_1, Q_2, these could prove infeasible in the aggregate for adverse θ_i values. What this model is actually illustrating is the way in which contracts insure workers against *interfirm* stochastic variations in demand, prices or technology, around a given and known mean value of θ_i, i.e. in a given period, μ is known but its stochastic across-firms variation represents a social diversifiable risk. Our result that wages are rigid (Q_1 is state invariant) means that workers' wages do not rise or fall with the fortunes of their particular employer. However, wages are not insensitive to changes in μ, the economy-wide mean value of θ_i. In other words all contracts are conditioned on this mean. Thus in a one-period model, wages are not rigid with respect to the economy-wide level of aggregate demand but only with respect to demand or technology fluctuations relating to particular products (firms).

Intertemporal models of labour contracts can be constructed, which although more complex are essentially analogous to our timeless model. In such models savings and dissavings (by firms, which are assumed to have greater access to capital markets than workers) allow contracts to be written in which risk averse workers can insure themselves against economy-wide shocks as well as interfirm demand variations, given that the mean and distribution over time of such shocks is known.

Asymmetric Information

The basic contract model we explained assumed that the state of nature θ_i was observable *ex post* to both contracting parties. A major development in the contract theory literature examines the implications of relaxing this assumption (Hart, 1983). We do not have the space to survey this literature, but we consider a very simple case which illustrates one aspect of the problem. Assume, as is commonly done, that while the firm can observe the θ_i outcome the worker cannot. In such circumstances there must be some way of ensuring that employers tell the truth (about *ex post* θ_i). One way of achieving this is to have the contract stipulate that when the employer says that θ_i is adverse he can only obtain a limited supply of labour, while if a favourable θ_i is declared then the contract requires some minimum level of employment (or hours).

Figure 7.8 illustrates one example of this 'observability problem' and shows how it can generate involuntary unemployment. Let θ_1 be the marginal product in the good state and θ_2 in the bad. Both θ_1 and θ_2 are known to employers but not to workers. In the good state let the contract specify H_1 hours of work and

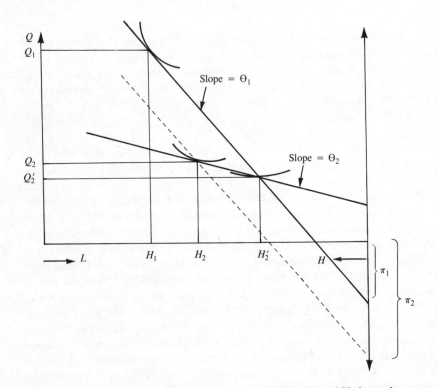

Figure 7.8 An Asymmetric Information Contract with 'Involuntary' Underemployment in the Bad State

Q_1 consumption (payments to the worker). The firm earns profits of Π_1. What should the contract specify about the bad state? If it were to specify H_2 and Q_2, maintaining equality between the MRS and MRT, then the firm has an incentive to cheat; if it claims the good state is actually the bad, it would earn profits of Π_2, greater than those earned by an honest disclosure of Q_1. However, if the contract were to specify that in a bad state the firm could not require hours in excess of H_2' from its workers, then this incentive is removed (at Q_2', $\underline{H_2}'$ profits in the good state are again Π_1). But note that H_2' implies involuntary unemployment in the bad state (MRS less than MRT). Note also that this is a possible but not a necessary result of asymmetric information. The theoretical literature on contracts with asymmetric information analyses the restrictions that must be imposed on the utility function to make such a result possible, but ultimately whether such contracts imply unemployment or underemployment in some states of nature is an empirical question — the fact that they can is not proof that they do.

Contract Theory — Evaluation

How useful is contract theory as a contribution to the understanding of unemployment? There is no professional consensus on this point as the following quotations illustrate:

> Under optimal contracts, real wages will be smoothed in the face of changes in the marginal revenue product of labour relative to what would be predicted by an auction market. And all of them [implicit contract theories] provide a rationale for the existence of *ex post* Pareto inefficiency and involuntary unemployment. (Schultze, 1985)

while on the other hand:

> Contract theory neither resolves nor illuminates questions of Keynesian unemployment based on nominal wage and price rigidities, money illusion and non market clearing. Explanations for 'sticky' wages and prices that impede efficient labour utilisation must be sought in other quarters. (Rosen, 1985)

The apparently contradictory nature of these statements is partially resolved by noting that the quotation from Schultze refers to contracts generating *real* wage stability while Rosen highlights the inability of contract theory to explain *nominal* wage rigidity. In fact the theme of the article from which the Schultze quotation comes is precisely to enquire whether modifications to new micro-theory, including contract theory, can help to explain the macroeconomic stickiness of nominal wages which prevent the economy successfully adjusting to aggregate demand shocks.

Contract theory has been criticised on a number of other grounds apart from its inability to explain nominal wage stickiness. For example, the theory does not seem well suited to the explanation of quit behaviour. In particular, if workers' quit propensity increases during business cycle upswings, as seems to be the case, this poses problems for contract theory because firms need to collect insurance premiums from workers in good times if they are to make payments in bad times. But theories of firm-specific human capital and/or job search, when used in conjunction with implicit contract theory, may provide a fuller explanation. Such theories are also needed to explain why lay-off behaviour generates unemployment; it will only do so if the laid-off workers (of firms with adverse θ_i shocks) do not search for other jobs or, if they do, why they are not hired by other firms (experiencing favourable outcomes). Some contract theories simply assume interfirm labour immobility, but this is both unsatisfactory and unnecessary; it is possible to build models in which on-the-job search leading to quitting or off-the-job search, by temporarily laid-off workers resulting in permanent separations, is optimal for all parties. Clearly such models will be more complex than the basic contract model used in this chapter.

One thing is clear, however: no explanation of unemployment which simply looks at the behaviour of one firm and its representative workers will be satisfactory. Unemployment is a *market* phenomenon and a satisfactory explanation must address itself to the question of lay-offs exceeding hires, in the market as a whole, not just for a single firm. [24]

Closely related to this point is that of how contracts can or should take account not only of different realisations of a known probability distribution of states of the world, but also of changes in the parameters of this distribution (due to wars, the emergence of the cartels of oil producers, etc.). Implicit contract theory has concerned itself with temporary rather than permanent changes in the economic environment. Contracts which do not allow wages and employment to move towards market clearing in the face of such changes are obviously socially inefficient. Because they may also be costly to individual firms, some incompleteness in the insurance contract will be required to promote labour mobility in response to permanent changes in demand or technology (see Stiglitz, 1984).

If contract theory has not lived up to its early promise of explaining the wage rigidity underlying aggregate disequilibrium unemployment, it has nevertheless taught us much about appropriate ways of modelling the labour market. While we can retain the standard neoclassical objectives of utility and profit maximisation, in many other ways the labour market of contract theory is radically different from the conventional neoclassical labour market in which demand and supply decisions are decentralised and depersonalised by all agents being price takers responding with quantity adjustments when flexible market prices signal excess supply or demand. In such a market all firms are identical and workers homogeneous. In markets dominated by implicit contracts, resource allocation relies heavily on the 'invisible handshake' rather than the invisible hand (Okun, 1981, p. 87).

Bilateral negotiation rather than decentralised markets determines how prices and quantities should respond to external changes. Thus current wages do not allocate labour resources as in the conventional model, although the value of contracts themselves may have an allocative role. Furthermore, continuity of association between workers and firms becomes necessary for implicit contracts to be viable; because the essence of such contracts is the taxing and subsidising of the workers' consumption (income) in good and bad times the system would break down if workers quit when their MRP was high or firms reneged on making insurance payments when MRP was low. To prevent such outcomes the rents flowing from continuity of association (e.g. returns to firm-specific training) are shared between the parties. In addition the need to enforce contracts informally makes the regulation of a firm and the goodwill of its labour force valuable commodities in a way which simply does not arise in a depersonalised world of homogeneous workers and firms. Firms which fail to honour contracts will suffer damage to their reputations which will affect their ability to hire good workers in the future. The penalty may be more immediate if dissatisfied employees go slow or throw a spanner in the works. Similarly there will be returns to workers whose reputations are enhanced by surviving the screening of applicants and monitoring of performance that are natural adjuncts to continuity of association.

The existence of implicit contracts and continuity of association may also play a role in generating dual or segmented labour markets (Doeringer and Piore, 1971). Not only may firms require temporary, non-contractual, labour for exceptionally favourable outcomes, as explained above, but, in addition, if enough firms adopt the strategy of a high-productivity low-turnover workforce, as implied by firm-specific training models, efficiency wage models (see below) and contract theory models, opportunities will be created for other firms to adopt cheaper but less productive casual labour employment strategies. Such firms will minimise screening and other hiring costs, will offer little on-the-job training, will tend not to enter into risk shifting contractual agreements, etc. As a result workers will feel little attachment to such firms (they may regard themselves as being in 'dead-end jobs'), quit rates will be high and wages more flexible than in contract markets.

7.4 Efficiency Wage Theory

We demonstrated in Chapter 3 that if the productivity of workers depends on the wage, an excess supply of labour may not provide firms with an incentive to cut wages, because in doing so the reduction in productivity may outweigh the savings made by paying lower wages, thereby actually increasing unit labour costs. The efficiency wage, w^*, is the wage which minimises wage costs per efficiency unit. Thus in Figure 7.9, although there is excess supply, U, at w^* the wage is not lowered for the reason given above. Note that, unlike search theory, for example, the efficiency wage model generates *involuntary* unemployment.

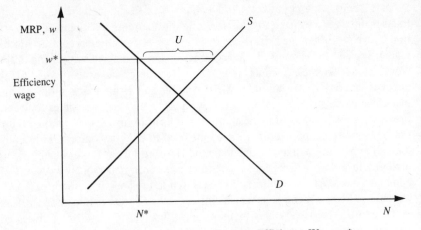

Figure 7.9 Unemployment With an Efficiency Wage w^*

There is a supply of unemployed workers willing to work at w^* or less but the wage–productivity relation prevents them being hired.

First we outline the analytical structure of efficiency wage models, then discuss possible sources of the wage–productivity relation and examine some general implications.

A Basic Efficiency Wage Model

The basic model was set out in Chapter 3 in the section 'Labour efficiency and wages', pp. 90–91. The reader should revise this section and, in particular, make sure that equation (3.16) is understood. This we repeat as equation (7.16). As the cost-minimising firm in this model has to choose employment as well as the wage we add the first-order condition with respect to employment, N (equation (7.16):

$$1 = \lambda Q_L \left(\frac{dE}{dw} \right) \tag{7.16}$$

$$w = \lambda Q_L E \tag{7.17}$$

where

$$Q_L = \frac{\partial Q}{\partial L}$$

therefore

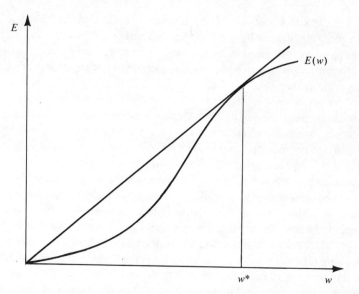

Figure 7.10   Choice of w^* to Maximise Efficiency per £ of Wage Outlay

$$w = \frac{E}{dE/dw} \tag{7.18}$$

This is the efficiency wage w^*. Note that the elasticity of E with respect to w^* is unity, as it must be if wage cost per efficiency unit is minimised. Note also that when we solve for N from (7.17) it will be state-dependent, i.e. it will depend on K in the production function $Q = F(K,L)$. w^*, however, is not state-dependent, depending only on the relation $E = E(w)$. Thus a change in K, due to a recession for example, will affect N but not w^*; wages are sticky so employment adjusts. Figure 7.10 illustrates the solution for w^*.

Rationales for the Wage−Productivity Relation

The theory originated in development economics (Leibenstein, 1957) where the relationship was a nutritional one: productivity depends on nutrition and nutrition depends on wages. While it still may have some relevance in that setting the applicability of this version to more developed economies is doubtful: few if any workers are so undernourished and so poor that their productivity would be affected by a wage change.

Even if this version of the theory is irrelevant, however, there are a number of features of developed economies' labour markets which could induce employers to set and stick to a cost-minimising efficiency wage. Consider the problem of labour turnover, caused by quits, firings and hirings. This is costly to firms as they have to pay hiring and training costs and, in some circumstances, severance pay. If a firm's labour force search on the job, then the probability of quits (or, more generally, turnover) is reduced by paying higher wages, because the probability that a worker will get a better offer elsewhere is reduced. Similarly high wages can increase the quality of applicants[25] thereby reducing screening costs, and possibly training and other costs as well (such workers are less likely to be dismissed for not measuring up to the job). All in all it seems reasonable to suppose that turnover is a decreasing function of the wage. In Figure 7.11 we draw a convex turnover function $T(w)$.[26] Convexity also seems a plausible assumption — even at high wages there will be some irreducible labour turnover, while decreasing wages must at some point induce increasing turnover rates. The tangency between this turnover function and the per worker isocost function $\bar{C} = w + aT$, where a is the cost to the firm of a quit plus hire, yields the cost-minimising efficiency wage w^*. Even if this wage leads to unemployment, firms have no incentive to reduce it because to do so would increase turnover costs (by more than the reduction in the wage bill). Only if the turnover function itself depended on the rate or level of unemployment (e.g. lower quits in times of high unemployment) might wage cuts become desirable for the firm (in which case an unemployment equilibrium may not exist).

Recently another aspect of firms' attempts to minimise unit labour cost has been

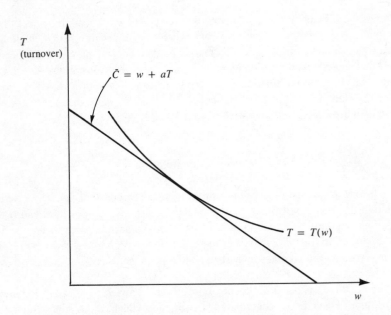

T
(turnover)

$\bar{C} = w + aT$

$T = T(w)$

w

Figure 7.11 Choice of w^* to Minimise Wage Plus Turnover Costs

analysed and shown to be capable of producing efficiency wage unemployment (Shapiro and Stiglitz, 1984). If firms are concerned about shirking by their workers, they may, where shirking is detectable, wish to discourage it by dismissing workers who are caught. But the threat of dismissal is only a disincentive to shirking if the dismissed worker must accept a lower wage at other firms which have vacancies or if there are no vacancies and unemployment is the consequence of being caught shirking. As all firms cannot increase relative wages, the unemployment result is a more likely outcome. Efficiency wages sufficiently high to result in unemployment are not reduced because the unemployment is required as a shirking penalty. This penalty is less severe the lower the unemployment rate and the higher the unemployment benefit.

Policy changes, such as changes in the level of unemployment benefit, can have different effects in the different versions of the theory. For example, in the shirking model an increase in unemployment benefit will reduce the effectiveness and firing as a penalty for shirking. To counter this, both wages and unemployment will increase. In the turnover model, however, the opposite possibility arises (Stiglitz, 1984; Shapiro and Stiglitz, 1984). Suppose an increase in benefit reduces the search intensity of low quality applicants by more than it does for high quality applicants. Then the productivity schedule of firms' applicants is increased at each wage, increasing the demand for labour. The equilibrium efficiency wage may increase or decrease. In Figure 7.12 (the left-hand panel of which is the same as Figure 7.10 with the axes transposed) we illustrate a hypothetical case where an increase in unemployment insurance eliminates unemployment. We do not necessarily believe that increasing unemployment benefit would in practice

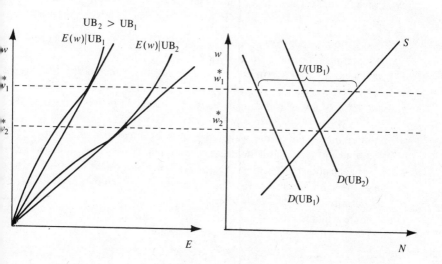

Figure 7.12 An Increase in Unemployment Benefit (from UB_1 to UB_2) Reduces the Efficiency Wage, Increases Labour Demand and Eliminates Unemployment

have this result, but we include the example to show that increases in unemployment benefit need not necessarily increase unemployment as is sometimes supposed. Ultimately the effect on unemployment of changes in unemployment benefit is an empirical question, which we consider in the next chapter.

Efficiency wage theories of unemployment in developed economies have only recently begun to be taken seriously. This makes an evaluation difficult and perhaps premature. The literature is less developed than that relating to search theory or contract theory. In some respects it is competitive with those theories. For example, contract theorists might argue that contracts could be written (involving, for example, vesting rules which entail ineligibility for pension rights for employees who quit within five or ten years of being hired) to deter turnover and/or shirking and that such contracts are Pareto superior to arrangements whereby firms set efficiency wages to reduce the costs of these activities. On the other hand, the efficiency wage theory may fill some gaps in the other approaches. For example, if the $E(w)$ relationship varies across firms for similar workers, then a distribution across firms of (efficiency) wages for these workers results.[27] We noted above that the absence of an explanation of the emergence and persistence of such a wage distribution was a weak link in the job search view of labour supply.

7.5 Bargaining Theory

We now pick up the analysis of employer–union bargaining introduced in Chapter 6, and examine in a little more detail its possible implications for wage rigidity and employment fluctuations. Because the analytic foundation was laid in Chapter 6 we restrict ourselves here to a diagrammatic exposition, beginning with Figure 7.13. This is essentially the same as Figure 6.2 with the following modifications:

1. We have added a reservation wage w_R. The union will not accept any bargaining outcome with $w < w_R$ because its members could achieve as much utility as w_R confers without being union members. The natural interpretation of w_R is that it is the level of unemployment benefit (plus the value of leisure). Alternatively w_R could be interpreted as the best alternative wage available to union members — whether that is the wage for non-union labour or the wage negotiated by a competing union.

2. Equilibrium (w_1, N_1) is determined here not as the Nash solution but by the intersection of the contract curve and what McDonald and Solow (1981) call the equity locus (in fact the arguments below apply equally where E is determined as the Nash solution). This is simply a locus showing how total revenue is divided between wages and profits. It is defined by $wN = kTR(N)$ where k is labour's share, assumed constant.

We now examine the effect of a change in aggregate demand. Take the case of a demand reduction. Assume the reservation wage is essentially determined by unemployment benefit, and that this is unaffected by the fall in demand. The

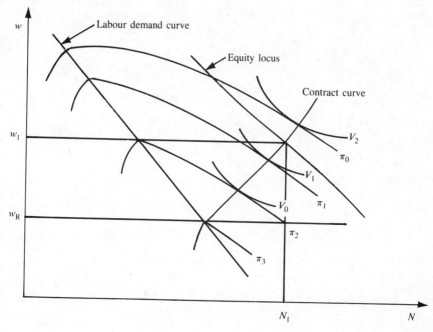

Figure 7.13 The Bargaining Model

effects of the fall in aggregate demand are illustrated in Figure 7.14 (in which, for clarity, we omit the isoprofit and indifference curves). The demand for labour is reduced (LD_1 to LD_2); thus the contract curve shifts north-westward (CC_1 to CC_2) and the equity locus south-westward (EL_1 to EL_2). As we have drawn the outcome, wages are unaffected and employment falls (N_1 to N_2).

It is important to realise that there is nothing in the way the model has been set up which requires wages to be completely rigid as in Figure 7.14 (McDonald and Solow note that such a result depends on the labour demand curve shifting iso-elastically, i.e. its elasticity unchanged at each wage). However, the fact that the shifts in the contract curve and the efficiency locus are offsetting with respect to the wage outcome and reinforcing with respect to the employment outcome offers a promising starting point for an explanation of empirically observed near-rigid real wages accompanied by procyclical employment fluctuations. A crucial assumption in producing this result was the assumption of the constancy of the reservation wage. Should this be determined by alternative labour market opportunities for the union labour force, rather than by unemployment benefit, such opportunities may deteriorate when aggregate demand falls. In this case the relative inflexibility of wages relative to employment result may not be robust; it will depend on how much w_R falls relative to the labour demand curve (the reader can verify this by redrawing Figure 7.14 with the new contract curve beginning at a lower level of w_R). One point worth noting is that, unlike implicit contract

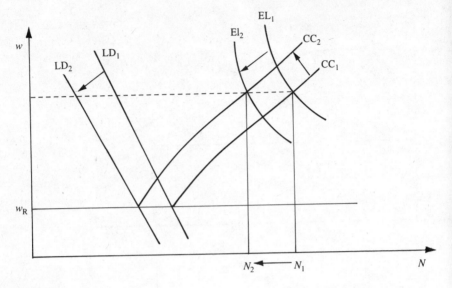

Figure 7.14 Effects of a Fall in Aggregate Demand in the Bargaining Model

theory where agreements are struck *ex ante*, the wage employment bargain is arrived at after the labour and product market conditions are known to both parties. Over time, experience with a series of short-term bargaining outcomes could lead to longer term *ex ante* implicit contracts specifying relatively stable wages and agreed rules for employment variability. We note finally that, as in other potential explanations of sticky wages, the bargaining model requires the agents whose behaviour determines the outcome to possess some degree of market power. The firm is not a price taker nor is its employment decision determined by the competitive $w = $ MRP criterion; although the wage–employment bargain is efficient (by definition there are no solutions which are Pareto superior to those on the contract curve), it is nevertheless true that it implies 'excessive' employment. The wage exceeds MRP; if it were a pure price taker the firm would prefer, for any given wage, to set employment at the level specified by its labour demand curve.

At this point, without assigning a separate section to it, mention should be made of an approach to wage rigidity which is gaining some currency, namely that of 'insider' wage setting. The basic idea here is that insiders, those with jobs, set wages at levels required to preserve their jobs. Such wage levels relate more to the demand conditions facing their employers than to 'outsider' pressure on wages exerted by the unemployed. Compare this to the setting of efficiency wages in Section 7.4, where wages depend upon outside opportunities (outside wages and unemployment benefit), and on the wage productivity relation $E(W)$.

Insider wage determination, if a valid description of actual wage setting, has the important implication that the NAIRU depends, at least in the short term, on the past history of unemployment (this phenomenon is known as hysteresis). If unemployment has been rising then insiders face an increasing probability of losing their jobs and so modify their wage demands, whereas if unemployment is simply *high*, but stable, they have no incentive to do so because their jobs are not at risk. Conversely when unemployment is *falling* insiders raise wage demands. The improvement in labour demand is taken in the form of wage increases by the insider work force rather than as extra output allowing increased employment of outsiders. Thus high recent unemployment means that reductions in unemployment are above the long-run NAIRU. Of course there are alternative explanations of why high recent unemployment increases wage pressure; the depreciation of human and physical capital and the effective detachment of the long-term unemployed from the labour market thereby removing or weakening the downward pressure they exert on wages.

7.6 Unemployment in General Equilibrium Theory [28]

All approaches to wage rigidity and unemployment we have considered up to this point have been partial equilibrium in nature, concentrating on the labour market alone and, even then, not fully considering the supply demand interactions leading to a final equilibrium. This has enabled us to examine some quite specific aspects of wage and employment determination but at the cost of ignoring general equilibrium considerations. In this section we draw the reader's attention to an emerging body of theory which examines the same issues in a general equilibrium context. Such theory is necessarily more abstract than the partial theories we have considered above. It is also technically demanding and any attempt to provide a rigorous treatment is well beyond the scope of this book. We limit ourselves to noting the existence of this theory, which has the potential for producing important contributions to an understanding of unemployment.

As long ago as 1959 Arrow pointed out a lacuna in Walrasian general equilibrium theory. Because, in that theory, all agents treat prices parametrically, there is no place in the theory to model the way in which agents change prices. Clearly this is unsatisfactory if we wish to describe the system out of equilibrium, or to consider whether or not a situation in which markets fail to clear could be described as an equilibrium. If the price vector ruling in an economy at any given time is not the Walrasian market clearing vector then the desired actions of agents (in response to actual prices) will be incompatible. Where this is the case agents will receive further signals that their desired transactions are infeasible. These signals are *quantity constraints*, or rations; i.e. firms may not be able to sell as much output as they wish (to maximise profits) at prevailing product prices, nor household members secure their desired employment at prevailing wage rates. These quantity constraints affect subsequent decisions — they become arguments in supply and demand curves. Under these circumstances it is possible that a short-run equilibrium (or equilibria) exists in which the desired actions of all agents, acting subject to existing price *and quantity* constraints are compatible. Such an equilibrium is clearly non-Walrasian and, in particular, it may be characterised by involuntary unemployment at the prevailing wage; individuals who cannot find employment would be prepared to accept a lower real wage if it enabled them to secure employment (or increased the probability of securing employment).

Now the question is whether there exist *long-run* equilibria which display similar properties, i.e. is it possible for the economy to settle at a long-run quantity-constrained (non-Walrasian) equilibrium? In terms of the labour market this amounts to asking why, if in the short-run equilibrium some individuals would trade off an increased probability of employment for a lower real wage, they do not, in the longer run when prices can change, lower their asking wage. Similarly, when employers observe unemployment, why do they not lower the wages they pay? To explain this, general equilibrium theorists introduce the notion of *conjectures*, which are simply the theories or beliefs held by agents about the effect of price changes (including wage changes) on the quantity constraints facing them. In a large economy with small agents and 'sufficient' information, agents might correctly conjecture that tiny price changes will remove any quantity constraints they face. A Walrasian (market-clearing) equilibrium will result. However, in smaller economies where agents are relatively large, where information is deficient, and where some types of market are absent, agents may correctly conjecture that price changes will not remove the quantity constraints facing them, or that the marginal cost in terms of price changes exceeds the marginal benefit in terms of relaxation of the quantity constraint before such constraints are removed.

To make the argument slightly more concrete we may refer back to some of the arguments we considered in the section on efficiency wages. If employers conjecture that wage cuts will induce higher quits and lower the quality of job applicants, and if job seekers believe that lowering their reservation wage will signal lower quality labour to prospective employers then it is rational for neither party to lower wages (or not sufficiently to eliminate involuntary unemployment) even though searchers would accept jobs at lower wages and firms would hire more labour of a given quality at a lower wage. What is interesting about such conjectural equilibria is that prices are not intrinsically sticky as in Keynesian unemployment equilibrium; in fact they are intrinsically flexible — a Walrasian equilibrium may exist — but conjectures as to the effect of price changes on quantity constraints cause the economy to become stuck in a quantity constrained equilibrium.

One problem with the notion of conjectural equilibria is that the characteristics of such equilibria clearly depend on the conjectures held by agents about the effects of price changes on the constraints facing them. Where do such conjectures come from? Do they have to be in some sense 'correct' or 'rational'? If not are they — and the general equilibrium theory on which they are based — arbitrary and unenlightening? Readers wishing to pursue these issues should consult Hahn (1977, 1978, 1980)[29] who has pioneered this approach.

7.7 Summary

Some readers may find the theories that we have examined in this chapter a trifle esoteric. Their purpose, however, and ours in explaining them in some detail, is an important one: to explain, or contribute to an explanation of, the way in which the relative inflexibility of real wages causes fluctuations in employment when aggregate demand changes, preventing the restoration of market clearing equilibrium in times of mass disequilibrium unemployment.[30]

The theories we discuss have been invoked to provide a theoretical underpinning to macroeconomic fixed price models such as Barro and Grossman (1976) and Malinvaud (1977). However, to dismiss these macro-models as being inconsistent, *ad hoc*, or even undeserving of serious consideration in the absence of a convincing explanation of *why* wages are inflexible, even when they are observed to be so, seems unreasonable. As Malinvaud himself argues:

> In contrast to what some economists seem to claim, the ability to explain an observed fact is not a precondition for a science to take this fact into account and to build on it new theoretical arguments. (Malinvaud, 1984, p. 21)

Nevertheless, no one would deny that such theories are more satisfactory if accompanied by a convincing explanation of why wages are sticky. The theories we have examined in this chapter go some way towards providing such an explanation. We do not claim that any one of them on its own offers a complete explanation. Even taken together they tell less than the whole story. Economists, ordinarily loath to invoke non-economic explanations to illuminate market behaviour, often agree that when it comes to explaining wage behaviour tradition and social convention may be important:

> We may predispose ourselves to misunderstand important aspects of unemployment if we insist on modelling the buying and selling of labour within a set of background assumptions whose main merit is that they are very well adapted to models of the buying and selling of cloth. (Solow, 1980, pp. 2–3)

Among these conventions is the public belief that wages should not be 'discriminatory', or 'exploitative', that as between different workers they should take account of 'fairness' and 'equity'. Of course, all these criteria are notoriously difficult to define precisely and yet they, more than any requirement to equate supply and demand, are the stated principles by which wages are set. Similarly wages are revised to compensate for cost of living increases, to restore traditional differentials, etc., rather than to reduce any supply–demand imbalances. Employers who took advantage of an excess supply of labour to recruit new workers on a lower pay scale than that applying to existing workers, or to dismiss existing workers and replace them with cheaper substitutes from the pool of the unemployed would be flouting convention in a way likely to attract social disapprobation or industrial opposition. None of this is to deny that market forces are also at work; conventions change, traditions die, new types of work and worker appear to which old rules are inappropriate. In the long run, supply and demand no doubt do influence wages. But the existence of these 'non-economic' factors surely does help to explain the apparent failure of employers and the unemployed to take advantage of the potential for mutually advantageous trade at lower than existing wages.

The theories we have examined combine with these non-economic factors to provide us with a fuller understanding of the relation between wages and unemployment. But they do more than this. Each of these theories contributes to an emerging picture of the labour market which differs radically from the market for cloth. Instead of impersonal relationships between fully informed buyers and sellers of homogeneous products, we have a market in which heterogeneity of labour, incomplete information, incomplete markets (capital markets, insurance markets), transactions costs, etc., enable mutual benefits to be derived from continued association between employers and workers. Once this happens both parties acquire some market power. This in turn means that they are not passive price takers, and sets economic theory the challenge of modelling how agents actually set and change (or do not change) wages and prices. Greater understanding of wage and price setting contributes to our understanding of unemployment in particular, and of the behaviour of non-clearing markets in general.

Appendix 7.1   Labour Supply Implications of Contract Theory

In an auction (non-contract) labour market an individual with no non-labour income can only consume what he or she earns (produces). With contracts the insurance element breaks this link. Insurance redistributes consumption: the 'premium' paid in good times reduces consumption below output and the insurance payment in bad times permits consumption in excess of output. This has important consequences for the analysis of labour supply as illustrated in Figure 7.15, in which we assume conventional indifference curves rather than the linear ones of equation (7.7). Let the good state be indexed by a marginal product θ_1 and the bad by θ_2. A contract guaranteeing equal utility in both states specifies H_1 hours of work and Q_1 consumption in the good state (point A) and H_2, Q_2 in the bad (point B). Points A and B are on the same indifference curve by definition. Thus in the bad state consumption exceeds output by Y_2. Because we are assuming no other source of non-labour income, this is the insurance payment in the bad state.

In the good state consumption Q_1 falls short of output by Y_1; this is the premium. But note that in each state MRS equals MRT. The worker acts as if labour supply and consumption are chosen to maximise utility given non-labour income of $-Y_1$ and a 'wage' of θ_1 in the good state and non-labour income and wage of Y_2 and θ_2 respectively in the bad.

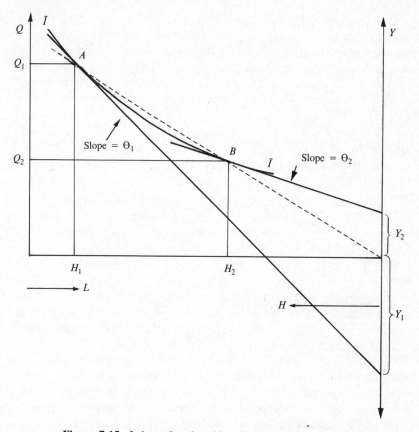

Figure 7.15 Labour Supply with a Constant Utility Contract

Compare this result with standard labour supply analysis in which an individual has no non-labour income. An increase in the wage from θ_2 to θ_1 would have ambiguous effects (Q and L normal goods). But in the contract case the income effect of the wage increase is negated by the 'as if' reduction of non-labour income from Y_2 to $-Y_1$. In this case the income effect of the wage increase is completely negated so we are left with a pure substitution effect; the individual simply moves around the indifference curve $\tilde{I}$. In general the taxes and subsidies (insurance premiums and payments) eliminate or ameliorate the income effects of insurable risks, producing more elastic labour supply responses, being exclusively or essentially substitution effects. Rosen (1985) aptly summarises:

> Contracts embody an implicit non-linear pricing mechanism that eliminates the income effects of insurable risks in the traditional consumption–leisure choice problem. They thereby ... promote elastic labour supply responses to external stimuli.

The implicit prices in the above analysis are the marginal wages θ_1 and θ_2 which, of course, may be quite different from measured average wage rates. These are generally measured by earnings divided by hours worked. As we have drawn the figure, the average wage, so measured, is equal at points *A* and *B* (in the good and bad states). However, it would be wrong to conclude that wage rigidity has increased employment fluctuation in this case. The volatility of employment comes not from rigid measured wages but from the use of *flexible* implicit wages and lump sum taxes (the insurance payment/premium) to shift risks.

Appendix 7.2   Staggered Contracts — Some Macroeconomic Implications of Contract Theory

In the main text we used relatively straightforward microeconomic analysis to show that long-term contractual arrangements between firms and workers can be advantageous to both parties, and hence efficient in a micro sense. However, macroeconomic theorists have asked whether such arrangements have an external cost, not considered by the contracting parties when setting the terms of the employment contract (Taylor, 1983). In particular the question arises as to whether the unemployment costs of disinflationary monetary or fiscal policies are greater than they would be in the absence of such employment contracts. In fact, as all contract theory variables are in real terms, the basic theory provides no scope for any real effects of known changes in the money supply.

In order to analyse this question, we slightly reinterpret the basic notion of contract theory and make one crucial assumption which was irrelevant in the micro context. The reinterpretation is that instead of attempting to stabilise the real wage, employment contracts stabilise the wage relative to the opportunity wage (i.e. the wage for similarly skilled workers in the same or related industries and occupations). The contract thus provides the worker with insurance against having to incur moving costs if the wage he receives deteriorates relative to the going wage. The assumption we make is that wage contracts are unsynchronised (staggered). This assumption can be justified simply as being descriptively accurate of wage setting procedures in many unplanned economies or, possibly, deduced as an equilibrium outcome of a wage-setting model in which there is an advantage to individual firms in being the last to set the wage (Okun, 1981).

Why might staggered contracts have the side-effect of generating or accentuating unemployment? There are two possible reasons:

1. Staggered wage setting generates a time path of nominal wages and, simultaneously, a demand for money with which to make the wage payments. If the nominal money supply does not change to meet this demand, interest rates will have to rise to equate money supply and demand. This will reduce expenditures, output and employment.
2. If prices are determined as a constant percentage mark-up over nominal wages then failure of the money supply to match the growth of nominal wages will reduce aggregate demand, and hence employment, via the real balance effect.

To make some of these points more concrete, consider two possible wage-setting rules in an economy where annual wage settlements are made by 50 per cent of workers on 1 January and by the other 50 per cent on 1 July. Six-monthly periods are subscripted, w represents the logarithm of the nominal wage.

Rule 1

$$w_t = w_{t-1} + \tfrac{1}{2}(w_{t-1} - w_{t-3})$$

This rule states that contracts made in period t will add to the 'reference wage' (i.e. the wage set six months earlier) one-half of the past year's wage growth. When wage inflation is constant, rule 1 ensures that the group currently settling always matches the prevailing wage over the duration of the contract, i.e. under constant wage inflation rule 1 implies:

$$w_t = \tfrac{1}{2}(w_{t-1} + w_{t+1})$$

Rule 2

$$w_t = w_{t-2} + (w_{t-2} - w_{t-3})$$

Rule 2 states that the group currently signing its annual wage contract receives the same percentage increase as the last group to settle. It maintains the percentage differential that any group receives above or below the reference wage, i.e. the most recently settled wage.

If wage setting follows either of rules 1 or 2 mechanically, then reduction in the money supply or its rate of growth will have no effect on wage inflation, which is determined exclusively by the equations above. If prices are set as a constant percentage mark-up over wage costs then price inflation will be unaffected also. However, unemployment will increase as the value of real balances, aggregate demand, output and employment all fall.

This conclusion would be modified if wage-setting behaviour was influenced by unemployment (which could enter with a negative coefficient on the right-hand side of the equations describing rules 1 and 2). The more responsive wage setting is to unemployment, the lower the unemployment cost of monetary disinflation. Note that under mark-up pricing this has nothing to do with real wages. Rather, responsiveness of wages and prices is necessary to preserve the real value of money balances.

The non-neutrality of monetary disinflation in the above analysis results from the expectational assumptions built into the wage-setting rules. The term $(w_{t-1} - w_{t-3})$ on the right-hand side of the wage-setting rules can be thought of as being the expectation of wage growth over the term of the contract, i.e.

$$(w_{t-1} - w_{t-3}) = (w_{t+1}^e - w_{t-1})$$

However, this expectation is simply the extrapolation of wage growth over the last full year for which parties to the current wage contract have data. If expectations are allowed to be *rational* rather than extrapolative then it can be shown

(Taylor, 1983) that the unemployment cost of monetary disinflation can be reduced or even eliminated. Basically what happens is that a credible disinflationary policy can reduce to zero expected, and therefore actual, wage growth. As the previous equation shows, if the monetary authorities can convince the group setting wages in period t that all future wage settlements, w_{t+1} and beyond, will equal w_{t-1} then as long as either of rules 1 or 2 continue to describe wage setting there will be no further inflation beyond the settlement $(w_t - w_{t-2})$, and its elimination will not have caused any unemployment.

Thus we see that the relevance of the staggered contract model as an explanation of the non-neutrality of monetary disinflation depends on the extent to which wage-setting mechanically follows rules such as those described in our equations. If such rules are modified by actual or expected unemployment, and/or by rational expectations, then the unemployment costs of reductions in the growth of the money supply will be reduced.

Notes

1. In some modern versions, part of N_eN is voluntary leisure, being taken currently in the belief that current real wages are unusually low relative to (the present value of) future real wages. In other words, according to this view, when we observe fluctuations in actual employment and unemployment we are actually observing intertemporal work—leisure substitution (which could also arise due to changes in current versus future interest rates). See Lucas and Rapping (1969).
2. This includes, for our purposes, what is sometimes called structural unemployment, which arises because of differences in the industrial, occupational or regional mix of labour supply and demand. Structural unemployment due to capital shortages (i.e. the labour requirements of the existing stock of capital is insufficient to employ all those prepared to work at the current wage) is, in our framework, disequilibrium unemployment.
3. In practice some unemployed workers become discouraged and leave the labour force altogether. This would be illustrated in Fig. 7.1 by inward shifts of the S and LF schedules.
4. Suggestive empirical evidence can take several forms:
   (i) Direct testing of the explanatory and predictive power of labour market models based on market clearing and disequilibrium conclude that the latter are more compatible with the data. (See, for example, Hall *et al.*, 1987).
   (ii) Estimates of the natural rate of unemployment, or the NAIRU (the non-accelerating inflation rate of unemployment), find this to be lower than the actual rate in most countries, suggesting the existence of disequilibrium unemployment (although such studies also show increases in the NAIRU).
   (iii) Claims that increases in unemployment duration are induced by increases in the real value of unemployment compensation (or the ratio of such compensation to resources available when in work) are not rejected by empirical studies, but the induced increases in frictional unemployment explain only a very small part of changes in measured unemployment. The same is true of increased labour force participation for groups (women, young workers) with longer mean search durations.
   (iv) Some studies (discussed in more detail in the following chapter) find that the

probability of leaving unemployment is significantly affected by variables measuring aggregate labour demand or the tightness of the labour market.

(v) Given what we know about labour supply and demand elasticities, there does not seem to be enough variation in real wages to be consistent with market clearing.

(vi) Individual labour supply seems to be explained better in models in which unemployment is allowed to act as a constraint on labour supply decisions (Blundell *et al.*, 1987).

5. Formal analysis of job search models began with Stigler (1962), but really took off in the early 1970s. However, some of the basic ideas have been around since the 1930s (see Hicks, 1932; Hutt, 1939). The job search literature is now enormous. Useful surveys are Lippman and McCall (1976) and Pissarides (1985). Chapter 2 of Okun (1981) provides further useful insights.

6. We assume that jobs do not differ in non-pecuniary characteristics, but, if they do, the analysis can accommodate this by confronting searchers not with wage offers but with job offers incorporating both wages and non-pecuniary characteristics.

7. We make this assumption to avoid the need to introduce discounting into our formal exposition of job search. Discounting complicates the model without adding significantly to the insight it provides. When we discuss the comparative statistics of the job search model, however, we will provide an intuitive argument about the effect of changes in the interest rate.

8. Our treatment here is somewhat intuitive. Although we explain the logic of the reservation wage approach we do not *prove* that it is the optimal strategy. A rigorous derivation can be found, for example, in McCall (1970).

9. For example if $p = 0.2$ there is one chance in five in any period that $w \geq w_R$. Thus it will take, on average, five periods to receive an acceptable wage offer. Because p deceases as w_R increases, unemployment duration and the reservation wage are, *ceteris paribus* positively related.

10. If any search at all takes place the cost of $(C - UB)$ during the first period is unavoidable. The probability of incurring $(C - UB)$ twice is $(1 - p)$ the probability of not having received an acceptable offer during the first search period. The probability of incurring the cost three times is $p(1 - p)$, the probability of not receiving an acceptable offer in the first period but doing so in the second. By extension the expected costs are

$$(C - UB)[1 + (1 - p) + p(1 - p)^2 + p(1 - p)^3 + \ldots]$$

i.e.

$$\frac{C - UB}{p}$$

This, of course is nothing but the per period cost $(C - UB)$ multiplied by $1/p$, the number of periods (expected search duration) the cost is expected to be incurred.

11. This is an appropriate point at which to note the formal similarity between the human capital model introduced in Chapter 5 and the job search model. Both are concerned with deriving an optimal 'stopping rule'; in the human capital model the individual must decide when to cease formal education and join the labour market, in the search model when to stop searching and accept a job offer. In both cases the rule is to stop when the marginal costs of continuing are just equal to the marginal benefits. Even the costs and benefits are similar — in both cases there are both direct costs and foregone earnings while the main benefit is an expected earnings differential.

12. In fact the optimal strategy may not even be a reservation wage strategy.

13. Formal models of employer search can be constructed along parallel lines to models of employee search (see Lippmann and McCall, 1976).

14. *Employment and Training Report of the President, 1977*, quoted in Fleisher and Kniesner (1980).

15. This could be due to a process of natural selection and/or because workers have more limited access to capital markets, making them less able to diversify the assets in their wealth portfolios (prominent among which is human capital which in general cannot be used as collateral for consumption loans; firm-specific human capital cannot, by definition, be used as a hedge against firm-specific risks).

16. These findings are not incompatible with the claim that the US labour force has very high turnover, nor with the fact that the typical job in the US labour market is brief. The latter finding comes from the analysis of the distribution of durations across *jobs*. Hall's findings all relate to the distribution of job durations across *workers*. (In the next chapter we draw a similar distinction with respect to unemployment duration; while a typical unemployment spell is relatively short, the average unemployment duration of an individual in the unemployment stock is much longer.) For the UK, Main (1982) also finds that the major part of male employment is accounted for by lifetime jobs, finding the average completed length of a job for males aged 21 and over is about 20 years.

17. The basic model appeared in the literature in the mid-1970s (Azariadis, 1975; Baily, 1974; D.F. Gordon, 1974). The model we present contains the essence of these models but the exposition is closer to Rosen (1985).

18. A more general utility function would require contracted hours to be specified for each state of nature. In such models, whether the solution involves lay-offs or work sharing will depend on both the production technology (whether the labour input can be defined simply in terms of worker-hours or whether workers and hours per worker need to be considered separately) and on the level of state-financed unemployment insurance. On the role of technology see Feldstein (1976) and Baily (1977). The reliance on unemployment insurance to generate lay-offs is sometimes claimed to be a weakness of contract models as an explanation of unemployment, because previous episodes of mass unemployment occurred when such benefits were less universal and less 'generous' than they are today. However, it may simply be that contract theory is more relevant to contemporary unemployment than as an explanation of the Great Depression of the 1930s.

19. If firms as well as workers are risk averse the maximand would be the expected utility of profits.

20. In some models utility is maximised subject to a profit constraint. Duality ensures the two solutions are equivalent.

21. See Chapter 3, note 9.

22. Such firms have excess demand for labour. This does not necessarily mean that they would wish to increase n ($\theta_i > \tilde{\theta}$ may be a relatively rare occurrence, and if firms have to make payments, Q_2, increasing n can be costly). However, they may, under such circumstances, wish to avail themselves of temporary labour. This may offer a partial explanation of dual labour markets — the internal, or primary, market comprising workers with a contractual obligation to the firm (explained and sustained by firm-specific human capital), the external, or secondary, market of lower-productivity, high-turnover workers. Often immigrant workers fill this role.

23. Payment by the firm of Q_2 emphasises that we are modelling *temporary* lay-offs (lay-offs subject to recall). Feldstein (1975) claims that, in the US, over 70 per cent of all lay-offs are temporary. In a formal sense contract models can be adapted to explain permanent lay-offs by reinterpreting ρ as the probability of permanent separation and Q_2 as severance pay.

24. In moving from single firm analysis to the whole labour market, certain externalities associated with the types of contracts we have been discussing may emerge. One such — the macroeconomic implications of the contracts of different groups of workers being unsynchronised — is discussed in Appendix 7.2.
25. If higher productivity searchers have higher reservation wages, for example, the quality mix of applicants to high wage firms will be superior to the mix applying to and accepting low wage offers. The positive correlation between reservation wages and productivity requires some heterogeneity in the labour market. In a completely homogeneous market, all firms would pay the same wage and there would be no incentive for higher productivity individuals to have higher reservation wages. On the other hand, if there is an informal or self-employment sector an individual's productivity in this sector will set the lower bound on the reservation wage. If we then, not implausibly, assume a positive correlation between productivity in the industrial and the informal sector we can deduce the positive correlation between a firm's wage and the productivity of its job applicants. Because of this relation job seekers will not reduce wages because to do so signals lower productivity and reduces the probability of employment. Similar considerations apply to turnover. If alternative employments exist where wages reflect productivity, then if a firm were to cut wages in times of unemployment it would find that its most productive workers would quit (Weiss, 1980).
26. Where the firm has an unchanging labour force, quits equal hires in any period, so T can be thought of as the average quit probability of a member of the firm's labour force. The $T(w)$ function and parameter a in the isocost function require redefinition when the firm's labour force is expanding or contracting.
27. The left-hand panel of Figure 7.12 can be reinterpreted to illustrate this if the two $E(w)$ schedules are thought of as applying to different firms rather than different levels of unemployment benefit.
28. This section can be omitted without loss of continuity.
29. The 1980 reference is relatively non-technical, the other two are analytically demanding.
30. Job search theory is on a slightly different footing although searchers' initial failure to adjust the reservation wage downwards, when the whole wage distribution deteriorates, is a type of wage stickiness. Although search unemployment is in a sense an equilibrium rather than disequilibrium phenomenon, the search model is widely used to examine certain aspects of recent unemployment history, in particular the role played by unemployment insurance in explaining observed increases in unemployment.

8

Empirical Aspects of Unemployment

This chapter deals with empirical aspects of unemployment (although a little more theory is required along the way). The chapter is divided into three main sections. [1] The first examines the definition and measurement of unemployment and provides comparative data on unemployment rates, durations of unemployment and the unequal distribution of unemployment. The second section deals with the vexed question of the role played by real wages in generating and sustaining unemployment. This issue, and the related one of changes in the Non-Accelerating Inflation Rate of Unemployment, the NAIRU, are examined in the context of the recessions that afflicted virtually all industrialised economies in the first half of the 1970s and the early 1980s. The emphasis is mainly, but not exclusively, on the British and US recessions and recoveries. The final part of the chapter examines in more detail some specific policy issues relating to unemployment.

A. Facts

8.1 Introduction — Unemployment from the 1920s to the Present

The Great Depression of the 1930s will be little more than history to most readers of this book. [2] For many of those who lived through it, however, the unemployment of that era caused untold and never-to-be-forgotten hardship and deprivation. The human cost cannot of course be conveyed by a few figures, but to indicate the magnitude of the malfunctioning of the UK and US economies, Table 8.1 shows the unemployment rates that prevailed. In the UK the peak rate of 22.1

Table 8.1 Unemployment in the Geat Depression: UK and US (%)

	1927	1928	1929	1930	1931	1932	1933	1934	1935	1936	1937
UK	9.7	10.8	10.4	16.1	21.3	22.1	19.9	16.7	15.5	13.1	10.8
US	—	—	3.2	8.7	15.9	23.6	24.9	21.7	20.1	16.9	14.3

Sources: UK: Department of Employment and Productivity (1971).
US: US Department of Labor (1985). Darby (1976) believes this series overestimates US unemployment rates because it includes employees on Government contracyclical programs ('emergency workers'). Excluding these workers mainly affects the post-1933 unemployment rates, reducing them, on average, by over 25 per cent.

per cent in 1932 represented about 2.8 million unemployed persons. The peak American rate of 24.9 per cent in 1933 represented about 12.8 million unemployed.

The world of the 1950s and 1960s (into the early 1970s) was an altogether more congenial one in terms of the economic performance of most industrialised countries. Table 8.2 shows that the record of the UK and the US in terms of both unemployment and inflation was an enviable one by today's standards. This is particularly so with respect to UK unemployment and US inflation. But for both countries unemployment was consistently below the levels reached and sustained subsequently.

Indeed, in the UK between 1950 and 1970, the unemployment rate never reached per cent. In the US, unemployment was higher — exceeding 6 per cent in 1958 and 1961 — but again well below the peak rates of the early 1980s. In the US, in particular, the fluctuations during the period reflect the tightening of the labour market during the Korean and Vietnam wars, resulting in average unemployment of just above 3 per cent during 1950–3 and under 4 per cent during 1966–9.

In the early 1980s unemployment in the developed economies of the West reached levels unprecedented since the Great Depression. While it is no doubt true that unemployment today causes less hardship and deprivation than in the

Table 8.2 Unemployment and Inflation, 1950–1974, UK and US (%)

	1950–1954	1955–1959	1960–1964	1965–1969	1970–1974
UK					
Unemployment	1.7	1.7	1.9	2.1	3.0
Inflation	5.2	3.4	2.8	4.3	9.6
US					
Unemployment	4.0	5.0	5.7	3.8	5.4
Inflation	2.5	1.7	1.2	3.4	6.1

Sources: UK: Department of Employment and Productivity (1971); Employment Gazette (various issues).
US: US Department of Commerce (1984).

1920s and 1930s (due mainly to the greater coverage and level of support offered by state benefits for the unemployed) it nevertheless appears that today's unemployment is even more deep rooted than during the earlier historical episode. Thus comparing Tables 8.1 and 8.3 reveals that the upward trend of unemployment in developed countries was sustained longer in the 1970s and 1980s than in the 1920s and 1930s. In addition the long-term unemployed, who suffer most from unemployment both materially and psychologically, are relatively more numerous today. For example in the UK in 1985 over 40 per cent of the unemployed were without a job for over a year — twice as high a proportion as the maximum reached during the Great Depression.[3]

Table 8.3, using internationally comparable unemployment definitions (Tables 8.1 and 8.2 use national definitions), charts the pervasive and inexorable increases in unemployment during the 1970s and early 1980s. By 1975 the effects of the first oil shock (amongst other factors) had made themselves felt in all the countries in the table, although there were substantial differences between countries: while Germany's unemployment rate was $4\frac{1}{2}$ times its exceptionally low 1970 level, Sweden had virtually recovered from a relatively depressed 1973 level to record unemployment not significantly different from its 1970 level. In fact Sweden's comparative performance over the whole period is remarkable, as is Japan's.[4] It is also noteworthy that the USA is the only country for which the unemployment rate had fallen substantially by 1979 compared with the 1975 figure (Germany also records a reduction but it is much smaller in both absolute and percentage terms). Of course the US rate rises again with the impact of the second oil shock of 1979−80 but the unemployment caused (in large part) by the first shock did not become as deeply entrenched as it did in countries like France and the UK. It is argued below that this difference is associated with greater real wage flexibility in the US. In many European countries, by contrast, wage increases attempted to keep up with rising import prices. Combined with contractionary

Table 8.3 Comparative Unemployment Rates, 1970−1986 (%)

	1970	1973	1975	1979	1980	1981	1982	1983	1984	1985	198
US	4.8	4.8	8.3	5.8	7.0	7.5	9.5	9.5	7.4	7.1	6.
Japan	1.1	1.3	1.9	2.1	2.0	2.2	2.4	2.6	2.7	2.6	2.
Germany	0.8	0.8	3.6	3.2	3.0	4.4	6.1	8.0	7.1	7.2	6.
France	2.4	2.6	4.1	6.0	6.4	7.3	8.1	8.3	9.7	10.1	10.
UK	3.1	3.3	4.3	5.1	6.9	10.6	11.4	12.6	11.7	11.2	11.
Italy	5.0	6.2	5.8	6.5	7.5	8.3	9.0	—	10.2	10.5	—
Canada	5.6	5.5	6.9	7.4	7.4	7.5	10.9	11.8	11.2	10.4	9.
Australia	1.6	2.3	4.8	6.2	6.0	5.7	7.1	9.9	8.9	8.2	8.
Sweden	1.5	2.5	1.6	2.1	2.0	2.5	3.1	3.5	3.1	2.8	2.
Mean	2.9	3.3	4.6	5.1	5.4	6.2	7.6	8.5	8.3	8.0	7.

Source: OECD (1985a, 1986, 1987).

monetary and fiscal policies this led to a profit squeeze and substantial increases in unemployment.

8.2 The Structure and Distribution of Unemployment

Measurement of Unemployment in Official Statistics

Definitions of unemployment used in official statistics do not necessarily bear a close relationship to the definitions used by economists. For example, in the UK, unemployment is now measured by the number of people claiming benefit at unemployment benefit offices on the day of the monthly count and who, on that day, were unemployed and 'able and willing to do any suitable work'.

In the US, to be unemployed a person has to be available for work in the survey week and must be actively seeking work (unless on temporary lay-off), which means having engaged in some specified method of job search during the previous four weeks. These definitions clearly do not correspond to the unemployment concepts illustrated in Figure 7.1 of the previous chapter. In particular, the official statistics tell us nothing about job seekers' reservation wages — the minimum wage at which they would accept a job offer. It is probable that even if at any particular time the levels of unemployment measured in the above ways do not correspond with economists' definitions of either equilibrium or disequilibrium unemployment, *changes* in officially measured unemployment correspond more closely to *changes* in unemployment as defined in economic theory.

Quite apart from the fact that official unemployment statistics make no reference to wage rates, they may have other shortcomings which lead to overestimates or underestimates of 'true' unemployment. In the UK, some unemployed may be ineligible for benefits (many married women for example), while some eligible claimants may not claim. On the other hand, some claimants may not be genuine job seekers, while others may already be working in the 'black economy'. Should persons on government employment and training programs, many of whom would be unemployed in the absence of such programs, be excluded (as they are) or included (as some believe they ought to be)?[5] Some unemployed may temporarily drop out of the labour force, and hence the unemployment statistics, due to becoming discouraged by unsuccessful job search, although if offered work they would accept it. It could be argued that these discouraged workers should be included in measured unemployment.[6] Similarly those involuntarily put on short-time working are really disguised unemployed, as are trained nuclear physicists working as cab drivers (i.e. those accepting jobs well below the skill level for which they were trained).

Although official unemployment statistics do not enable us to identify an excess supply of labour at prevailing wage rates, it is nevertheless important to realise that changes in supply as well as demand affect measured unemployment. Figure 8.1 shows how both reductions in employment *and* increases in the labour force

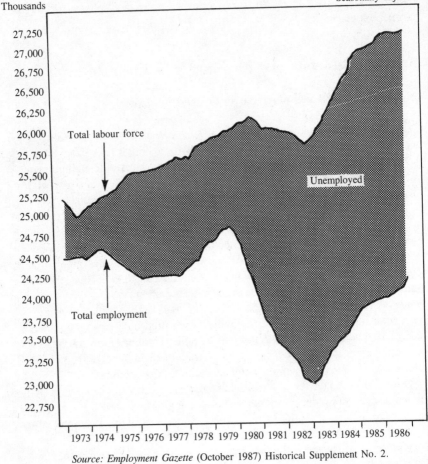

Source: *Employment Gazette* (October 1987) Historical Supplement No. 2.

Figure 8.1 (a) Working Population and Employed Labour Force: Great Britain, 1973–1986

(being the net effect of population growth and changes in activity rates — see Chapter 3) contributed to the growth of unemployment in Britain and the US in the 1970s and 1980s. It can be seen from the figures that unemployment is the difference between two much larger magnitudes, total labour force and total employment. Relatively small changes in one or both of these can result in large proportionate changes in unemployment. Figure 8.1(b) for the US shows especially graphically the need for sustained job creation if increased unemployment is not to result from labour force growth.[7]

The aggregate unemployment rates we have examined above conceal many

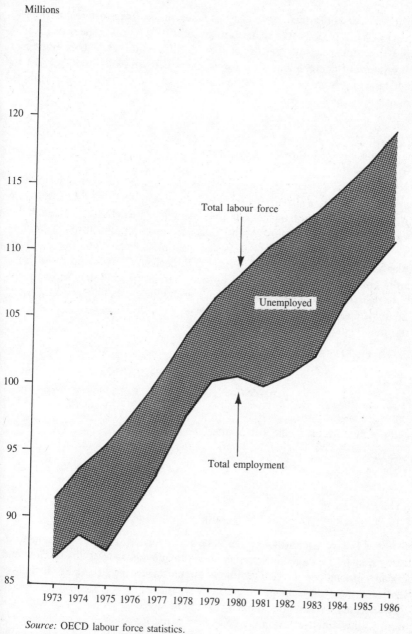

Source: OECD labour force statistics.

Figure 8.1 (b) Working Population and Employed Labour Force: USA, 1973–1986

disparities in unemployment by age, sex and race, and between different industries, occupations and regions. We shall examine some of these differences in this section. Before doing so, however, we analyse the distinction between the incidence and duration of unemployment: a distinction which is crucial both in order to understand the nature of unemployment and in order to devise effective policies to alleviate it.

Unemployment — Inflows and Duration

Unemployment is a *stock*, i.e. a measure of the total number who are unemployed at any instant. But the size of this stock is determined both by the *rate of inflow* into unemployment and the length of time unemployed individuals remain in the stock — the *duration* of unemployment. Take a hypothetical economy with a labour force of 50 million persons with measured unemployment of 5 million in a particular year, i.e. an unemployment rate of 10 per cent. This could result from 5 million persons being unemployed for one year, from each member of the 50 million labour force having a spell of 5.2 weeks of unemployment during the year, or from any other combination of inflow and duration whose product is 5 million. Thus

$$U = I \times D$$

Unemployment = inflow into unemployment per week[8] × average duration of unemployment in weeks[8]

Dividing through by L, the size of the labour force,

$$\frac{U}{L} = \frac{I}{L} \times D$$

Unemployment rate = rate of inflow × average duration

Note that D, average duration, can only be calculated from these formulae in a 'steady state' i.e. when inflow into unemployment is equal to the outflow and both are constant over time. Under these circumstances the size of the unemployment stock (and the unemployment rate) is constant.

To understand further the implications of this stock-flow process, consider the following hypothetical example.[9] Suppose that each week 20 people become unemployed, and they will remain so for exactly one week, and one person begins a 20-week spell of unemployment. After 20 weeks the system reaches a steady state in which inflow equals outflow and 40 people are unemployed. What is the mean duration of a completed spell of unemployment? Because we are in a steady state we can use our formula

$$U = I \times D$$

i.e. $D = \dfrac{U}{I} = \dfrac{40}{21} = 1.9$ weeks

This is also the expected duration for any week's inflow, i.e. the weighted average of the eventual duration of the 21 spells beginning each week:

$$D = \left(\frac{20}{21} \times 1 \right) + \left(\frac{1}{21} \times 20 \right) = 1.9 \text{ weeks}$$

Note that the average probability of leaving unemployment (the *exit probability*) in any given (steady state) week is simply the reciprocal of D. 21 people have a 100 per cent probability of leaving unemployment and 19 have a zero probability; the average is

$$\left(\frac{21}{40} \times 1 \right) + \left(\frac{19}{40} \times 0 \right) = 0.525 = \frac{1}{1.9}$$

However, the average length of a complete spell is not the only possible measure of duration, nor is it the one most commonly found in officially published statistics. The latter are derived from surveying the currently unemployed and therefore cannot refer to completed spells. Such surveys ask those experiencing a spell of unemployment how long that spell has so far lasted. What the answers describe therefore is the *duration of incomplete (or interrupted) spells* of unemployment. Let us calculate this half way through a steady-state week in our numerical example. The 20 people entering unemployment in that week will have half a week to go before leaving unemployment. So will those in the 20-week spell which began 19.5 weeks ago. The individual with a 20-week spell which began 18.5 weeks ago still has 1.5 weeks to serve, etc. So the mean value of an incomplete spell, D_x, is

$$D_x = \left(\frac{21}{40} \times 0.5 \right) + \left(\frac{1}{40} \times 2.5 \right) + \ldots \left(\frac{1}{40} \times 19.5 \right) = 5.25$$

which is also the average length of time taken to leave unemployment of all those currently unemployed).

Why is the average incomplete duration 2.75 times the average length of a complete spell of unemployment? Basically, in this example, because the long-term unemployed (those with 20-week spells) are more heavily represented in the unemployment *stock* than in the unemployment *flows* (into and out of unemployment). In practice this can arise either because different groups of unemployed (e.g. the skilled versus the unskilled) have different exit probabilities and/or because an unemployed person's exit probability declines with the length of time a person has already been unemployed — due to the depreciation of skills or simply because prospective employers are more likely to think that there is 'something wrong' with applicants the longer they have been unemployed. [10]

One implication of the build-up of the longer-term unemployed in the stock is that although the mean complete duration of unemployment may be quite low, implying, on average, rapid turnover of the unemployed, it will still be true that such high turnover individuals will on average form a relatively low proportion of measured unemployment. Thus, in our numercial example, although only one in twenty of all individuals becoming unemployed will remain so for 20 weeks, such individuals comprise 50 per cent of measured steady state unemployment.

For a given aggregate unemployment rate (or level) the social costs will depend on the relative importance of the inflow and duration components. Furthermore the policies required to alleviate high-inflow—low-duration unemployment are unlikely to be appropriate for dealing with long-duration unemployment. In terms of jobs, one is tempted to simplify heroically and claim that rapid turnover indicates a need for better jobs while long durations imply a need for more jobs.

In the UK, statistics on the flows into and out of unemployment are published regularly. Table 8.4 gives annual averages for these flows and the corresponding stock of unemployment, illustrating that these flows are large relative to the stock. The implied completed durations, using the steady state formula, are 9.5 months for males, 7.3 for females and 8.7 for the combined labour force. If everyone in the stock had the same duration these would be the required times for the stock to be completely renewed. We shall see shortly how far this is from describing the actual situation.

Nevertheless, the large flows — relative to the stock — do imply considerable turnover among the unemployed. Even though total unemployment changes relatively slowly from month to month, the actual individuals making up this total are not an unchanging group, although, as we document more fully below, there is a large minority of individuals, the long-term unemployed, who do stay in the unemployment stock for long periods.

Turning to durations, Table 8.5 gives recent figures for Great Britain. As in our hypothetical examples above, and for the reasons there discussed, incomplete durations exceed complete durations (for both means and medians). The difference

Table 8.4 Unemployment Flows and Stocks, UK, 1984/5[a,b] (000)

	Monthly inflow	Monthly outflow	Unemployment	$\frac{Inflow}{U} \times 100$	$\frac{Outflow}{U} \times 100$
Male	227.6	226.4	2,170.7	10.5	10.4
Female	129.5	126.9	949.6	13.6	13.4
Total	357.1	353.3	3,120.3	11.4	11.3

Source: Department of Employment, Employment Gazette, August 1985.
Notes: (a) School-leavers excluded (under 18).
          (b) July 1984—June 1985.

Table 8.5 Incomplete and Complete Unemployment Durations, GB, 1985[a] (weeks)

	Males	Females	Total
A Incomplete durations			
Mean	na	na	71.9[c]
Median	45.3	29.1	39.3
B Complete durations			
Mean[b]	37.7	31.6	35.5
Median	16.2	15.7	16.0

Source: Department of Employment, *Employment Gazette*, October 1985.
Notes: (a) Mean complete durations are for the second quarter of 1985. Other figures refer to July 1985.

(b) Mean complete durations are calculated as

$$\frac{1}{\text{quarterly exit probability}} \times 13$$

(c) This figure refers to UK not GB. Mean incomplete duration is calculated from grouped data and is therefore subject to error. The 5 per cent of unemployed in July 1985 with incomplete durations in excess of 5 years are (conservatively) assigned durations of 5.5 years for the purposes of this calculation. Those with durations of up to two weeks are assigned durations of one week. Mid-points of published intervals are used for other durations.

between the medians and means is striking: the duration distributions are positively skewed.

International comparisons are difficult, as flow and completed duration statistics are not regularly published outside the UK. Table 8.6, relating to incomplete durations, however, does indicate that turnover is substantially greater in the US than the UK. Compared to the US, durations are longer in the UK and increased more rapidly in the early 1980s. Comparative data on completed durations are even

Table 8.6 Mean Incomplete Duration of Unemployment by Age and Sex, US and UK, 1980 and 1984 (weeks)

		Youths[a]		Adults	
		M	F	M	F
US	1980	10.4	8.7	15.6	11.7
	1984	14.7	11.3	25.1	16.9
UK	1980	17.3	16.0	52.9	39.4
	1984	49.8	39.9	84.1	58.1

Source: OECD (1985b).
Note: (a) Ages 16–24.

harder to come by but Table 8.7 again compares the United States and United Kingdom. In spite of the fact that the age groups are not strictly comparable, the message is again resoundingly clear: individuals are unemployed for very

Table 8.7 Average Completed Unemployment Durations, US and UK, 1981 (weeks)

	US[a]	UK
Teenagers[b]		
M	8.2	20.2
F	7.7	17.2
Young adults[c]		
M	10.8	33.5
F	8.2	27.1
Prime-aged adults[d]		
M	11.2	43.4
F	9.0	36.1

Source: OECD (1983).
Notes: (a) Whites only.
(b) UK: ages 16–18; US: 16–19.
(c) UK: ages 18–24; US: 20–24.
(d) UK: ages 25–44; US: 25–29.

(a) STOCK AND FLOW, MALES, GREAT BRITAIN
JAN 1949 TO JAN 1986

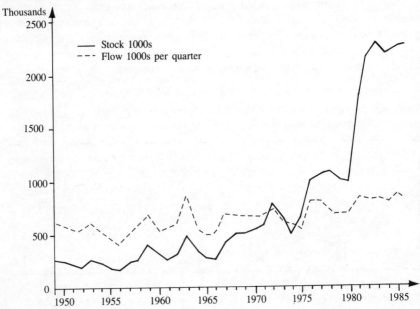

(b) MEDIAN DURATION OF UNCOMPLETED SPELLS OF
UNEMPLOYMENT: GB 1962–1985, Males

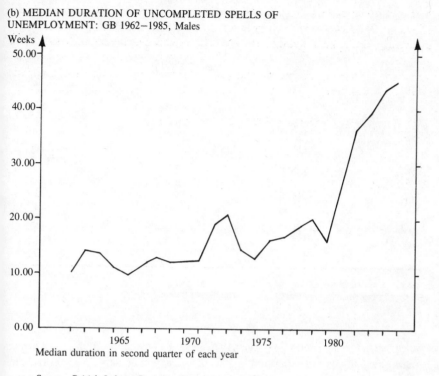

Median duration in second quarter of each year

Source: British Labour Statistics, Department of Employment and DHSS.

Figures 8.2 (a) and (b)   Inflow, Duration and Unemployment, Males, GB

much longer in the UK than in the US; up to four times as long (prime-aged women) and not less than twice as long for any group. Within each country there is, in addition, a clear pattern of duration increasing with age.

One remarkable feature of the increase of unemployment in Britain in recent years, especially from the late 1970s to the mid-1980s, is the extent to which it is attributable to increases in the time spent unemployed rather than to increased inflow into unemployment. Figure 8.2(a) shows that while male inflows are subject to considerable short-term fluctuations they do not exhibit any marked upward trend. Unemployment, however, has continued to show a pronounced upward trend implying that unemployment durations increased substantially. This is shown in Figure 8.2(b). (The increase in female unemployment in the 1970s and 1980s is more evenly distributed between increased inflows and durations.) The increase in durations is shown directly in Table 8.8. Median values of both complete and incomplete unemployment durations have increased even over the short period for which such figures have been collected. But major increases in duration

Table 8.8 Median Unemployment Durations, Complete and Incomplete, GB, 1982−1985 (weeks)

		Complete	*Incomplete*
1982	Q4	11.3	28.7
1983	Q1	14.3	30.3
	Q2	16.7	34.1
	Q3	11.4	34.9
	Q4	11.6	32.4
1984	Q1	14.2	32.5
	Q2	16.9	36.3
	Q3	11.2	38.1
	Q4	11.9	34.5
1985	Q1	14.1	34.2
	Q2	16.0	37.3
	Q3	10.9	39.3

Source: Department of Employment, *Employment Gazette*.
Note: Incomplete durations refer to the first month of the quarter.

occurred before this period, between 1970 and 1981 especially. By way of a benchmark, median complete duration in 1971/2 was approximately $2\frac{1}{2}$ weeks and median incomplete duration was about 15 weeks (Stern, 1979; *Employment Gazette*, 1974).

In the United States, although durations were much shorter than in the UK, they also increased substantially in the early 1980s, as Table 8.6 showed.

Long-Term Unemployment

One aspect of the increase in average unemployment duration causing particular concern in both countries is the growth in the number and proportion of long-term unemployed: widely, if arbitrarily, defined as those unemployed for a year or longer (Table 8.9).

Table 8.9 Percentage of Long-Term Unemployed[a] in Total Unemployment

	1979	*1980*	*1981*	*1982*	*1983*	*1984*	*1985*
UK	24.8	21.5	22.0	33.6	26.5	39.8	41.0
US	4.2	4.3	6.7	7.7	13.3	12.3	9.5

Source: OECD (1986).
Note: (a) Unemployment in progress 52 weeks or more.

In the UK, while total unemployment increased by 88 per cent between 1980 and 1985 (July), those unemployed for over 52 weeks increased by 260 per cent (from 369 thousand to 1.3 million). The increase in long-term unemployment is not limited to the UK and US, it has occurred in most other OECD countries, including those such as Germany and Sweden with relatively low aggregate unemployment.

If anything, these figures underestimate the numbers (and proportions) of long-term unemployed due to differential discouraged-worker effects, i.e. the proportion of the outflow from unemployment who are withdrawing from the labour force due to repeated disappointments in job applications is greater for the long-term unemployed than for those leaving shorter-term unemployment, i.e. there is likely to be considerable disguised long-term unemployment.

Who are the long-term unemployed? Table 8.10 shows, for the UK, the distribution of those with unemployment in progress of over 52 weeks by age and sex. It is commonly believed that the long-term unemployed are mainly older workers. The table shows this not to be the case. While it is true that the probability of entering a spell of greater than 52 weeks is highest for the 55 and over age group,[11] sufficient numbers of young and prime-aged workers are long-term unemployed for these two groups to constitute 85.5 per cent of all long-term unemployed. It is also noteworthy that, over time, the age structure of the long-term unemployed has changed very significantly. Whereas in 1985 over one-quarter of the long-term unemployed in the UK were under 25 years of age, the corresponding figure in 1973 was about 6 per cent. Also, at that time only 9 per cent of the long-term unemployed were women, compared to nearly 25 per cent in 1985. Nor is it true that it is only the unskilled and semi-skilled who remain unemployed for long periods. For example, in Britain the 1983 Labour Force Survey showed that 57 per cent of the long-term unemployed were skilled workers (including managerial and professional). These trends indicated that, while certain groups are more prone to long-term unemployment (those with outdated skills, less adaptability, health problems etc. all possibly correlated with age), in a deteriorating labour market individuals from groups previously less at risk increasingly get drawn into long-term unemployment. This trend is exacerbated by the fact that the probability of 'exiting' or 'escaping' from unemployment tends to decline with length of time that a person has already been unemployed. This is shown for Britain in Table 8.11. The declining escape probability may be partly

Table 8.10 Age and Sex Distribution of the Long-Term Unemployed, UK, July 1985

	Under 25	25–54	55 and over	All ages
Male	17.9	47.5	11.3	76.7
Female	8.6	11.5	3.2	23.3
Total	26.5	59.0	14.5	100.0

Source: Department of Employment, Employment Gazette (Oct. 1985).

Table 8.11 Probability of Leaving Unemployment by Duration Already Reached, GB

Duration already reached	Probability (per cent) of leaving unemployment within:		
	3 months	6 months	1 year
Inflow	49	66	81
3 months	3	51	76
6 months	28	46	72
1 year	34	48	64
2 years	—	—	39
3–4 years			26

Source: Department of Employment, *Employment Gazette* (Sept. 1986). Based on observations January 1985–January 1986.

due to skill depreciation and waning search motivation but, in addition, prospective employers may interpret long-term unemployment as a signal that the applicant has already been rejected by a number of other employers and feel that to
hire such applicatns is too risky. The decline of the exit probability as incomplete
duration increases is known as 'state dependence'. When analysing how exit probabilities differ between individuals it is difficult in practice to separate the state
dependence effect from the effects of individuals belonging to different
age/sex/skill/regional groups ('heterogeneity' rather than 'state dependence').
Table 8.11 reflects both influences.

Repeated Spells of Unemployment

In the steady state formula $U = I \times D$, which we have used above, individuals
who begin more than one spell of unemployment in the period would appear more
than once in the inflow into unemployment in the time period chosen. I is the
number of spells of unemployment which begin during the period. If we define
I_f as the number of persons who become unemployed during the period and S
as the average number of unemployment spells per person, we can rewrite the
basic identity as

$$U = I_f \times S \times D$$

or, dividing by L,

$$\frac{U}{L} = \frac{I_f}{L} \times S \times D$$

which can also be expressed as:

Unemployment rate	average risk of a member of the = labour force entering unemployment	× average no. of spells per person entering unemployment	× Average duration of an un- employment spell

Of course if the time period used is very short it will be difficult for any person to become unemployed more than once so that S is very close to unity and we could simply revert to the formula $U = I \times D$. However, in studying inequalities in unemployment, it is important to take account of multiple spells. Thus if, for example, teenagers and young adults have shorter durations on average than old workers, but are more prone to repeat spells, then it would be possible for young workers on average to spend as much time unemployed during a given period (two years, say) as older workers, even though the latter have, on average, longer complete durations. Good data on repeated spells are hard to come by, ideally requiring longitudinal data on cohorts of individuals. Using less than ideal data, a number of studies have provided evidence of the pervasiveness of multiple spells. A study in the UK (Smee and Stern, 1976) relating to the year June 1971 to June 1972 (at that time a year of high unemployment) found that the average male claimant of unemployment benefit had 1.8 spells during that year, while, remarkably for such a short time span, 1.7 per cent of male claimants had 10 or more spells. The distribution is shown in more detail in Table 8.12. Thus, even during one year, the 66 per cent of persons with only one spell of unemployment account for only 35 per cent of all spells. A number of more recent studies quoted in OECD (1983, 1985) document the tendency for teenagers and young adults to be the groups most prone to multiple spells of unemployment. Thus in France, between October 1977 and March 1978, 13.5 per cent of all male teenage unemployed had two or more spells compared with 8.7 per cent of all unemployed adults.

Moylan et al. (1982), in a study of male unemployment in the UK during the period Autumn 1978−Autumn 1979, found that 35 per cent of their sample had more than one spell of unemployment. For the whole sample the median duration of the first unemployment spell was 15 weeks but the median time spent unemployed during the year was 22 weeks. For the subsample who experienced

Table 8.12

Percentage of male claimants with:						
1 spell	2 spells	3 spells	4 spells	5 spells	6+ spells	Total
66	20	7	3	1	3	100
Percentage of all spells:						
35	22	11.1	6.4	2.7	22.8	100

more than a single spell the median time spent unemployed was just under six months. This group was slightly younger on average than the sample as a whole.

With this background in the analysis of inflows, duration and multiple spells, we are in a position to analyse inequalities and disparities in the unemployment experience of different groups. We concentrate on the effects of age, sex and occupation/industry but also refer briefly to the effects of other factors such as marital status, race and region.

Age and Unemployment

One of the main factors influencing a person's unemployment experience is age. In this section we provide some evidence on the age–unemployment relationship and discuss some of the factors which generate it. The problem of youth unemployment is highlighted.

Table 8.13 illustrates a broadly similar distribution of unemployment by age in the UK and US. In both countries over 50 per cent of the unemployed are prime-aged (25–44) workers but teenagers and younger adults, at around 40 per cent of the total unemployment in each country, are clearly over-represented in unemployment relative to their numbers in the labour force. This is shown clearly in row 1 of Table 8.14. Unemployment rates by age for Great Britain start at high levels, declining during prime working ages and rising again slightly for older members of the labour force.

The next two rows of Table 8.14 show that the high unemployment rates for young people result from the high probability of entering unemployment for the under 25s. Quarterly probabilities of entering unemployment decline with age. Median durations, on the other hand, follow a U-shaped pattern (for 18-year olds and above). The high youth rates for the UK are not an isolated phenomenon as Table 8.15 shows. Even though youth unemployment rates differ from country to country they are universally higher than the overall unemployment rate, twice as high on average (Germany is an exception). With the exception of the US, youth unemployment rates increased substantially between 1980 and 1984, but not in relation to total unemployment.

Table 8.13 Unemployment by Age, UK and US, 1984 (Percentage of total Unemployment)

	19 and under	20–24	25–34	35–44	45–54	55 and over	Total
UK	15.9	22.3	23.5	14.5	12.9	10.9	100
US	17.5	21.5	27.8	15.6	9.8	7.8	100

Sources: UK: Department of Employment, *Employment Gazette* (Oct. 1985).
US: US Department of Labor (1985).

Table 8.14 Unemployment Rates, Inflow Probabilities and Durations by Age, GB, 1985

	Under 18	18–19	20–24	25–29	30–34	35–44	45–54	55+	All ages
Unemployment rates (%)[a]	18.3	24.4	20.2	15.6	11.9	8.8	9.3	10.9	13.2
Likelihood of becoming unemployed (%)[b]	15.8	10.2	8.6	5.3	3.7	2.6	2.1	2.1	4.7
Median duration[b] (completed spells in weeks)	6.8	18.6	18.1	19.2	17.5	15.2	14.4	20.0	16.0

Source: Department of Employment, *Employment Gazette* (Oct. 1985).
Notes: (a) July 1985.
      (b) April–July 1985.

Table 8.15 Youth[a] Unemployment in Selected OECD Countries, 1980, 1984

	1980		1984	
	Youth rate	Youth rate / Aggregate rate	Youth rate	Youth rate / Aggregate rate
US	13.3	1.9	13.3	1.8
Japan	3.6	1.8	4.9	1.8
Germany	3.9	1.3	10.1	1.2
France	15.0	2.3	26.1	2.7
UK	14.1	2.0	21.8	1.7
Italy	25.2	3.4	34.1	3.3
Canada	13.2	1.8	7.9	1.6
Australia	12.3	2.1	16.1	1.8
Sweden	5.1	2.6	6.0	1.9
Mean	11.7	2.1	16.7	2.0

Sources: OECD (1985, Table 10.2).
Note: (a) 'Youth' refers to persons aged 24 and under.

Why do young people have such high probabilities of entering unemployment? Firstly many of them are entering the labour force for the first time (nearly 50 per cent of teenage unemployed in the US — see Table 8.16), a source of 'recruitment' into unemployment which is ruled out by definition for the majority in older age groups. While searching for the type of employment which might be suitable for a career, young workers are likely to sample a number of jobs. If we exclude new entrants, then Table 8.16 shows that US teenagers do have a higher propensity to quit than do older workers (15.1 per cent compared to 10.6 per cent).

Table 8.16 Reasons for Entering Unemployment by Age, US, 1984 (per cent)

	Ages 16–19		Ages 20 and over	
Job losers	18.1	35.9[a]	59.0	62.2[a]
(lay-offs)	(4.3)	(8.5)	(15.8)	(16.6)
(other)	(13.8)	(27.4)	(43.2)	(45.6)
Job leavers	7.6	5.1	10.1	10.6
Re-entrants	24.6	49.0	25.7	27.2
New entrants	49.7	—	5.2	—
Total	100.0	100.0	100.0	100.0

Source: US Department of Labor (1985).
Note: (a) Columns 2 and 4 exclude new entrants.

This may also be due to the fact that many of the jobs available to young workers are menial and dead-end, which in turn may be partly due to the low skill levels and lack of firm-specific human capital possessed by young people. These and other factors mean that continuity of association between worker and firm has not yet been established. The costs to either party of severing the association are low. The relatively short durations of the young unemployed suggest that the types of jobs in which teenagers are employed are relatively easy to find. But care is needed in this interpretation. Firstly, as we have seen above, although median unemployment durations for young persons are relatively short, the young form over a quarter of the long-term unemployed in the UK (the comparable figure for the US is just over 5 per cent). Secondly, the relatively short durations may be illusory if young people are particularly prone to multiple spells of unemployment. This can happen if youths become discouraged by unemployment and leave the labour force only to re-enter the stock of unemployed after a short period. In many respects such a sequence is best regarded as a single unemployment spell. Table 8.16 shows that, in fact, the proportion of inflow (excluding new entrants) into unemployment accounted for by labour force re-entrants is much higher for teens than for older workers in the US. In the US, in 1983, 36.4 per cent of males and 34.6 per cent of females aged 16–19 who were unemployed experienced multiple spells.

At the other end of the age spectrum older workers, although their probability of entering unemployment is relatively low, have long durations if they are unfortunate enough to become unemployed. Physical and mental powers, adaptability, etc. may begin to wane (or employers believe this to be the case) towards the end of the working life. Job search motivation may also be weaker for older workers. In addition, reservation wages of older searchers may be unrealistically high if based on the wage received in last employment, which in turn may have reflected seniority rather than current productivity.

Table 8.17 Male and Female Unemployment 1972–1984, UK and US

	Unemployed women as percentage total unemployment		Unemployment rates			
			UK[a]		US	
	UK	US	M	F	M	F
1972	14.5	45.5	5.0	1.6	5.0	6.6
1974	14.5	47.3	3.6	1.1	4.9	6.7
1976	22.5	45.5	7.3	4.0	7.1	8.6
1978	26.9	49.4	7.3	5.0	6.3	7.0
1980	29.0	44.1	8.3	4.8	6.8	6.7
1982	26.8	42.1	15.0	7.9	10.3	8.9
1984	30.6	44.4	15.7	9.4	7.4	7.6

Sources: UK: Department of Employment, *Employment Gazette* (various issues).
         US: US Department of Labor (1985).
Note: (a) 1972–1978 rates refer to GB.

Male–Female Unemployment Differentials

Men and women tend to have different skills, labour market experience and are not equally represented across all sectors/industries, so it is not surprising that they differ in their unemployment experience. In the UK for example (see Table 8.17) women accounted for just over 30 per cent of total unemployment in 1984 and have significantly lower unemployment rates than men (due both to lower inflow probabilities and shorter durations). In both respects, however, Table 8.17 shows that the position of women has deteriorated. In the US, by contrast, women are more equally represented in the unemployment stock and have similar unemployment rates to men.

Unemployment by Occupation and Industry

Unemployment in all countries is very unequally distributed by skill (occupation) and industry. Table 8.18 illustrates this for Britain by looking not at unemployment itself but at redundancies — a major component of the inflow into unemployment.

Table 8.18 indicates the extent to which the recent recession in Britain was concentrated in manufacturing industries with construction also having high redundancy probabilities. Comparably great disparities exist in other countries also. In the US in 1984, when the overall unemployment rate was 7.5 per cent, the unemployment rate in construction was 14.3 per cent, while in the industrial group-

Table 8.18 Confirmed Redundancies by Industry, GB, 1980 and 1984

	Redundancy rates per thousand employees		Percentage of total redundancies	
	1980	*1984*	*1980*	*1984*
Agriculture forestry & fishing	3.5	0.7	0.2	0.1
Energy & water supply	4.9	15.0	0.7	3.9
Manufacturing industries	59.6	27.9	81.5	63.3
Construction	29.5	23.5	7.1	9.5
Services	3.9	4.1	10.4	23.2
All	22.1	11.5	100.0	100.0

Source: Department of Employment, *Employment Gazette* (May 1985).

ing 'finance, insurance and real estate' it was only 3.7 per cent.[12] However, in manufacturing the rate was 7.5 per cent — identical to the overall rate. The US recession was less concentrated in manufacturing than was the case for the UK.

The occupational or skill structure of unemployment is perhaps more revealing than the industrial structure. In 1981 non-manual workers comprised 71 per cent of total unemployment in GB.[13] Again, similar patterns of unemployment by skill and occupation are observed in the United States: in 1983 when the overall unemployment rate was 9.6 per cent, managerial and professional workers had an unemployment rate of only 3.3 per cent, while the rate for 'operators, fabricators and laborers' was 15.5 per cent. Looking at what is essentially the same phenomenon from a different perspective we see in Table 8.19 that years of education are strongly negatively correlated with unemployment and increases in unemployment. Evidently education confers access to occupations/jobs with greater employment stability.

Unemployment by Race

In the US, and to a lesser extent in the UK, there are substantial differences in the unemployment rates of different racial and ethnic groups. In the US in 1984, the unemployment rate for white males (ages 16 and above) was 6.4 per cent, while for black males it was 26.4 per cent. For white and black women the

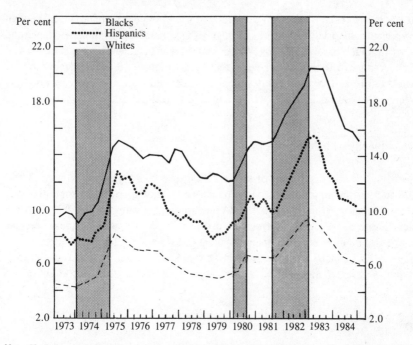

Note: Shaded areas indicate recessions as designated by the National Bureau of Economic Research.

Figure 8.3 Unemployment Rates of Blacks, Hispanics and Whites, Quarterly Averages, Seasonally Adjusted 1973−84

Table 8.19 Unemployment Rates (%) by Education, USA, 1978, 1985

	1978	1985	% increase
1−3 years high school	12.4	15.9	28.0
4 years high school	6.2	8.0	29.0
1−3 years college	4.6	5.1	10.9
4+ years college	2.5	2.6	4.0
Overall unemployment rate	6.1	7.2	18.0

Source: Summers (1986).

unemployment rates were 6.5 per cent and 15.4 per cent respectively. The proportionate disparity for teenagers is roughly the same, although of course the actual
rates are much higher. In 1984, 41 per cent of black teenagers were unemployed
compared to 15.6 per cent of white teenagers. Figure 8.3 (which refers to persons aged 16 and over) illustrates the differences dramatically, showing also how
white—nonwhite disparities are accentuated during recession.

Unemployment by Region

Finally,[14] in this discussion of the structure of unemployment, we note that in
all countries unemployment tends to be very unevenly distributed geographically.
For example in Britain in April 1984 unemployment rates ranged from 9.4 per
cent (South East) to 17.7 per cent (North), with corresponding annual percentage probabilities of entering unemployment of 13.3 and 17.2, and completed durations of 12.3 and 16.5 weeks. In the US, regional differences also exist but, due
in part to greater mobility of labour, are less persistent than in the UK.[15]

B. Causes

8.3 Real Wages and Unemployment

It is frequently claimed that the explanation of the mass unemployment documented
in the early part of this chapter is to be found in 'excessive' or 'too high' real
wages. The corollary, implicit or explicit, is that real wage cuts are required to
reduce unemployment.

Rather than discussing what has become known as the 'real wage debate' in
the abstract, it is instructive to relate it to the dramatic and pervasive increases
in unemployment that occurred in the 1970s and, particularly, the early 1980s.
Of course this was a period during which deterioration across a whole range of
macroeconomic indicators (inflation, GDP growth, productivity growth, as well
as unemployment) indicated a deep malaise throughout most of the industrialised
world (*all* OECD countries for example). Naturally the causes of such a
phenomenon are not simple to analyse nor, as yet, does a consensus exist among
professional economists as to the respective roles of different factors in explaining the magnitude and persistence of the world recession. With respect to
unemployment in OECD countries, however, it is widely agreed that the *supply
shocks* (mainly the oil price increases of 1973—4 and 1979—80, but also increases
in commodity prices, exchange rate depreciations and competition from the newly
industrialised countries) and the policy responses to these shocks are crucial
elements of any explanation. We will therefore consider firstly what elementary
theory has to tell us about the impact of supply shocks, concentrating on the role

of real wages, and subsequently examine some empirical evidence relating to these questions.

We begin in a microeconomic setting (the theoretical background is discussed in Chapters 3 and 4). Writing the production function as

$$Q = F(N,M,K) \tag{8.1}$$

where M refers to raw material inputs (including oil), in the short run with capital fixed ($K = K_1$) the labour demand function for profit-maximising[16] firms can be written

$$N_d = N_d\left(\frac{W}{P}, \frac{P_M}{P} : K_1\right) \tag{8.2}$$
$$\quad\quad\quad - \quad - \quad +$$

where P_M is the price of raw materials, P is the product price, and the signs indicate whether the dependent variable N_d will increase ($+$) or decrease ($-$) when the independent variable increases.

The labour demand function is shown in Figure 8.4, in which it can be seen

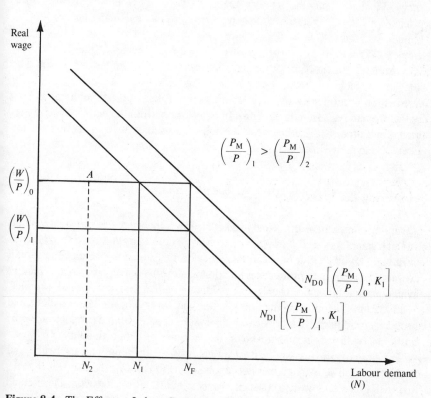

Figure 8.4 The Effect on Labour Demand of an Increase in the Price of Raw Materials

that, when materials prices increase, the demand for materials falls and, as materials and labour are complementary in production, the labour demand curve shifts inwards. If the real wage stays unchanged at $(w/P)_0$, labour demand falls from N_F to N_1. To maintain labour demand at N_F (full employment) the real wage must fall to $(w/P)_1$ assuming labour supply is completely inelastic (if it is not then the required fall in the wage is less). The amount by which the real wage must fall in order to maintain full employment, $(w/P)_0 - (w/P)_1$, is often referred to as the *wage gap*.

Two observations about economic policy are in order here. Firstly, any form of indexation of nominal wages to prices, either via formal indexation or due to 'real wage resistance' in collective bargaining, while maintaining living standards of those in work, will prevent the required fall in the real wage in response to the adverse supply shock.[17] Secondly, we note the effect of a contractionary monetary or fiscal policy in the circumstances of an adverse supply shock. Such policies were, of course, widely adopted in Europe following the oil shocks because it was believed that expansionary or 'accommodating' policies would trigger off accelerating inflation. By reducing aggregate demand (AD) such contractionary policies, if severe enough, can exacerbate the unemployment effects of the supply shock. Firms find that they cannot sell as much as they would like to at existing prices. This is reflected by firms being off their labour demand curves, e.g. at point A in Figure 8.4. At the real wage w_0/P_0 profit maximising firms would employ N_1 but they are constrained from doing so in the goods market. $N_1 - N_2$ is, of course, 'Keynesian', or demand deficient, unemployment, which could be alleviated without any reduction in the real wage if AD was increased (conversely, a reduction in the real wage cannot on its own restore full employment as long as the demand constraint is binding). In other words from the output and employment point of view the deflationary policies followed by many governments are likely to have aggravated the consequences of the supply shocks of the 1970s.

Measuring the Wage Gap[18]

Assuming competitive firms and market clearing, the wage gap can be measured and calculated as $(w/P - MP_L^f)$ where MP_L^f is the marginal product of labour at full employment. But how can this latter be measured? In principle one could estimate an aggregate production function and evaluate MP_L at $L = L_f$. Readily available data, however, usually reveal labour's average, not marginal, product. With a Cobb–Douglas production function, however, knowledge of the average product would be sufficient because the marginal and average products are proportional (with labour's share being the constant of proportionality).[19]

This property forms the basis of an analysis of the wage gap by Bruno and Sachs (1985). The average product of labour, AP_L, is measured at cyclical peaks and is assumed to grow at a constant exponential rate between peaks. This method yields an index of the wage required to maintain full employment, which is subtracted from an index of the actual real wage to give a real wage gap index.[20]

Table 8.20 presents a selection of Bruno and Sachs' results. Several points of note emerge from the table. Firstly, looking at the averages, we see that after the middle and late 1960s when the gap was negligible, it increased steadily throughout the 1970s and into the 1980s in the major OECD countries taken together. This coincides with a period of high and rising unemployment.[21] The differences between the UK and the US are equally interesting. While in 1973 both countries had an equal (percentage) wage gap, by the mid-1970s the gap had been eliminated in the US but was still growing in the UK. Although other factors undoubtedly played a part, it is surely no coincidence that US unemployment fell during the mid/late 1970s while UK unemployment continued to rise. A real wage gap again emerged in the US during the second recession at the end of the 1970s but by this time the UK wage gap was running at more than twice the US level.

In Chapter 7 we examined some theoretical reasons for rigid real wages. However, the differences between countries in their real wage/unemployment histories suggests that a fuller explanation must include structural and institutional differences between countries in their wage setting mechanisms. Thus Bruno and Sachs argue that the low degree of indexation of wages to prices, coupled with relatively long (three-year) wage–employment contracts, produce much greater moderation in real wage growth in the US.[22] By contrast, more extensive indexation and/or frequent bargaining prevents such moderation in many European countries. Apart from the US, those countries that performed better in terms of wage moderation and unemployment have (nominal) wage setting mechanisms characterised by a high degree of 'corporatism'; negotiation is highly centralised with bargaining between functional groups (trades union councils, employers federations, central government) rather than plant level negotiation with rank and file voting. Countries cited as having a high degree of corporatism are Germany and Sweden, while countries such as Australia, France and the UK do not have strongly corporatist structures; wage setting is decentralised, plant level voting/ratification is common, contract duration is short, etc. Bruno and Sachs construct an 'index of corporatism' (high values of the index are associated with

Table 8.20 The Real Wage Gap, 1965–1981 (%) (1965–9 average = 0.0)

	1965	1969	1973	1975	1979	1981
UK	-1.5	1.1	3.1	9.9	14.1	19.3
US	1.2	0.0	3.1	-0.1	6.1	8.1
OECD Big Six (average)	0.4	-0.2	3.7	7.4	8.0	10.4

Source: Bruno and Sachs (1985, p. 180).
Notes: The OECD Big Six are Canada, France, Germany, Japan, UK, US.
The 1981 figure for the Big Six excludes Canada and Japan for which 1981 data were unavailable.

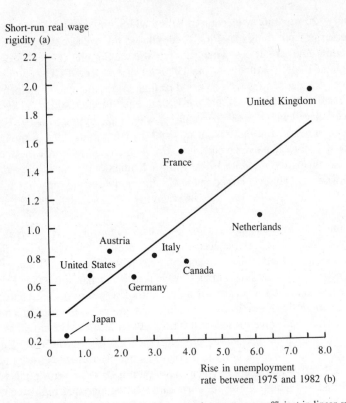

Figure 8.5 Short-Run Real Wage Rigidity and Unemployment

Notes: (a) Short-run price coefficient divided by unemployment rate coefficient in linear specification (money wage equations). (b) Percentage points.

a strongly corporatist structure) and show that it is negatively correlated with the real wage gap.

The inter-country correlation between wage rigidity and unemployment increases (between 1975 and 1982) is strikingly confirmed in Figure 8.5. The index of real wage rigidity on the vertical axis depends positively on the responsiveness of money wages to price changes and negatively on the responsiveness of money wages to unemployment.[23]

Real Wages in Econometric Models of the Labour Market

An alternative method of examining some of the above issues is to estimate econometrically a model of the labour market in which employment, unemployment and real wages are endogenous outcomes. Such models can be used to simulate the effects of alternative policy options. Furthermore because such models emphasise that real wages are determined by interactions of supply, demand and adjustment mechanisms within the labour market, they help to dispel the erroneous notion that real wages are exogenous policy instruments that can be manipulated directly and at will to bring about desired macroeconomic outcomes such as the reduction of unemployment.

The basic elements of such a model (some of which have been discussed separately in earlier chapters) are as follows:

1. *A labour demand schedule*

$$N_{dt} = N_{dt}(w_{pt}, \mathbf{Z}_{dt})$$ (8.3)

where w_{pt} is the *real product wage in period* t which is equal to $w_t(1+\tau_1)$ where w_t is the real pretax wage in period t and τ_1 is the rate of wage tax paid by employers. $\mathbf{Z}_{dt}$ is a vector of exogenous variables affecting the demand for labour. The real prices of other factors of production and, in some models, the size of the capital stock and output (aggregate demand)[24] and its lags are the types of variables typically included in $\mathbf{Z}_{dt}$. Lagged employment may also appear in order to capture the effects of adjustment costs.

2. *A labour supply schedule*

$$N_{st} = N_{st}(w_{ct}, \mathbf{Z}_{st})$$ (8.4)

where w_{ct} is the real consumption wage in period t which is equal to $w_t(1 - \tau_2)/(1 + \tau_3)$ where τ_2 is the income tax rate and τ_3 is the indirect tax rate[25] and $\mathbf{Z}_{st}$ is a vector of exogenous determinants of labour supply such as the size of the labour force, the real interest rate, etc.

3. *Choice of equilibrium versus disequilibrium framework*
   If we are to assume that observed wages and employment are equilibrium outcomes then the model is closed simply by specifying

$$N_{dt} = N_{st}$$ (8.5)

If, on the other hand, we wish to examine a disequilibrium framework then it is usual to allow employment (N_t) to be determined by the condition

$$N_t = \min(N_{dt}, N_{st})$$ (8.6)

which simply states that employment is determined on the short side of the market.

4. *A wage adjustment equation*

$$(w_t - w_{t-1}) = f[(N_{dt} - N_{st}), \mathbf{Z}_{wt}]$$ (8.7)

where $\mathbf{Z}_{wt}$ is a vector of factors causing wages to deviate from their equilibrium values, e.g. the degree of corporatism in the economy (see above).

Equation (8.7) states that the speed of adjustment of wages towards their market clearing level depends on the extent of excess demand and on the Z_{wt} factors
   Equation (8.7) (like (8.3) and (8.4)) is called a *structural equation* which means that its right-hand side contains endogenous variables. It can be transformed into a *reduced form equation* in which the right-hand side variables are all predetermined (i.e. not determined within the model in period t):

$$w_t = w_t(Z_{dt}, Z_{st}, Z_{wt}, \tau, w_{t-1}) \qquad (8.8)$$

where τ are the tax variables.

A similar reduced form wage equation can be derived from the market clearing model. It would not contain Z_{wt} or w_{t-1} which pertain to the disequilibrium specification only (although these variables could appear in alternative specifications of equilibrium versions of the model). Furthermore the form of (8.8) will depend on the solution to (8.6).
   The solution of the model also produces a reduced form equation explaining employment by the same set of predetermined variables:

$$N_t = N_t(Z_{dt}, Z_{st}, Z_{wt}, \tau, w_{t-1}) \qquad (8.9)$$

Note that, when the size of the labour force, L_t, is exogenous, we can translate any results relating to employment into corresponding unemployment results simply by using the identity $U_t = L_t - N_t$. More detailed models may make the size of the labour force itself an endogenous variable.
   Models with a structure described by equations (8.3)–(8.7), or similar, can be estimated (either on their own or as part of a larger macroeconomic model using time series data.[26] Once estimated, it may be possible to derive elasticities of employment, unemployment and real wages with respect to exogenous variables, including those, such as the tax rates, which are under the control of policy makers. Alternatively it is possible to conduct simulation exercises whereby the value of a policy variable is changed and the model is used to predict changes in the endogenous variables.
   It is important to realise that the real wage is not one of the exogenous variables that can be altered in such simulations. With the full structure of the model before us we can see that it is not possible to make statements about causality between the two endogenous variables, unemployment and real wages.[27] These two variables are positively related via equations (8.3) and (8.4) and negatively related via equation (8.7). All the model can do is track the behaviour of both wages and unemployment when exogenous variables change. Of course it is true that estimation of the model will generally provide estimates of the coefficients of the labour demand curve, and thus of the elasticity of employment or unemployment with respect to the real wage, but this is of limited relevance for macroeconomic policy because the real wage is an endogenous variable, not a policy instrument.[28]
   The above argument does *not* imply that real wage behaviour is irrelevant to the unemployment problem — on the contrary, we have shown that it is crucial

Indeed if the government could control real wages the parameters of a macroeconometric model could be used to forecast the consequences. Usually, however, government cannot directly control real wages (except perhaps in the public sector where it can relate nominal wage settlements to the rate of infla- tion), but will have to do so by making changes in the tax variables, τ, and/or those variables in the $\mathbf{Z}$ vectors which are under its control. One such is the rate of unemployment benefit (which is an element of the $\mathbf{Z}_{st}$ vector). Andrews (1986), surveying four models of the type described above (using post-war data for the UK), reports estimated elasticities of the real wage with respect to unemployment benefit varying between 0.03 and 0.39 while the elasticity of unemployment with respect to benefits ranges from 0.13 to 2.8. While the range of these estimates is very large (too large perhaps to be of real use to policy makers) it does at least take account of the interdependence between wages and employ- ment (unemployment). Estimates of the effect of benefits on unemployment calculated from cross-section data (see below) are not able to take this interdependence into account, even though such studies are preferable in other respects.

8.4 Increases in the Non-Accelerating Inflation Rate of Unemployment

The main constraint on using Keynesian demand expansion to reduce mass unemployment in the 1970s and 1980s has been the fear that such policies would not only increase inflation but trigger off accelerating inflation. To understand the basis for this fear and to assess its validity we have to explain the concept of the natural rate of unemployment, or more accurately the non-accelerating inflation rate of unemployment (NAIRU). We do this briefly; further discussion and explanation can be found in virtually any modern macroeconomic textbook. Consider the following simple set-up:

$$\dot{W} = \alpha_0 + \alpha_1 U + \dot{P}_e + \alpha_2 \mathbf{Z}_w \tag{8.10}$$

$$\dot{P} = \beta_0 + \dot{W} + \beta_1 \mathbf{Z}_p \tag{8.11}$$

$$\dot{P}_e = \dot{P}_{-1} \tag{8.12}$$

Dots above variables indicate the time rate of change, e.g.

$$\dot{W} = \frac{(dW/dt)}{W}$$

Equation (8.10) (which is very similar to (8.7) above) states that money wage inflation depends on expected price inflation, negatively (i.e. $\alpha_1 < 0$) on unemployment, and on a vector of 'wage push' factors (union militancy, taxes, unemployment benefit rates etc.). Equation (8.11) shows price inflation as a mark- up over wage inflation, modified by variables in the $\mathbf{Z}_p$ vector (productivity

growth, extent of competition in product markets, etc.). Equation (8.12) is a highly
simplified view of expectations formation which simply states that, in any given
period, expected inflation is equal to actual inflation in the previous period.

Substituting (8.10) into (8.11) yields

$$\dot{P} - \dot{P}_e = \beta_0 + \alpha_0 + \alpha_1 U + \alpha_2 \mathbf{Z}_w + \beta_1 \mathbf{Z}_p \tag{8.13}$$

i.e. there is a trade-off between *unanticipated* inflation and unemployment.
However, in a steady state equilibrium, inflation becomes fully anticipated, i.e.
$\dot{P} = \dot{P}_e$. Thus from (8.13) the steady state equilibrium level of unemployment is

$$U = \frac{-(\beta_0 + \alpha_0) - (\alpha_2 \mathbf{Z}_w + \beta_1 \mathbf{Z}_p)}{\alpha_1} \tag{8.14}$$

This is the NAIRU. There is no long-run ($\dot{P} = \dot{P}_e$) trade-off between inflation
and unemployment,[29] but any attempt to hold unemployment below its natural
rate will cause inflation to accelerate. To see this, suppose that the unemployment rate were less than the NAIRU. Equation (8.13) would then imply that actual
inflation exceeds expected inflation. Then (8.12) implies that in the subsequent
period expected inflation would have increased, and so, via (8.10) and (8.11),
actual wage and price inflation, w, $\dot{P}$ and $\dot{P}_e$ will all continue to increase as long
as the actual unemployment rate remains below the NAIRU. Thus if the actual
unemployment rate is equal to the NAIRU or less, attempts to reduce it by
aggregate demand expansion will cause inflation to accelerate. Policy should
instead be directed to reducing the natural rate itself by operating on variables
in the $\mathbf{Z}_w$, $\mathbf{Z}_p$ vectors. Conversely, if the actual unemployment rate exceeds the
NAIRU, demand expansion can be pursued without fear of triggering off
accelerating inflation. For policy purposes it is thus important to know what the
NAIRU is in practice.

Table 8.21 provides a set of estimates of the NAIRU (or natural rate of
unemployment) for the UK, Germany, Japan and the USA, and compares these
estimates with actual unemployment rates. The method used for estimating the
NAIRU is discussed in Appendix 8.2.

It must be stressed that these estimates depend both on the model specification
and econometric estimation techniques used by the authors, who stress the
approximate and tentative nature of their results. Other economists might particularly question whether the natural rate in the early 1980s is really as high
as Table 8.21 suggests. Bearing this in mind, the table indicates that during the
mid-1970s the natural rate was considerably higher in all countries than it was
in the early 1960s. However, in spite of the recession following the second oil
price shock, only in the UK (of the countries shown) did the natural rate continue
to increase into the 1980s. Further, the closeness of the calculated natural rate
to actual unemployment rates indicates limited scope for using aggregate demand
to reduce mass unemployment without triggering off accelerating inflation.

The implication of the figures in Table 8.21 is that while there is some scope

Table 8.21 Natural and Actual Unemployment Rates, UK, Germany, Japan and US

	1957–66	1967–74	1975–78	1979–82
UK				
Natural rate	2.03	4.25	7.53	10.47
Actual rate	2.03	3.78	6.80	11.28
Germany				
Natural rate	2.03	1.06	3.82	3.34
Actual rate	1.38	1.12	3.89	4.51
Japan				
Natural rate	1.56	1.89	2.47	2.37
Actual rate	1.56	1.25	2.04	2.18
USA				
Natural rate	5.18	4.71	7.80	6.20
Actual rate	5.18	4.35	7.05	7.31

Source: Layard and Nickell (1985a).
Note: The UK unemployment rates are for males only.

for reducing unemployment by expanding aggregate demand during the oil shock-induced recessions, this scope was limited. In such circumstances policy should be directed as well towards reducing the NAIRU. This can be achieved by operating on terms in the wage push vector Z_w — all the models we have examined place paramount importance on wage push factors in determining employment and unemployment outcomes in the labour market. Referring to Figure 8.8 in Appendix 8.2, reduction in wage push shifts the wage-setting line inwards, lowering the NAIRU at any feasible real wage determined by pricing behaviour.

The most direct way of attempting to reduce wage push is by means of incomes policy. This is discussed in more detail in Section 8.6. Other methods that might be used to achieve the same objective include:

(i) tax reductions (taxes increase wage push by driving a wedge between the production and the consumption wage, tax cuts increasing the latter relative to the former);

(ii) training, mobility and labour market coordination policies which reduce the mismatch between the unemployed and the vacancies they seek to fill;

(iii) policies, e.g. exchange rate policy, to control relative import prices (increases in import prices reduce the real consumption wage, and, if this is resisted by labour, unit labour costs will increase);

(iv) policies to reduce union wage pressure — these could take the form of legislation to reduce trade union power such as introduced by the Conservative Government in the UK since it came to power in 1979; wage-setting agreements with trade unions, whether in the shape of formal incomes policy or centralised mechanisms whereby unions explicitly take account of the macroeconomic context (such as in Germany and Sweden) are alternatives.

C. Cures

This section discusses several policy-related aspects of unemployment in more detail. It does not consider all possible policies, but rather concentrates on a number of issues which have received much attention in both the academic and public debate on unemployment. These are:

  (i) the effects of unemployment insurance;
 (ii) targeted policies, taking marginal employment subsidies and job guarantees for the long-term unemployed as examples;
(iii) incomes policies;
(iv) work-sharing.

8.5 Unemployment Insurance and Unemployment

During the high unemployment periods of the 1970s and 1980s much attention has been paid to the possibility that increases in the level of income available to persons out of work (unemployment insurance, henceforth UI) relative to income in work may have increased the incentive for workers to quit their jobs and a disincentive for the unemployed to return to work. In other words some of the observed increases in unemployment may have been induced by increases in unemployment benefits relative to income in work, i.e. by increases in the *replacement ratio*. This has suggested to some economists and policy makers that a reduction in the replacement ratio engineered by a reduction in unemployment benefit may be an effective method of reducing unemployment. For example Professor Minford (Minford, 1985) has suggested that the replacement ratio in the UK should not be permitted to exceed 70 per cent.

In the light of suggestions of this type it is worth pointing out that even if it could be clearly established that unemployment benefits were responsible for a substantial increase in the 'natural' or equilibrium rate of unemployment — and we argue below that this claim is *not* clearly established — it would not automatically follow that benefits ought to be reduced. The whole purpose of unemployment insurance is to provide an adequate income to those who become unemployed, often through no fault of their own. What is 'adequate' in this context is of course a social value judgement, but once this judgement has been made the consequences, including a possible increase in the NAIRU, must be accepted. A related point is that if 'generous' benefits enable the unemployed to search longer, and thus find employment which is better suited to their skills and preferences, this improves the overall efficiency of the labour market. At the very least any reductions in unemployment that may result from decreasing the replacement ratio must be set against the increased hardship to the unemployed that such a reduction implies.

In this section we examine how the relationship between UI and unemployment may be investigated empirically. Before doing so, however, we briefly explain the mechanism by which lower unemployment benefits may reduce unemployment. This is done with the aid of Figure 8.6 (refer back to the discussion of Figure 7.1 if uncertain about the analysis used here).

By reducing the income support received while unemployed, lower benefits would increase the willingness of individuals to hold jobs at any given wage. The supply curve would thus move outwards from S_1 to S_2. Assuming flexible wages (Figure 8.6(a)) this lowers the real wage from w_1 to w_2, increasing employment from N_1 to N_2 and reducing voluntary unemployment from U_1 to U_2. This is a reduction in the equilibrium rate of unemployment. If the reduction in benefits induced some of the unemployed to drop out of the labour force altogether the LF line would shift inwards, reducing unemployment even more. Where real wages are inflexible downwards, as illustrated in Figure 8.6(b), both employment and unemployment would be unaffected (unless the labour force is reduced), i.e. $(U_{1A} + U_{1B}) = (U_{2A} + U_{2B})$. All that has changed is the distribution of total unemployment as between its voluntary and involuntary components, the latter increasing.

The analysis just described summarises the main potential effects of a change in the level of UI at the level of the aggregate labour market. It has the advantage of including demand as well as supply in the analysis. In particular it shows the

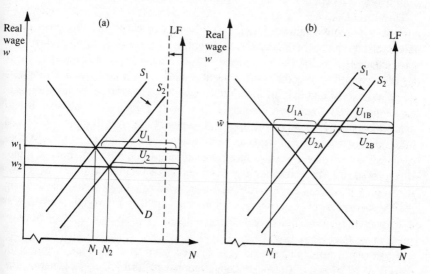

Figure 8.6 The Effects of Reducing Unemployment Benefit

effect of a change in UI on the demand for labour via the effects on the wage; an increase in UI increases the market clearing wage, reducing the quantity of labour demanded. However, if we are to really understand the *mechanism* by which these changes occur, it is necessary to model the way UI affects labour market turnover, i.e. its effect on individual decisions about which labour market state — employment, unemployment, or outside the labour force — to choose in any particular period. For this purpose the search and contract models discussed in Chapter 7 provide the relevant framework.[30] We saw in our discussion of job search that increases in UI raise the reservation wage and prolong unemployment duration. Of course theory on its own can tell us nothing about the magnitude of this effect; it may be small or even zero. For example if the lack of job offers drives the reservation wage so low that it is below the lowest wage offer likely to be received in practice (virtually any offer would be accepted, search is for a vacancy rather than a higher wage offer) then an increase in UI could have a negligible effect on unemployment, or none at all.

There is a vast literature on the effects of unemployment benefit on voluntary unemployment. What follows is necessarily very selective, conveying the principal ways of looking at the problem and the general thrust of the results.

The first type of evidence suggesting that UI might have had an effect on the natural rate of unemployment is provided by the increase over time of the amount of unemployment existing at given levels of vacancies. For example, in Britain during the 1970s, the unemployment rate increased by two-thirds at given vacancies while unemployment duration rose by 150 per cent at given vacancy duration (Jackman *et al.*, 1985). Increased numbers of unemployed at any given level of vacancies is certainly consistent with the unemployed being more choosy about which jobs to accept — one of the implications of higher UI in job search models.

The shift of the $U-V$ curve, however, can only offer suggestive evidence of the effect of the real value of UI on unemployment because there are other possible explanations of the increase in the numbers unemployed at given levels of vacancies. Shifts in the $U-V$ curve may also reflect changes in attitudes towards UI which would not emerge in cross-section studies, i.e. an increased willingness to claim benefits and live off them while searching. Similarly if eligibility tests for claiming UI (requiring claimants to provide evidence of job search and availability for work) have been applied less rigorously over time, this too could effect duration of unemployment, even at given real levels of benefits. Other explanations of the $U-V$ shift may have nothing to do with UI. For example, if factors such as sectoral shifts in product and labour demand resulted in a growing mismatch between those becoming unemployed and the jobs available to them, the $U-V$ curve would be observed shifting outwards, as it would be if *employers* were becoming more choosy in their recruitment, possibly as a result of employment protection legislation.

Superior, in principle, is evidence derived from studies which examine the effects of UI directly. These can take a number of forms, but the general principle is to estimate equations which explain one or more of the labour market transitions relevant to unemployment, including UI as one of the group of explanatory variables. The transitions of particular interest are:

(i) the flow from employment into unemployment via lay-offs;
(ii) the flow from employment into unemployment via quits;
(iii) the flow from unemployment into employment (hires and rehires);
(iv) the flow from unemployment into non-participation (i.e. out of the labour force);
(v) the flow from non-participation into unemployment.

In the UK, empirical work has concentrated on the possible effects of UI on flows out of unemployment, (iii) and (iv), or, equivalently, on the duration of unemployment. This is partly due to data limitations, but also because, as we showed earlier in this chapter, increases in UK unemployment in the 1970s and early 1980s were largely the result of increased durations. In the US, while there are also many studies of the effects of UI on duration, the effect on inflows into unemployment, (i) and (ii), have been studied more than in the UK. This partly reflects the fact that variations in inflows are more important in explaining variations in unemployment in the US and partly because different institutions make it more likely a priori that UI will affect inflows.[31]

Contract theory, discussed in Chapter 7, suggests a completely different connection between UI and lay-offs: higher real values of UI will make workers more willing, *ex ante*, to enter into contracts with temporary lay-off provisions or with higher lay-off probabilities (even those, *ex post*, lay-offs are determined by employers, and workers prefer continued employment to being laid off). Positive effects of UI on lay-offs in the US have been found in empirical work by Feldstein (1975, 1976).

Before examining the relationship between UI and unemployment, it would be instructive to ascertain the facts about changes in the real value of UI relative to income in work, i.e. to chart what has been happening to the replacement ratio (henceforth R) over time. Unfortunately this is not as easy to do as might be supposed. This is because both conceptual and measurement problems make it difficult to define and measure R appropriately and accurately. Often, especially in aggregate time series studies, R is measured as a labour force average, for example as the average level of UI divided by average earnings. Sometimes this average will be hypothetical, not actual: UI is calculated by applying eligibility rules to an 'average' family (usually taken to be a married couple with two children, spouse not working). Such methods fail to capture the diversity of circumstances of the unemployed and may seriously misrepresent the position they face: not all unemployed households claim all the benefits to which they are entitled (this can affect income in work as well as unemployment income), entitlement rules themselves may not always, or in all places, be applied with equal strictness and in any case depend on household composition and earnings. Furthermore the presumed 'typical' household is often not at all typical of the unemployed (for example in Britain only about 25 per cent of the unemployed, at the most, are heads of households comprising a married couple with two children in which the spouse is not working — between 40 per cent and 50 per cent of the unemployed are in fact single).

Conceptual problems in calculating R arise in deciding whether the ratio should be *backward looking* — to what extent does UI replace income in the unemployed's previous job (where there was one) — or *forward looking* — how large is UI relative to the income an unemployed person could reasonably expect in employment. If skills depreciate or become obsolete, or if labour market conditions, and/or the searchers' expectations of them, are changing, then these alternative measures of R can differ substantially. The backward looking measure is probably more relevant to judging the adequacy of UI, while the forward looking measure better captures its disincentive effects. Obviously the forward looking measure poses severe measurement problems because expected income in work is not observable. It is usually imputed from the earnings of those in work with similar characteristics to the unemployed person whose R one is trying to calculate. From our discussion in Chapter 2 it should not be difficult to see that this approach may be subject to sample selection bias.

Using data on benefits and employment incomes by family type, and weighting these by the proportions of each family type in unemployment, Layard and Nickell calculate the following replacement ratios for Britain (per cent):

1956–60	1961–5	1966–70	1971–5	1976–80	1980–3
39.3	43.8	51.0	48.1	48.6	52.8

Basically, R increased in the 1950s and 1960s, but has been untrended since then. So, on the basis of this time series, it is not plausible a priori that the large increases in unemployment in the 1970s and early 1980s could have been caused by increases in UI relative to earnings.

However, to show how much is concealed by the use of averages as well as to show the effect of changing the definition of R, Table 8.22 shows the enormous variation *in the actual* replacement ratios faced by a group of unemployed

Table 8.22 Percentage Distribution of Average Replacement Ratios for those in Weeks 5–13 of a Spell of Unemployment: UK, Males, 1973–1977

	<25	25–49	50–79	80–99	100+	Total	<50	≥80	Mean R	CV
R_1	4	29	47	16	4	100	33	20	63.5	0.63
R_2	7	39	41	9	4	100	46	13	56	0.55

Source: Atkinson and Micklewright (1985); FES data.

Notes: R_1 is the ratio of after-tax incomes (including income unrelated to employment status) out of work and in last job.

R_2 excludes income unrelated to employment status (pension, wife's income, etc.) from both numerator and denominator.

CV is the coefficient of variation (standard deviation divided by mean).

males in the UK. The table also shows that changing the definition of R can have substantial effects both on its mean value and distribution.

Having discussed the measurement of R we can now briefly discuss the methodology and results which investigate the extent to which changes in this variable (or sometimes income in work and out of work — the numerator and denominator of R — treated as separate variables) can explain changes in unemployment rates or durations, other factors having been controlled for as suggested by theory and permitted by the data.

Macroeconomic time series studies, more common in Britain than in the US, produce widely varying results. The British studies initially focused on the question of whether the increases in unemployment from 1967 into the early 1970s could be attributed to increases in R caused by the introduction of the Earnings Related Supplement in 1966. Gujarati (1972) and Maki and Spindler (1975), among others, claimed to have demonstrated empirically that increases in UI substantially increased unemployment. However, the results were subsequently shown to be not at all robust to variations in the set of explanatory variables or to the choice of period over which the effect is estimated (see Atkinson, 1981). One reason for the lack of robustness is presumably the somewhat *ad hoc* nature of the equations estimated; these being only tenuously related to any underlying analytical structure. However, studies in which the effect of UI is embedded in structural models of the labour market still produce bewilderingly different results. For example Layard and Nickell (1985a) find an elasticity of unemployment with respect to UI of about 0.7 while Minford (1985) reports an elasticity of 4.0.

Applying the time series method to an earlier historical period of high British unemployment, from 1921 to 1938 when unemployment never fell below 9.5 per cent, Benjamin and Kochin (1979), in a controversial study, concluded that 'the persistently high rate of unemployment in interwar Britain was due in large part not to deficient aggregate demand but to high unemployment insurance benefits relative to wages', and, more specifically, that 'over the period as a whole the insurance system raised the average unemployment rate by about five to eight percentage points'. This has proved to be a highly contentious conclusion, in part because it offers an alternative explanation of the same unemployment episode that led Keynes to formulate his General Theory, which propounded a view of an involuntary unemployment equilibrium due to deficient aggregate demand. However, as with previous studies, Benjamin and Kochin's conclusions are sensitive to the conventions adopted in measuring R. For example Metcalf *et al.* (1982) dispute the high values of R used by Benjamin and Kochin, claiming that, when correctly measured, replacement ratios were no higher, and generally lower, during the inter-war years than in the post-war era of low unemployment.

The problem of measuring R accurately, even of giving a meaningful interpretation of an average replacement ratio, suggests that studies based on individual data — enabling the true R faced by each individual to be identified — are likely to produce more reliable results. In general this is true, but it is worth noting that studies based on microeconomic data (usually from a single cross-section, although the use of panel data, in which surveys of individuals are repeated over time, is becoming more common) have certain shortcomings of their own. These relate to the difficulty of using results, which show how *individuals'* unemployment duration is affected by UI, to predict the effect of a change in UI on the *aggregate* level of unemployment. This is not straightforward.[32] Suppose that in the cross-section there are some individuals who are unaffected by UI. The estimated duration elasticity is an average which, while influenced by these individuals, will turn out to be positive as long as some individuals *do* prolong their duration when UI increases. This will, on average, increase the vacancies available to those who are unaffected by UI and increase their probability of leaving unemployment, i.e. duration will actually be shortened for this group. It is conceivable that there is no affect on aggregate unemployment even though the cross-section evidence shows duration to be a positive function of UI.

A similar problem related to the heterogeneity of individuals can arise if cross-section studies focus on durations, ignoring the effect of UI on quits. An increase in UI could increase the duration of those currently unemployed, but induce quits by individuals likely to find jobs again quickly. In these circumstances the average duration of unemployment could actually fall, even though UI increases expected duration for each individual, because the stock of unemployed persons now contains a higher proportion of short duration individuals. Nor would aggregate unemployment fall when UI increased, even where cross-section evidence shows UI to increase duration, if the real wage was rigid at a level above market clearing level. The increase in UI would then simply reallocate total unemployment, increasing the voluntary component (this can be seen by referring back to Figure 8.6). Finally, a more obvious point is that the results of a cross-section study may simply be inapplicable to periods other than that to which the data apply. This may be particularly important when the macroeconomic climate is changing. It may be misleading to predict the effect of UI on duration, in a time of high unemployment, on the basis of results derived from a cross-section taken when the labour market was tighter. Cross-section studies sometimes do attempt to pick up the effect of changing labour market conditions by allowing an index of labour market tightness, say the ratio of vacancies to unemployment, to vary regionally. However, it is unlikely that this method will accurately simulate the effects on re-employment probabilities of changes in the aggregate unemployment rate (or the aggregate V/U ratio).

Most cross-section studies utilise data from surveys of currently unemployed individuals. Thus it is not possible to estimate directly the effects of UI on completed duration. Instead, it is recognised that a spell of unemployment is a probabilistic process in which, during each period making up the spell, the individual has some chance of leaving unemployment. This chance depends on individual characteristics, including R and, possibly, the amount of time already spent unemployed. One then estimates the conditional probability of an individual still being unemployed in period t, given that he or she entered unemployment n periods earlier. From this the probability of leaving unemployment (the 'escape' probability, or the 'hazard' as it is sometimes known) can be derived, and from this in turn the expected duration of unemployment can be estimated.[33]

While studies of this type have themselves produced rather a wide range of
stimates of the effects of UI (see Atkinson and Micklewright, 1985), although
ot as wide a range as do time series studies, a recent British study (Narendranathan
al., 1985), using superior data to earlier studies,[34] produced results which are
oth highly significant in statistical terms and which appear to be robust to alter-
ative specifications of the model and composition of the sample on which it is
stimated. The main results (all referring to males only) are as follows:

1. The elasticity of expected unemployment duration with respect to unemployment benefits lies between 0.3 and 0.35. This is lower than previous cross-
   section estimates for Britain (Lancaster and Nickell, 1980; Nickell, 1979).
   As the earlier results come from periods of lower unemployment, the
   implication is that the benefit elasticity falls as aggregate unemployment
   increases. This accords with intuition.
2. The conditional probability of leaving unemployment does not fall with duration (in terms of the footnote on the previous page the coefficient α is
   estimated as being not significantly different from unity). In terms of job
   search theory this implies that the reservation wage must be falling as the
   unemployment spell is extended. It is known that the longer persons are
   unemployed, the fewer job offers they receive; employers believe that skills
   have depreciated, or simply that being unemployed for a long time is
   evidence that the individual has 'adverse' characteristics as a potential
   employee). This would, *ceteris paribus*, lower the escape probability. If
   this is not happening the reservation wage must be falling to offset the reduction in the frequency of job offers.
3. After six months of unemployment UI ceases to have any effect on the escape
   probability (except for teenagers). In terms of search theory this means that
   the expected utility from prolonging unemployment has fallen to a level
   where the probability of accepting a job offer approaches unity. As we
   argued above, increases in UI will not increase unemployment in these circumstances and this result can and has been used in support of increasing
   the level of UI paid to the long-term unemployed, who after all suffer most.
   This should not affect the aggregate unemployment rate.
4. The escape probability falls with age, as does the elasticity of expected duration with respect to UI (0.8 for teenagers, 0.4 for men aged 20–24, 0.2
   for ages 25–44 and zero for men over 45).

The methodology followed in this study and the results obtained are fairly
presentative of cross-sectional and longitudinal studies both in the UK and the
S, although of course each study will differ as to details. However, it is worth
ting the results of an American study which attempts to evaluate the effects
changes in UI on each of the transition probabilities listed on p. 269, rather
an just the flows out of unemployment, as in the case of Narandranathan *et al.*
Using longitudinal data from the March and April 1978 Current Population
rveys, Clark and Summers (1982) find, contrary to results from the British
dies quoted, that UI does not seem to significantly reduce the flow from
employment into employment or out of the labour force, i.e. duration of the

currently unemployed does not increase. However, they find that the transition from employment are significantly affected: increases in UI increase the flo⟨ from employment to unemployment (mainly via lay-offs) and reduce the flo⟨ from employment out of the labour force. These flows are not even examine in most British studies, and indeed the sensitivity of the employment−employ ment flow to UI may be much greater in the US due to the greater importanc of temporary lay-offs in the US. Finally Clark and Summers find that transition into the labour force are affected by UI — in particular an increase in UI wi increase the flow into unemployment. Overall, increases in UI positively affec labour force participation (mainly by reducing the flow from employment o⟨ of the labour force). Thus increases in UI tend to increase *both* employment an unemployment. Because it covers a wider range of labour market transitions, th Clark and Summers approach should predict the effects of changes in UI o unemployment more accurately than studies concentrating on duration alon⟨ Whether this is true in practice will depend on the accuracy with which each ⟨ the transition probability functions is estimated in the Clark and Summe⟨ approach. If good and bad estimates have to be combined, it is not obvious th: the overall prediction will be more accurate than one derived from studies of t⟨ probability of leaving unemployment.

8.6 Incomes Policy

If wage pressure could be reduced at any given level of aggregate demand (⟨ any level of unemployment) the NAIRU would fall (see Appendix 8.2).[35] By t⟨ same token, attempts to increase employment by demand expansion would ⟨ frustrated if real demand effects were dissipated in wage inflation (followed ⟨ price inflation).

   One method of alleviating wage pressure is by using wage controls or, mo⟨ generally, *incomes policy*. Some economists would argue the case for incom⟨ policy more strongly, claiming that it is an essential adjunct to the demaⁿ expansion required to significantly lower unemployment.[36] To ardent fr⟨ marketeers on the one hand and trade unionists on the other, incomes polic⟨ are anathema because, by their nature, they intervene to modify the effects market forces or free collective bargaining. Historically incomes policies ha⟨ been used more in Europe than in the US, and have been more favoured by le⟨ of-centre than right-of-centre governments, wherever located. However, fe governments are prepared to forswear the use of incomes policy, at least as temporary last resort, if inflation threatens to get out of control. The two ma⟨ periods of incomes policy in the US occurred during 1962−6, the 'wa⟨ guideposts' period, and during 1971−4 when the Nixon Administration impos⟨ four phases of controls. In the UK an incomes policy of one sort or another w⟨ in force for most of the 1970s until the Conservative Party came to power 1979. The main exception was from August 1974 to August 1975 when the new returned Labour Government claimed to have a 'social contract' with the trade unions. Wage inflation approached 30 per cent and price inflation 26 per cent during this period.

Critics of incomes policies make the following points:

1. Controls prevent relative wages performing their allocative function by preventing their increase in excess demand markets.
2. Wage drift, the excess of actual earnings growth over the negotiated growth of wage rates, undermines the policy while it is in force. Wage drift can occur by employers simply breaking the rules if monitoring is ineffective, or by more subtle methods such as reducing the normal work week so that overtime rates come into force sooner, enabling earnings for a given number of hours worked to increase, or by reclassifying the job of a given worker so that in effect he can be paid more for doing the same work.
3. Incomes policies are difficult to sustain for any length of time. They always break down when employers need to increase pay to get the right kind of labour and/or when strong trade unions become concerned about their relative positions, or simply become fed up with constraints on free collective bargaining.
4. After incomes policies break down everyone joins in a rush to 'catch up' for perceived losses sustained while the policy was in force. There is a wage explosion and the economy is worse off than if there had never been a policy at all.

These claims are not at all easy to test empirically. One cannot judge the success or failure of an incomes policy simply by comparing inflation during the policy with the pre-policy inflation rate, because other things apart from the wage controls (import prices and/or government monetary and fiscal policy, for example) may also have altered and be affecting inflation during the 'policy-on' period. What one needs is a benchmark to indicate what inflation *would* have been in the absence of the incomes policy, given that the policy itself is unlikely to be the only way in which the policy-on and policy-off periods differ from each other. Similarly one requires a benchmark to test whether any gains are thrown away in a rush to offset the effects of the policy once it is discontinued. To be more specific, the required benchmark is an empirical equation which can accurately predict wage growth in the absence of incomes policy. In practice there is little agreement about the variables which should enter as explanatory variables in such an equation. A related problem is that estimated wage equations tend to be rather unstable: an equation which fits the data well during one period often breaks down when applied to data from a different period.

Using, as a benchmark, predictions from a policy-off wage growth equation, Reid (1981) evaluates the effectiveness of US wage controls. To give a flavour of his results we quote his evaluation of phase IV of the Nixon controls. This phase ran from 1973:III to 1974:I. The wage equation estimated from policy-off data predicts that wages would have grown by 9.2 per cent during the phase IV period if there had been no controls. Actual wage growth was 7.2 per cent, indicating a degree of success for the policy even though the guideline (target) of 5.5 per cent was exceeded. However, in the three quarters following the end of the guideline policy, wages were predicted by the equation to grow at an annual rate of 10.6 per cent. Actual wage growth was 11.5 per cent indicating that catch-up attempts were at least partially successful, offsetting almost half of the 2 per cent restraint achieved while the controls were in force.[37]

Recently attention has turned to the possibility of devising an incomes policy which would overcome some of the major objections to the more traditional forms of control, enabling it to become a more permanent feature of the economic environment. These policies are known as *tax-based incomes policies* (TIPs) (Wallich and Weintraub, 1971; Jackman and Layard, 1986). As their name suggests they are designed to work via the tax system, providing incentives to firms to exercise restraint in reaching wage settlements by taxing wage increases above some annually agreed norm.

Incomes policy of whatever kind requires consensus if it is to be successfully sustained. In the case of TIPs this is more likely to be obtained, especially if the norm, or reference level, of wage increases is agreed by tripartite negotiation between government, employers and unions. What are the principles involved in setting this norm? Firstly the government will have a *target* rate of wage increases. This will be closely related to the underlying rate of productivity growth. If productivity were growing at x per cent per year, money wages could also grow at this rate without increasing real unit labour costs. However, if price inflation is currently running at, say, y per cent $(y > x)$ it may impose excessive strains upon the economy to attempt to reduce this to zero in the first year of the policy. Therefore a realistic target may be to hold inflation constant in the first year, reduce it by 1 per cent in the next year, etc. Thus wage growth targets would be $(x + y)$ in year one, $(x + y - 1)$ in year two, etc. However, if these targets are to be achieved, the pay norms will have to be lower because the policy will allow some firms to exceed the norm. Thus reasonable reference levels for increases in hourly earnings may be, for example, $(x + y - 3)$ in year one, $(x + y - 4)$ in year two, etc. Now, if a firm agrees to (and achieves) hourly earning growth less than or equal to the norm, it pays no tax.[38] On the other hand, if it grants increases in hourly earnings, z, in excess of the reference level, it pays tax on the excess according to the formula

$$T = t[z - (x + y - 3)]N$$

in year one (N is the size of the firm's labour force). If the tax rate t were 100 per cent this would double the cost to the firm of every £ or $ increase in hourly earnings granted in excess of the norm. Clearly this is a disincentive. Nevertheless firms which really need to increase relative wages for recruitment or retention purposes, or to reward internal productivity gains, can do so if they are prepared to pay the tax. It is an undesirable side-effect of TIPs that firms achieving above average productivity gains are likely, on balance, to pay above average taxes. It is little consolation that many existing profits taxes have the same effect.[39]

8.7 Targeted Employment Policies

Policies aimed at increasing labour demand will be cheaper and more effective if they are *targeted*. Direct targeting attempts to focus demand on underemployed groups, i.e. on groups where there is excess labour supply. This will reduce wage pressure for any given increase in aggregate demand. Where possible, targeting should be to low wage groups (which may be the same as above) because this reduces the budget deficit cost per job. Groups hit particularly hard in recent recessions, and therefore candidates for direct targeting, are the long-term unemployed, the unskilled, youths and labour in depressed regions. Indirect targeting attempts to increase demand in sectors and activities which use underemployed and low wage groups intensively: construction and the maintenance and modernisation of infrastructure are possible examples.

The net cost per job to the budget will depend both on the wage and on how much of a given amount of government expenditure goes directly on to job creation and how much 'leaks'. With across-the-board tax cuts, for example, there will be leakage into imports, while at the same time the government has no control over whether the jobs created are high or low wage jobs. A related point is that targeted subsidies are likely to involve less *deadweight* expenditure than across-the-board policies, i.e. less of the subsidy will go to those who would have been employed anyway. Of course benefits per job, as well as cost per job created, have to be considered.

Employment Subsidies

The use of targeted marginal employment subsidies to increase employment (and reduce unemployment assuming the labour force to be fixed) has attracted growing attention from academic economists as well as policy makers.[40]

In essence, employment subsidies shift the relevant segment of the labour demand curve outwards, thus increasing employment (provided that the labour supply curve is upward sloping). Such subsidies may therefore be regarded as a means of offsetting the 'distortionary' effect on employment of income maintenance policies such as minimum wage legislation or unemployment benefits.

The payment of employment subsidies is almost always for a limited period — usually between six months and two years — emphasising that the objective of the subsidy is to encourage recruitment rather than to subsidise the wages of existing workers.[41] Most such policies are targeted, firstly, by attempting to restrict the subsidy to the employment of workers who would be unemployed in the absence of the subsidy, and secondly, by making only certain groups of workers — the low paid, the unskilled, youths, the long-term unemployed — eligible for the subsidy.

Even though targeting attempts to restrict expenditure on employment, there will inevitably be some deadweight expenditure, as defined above. Further, an assessment of employment subsidies must allow for the possibility of *displacement*, an increase in the employment of the targeted group at the expense of non-subsidised workers. For example, a subsidy to private employers to hire from the pool of long-term unemployed may mean that they hire fewer short-term unemployed than they would have done in the absence of the subsidy (we argue below that such a switch is desirable on anti-inflationary as well as equity grounds). Likewise, subsidisation of youth employment may simply mean that employers replace adults by youths without creating any net increase in their workforce. In these cases the subsidy redistributes unemployment, but does not reduce it.

If we ignore any tax increases required to finance employment subsidies, then, apart from any substitution effects that such subsidies may have, there will be scale effects or profit effects. That is to say, subsidies will increase profit levels which, in turn, in competitive product markets, will induce new firms to enter the industry, increasing output and employment. However, in assessing the effectiveness of employment subsidies, it is necessary to consider how they are to be financed. As we are interested in non-inflationary policies for reducing unemployment, let us impose the condition that the subsidy must be self-financed by a payroll tax. The self-financing requirement means that in the aggregate we can assume that profit levels are unaffected so that there is no net profit or scale effect.

If the wages and employment of homogeneous labour are determined competitively, then it is obvious that a self-financing subsidy on all employment cannot be used to increase employment. Let the subsidy per worker be s and the payroll tax used to finance the subsidy be t. Self-financing requires $s = t$ so both the average and, more importantly for employment, the marginal cost of labour is unchanged. However, even in the absence of the self-financing requirement, a subsidy on all employment would be very wasteful because of the amount of deadweight expenditure involved. It is better to try to devise a *marginal* employment subsidy which helps firms to hire extra labour or retain workers they would otherwise have dismissed. A marginal subsidy delivers more punch per £ than an across-the-board subsidy.

In practice, avoiding deadweight (limiting the subsidy to workers who would otherwise be unemployed) is extremely difficult. For the sake of argument let us say that a subsidy, s, will be paid for each worker hired in excess of N^*, where N^* is, say, 95 per cent of the previous year's employment level. We again impose the condition that the scheme must be financed by a payroll tax of t per employed worker. The marginal cost of labour, up to and including N^*, is $(w + t)$ where w is the pre-tax and pre-subsidy wage. The marginal cost of employment beyond N^* is $(w + t - s)$ so that, as long as s is greater than t, marginal cost will be reduced. Of course s will be greater than t (as long as N^* is greater than zero) as can be easily seen from the self-financing requirement $Nt = (N - N^*)s$. Taxes and subsidies do not figure in the *average* cost of labour, which is simply the market wage.

The above analysis is illustrated in Figure 8.7 where the tax-subsidy program changes the labour demand schedule (drawn with respect to the market wage — taxes and subsidies change labour costs to employers at given market wages) from N_{D1} to the broken schedule N_{D2}.[42] If the original wage is the market-clearing w_0 then voluntary unemployment falls from I_1 to U_2, employment increasing from N_1 to N_2. If originally the wage was fixed at w_1, i.e. above market clearing, due for example to minimum wage legislation, the disequilibrium unemployment of U'_1 is eliminated, the increase in employment being from N'_1 to N_2. Figure 8.7 shows why a marginal subsidy can be effective even with self-financing — the tax, because it is widely spread, increases labour costs by less than the subsidy reduces them for marginal workers.

Where wages are not determined by market forces, but are administered by firms, the effectiveness of employment subsidies will depend in part on the type of subsidy chosen. Suppose for example that firms set wages above market clearing

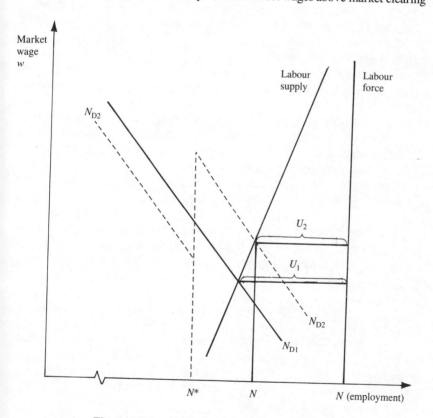

Figure 8.7 A Marginal Employment Subsidy

to reduce turnover costs (see the section on efficiency wages in Chapter 7). In this case a subsidy which is proportional to the wage would reduce the marginal cost of using wage increases to reduce turnover. But it would also reduce the marginal benefit from reduced turnover because the wage subsidy reduces the cost of a new hire. With both the costs and benefits of reduced turnover having fallen, equilibrium unemployment will be unaffected. A flat-rate *per capita* subsidy like *s*, on the other hand, will not affect the marginal cost of using a wage increase to reduce turnover, but net turnover costs are reduced because the subsidy offsets some of the costs of a new hire. Firms become less averse to quits, so wages can be reduced and thus unemployment can fall. This argument also works in reverse, suggesting that *per capita* labour taxes are more harmful to employment than *ad valorem* (proportional to wages) taxes.

Job Guarantees for the Long-Term Unemployed

We have seen above that one of the most disturbing features of recent unemployment episodes has been the growth of long-term unemployment (unemployment spells lasting a year or more). Not only has long-term unemployment been higher than in previous recessions, including those of the 1920s and 1930s, but today long-term unemployment affects all age and skill groups, not just the elderly, the sick and the unskilled. Furthermore long-term unemployment imposes greater private and social costs than short-term unemployment. Financial hardship increases as unemployment or other forms of state support become exhausted or reduced (in some countries), as savings and stocks of real goods and services are run down, etc. In addition, physiological and psychological health problems are likely to increase,[43] and re-employment prospects are likely to be reduced. Of course recovery of the economy from recession, i.e. resumed economic growth, will eventually have an impact on long-term unemployment but the time lag may be considerable. In the US,[44] long-term unemployment in 1985 was still over three times its 1979 level. In the UK, six years of economic growth (1981–6) increased rather than decreased both the numbers of long-term unemployed and their share in total unemployment. Not until 1987 did long-term unemployment begin to fall. Thus in terms of the welfare of the unemployed and their families, the case for special policies to relieve long-term unemployment seems overwhelming.

There is, however, another and potentially crucial argument. Recently most Western governments, in setting their economic objectives, have given top priority to the control of inflation. As part of their anti-inflationary policy, governments use unemployment to moderate wage pressure, reasoning that the existence of an alternative labour force — the unemployed — 'beating at the factory gates' will both moderate the wage demands of those in work and stiffen the resistance of their employers to such demands.[45]

Evidence is emerging that the long-term unemployed do not exert the same downward pressure on wages as those who have been unemployed for a shorter period of time.[46] The long-term unemployed become progressively detached from the labour market and cease to 'beat on the factory doors', or their beating is ignored by employers who interpret long-term unemployment as a sign of skill erosion or adverse (from the employment perspective) individual characteristics. Thus any policy which reduces the number of the long-term unemployed, while leaving short-term unemployment unaffected, will not generate wage inflation, *ceteris paribus*. As the entry into long-term unemployment is largely determined by the level of short-term unemployment the implication is that long-term unemployment should, where possible, be reduced by increasing the escape probability from, rather than the inflow into, long-term unemployment. This leaves the level of short-run unemployment unchanged.

Of course, many countries already have policies directed at the long-term unemployed. Ignoring early retirement, which we deal with under work sharing, these policies involve one or more of the following: (i) creation of temporary jobs, usually in the public sector; (ii) job subsidies to the private sector; and (iii) training measures. In most countries, however, such policies are limited in size relative to the scale of the problem. In the UK, for example, at the time of writing, the Community Programme offers community work (often part-time) to the long-term unemployed for up to a year, but there are only enough places for, at most, one in five of the eligible unemployed. The programme has also been criticised, as have temporary community work schemes in general, for being unattractive to the long-term unemployed, both because of the low wages they offer relative to unemployment benefit and the low-technology labour-intensive nature of the work which ill prepares participants for private sector employment when they leave the scheme.

One exception to the inadequate scope of these measures is to be found in the approach followed in Sweden. There, unemployment benefit is paid (on a relatively generous scale) for a maximum of ten months (on average) but, before the expiry of benefit, every unemployed person receives an offer of a job (private sector jobs, and even some in the public sector, being supported by recruitment subsidies) or a place on a training scheme. Of course, the gross costs of such a policy are high: close to 2.5 per cent of GDP is spent on special employment measures (Jackman *et al.*, 1985), but the net costs must be substantially less after accounting for increased tax receipts, savings on benefit payouts, etc. Sweden in 1985 had an unemployment rate of 2.8 per cent relative to the OECD average of 8 per cent and a European average of 11 per cent. Long-term unemployment was 11.4 per cent of total unemployment relative to 41 per cent in the UK.

Work Sharing

We turn, finally, to a brief discussion of work sharing. Work sharing can take a number of forms. It is worthwhile to distinguish three of these:

282 THE ECONOMICS OF LABOUR MARKETS

1. *Early retirement*   An unemployed worker takes over the job of a currently employed worker who leaves the labour force prior to the normal retirement age.
2. *Job sharing*   New jobs are split so that the number of new recruits exceeds the number required if they all worked full-time. It is usual to think simply of the job being split in two but this need not necessarily be the case — a wide variety of reallocations may be possible (see Drèze, 1986).
3. *Shorter hours*   Existing workers have their hours (e.g. weekly hours) reduced to create extra jobs.

Clearly, items 2 and 3 are similar except that 2 does not alter hours of work for existing employees.

Economists are divided about the effectiveness of work sharing. Unlike the other policies we have discussed, it can be plausibly argued that work sharing does nothing to increase output or *net* employment measured in full-time equivalents. In this case work sharing has the limited objective of redistributing the burden of unemployment. This is not an unimportant objective, but the point is that it could be achieved at no extra inflationary cost by policies which increase output and employment. Both approaches add to inflationary pressure by reducing unemployment (unless, according to the argument above, the reductions are drawn from the long-term unemployed).

If it could be shown to reduce the NAIRU, the case for work sharing would be much stronger. In terms of the model of the NAIRU outlined in Appendix 8.2, this could happen if *either* work sharing increased the feasible real wage *or* reduced wage pressure at given unemployment. In terms of the feasible wage, work sharing is more likely to reduce it (increasing the NAIRU, *ceteris paribus*) than increase it. Work sharing of types 2 and 3 will impose additional fixed costs and adjustment costs[47] on firms, increasing unit production costs. The feasible wage must fall to compensate. Similarly the feasible wage will fall if unit wage costs are increased by workers' efforts to increase the hourly wage in order to offset reductions in weekly earnings caused by reductions in weekly hours. Models of union wage setting can easily produce such a result, as shown in Appendix 8.3. Similarly, if short-time working were to modify wage pressure, given the number of fully unemployed workers, then work sharing, by reducing hours per worker, would reduce the NAIRU, but there is no evidence for this.[48]

As work-sharing on a significant scale does not occur spontaneously, any government wishing to reduce unemployment by these means will have to improve the incentives to workers and firms. Older workers must be bribed to retire earlier than otherwise (by an allowance until pension age and modification of pension rules so that early retirement does not reduce the full pension when it becomes due). Workers wishing for full-time jobs and incomes must be compensated for taking part-time work. Firms must be compensated for the increased costs that job sharing imposes. Indeed such subsidies are provided in many countries, especially, but not exclusively, in Europe.[49]

The Job Release Scheme, introduced in the UK in 1976, is fairly typical of early retirement schemes. It provides a weekly allowance from the date the applicant leaves work until he or she becomes eligible for the full state pension *provided that the employer replaces the applicant by a worker who would otherwise be unemployed.* The scheme is open to 64-year-old men and 59-year-old women (pension age is 65 for men and 60 for women). Extensions and modifications of the scheme could reduce the eligibility age and/or stipulate that the replacement should be drawn from the pool of youth unemployed or long-term unemployed. A similar scheme, including mandatory replacement, ran betwen 1981 and 1983 in France under the '*Contrats de Solidarité*' programme. Belgium, The Netherlands and Germany also have early retirement schemes.

Job sharing and hours-reduction schemes are less widespread. In Britain an example of the former is the Job Splitting Scheme, which pays a grant to employers who split an existing job into two part-time jobs which are kept filled for at least 12 months. One or both of the part-time jobs must be filled by a worker who would otherwise have been unemployed. The scheme is cheap to run — in fact the cost is negative because the grant is less than the savings in unemployment benefit. However, because of low take-up, the effect on unemployment is negligible. Low take-up also plagues schemes which subsidise firms to reduce the standard working week in return for increased recruitment.[50] This is not surprising because in a recession many firms hoard labour, i.e. in order to protect investments in recruiting and training they retain workers even though their wage exceeds the marginal revenue product. In such circumstances reductions in weekly hours, or wages for that matter, will not induce recruiting.

8.8 Summary

Although lengthy, this chapter is by no means an exhaustive or comprehensive survey of empirical and policy analysis of unemployment. If nothing else, the vast literature produced on these topics in recent years testifies to the determination of the economics profession to address the major economic problems of the day. It would be reassuring to be able to claim that all this activity has produced a professional consensus both as to the causes of and the cures for the human misery and waste of resources that lie behind the bald statistics of mass unemployment. That would be an exaggerated claim. However, as the chapter shows, progress has been made. Few economists would deny that we are now better placed to understand and combat recessions than we were when the comfortable world of low unemployment and inflation began to yield to a much harsher reality in the early/mid 1970s, a change which in itself was only a forerunner to the far more devastating recession of the early 1980s.

The first section of the chapter dealt with the factual background. Recent unemployment was contrasted both with the experience of the 1920s and 1930s as well as with the period 1950–73, which for the UK was a 'golden age' as far as employment was concerned, with the unemployment rate never above 5 per cent of the labour force (never above 3 per cent between 1950 and 1970). During this period US unemployment, while higher than in the UK (although US inflation was lower) was still substantially lower than the levels reached in 1975–6 and 1980–3. The unemployment of the 1970s and early 1980s, while never reaching the same percentage rates as during the peaks of the 1930s, has been in other respects (such as its persistence and the proportion of long-term unemployment) at least as severe as that of the Great Depression.

In examining the structure of unemployment, we stressed the important distinction between inflows into the unemployment stock and the unemployment duration of those in the stock. Inflows and durations are influenced by different factors (and unequally by the same factors). This must be borne in mind when considering policies to alleviate unemployment. Thus, for example, if increases in unemployment are largely the result of increased durations, policies must be targeted at reducing duration rather than inflow. Inequality in the distribution of unemployment across demographic groups is also easier to explain when one looks separately at the inflows and durations of these groups. For example the young and the old both experience above average unemployment, but for different reasons. Young people are more likely to become unemployed but tend to remain so for less time than older workers.

In looking at empirical studies of unemployment growth in the second part of the chapter, we placed much emphasis on the role of the real wage, and in particular on its failure to adjust to the supply shocks caused by increases in the price of oil, raw materials and commodities as well as by competition from newly industrialised countries. We found that real wage rigidity did play a part in explaining increases in unemployment. The policy implications of this finding are not obvious, however, as the real wage is determined by supply and demand interactions in both labour and product markets and cannot usually be directly influenced by government policy.

To see what role may exist for expansionary monetary and fiscal policy we examined the concept of the non-accelerating inflation rate of unemployment, the NAIRU, and the factors that may have led to its increase. Empirical analysis of the NAIRU and its relation to actual unemployment rates suggests that the part to be played by general macroeconomic expansion in reducing unemployment must be limited if inflation is to be contained at low levels.

This highlights the need to target spending increases so as to minimise 'leakage' into imports or into increasing the demand for already employed labour. Expenditure should be targeted at groups and sectors where net employment growth is likely to be greatest and where this is least likely to increase the pressure on nominal wages (and subsequently prices). We examined several specific policies to see how they measured up to these criteria: reducing unemployment insurance, marginal employment subsidies, job guarantees for the long-term unemployed, incomes policies and work sharing. Of these, employment subsidies, specific help for the long-term unemployed and incomes policies (tax-based) seem the most promising.

Appendix 8.1   The Wage Gap — Further Empirical Analysis

he relationship between the wage gap and unemployment can be tested directly sing regression analysis. We look at two such equations from Bruno and Sachs 985). The first, equation (8.15), simply relates unemployment to the wage gap:

$$U_t = \alpha_0 + \alpha_1 U_{t-1} + \alpha_2 WG_t + \text{time trend} \qquad (8.15)$$

here U_t is the unemployment rate at time t, WG_t is the wage gap defined as $w/P)_t - (w/P)_f]/(W/P)_f$. Lagged unemployment is included to allow for lagged sponses of labour supply and demand to changes in the real wage. The second quation (8.16) adds a variable — real money balances (measured in logarithms id lagged one period) to capture aggregate demand effects on unemployment.[51]

$$U_t = \beta_0 + \beta_1 U_{t-1} + \beta_2 WG_{t-1} + \beta_3 \ln\left(\frac{M}{P}\right)_{t-1}$$
$$+ \text{ time trend and shift variables} \qquad (8.16)$$

here (M/P) measures real money balances and the shift variables allow both e slope and intercept to change after 1973 to allow for the changes in the growth full employment output (against which excess aggregate supply and demand e measured). Table 8.23 provides estimates, for the UK, Germany and the US, the crucial parameters in equations (8.15) and (8.16), along with the R^2 value.

ble 8.23 Unemployment Equations, UK, Germany, USA, 1961–1981

	Equation					
	UK		Germany		USA	
efficient ariable)	(8.15)	(8.16)	(8.15)	(8.16)	(8.15)	(8.16)
, $\hat{\beta}_1$ (U_{t-1})	1.13	0.63	0.55	0.38	0.62	0.19
	(5.48)	(2.78)	(4.44)	(3.72)	(3.43)	(2.60)
$(WG)_t$	23.61		18.37		10.67	
	(4.20)		(3.53)		(1.07)	
$(WG)_{t-1}$		21.97		10.85		-8.97
		(3.89)		(2.55)		(1.73)
$(\ln(M/P)_{t-1})$		-5.15		-8.93		-24.49
		(1.84)		(3.52)		(1.55)
	0.91	0.95	0.90	0.95	0.56	0.93

urce: Bruno and Sachs (1985, Tables 9.4, 10.6).
te: The dependent variable is the unemployment rate (expressed as a percentage of the labour force).

The equations are estimated using data covering the period 1961−81. The figures in parentheses are t-statistics.

In equation (8.15) the estimated $\hat{\alpha}_2$ is positive in each country as expected (an increase in the wage gap increases the unemployment rate) and is statistically significant in the UK and in Germany, but not in the US equation, which also performs worse in terms of overall explanatory power.

Adding the real money balance term (and the shift variables) to the equation increases its explanatory power in each country. This demand variable has the 'correct' sign (an increase in demand reduces unemployment) in each country but its statistical significance is low in the US equation in which the wage gap variable coefficient now assumes the wrong sign.

Several interesting exercises can be conducted using these regression results.

1. The coefficient estimate $\hat{\beta}_2$ can be used to calculate the one-year effect of a 1 per cent change in the wage gap.[52] Thus if the wage gap were reduced by 1 per cent the unemployment rate would fall by 0.2 per cent in the UK, by 0.1 per cent in Germany and *increase* by 0.1 per cent in the US (remember, however, that this perverse result is based on a coefficient that is not statistically different from zero).

2. The long-run effect (i.e. when $U_t = U_{t-1}$) of a 1 per cent change in the wage gap is calculated as $0.01[\hat{\beta}_2/(1-\hat{\beta}_1)]$. For the UK this long-term effect of a 1 per cent reduction in the wage gap is to reduce the unemployment by 0.6 per cent, in Germany by 0.2 per cent and in the US to raise the unemployment rate by 0.1 per cent.

3. The short- and long-run effects of eliminating the wage gap completely (rather than reducing it by 1 per cent) can be similarly calculated. Thus Table 8.20 showed the real wage gap in the UK to be 19.3 per cent in 1981. If this were eliminated, the short-run effect on the unemployment rate can be calculated from the coefficient estimates from equation (8.16):

$$\Delta U = \hat{\beta}_2 \Delta WG_{1981} = 21.97 \times (-0.193) = -0.42$$

The long-run effect is even more substantial with 11.5 percentage points removed from the unemployment rate.[53]

4. Equation (8.16) can also be used to decompose the observed increase in unemployment over a given period to its proximate causes. Ignoring the time trend and shift variables, the three causes of changes in U_t are changes in inherited unemployment (U_{t-1}), changes in the wage gap and changes in the growth of real money balances. Bruno and Sachs decompose the change in the unemployment rate throughout the 1970s and into the 1980 relative to the average rate prevailing over the period 1965−9. The method they use to achieve this decomposition need not detain us here: interested readers should consult the original. Table 8.24 shows a selection of their results.

Table 8.24 Decomposition of Unemployment Changes by Cause, UK, Germany and US

	Period		
	1965/9–1973/5	1965/9–1976/8	1965/9–1979/81
United Kingdom			
Total effect (increase in U rate) of which:	1.0	3.6	5.6
Inherited U effect	0.6	1.9	2.5
Wage gap effect	1.2	1.8	2.5
Money supply effect	–0.7	–0.1	0.5
Other	–0.1	0.1	0.1
Germany			
Total effect of which:	1.7	3.3	2.8
Inherited U effect	0.2	1.3	1.1
Wage gap effect	0.8	1.2	1.0
Money supply effect	0.5	0.9	0.6
Other	0.2	–0.1	0.1
USA			
Total effect of which:	2.5	3.1	3.0
Inherited U effect	0.3	0.8	0.5
Wage gap effect	–0.2	–0.1	–0.5
Money supply effect	2.3	2.5	3.2
Other	0.1	–0.1	–0.2

Source: Bruno and Sachs (1985, Table 10.8).

In reading Table 8.24 it is important to realise that the inherited unemployment effect will incorporate past wage gap and money supply effects, so that these factors have greater cumulative (long-term) impact than is indicated by the separable effects measured in the table. Bearing this in mind, the table again highlights the difference between the European and US experience. The growth in the wage gap contributed significantly to European unemployment while real money supply growth shows up much more strongly in the US, where excessive growth of real wages is not a significant factor.

Appendix 8.2   Estimating the Non-Accelerating Inflation Rate of Unemployment (NAIRU)

The NAIRU is not of course directly observable. One simple and direct method of calculating it would be to estimate an equation of the form

$$(\Delta \dot{P})_t = \alpha_0 + \alpha_1 U_t + \alpha_2 \mathbf{Z}_t$$

where $(\Delta \dot{P})_t = \dot{P}_t - \dot{P}_{t-1}$

With non-accelerating inflation the left-hand side equals zero so we solve for the natural rate as

$$U_t = \frac{-\hat{\alpha}_0 - \hat{\alpha}_2 \mathbf{Z}_t}{\hat{\alpha}_1}$$

where $\hat{\alpha}_0$, $\hat{\alpha}_1$, $\hat{\alpha}_2$ are the estimated coefficients and $\mathbf{Z}_t$ is the vector of actual values of the $\mathbf{Z}_t$ variables in period t.

A second method of calculating the NAIRU is to estimate the coefficients of equations (8.10) and (8.11) (requiring unobservable expectations to be modelled) and to use the estimates to calculate the NAIRU using equation (8.14).

Layard and Nickell (1985a) use a third alternative approach based on the long-term solution (i.e. when there are no wage or price 'surprises') to a three-equation structural macroeconomic model centred on the labour market. Unlike most NAIRU models it is specified in *levels* of wages and prices rather than rates of change (the latter enter in the way expectations are modelled). In a highly simplified form, their model is captured by the following equations:

Employment

$$L - U = f_1 \left(\frac{W}{P}, \mathrm{AD} \right)$$
$$\phantom{L - U = f_1 \left(\frac{W}{P}} {}_{-} \quad {}_{+}$$

Prices

$$\frac{P}{w} = f_2 \left[(L - U), \frac{P}{P_e} \right]$$
$$\phantom{\frac{P}{w} = f_2 \left[} {}_{+} \qquad {}_{-}$$

Wages

$$\frac{W}{P} = f_3\left(\underset{-}{U}, \underset{-}{\frac{P}{P_e}}, \underset{+}{\mathbf{Z}_w}\right)$$

L is the labour force, which is assumed to be fixed. Employment, N, is equal to $L - U$. The capital stock is also assumed to be fixed.

The employment equation should require no further explanation, except to reiterate that it is only in the case of imperfect competition that labour demand depends on aggregate demand as well as on the real wage. The price equation is based on firms setting prices as a mark-up over marginal costs. As marginal cost rises with N so does the mark-up over wages, assuming that the mark-up over MC is fixed. If prices are higher than expected, firms sell less than expected, MC and P fall, and so the mark-up over wages falls. The wage equation is familiar, except that if prices are higher than expected the real wage turns out to be lower than expected. The price equation can be thought of as determining the *feasible real wage* and the wage equation the *target real wage*. Equilibrium requires the two to be equal.

The long-run solution of the model, i.e. when $P = P_e$, solves for unemployment, the real wage and AD as functions of L, K and the exogenous vector of wage push variables, $\mathbf{Z}_w$. This solution value of U is the NAIRU. This is the method used by Layard and Nickell to calculate the values of the NAIRU shown in Table 8.21. The value of AD is the level of demand consistent with it. If demand is lower than this, unemployment will exceed the NAIRU.

Figure 8.8 illustrates the solution using the price and wage equations only.[54]

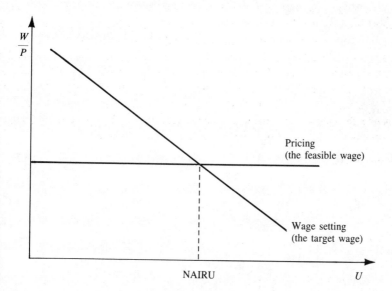

Figure 8.8 Determination of the NAIRU

Prices are assumed to be set as a constant proportional mark-up over wages rather than over marginal cost (a constant mark-up over MC would make the feasible real wage line upward sloping).

Appendix 8.3   Unemployment Policy in the Monopoly Union Model

Most of the policy discussion in Chapter 8 has implicitly assumed the existence of labour markets in which real wages are competitively determined or else set by firms (efficiency wages). But what if unions set wages? Do our conclusions still hold? On the whole, yes. We illustrate this with the simplest possible model — a version of the monopoly union model of Chapter 6. The whole labour force, L, is unionised. Unions are assumed able to set the real wage per worker, w, but firms then determine employment according to their labour demand curve. Unions care about both employment and wages. Unemployed workers receive benefit B. L, B and ϵ, the elasticity of the demand function $N = N(w)$ are parameters. Thus unions maximise

$$\Omega = wN + (L - N)B$$

$$\therefore \quad \Omega = N(w - B) + \text{constant} \tag{8.17}$$

i.e. unions maximise the 'rent' earned by its employed members. (Note that this equation is equivalent to equation (5.5) with a linear utility function and with unemployment benefit, B, replacing the non-union wage, w_0.) They do this by choosing the wage subject to the firm's demand curve. Once w is chosen, N is determined and, given that L is fixed, unemployment U is determined as $L - N$.

Formally unions set $\partial\Omega/\partial w = 0$:

$$\frac{\partial\Omega}{\partial w} = N'(w - B) + N = 0 \tag{8.18}$$

where $N' = \dfrac{\partial N}{\partial w}$

$$\therefore \quad w - B = -\frac{N}{N'} \tag{8.19}$$

$$\therefore \quad w - B = \left(\frac{1}{\epsilon}\right)w \tag{8.20}$$

where $\epsilon = \left(\frac{\partial N}{\partial w}\right)\frac{w}{N}$

$$\therefore w = B\left(\frac{\epsilon}{1 + \epsilon}\right) \tag{8.21}$$

(note that for $w > B$ the absolute value of the elasticity, $|\epsilon|$, must exceed unity, as in the case of monopoly firms)

$$U = U(B, \epsilon) \tag{8.22}$$
$$+ \quad +$$

Policy 1: Changes in Unemployment Benefit

Equations (8.21) and (8.22) clearly indicate that an increase in B increases the wage the union will set, reduces employment and increases unemployment. Thus conclusions about the effect of benefits on unemployment need not rest solely on job search theories.

Policy 2: Employment Subsidies

Let there exist two employment subsidies, a per capita subsidy of s per worker and a proportional wage subsidy of θ. Employers' cost per worker is thus

$$C = [w(1 - \theta) - s] \tag{8.23}$$

Employers' labour demand elasticity with respect to C is

$$\epsilon_c = \left(\frac{\partial N}{\partial C}\right)\left(\frac{C}{N}\right) = \left(\frac{\partial N}{\partial w}\right)\left(\frac{\partial w}{\partial C}\right)\left(\frac{C}{N}\right) \tag{8.24}$$

$$= \left(\frac{\epsilon}{w}\right)\left(\frac{1}{1 - \theta}\right)[w(1 - \theta) - s]$$

$$\therefore \epsilon = \frac{\epsilon_c w(1 - \theta)}{w(1 - \theta) - s} \tag{8.25}$$

We know from (8.22) that an increase in $|\epsilon|$ will reduce unemployment. Equation (8.25) shows that s, the per capita subsidy, does increase $|\epsilon|$ and thus reduces unemployment. So does θ, but only where $s > 0$. If $s = 0$, $\epsilon = \epsilon_c$ and unemployment is unaffected.

Policy 3: Work Sharing

Reinterpret ϵ as the elasticity of the demand for *man-hours* with respect to the *hourly* wage, w, from the firm's labour demand function $NH = f(w)$, where

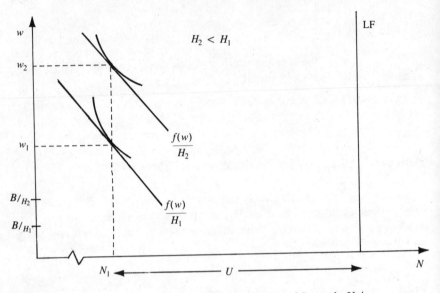

Figure 8.9 Response to Work Sharing by a Monopoly Union

H is hours worked per person (per period). In this case unions choose the wage and employers set man-hours. The union's objective function becomes

$$\Omega = NwH + (L - N)B \qquad (8.26)$$
$$= N(wH - B) + \text{constant}$$

Thus

$$\frac{\partial \Omega}{\partial w} = f'w + f - \left(\frac{B}{H}\right)f' = 0 \qquad (8.27)$$

$$\therefore w = \frac{B}{H} - \frac{w}{\epsilon}$$

where $\epsilon = \left(\frac{\partial NH}{\partial w}\right)\frac{w}{NH} = \frac{f'w}{f}$

$$w = \frac{B}{H}\left(\frac{\epsilon}{1 + \epsilon}\right) \qquad (8.28)$$

(note again that for $wH > B$, $|\epsilon| > 1$)

The success of work sharing depends on hourly pay not increasing when hours per person fall, so that extra employment is possible without increasing the overall wage bill. Now (8.28) shows clearly that if hours per person are reduced, the union-set wage will increase to offset the reduction in earnings. Any increase in the wage will reduce employers' willingness to hire extra workers to make up for the reduction in hours, i.e. the total demand for man-hours will fall. In our simple model the conclusion is dramatic: namely the union will increase the hourly wage to the point where existing workers receive the same income with reduced hours. A cut in hours worked per person will not produce *any* extra employment (will not reduce unemployment). This is easily seen by noting that the elasticity of w with respect to H is equal to -1. Thus a 1 per cent reduction in hours per employed worker will induce a 1 per cent increase in the hourly wage. Workers are no cheaper, so no more will be employed. Unemployment is unaffected by the reduction in hours per worker. This is illustrated in Figure 8.9.

Notes

1. The three sections are immodestly subtitled Facts, Causes, Cures. This is for expositional purposes only; we are well aware of how complex these issues are and do not claim that our treatment is either comprehensive or definitive. We hope it is useful.
2. This watershed episode in economic history is well described in Kindleberger (1973). Recent research relating to British inter-war unemployment is surveyed in Hatton (1986).
3. Source: *Charter for Jobs*, Economic Report No 1, September 1985.
4. Formal arrangements whereby redundant workers are kept on the payroll in exchange for lower unit wage costs via bonus reductions may have disguised growing excess supply of labour in Japan.
5. In the UK in the latter part of 1985 it is estimated that measured unemployment would be increased by approximately 400 000 (12 per cent) in the absence of such schemes (*Employment Gazette*, 1985, various issues).
6. In the US in 1982, in the final quarter of 1982 it has been estimated that there were 1.8 million (16 per cent of total measured unemployment) such discouraged workers, (OECD, 1983), while in Britain the Department of Employment estimated that in the spring of 1984 there were 364 000 discouraged workers, or 12 per cent of measured unemployment. It is interesting to note that countries with very low measured unemployment rates have much larger numbers, proportionately, of discouraged workers. Thus, for example, in 1983 it has been estimated (OECD, 1987) that in Sweden discouraged workers amounted to 37 per cent of measured unemployment, while in Japan in the same year the corresponding figure was 250 per cent! Clearly if, as some argue, discouraged workers should be included in the unemployment count, the differences in measured unemployment rates across countries would be narrowed.
7. The magnitude of the problem confronting governments wishing to reduce unemployment is highlighted by specifying required employment growth as the difference between labour force growth and the unemployment target.

$$\text{Labour force (LF)} = \text{employment } (N) + \text{unemployment } (U)$$
$$\text{GB, 1985, (000s) } 27\ 036 \qquad 23\ 893 \qquad\qquad + 3143$$

By 1991 the GB labour force is forecast to be 27 561 000. Let us assume that a target level of 1.5 million unemployed is set for 1991. Then required employment is

$$27\ 561 - 1500 = 26\ 061$$

Thus the British economy would need to create 2.168 million (26.061 − 23.893) net new jobs in six years, i.e. 990 net new jobs per day. Of course, *net* job creation will be less than the *gross* requirement because as new jobs are created old ones continue to be lost. A rate of 150 000 redundancies per year would imply the creation of 1400 new jobs per day to achieve the *net* requirement of 990. The job creation requirements can be translated into economic growth requirements. The employment requirement in our example would require an annual output (GDP) growth rate of 1.5 per cent if output/worker (productivity) were constant, but a 4 per cent annual rate of GDP growth if productivity grows at 2.5 per cent per annum. This assumes that hours worked per employee remain constant. Should these fall, as Chapter shows they have done over a long period, then the GDP growth requirement to meet the given employment target is correspondingly reduced (in these circumstances productivity must be defined as output per employee-hour). In our example the required GDP growth rate (or the required net daily job creation) exceeds achieved growth over the period 1982—5, implying that the 1.5 million unemployment target for 199 is somewhat ambitious. Obviously the GDP growth required to meet a given unemployment target is greater, the greater is the forecast growth of the labour force (very modest in our example) and the greater the expected productivity growth.

8. Or per month or year; any period will do as long as it is used consistently.
9. Suggested by Clark and Summers (1979).
10. In practice, as in our numerical example, incomplete durations exceed completed durations. However, this need not always be the case. If everyone entering unemployment were to remain unemployed for the same length of time, then (in a steady state) complete duration would be double incomplete duration; if 20 people enter unemployment each week and each of them remained unemployed for four weeks then this is the average completed duration, while a survey half-way through a steady state week would yield an average incomplete duration of two weeks. Complete and incomplete durations would be equal if everyone in the stock had the same exit probability irrespective of when they became unemployed.
11. Thus in the UK, in July 1985, 55 per cent of all unemployed aged 55 and over have unemployment in progress of over 52 weeks. The corresponding proportion for those aged under 25 is 50 per cent and for prime-aged workers it is 35 per cent.
12. The concept of industry-specific unemployment rates (based on last full-time job) makes most sense when inter-industry mobility is low. An unemployed electrician for example, who previously worked in manufacturing may also be looking for work in non-manufacturing industries.
13. Source: *General Household Survey*. The manual/non-manual pattern differs markedly between men and women. 81 per cent of male unemployment is manual and 19 per cent non-manual. For women the corresponding proportions are 45 per cent and 5 per cent.
14. There are, of course, further dimensions of inequality in the incidence of unemployment that could have been considered. For example single persons have higher unemployment rates than married persons. In the US in 1985 the unemployment rate for single men was 12.7 per cent while for married men it was only 4.3 per cent (Summers, 1986).
15. For example the correlation between the 1976 and 1985 unemployment rates for individual states in the US was only 0.03, although the correlation between 1970 and 1985 rates was 0.54. See Summers (1986) for more on regional differences in unemployment in the US.
16. Cost minimisation yields the labour demand function

$$N_d = N_d \left(\frac{W}{P_M} : Q, K \right)$$
$$\quad\quad - \quad + \ +$$

Here the increase in the price of materials *increases* the demand for labour, *ceteris paribus*. However, this specification is unrealistic as it requires labour and materials to be substitutes rather than complements in production.

7. The macroeconomic implications of the supply shock can be traced out using the apparatus of aggregate supply and demand (augmented by a labour market and aggregate production function) now routinely utilised in macroeconomic textbooks such as Dornbusch and Fischer (1987). In brief, the increase in materials prices increases marginal costs of production thereby reducing the output supplied by firms at each price — the aggregate supply schedule moves inwards and there is excess demand for goods. At the same time, as Figure 8.4 shows, there is excess supply of labour. This combination is often described as 'classical unemployment'. If prices and nominal wages are flexible, price increases (and possibly nominal wage cuts as well) will reduce the real wage and eliminate unemployment. In practice changes are likely to occur in rates of change rather than levels of wages and prices, i.e. the fall in the real wage may result from a reduction in wage inflation relative to price inflation.

This section relies heavily on the empirical work of Bruno and Sachs (1985). It should be noted that some other empirical studies, e.g. Gordon (1986), do not find as strong a relationship between the wage gap and unemployment as do Bruno and Sachs.

$$Q = \alpha_0 L \alpha_1 K^{1-\alpha_1}$$

$$MP_L = \frac{\partial \theta}{\partial L} = \frac{\alpha_1 Q}{L} = AP_L$$

when $W = MP_L$, $\alpha_1 = WL/Q$ = labour's share.

The index is normalised at zero for the full employment–low inflation period 1965–9. As the whole analysis is conducted in logarithms the results should be interpreted as percentage differences of the real wage from its full employment level. Bruno and Sachs discuss the various types of bias to which these calculations are subject and conclude that, if anything, their results underestimate the wage gap. They also find that the estimates are robust with respect to alternative specifications of the production function. There is, however, one remaining conceptual pitfall in the empirical methodology used by Bruno and Sachs (and others) to measure the wage gap and analyse its effects. Suppose an *ex-ante* wage gap induces firms to adopt a more capital intensive production technology. This will raise labor productivity and reduce or eliminate the *ex-post* measured wage gap. A potential wage gap has reduced employment below its *ceteris paribus* level but an empirical wage gap analysis would not reveal this.

An increasing labour share of value added (at the expense of profits) and a declining real pretax return to capital are empirical counterparts to the rising wage gap over the period (see Bruno and Sachs, 1985, Chapter 8.1).

In fact, relatively fixed money wages enabled reductions in real wages as prices increased after the first oil shock.

Suppose we estimate, using time series data, a nominal wage equation of the following form (although in practice we may wish to add lagged values of prices and unemployment to the right-hand side)

$$\ln W_{nt} = \alpha_0 + \alpha_1 \ln P_t + \alpha_2 \ln U_t$$

the higher the elasticity of money wages with respect to prices and the lower the elasticity with respect to unemployment, the more rigid are *real* wages. Thus the absolute value of the ratio of the estimate of α_1 to the estimate of α_2 can be used as an index of real wage rigidity. For further details see Grubb *et al.* (1983).

In a labour demand function such as (8.3), aggregate demand does not appear as an argument. That equation referred to profit maximising firms in perfectly competitive markets. But if firms are either imperfect competitors (i.e. are not price takers facing horizontal demand curves for their output) or, which amounts to the same thing, are sales constrained (in which case they will be off their labour demand curve, e.g. at point A in Figure 8.4) aggregate demand can affect the demand for labour. Aggregate demand could have a similar effect even for competitive firms in a fuller model of the economy in which aggregate demand affects net investment and hence the capital stock.

25. The price level P_t is implicitly set equal to unity.

26. Estimation will involve simultaneous equation methods as ordinary least squares estimation is inappropriate for equestions containing endogenous variables on the right-hand side (the reduced form equations could therefore be estimated by OLS).

27. In fact because it suppresses pricing behaviour the labour market model of this section does not fully capture the endogeneity of the real wage. To explain the determination of w/P, it is necessary to explain how both nominal wages and prices are set. Price setting, although of course influenced by wage costs, is not primarily a labour market phenomenon. A small macroeconometric model in the general spirit of the model we discuss in this section but which also incorporates pricing behaviour (examining in particular the implications of average versus marginal cost pricing) is presented by Layard and Nickell (1985a) and discussed in Appendix 8.2.

28. Exogeneity of real wages and their uses as an instrument to reduce unemployment is surely implied by the following statement by the UK Chancellor of The Exchequer, Nigel Lawson, in the House of Commons (30 October 1984):

> The evidence suggests that, in Britain, a 1% change in the average level of real earnings will, in time, make a difference of between 0.5% and 1% to the level of unemployment. That will mean, in all probability, between 150,000 and 200,000 jobs.

29. If either $\dot{P}_e$ in equation (8.10) or $\dot{w}$ in (8.11) had coefficients less than unity there would be a long-run trade-off.

30. Appendix 8.3 shows that increase in UI will increase unemployment in a model where unions set wages — the search model is not the only one which can produce benefit-induced unemployment.

31. In the US the payroll taxes that a firm pays towards the financing of UI are partially determined by that firm's lay-offs. This system is often known as 'experience rating' Where experience rating is incomplete, so that contributions are not strictly propor tional to lay-offs, there is an incentive to lay off workers. To take an extreme exam ple, where the tax contribution has an upper limit, firms which have already pai this maximum face a zero marginal tax cost if they lay off another worker.

32. In what follows we ignore the general problem of partial versus general equilibriur to which we have referred on numerous occasions. In particular we make no allowanc for the fall in the real wage that would occur if UI were reduced (see Figure 8.6)

33. Those requiring a formal explanation of the estimation methodology should see Lan caster and Nickell (1980). The 'escape function' or 'hazard function' that is actuall estimated can take several forms but a commonly estimated one is

$$\theta_i = \exp[\mathbf{X}_i(n)\beta]\alpha n^{\alpha-1}$$

where θ_i is the escape probability for individual i

   $\mathbf{X}_i$ is a vector of personal characteristics including R (or UI and income work separately). Note that $\mathbf{X}_i$ has itself been made a function of dur tion. Many individual characteristics, including the value of R the individu faces, can change over a spell of unemployment.

   n is the period of time the individual has been unemployed (the incomple duration)

   α and β are coefficients (the latter a vector) to be estimated

α is restricted to be greater than 0. If α is estimated as being less than 1 this means that the escape probability increases with duration, while $0 < \alpha < 1$ implies a decreasing escape probability. If α is not significantly different from unity the escape probability is independent of how long the individual has been unemployed. These conditions can be easily seen by noting that

$$\frac{\partial \theta}{\partial n} = (\alpha - 1)\exp(X_i\beta)\alpha n^{\alpha-2}$$

34. The study is based on The Department of Health and Social Security's *Cohort Study of the Unemployed*. This is a sample of 2300 men taken from the unemployment inflow in autumn 1978. The data used by the study follow this sample for a year. Thus, unlike many earlier studies, it relates directly to a period of high unemployment (the average male unemployment rate was 7.6 per cent). Apart from containing good data on *actual* rather than hypothetical income of the unemployed, there is also information on completed unemployment spells rather than simply on incomplete spells. This enables more direct estimation of escape probabilities.

35. Note that the *real* wage need not fall. Nominal wage reductions are met by price reductions. Wage restraint aims not to reduce real wages but to reduce the level of unemployment required to prevent wage push setting nominal wages above feasible wages (given prices). In terms of Figure 8.8 in Appendix 8.2, if the mark-up over unit labour costs falls as unemployment increases, the feasible real wage line is upward sloping. A reduction in wage pressure at given unemployment *would* then reduce the real wage, which is now determined by both wage and price setting. In these circumstances the consumption real wage could be maintained by tax cuts made possible by the extra output and employment generated by the reduction in wage push.

36. A more sophisticated economic argument in favour of incomes policy is the following: firms bid up wages against each other in order to promote worker efficiency and reduce turnover. However, in doing so they do not take into account the fact that this increases real wages economy-wide and reduces aggregate employment, given aggregate monetary demand. A similar argument explains why firms do not reduce money wages when there is aggregate unemployment. Thus an externality exists, and incomes policy is the intervention required to offset it by preventing firms bidding up nominal wages against each other.

37. Further results for the UK, the rest of Europe and the US can be found in Fallick and Elliot (1981). A recent UK study which is notable for careful theoretical and econometric specification of the wage equation is to be found in Wadhwani (1985).

38. We are abstracting from any other taxes the firm may be required to pay.

39. Various suggestions have been made for ameliorating the effects of this distortion, and for making TIPs compatible with profit sharing (Layard and Nickell 1986). The basic idea is to exempt from the tax any payments to workers out of genuine growth in profits, while at the same time preventing firms from avoiding the tax by simply redefining part of a wage increase as a profit share payment. This is achieved by requiring that any tax-exempt part of a wage increase be related to changes in shareholders' profits.

40. See, for example, OECD (1982), Baily and Tobin (1977), Layard and Nickell (1980) and Haveman and Palmer (1982). For an analysis of the welfare implications of employment subsidies see Johnson and Layard (1986). In the United States the New Jobs Tax Credit was an example of a marginal wage subsidy for firms that increased employment. See Perloff and Wachter (1979) for an evaluation. UK examples include the now discontinued Small Firms Employment Subsidy and the Temporary Employment Subsidy (1975–9). For an evaluation of these programmes and those in other OECD countries, see OECD (1982).

41. This raises the question of what happens to the worker at the end of the period of subsidisation. It is possible that he or she will be dismissed only for the employer to hire another unemployed worker and receive the subsidy for a further period. This possibility highlights the difficulty of creating subsidies which genuinely relate to additional *net* employment. However, during the subsidised period the worker will have acquired skills, some of them firm specific. If the subsidy has been set correctly the acquired skills should make it more profitable for the firm to retain the worker at the unsubsidised wage than it would be to dismiss the worker and take on another subsidised, but less productive, recruit.

42. The subsidy in Figure 8.7 is a fixed percentage subsidy per worker. The reader may wish to draw a version of the figure in which the subsidy is set as a fixed percentage of the wage bill of workers recruited beyond N^*.

43. While statistical correlations between unemployment and indicators of ill-health, mortality, suicide, family breakdown, etc. are well established, the direction of causality is more difficult to pin down; it could be, for example, that ill health causes unemployment, not vice versa. Evidence that spouses and children of the unemployed have poorer health than spouses and children of the employed helps to establish the direction of causality from unemployment to ill health — the reverse causation is less credible in this case. For a summary of the evidence relating to the UK, and further references, see Jackman (1986).

44. The lower levels of long-term unemployment in the US and Canada relative to most Western European countries reflect in part the lower levels of public assistance for the long-term unemployed in North America.

45. At the end of the previous chapter we argued that the extent to which firms are prepared to replace their existing labour force with cheaper recruits from the unemployed is limited by adjustment costs (hiring and firing costs), by efficiency wage considerations (e.g. unwillingness to damage the firm's reputation as a good employer), as well as by social custom and convention and institutional impediments.

46. One method of testing this proposition would be to estimate an equation of the form

$$w = \alpha_0 - \alpha_1 U + \alpha_2\left(\frac{U_L}{U}\right) + \alpha_3 \mathbf{Z}_w$$

where w = real wage
U = total unemployment
U_L/U = share of long-term unemployment in total unemployment
$\mathbf{Z}_w$ = the vector of other wage push variables

(This equation can be thought of as an adaptation of the wage equation in Appendix 8.2, with the term P/P_e now included in the $\mathbf{Z}_w$ vector.) The equation says that, for a given level of unemployment, downward wage pressure is reduced the higher is the proportion of long-term unemployment. Conversely a reduction in the proportion of long-term unemployment will increase the downward pressure on wages exerted by a given level of unemployment. Layard and Nickell (1985a) estimate an equation similar to the above for Britain. Their version is estimated in log-linear form, with the logarithm of the unemployment rate replacing U in the second term. Thus the coefficient α_1 is the elasticity of the real wage with respect to the unemployment rate. This modification of the wage equation attempts to capture the notion that unions are concerned about their members, who are the employed, the 'insiders', rather than about the unemployed, the 'outsiders'. Wage moderation is only required to offset an *increase* in the probability of insiders losing their jobs and becoming outsiders, i.e. is only required when unemployment is increasing. Stable unemployment, no matter how high, will not, on average, reduce the number of insiders, so the latter group have no incentive to reduce real wages. In the estimated equation, the coefficient on the U_L/U variable is positive and statistically significant, implying that policies aimed at reducing long-term unemployment will, *ceteris paribus*, reduce wage inflation. High and growing long-term unemployment is a major factor explaining why wage inflation in the UK has remained relatively high (and stable) in the first half of the 1980s.

47. Apart from increased hiring and training costs firms will face increased costs if hours and workers ar not perfect substitutes in production, and/or if payroll taxes increase less than proportionately with hours per worker. An example of cost increases of the first type is where the production technology is such that there is a 'warm-up' period required for each worker to reach full productivity. An example of the second type would be the UK system of National Insurance contributions which are proportional to earnings, but subject to an upper limit. In such circumstances job sharing will increase labour costs if a single full-time worker earning more than the upper limit for NI contributions is replaced by two half-time job sharers for whom contributions are not constrained by the upper limit. Early retirement should not impose any of these costs because it does not affect work organisation.

48. Layard (1985a, p. 178) cites evidence showing that hours per worker have no effect on wage bargains once the level of unemployment has been controlled.

49. See Best (1981) for a discussion of work sharing in the US.

50. For example Drèze (1986) notes that while the French '*Contrats de Solidarité*' programme offered such inducements, 'out of some 12 500 contracts signed by September 30, 1982, only 4.5% were concerned with education in working time, and 10 times as many new hirings resulted from early retirement as from shorter hours'.

51. This equation is derived formally and explained in more detail in Bruno and Sachs (1985).

52. Because WG is defined as $[(W/P) - (W/P)_f]/(W/P)_f$, a 1 per cent decrease means WG falls by 0.01. Thus

$$\Delta U_t = \hat{\beta}_2 \Delta \text{WG} = \hat{\beta}_2(-0.01)$$

53. $\Delta U_t = \left(\dfrac{\hat{\beta}_2}{(1 - \hat{\beta}_1)} \right) \Delta \text{WG}_{1981}$

$= \left(\dfrac{21.97}{1 - 0.63} \right) (-0.193) = -11.5\%$

54. In the diagram the aggregate demand side of the model has been suppressed. It could be included by drawing the (un)employment equation as an upward sloping line, which in full equilibrium must pass through the same point at which the feasible and target wage lines intersect.

Bibliography

Aaron, H. and Burtless, G. (eds) (1984) *Retirement and Economic Behaviour*, The Brooking Institution.

Addison, J. and Siebert, W.S. (1979) *The Market For Labor: An Analytical Treatment*, Goodyear.

Allen, R.G.D. (1938) *Mathematical Analysis For Economists*, Macmillan.

Allen, S.G. (1984) 'Unionised construction workers are more productive', *Quarterly Journal of Economics*, vol. 99, pp. 251–274.

Andrews, M.J. (1986) 'Empirical models of the UK aggregate labour market: a survey', *Economic Perspectives*, vol. 4, pp. 175–223.

Arrow, K.J. (1959) 'Towards a theory of price adjustment', in M. Abramovitz (ed.) *The Allocation of Economic Resources*, Stanford University Press.

Arrow, K.J. (1973) 'Higher education as a filter', *Journal of Public Economics*, vol. 2, pp. 193–216.

Arrow, K., Chenery, H., Minhas, B. and Solow, R. (1961) 'Capital–labour substitution and economic efficiency', *Review of Economics and Statistics*, vol. 43, pp. 225–250.

Arrufat, J.L. and Zabalza, A. (1983) 'Female labour supply with taxation, random preferences and optimization errors', Discussion Paper No. 174, London School of Economics, Centre for Labour Economics.

Ashenfelter, O. (1972) 'Racial discrimination and trade unions', *Journal of Political Economy*, vol. 80, pp. 435–464.

Ashenfelter, O. (1978) 'Unemployment as a constraint on labour market behaviour' in M.J. Artis, and A.R. Nobay (eds) *Contemporary Economic Analysis*, Croom-Helm.

Ashenfelter, O. (1980) 'Unemployment as disequilibrium in a model of aggregate labour supply', *Econometrica*, vol. 48, pp. 547–564.

Ashenfelter, O. and Heckman, J. (1974) 'The estimation of income and substitution effects in a model of family labor supply', *Econometrica*, vol. 42, pp. 73–85.

Ashenfelter, O. and Pencavel, J. (1969) 'American trade union growth: 1900–1960' *Quarterly Journal of Economics*, vol. 83, pp. 434–448.

Ashworth, J.S. and Ulph, D.T. (1981) 'Household models', in C.V. Brown (ed.) *Taxation and Labour Supply*, George Allen and Unwin, Ch. 9.

Atkinson, A.B. (1981) 'Unemployment benefits and incentives', in J. Creedy (ed.) *The Economics of Unemployment in Britain*, Butterworths.

Atkinson, A.B. and Micklewright, J. (1985) *Unemployment Benefits and Unemployment Duration*, Suntory-Toyota International Centre for Economics and Related Disciplines, The London School of Economics and Political Science.

Atkinson, A.B., King, M.A. and Sutherland, H. (1983) 'The analysis of personal taxation and social security', *National Institute of Economic and Social Research Review*,
no. 106, pp. 63–74.

Azariadis, C. (1975) 'Implicit contracts and underemployment equilibria', *Journal of
Political Economy*, vol. 83, pp. 1183–1202.

Baily, M.N. (1974) 'Wages and employment under uncertain demand', *Review of Economic
Studies*, vol. 41, pp. 37–50.

Baily, M.N. (1977) 'On the theory of layoffs and unemployment', *Econometrica*, vol.
45, pp. 1043–1063.

Baily, M.N. and Tobin, J. (1977) 'Macroeconomic effects of selective public employment and wage subsidies', *Brooking Papers on Economic Activity*, vol. 2, pp. 511–541.

Bain, G. and Elsheikh, F. (1976) *Union Growth and the Business Cycle*, Basil Blackwell.

Ball, R.J. and St Cyr, E.B.A. (1966) 'Short term employment functions in British manufacturing industry', *Review of Economic Studies*, vol. 33, pp. 179–207.

Barro, R.J. and Grossman, H. (1976) *Money, Employment and Inflation*, Cambridge
University Press.

Baumol, W.J. (1958) 'On the theory of oligopoly', *Economica*, vol. 25, pp. 187–198.

Becker, G. (1957) *The Economics of Discrimination*, University of Chicago Press.

Becker, G.S. (1964) *Human Capital*, Columbia University Press (for NBER); 2nd edn,
1975.

Becker, G.S. (1965) 'A theory of the allocation of time', *The Economic Journal*, vol.
75, pp. 493–517.

Becker, G.S. (1974) 'A theory of social interactions', *Journal of Political Economy*, vol.
82, pp. 1063–1093.

Benjamin, D.K. and Kochin, L.A. (1979) 'Searching for an explanation of unemployment in interwar Britain', *Journal of Political Economy*, vol. 87, no. 3, June, pp.
441–478.

Ben-Porath, Y. (1967) 'The production of human capital and the life cycle of earnings',
Journal of Political Economy, vol. 75, pp. 352–365.

Ben-Porath, Y. (1970) 'The production of human capital over time', in W. Lee Hansen
(ed.) *Education, Income and Human Capital*, NBER/Columbia University Press.

Best, F. (1981) *Worksharing: Issues, Policy Options and Prospects*, Upjohn, Kalamazoo,
Michigan.

Blundell, R.W. and Walker, I. (1984a) 'Empirical approaches to life cycle labour supply',
University of Manchester Econometrics Discussion Paper ES149.

Blundell, R.W. and Walker, I. (1984b) 'A life cycle consistent empirical model of labour
supply using cross section data', University of Manchester Econometric Discussion
Paper ES154.

Blundell, R.W. and Walker, I. (eds) (1986) *Unemployment, Search and Labour Supply*,
Cambridge University Press.

Blundell, R.W., Ham, J.C. and Meghir, C. (1987) 'Unemployment and female labour
supply', *The Economic Journal*, vol. 97, Supplement (Conference Papers), pp. 44–64.

Blundell, R.W., Meghir, C., Symons, E. and Walker, I. (1984) 'A labour supply model
for the simulation of tax and benefit reforms', in R.W. Blundell and I. Walker (eds)
(1986) *Unemployment, Search and Labour Supply*, Cambridge University Press, Ch. 13.

Boskin, M.J. and Hurd, M.D. (1978) 'The effect of social security on early retirement',
Journal of Public Economics, vol. 10, pp. 361–377.

Bowles, S. (1970) 'Aggregation of labor inputs in the economics of growth and planning:
experiments with a two level CES function', *Journal of Political Economy*, vol. 78,
pp. 68–81.

Bowles, S. (1973) 'Understanding unequal educational opportunity', *American Economic
Review* (Papers and Proceedings), vol. 63, pp. 346–356.

Bratt, C. (1982) *Labour Relations in 17 Countries*, Swedish Employers Federation,
Stockholm.

Break, G.F. (1957) 'Income taxes and incentives to work: an empirical study', *American Economic Review*, vol. 47, pp. 529–549.

Brechling, F. (1965) 'The relationship between output and employment in British manufacturing industries, *Review of Economic Studies*, vol. 32, pp. 187–216.

Brown, C.V. (ed) (1981) *Taxation and Labour Supply*, George Allen and Unwin.

Brown, C.V. and Levin, E. (1974) 'The effects of income taxation on overtime: the results of a national survey', *Economic Journal*, vol. 84, pp. 833–848.

Brown, C. and Medoff, J. (1978) 'Trade unions in the production process', *Journal of Political Economy*, vol. 86, pp. 355–378.

Brown, C.V., Levin, E. and Ulph, D.T. (1976) 'Estimates of labour hours supplied by married male workers in Great Britain', *Scottish Journal of Political Economy*, vol. 23, pp. 261–277.

Brown, M. (1966) *On the Theory and Measurement of Technical Change*, Macmillan.

Browning, E.K. (1985) 'A critical appraisal of Hausman's welfare cost estimates', *Journal of Political Economy*, vol. 93, pp. 1025–1034.

Bruno, M.N. and Sachs, J. (1985) *Economics of Worldwide Stagflation*, Basil Blackwell.

Burtless, G. and Hausman, J.A. (1978) 'The effect of taxation on labor supply: evaluating the Gary Indiana negative income tax experiment', *Journal of Political Economy*, vol. 86, pp. 1103–30.

Cain, G.G. (1976) 'The challenge of segmented labour market theories to orthodox theories: a review', *Journal of Economic Literature*, vol. 14, pp. 1215–1257.

Cain, G.G. (1986) 'The economic analysis of labor market discrimination: a survey', in O. Ashenfelter and P.R.G. Layard (eds) *Handbook of Labor Economics*, Elsevier.

Cain, G.G. and Watts, H.W. (eds) (1973) *Income Maintenance and Labor Supply*, Academic Press.

Cairnes, J.E. (1874) *Some Leading Principles of Political Economy Newly Expounded*, Macmillan.

Cameron, G.C. (1965) 'The growth of holidays with pay in Britain', in G.L. Reid and D.J. Robertson (eds) *Fringe Benefits, Labour Costs and Social Security*, George Allen and Unwin.

Carruth, A. and Oswald, A. (1985) 'Miners' wages in post-war Britain: an application of a model trade union behaviour', *Economic Journal*, vol. 95, pp. 1003–1020.

Carruth, A. and Oswald, A. (1987) 'On union preferences and labour market models: insiders and outsiders', *Economic Journal*, vol. 97, pp. 431–445.

Chiplin, B. and Sloane, P.J. (1976) *Sex Discrimination in the Labour Market*, Macmillan.

Chiswick, B.R. (1973) 'Racial discrimination and the labor market: a test of alternative hypotheses', *Journal of Political Economy*, vol. 81, pp. 1330–1352.

Clark, K.B. (1980) 'Unionisation and productivity: micro-econometric evidence', *Quarterly Journal of Economics*, vol. 95, pp. 613–639.

Clark, K.B. and Freeman, R. (1980) 'How elastic is the demand for labour?', *Review of Economics and Statistics*, vol. 62, pp. 509–520.

Clark, K.B. and Summers, L.H. (1979) 'Labor market dynamics and unemployment: a reconsideration', *Brookings Papers on Economic Activity*, 1979 (1) pp. 13–60.

Clark, K.B. and Summers, L.H. (1982) 'Unemployment insurance and labor market transitions', in M.N. Baily (ed.) *Workers, Jobs, and Inflation*, The Brookings Institution.

Coen, R. and Hickman, B. (1970) 'Constrained joint maximisation of factor demand and production functions', *Review of Economics and Statistics*, vol. 52, pp. 287–300.

Cogan, J.J. (1981) 'Fixed costs and labor supply', *Econometrica*, vol. 49, pp. 945–964.

Collier, P. and Knight, J.B. (1986) 'Wage structure and labour turnover', *Oxford Economic Papers*, vol. 38, pp. 77–93.

Collier, P. and Lal, D. (1986) *Labour and Poverty in Kenya 1900–1980*, Clarendon Press.

Comanor, W.S. (1973) 'Racial discrimination in American industry', *Economica*, vol. 40, pp. 363–378.

Craine, R. (1973) 'On the service flow from labour', *Review of Economic Studies*, vol. 40, pp. 39−46.

Cyert, R.M. and March, J.G. (1963) *A Behavioural Theory of the Firm*, Prentice-Hall.

Darby, M.R. (1976) 'Three-and-a-half million US employees have been mislaid: or, an explanation of unemployment 1934−41', *Journal of Political Economy*, vol. 84, pp. 1−16.

DeFina, R. (1983) 'Unions, relative wages and economic efficiency', *Journal of Labour Economics*, vol. 1, pp. 408−429.

Denison, E.F. (1967) *Why Growth Rates Differ*, Brookings Institution.

Doeringer, P. and Piore, M. (1971) *Internal Labour Markets and Manpower Analysis*, Lexington.

Dornbusch, R. and Fischer, S. (1987) *Macroeconomics 4th edition*, McGraw-Hill.

Dougherty, C.R.S. (1972) 'Estimates of labour aggregation functions', *Journal of Political Economy*, vol. 80, pp. 1101−1119.

Drèze, J.H. (1986) 'Work-sharing: some theory and recent European experience', *Economic Policy*, no. 3, October, pp. 562−619.

Fair, R.C. (1969) *The Short-Run Demand for Workers and Hours*, North-Holland.

Fallick, J.L. and Elliot, R.F. (eds) (1981) *Incomes Policies, Inflation and Relative Pay*, George Allen and Unwin.

Fallon, P.R. and Layard, P.R.G. (1975) 'Capital−skill complementarity, income distribution and output accounting', *Journal of Political Economy*, vol. 83, pp. 279−301.

Feldstein, M.S. (1967) 'Specification of the labor input in the aggregate production function', *Review of Economic Studies*, vol. 34, pp. 375−386.

Feldstein, M.S. (1975) 'The importance of temporary layoffs: an empirical analysis', *Brookings Papers on Economic Activity*, vol. 3, pp. 725−745.

Feldstein, M.S. (1976) 'Temporary layoffs in the theory of unemployment', *Journal of Political Economy*, vol. 84, pp. 937−957.

Fields, D.B. and Stanbury, W.T. (1971) 'Income taxes and incentives to work: some additional empirical evidence', *American Economic Review*, vol. 61. pp. 435−443.

Fleisher, B.M. and Kniesner, T.J. (1980) *Labour Economics*, 2nd edn, Prentice-Hall.

Freeman, R. (1978) 'A fixed effect logit model of the impact of unionism on quits', *NBER Working Paper No. 280*, National Bureau of Economic Research.

Freeman, R.B. (1980) 'The exit−voice tradeoff in the labor market: unionism, job tenure, quits and separations', *Quarterly Journal of Economics*, vol. 94, pp. 643−673.

Friedman, M. (1949) 'The Marshallian demand curve', *Journal of Political Economy*, vol. 57, pp. 463−495.

Friedman, M. (1951) 'Some comments on the significance of labour unions for economic policy', in McCord Wright (ed.) *The Impact of the Union* , Harcourt Brace Jovanovich.

Friedman, M. (1953) *Essays in Positive Economics*, University of Chicago Press.

Fuji, E.T. and Trapani, J.M. (1978) 'On estimating the relationship between discrimination and market structure', *Southern Economic Journal*, vol. 45, pp. 556−567.

Glaister, K.W., McGlone, A. and Ulph, D.T. (1981) 'Labour supply responses to tax changes: a simulation exercise for the UK', in C.V. Brown (ed.) *Taxation and Labour Supply*, George Allen and Unwin, Ch. 12.

Goldfarb, R.S. and Hosek, J.R. (1976) 'Explaining male−female wage differentials for the same job', *Journal of Human Resources*, vol. 11, pp. 98−108.

Gordon, D.F. (1974) 'A neoclassical theory of Keynesian unemployment', *Economic Inquiry*, vol. 12, pp. 431−459.

Gordon, R. (1986) 'Wage and price dynamics inside and outside of manufacturing in Europe, the US and Japan', Paper presented to Workshop at Centre for Labour Economics, LSE, June.

Gordon, R.H. and Blinder, A.S. (1980) 'Market wages, reservation wages and retirement decisions', *Journal of Public Economics*, vol. 14, pp. 277−308.

Greenhalgh, C. (1980) 'Male–female wage differentials in Great Britain: is marriage an equal opportunity?' *Economic Journal*, vol. 90, pp. 651–775.

Griliches, Z. (1969) 'Capital–skill complementarity', *Review of Economics and Statistics*, vol. 51, pp. 465–468.

Griliches, Z. (1977) 'Estimating the returns to schooling: some econometric problems', *Econometrica*, vol. 45, pp. 1–22.

Griliches, Z. and Mason, W.M. (1972) 'Education, income and ability', *Journal of Political Economy*, vol. 80, pp. 74–103.

Gronau, R. (1977) 'Leisure, home production and work — the theory of the allocation of time revisited', *Journal of Political Economy*, vol. 85, no. 6 (December) pp. 1099–1123.

Grubb, D., Jackman, R. and Layard, R. (1983) 'Wage rigidity and unemployment in OECD countries', *European Economic Review*, March/April, pp. 11–39.

Gujarati, D. (1972) 'Behaviour of unemployment and unfilled vacancies', *Economic Journal*, vol. 82, pp. 195–204.

Haessel, W. and Palmer, J. (1978) 'Market power and employment discrimination', *Journal of Human Resources*, vol. 13, pp. 545–560.

Hahn, F.H. (1977) 'Exercises in conjectural equilibria', *Scandanavian Journal of Economics*, vol. 79, pp. 210–226.

Hahn, F.H. (1978) 'On Walrasian equilibria', *Review of Economic Studies*, vol. 45, pp. 1–17.

Hahn, R.H. (1980) 'Unemployment from a theoretical point of view', *Economica*, vol. 47, pp. 285–298.

Hahn, F.H. (1987) 'On involuntary unemployment', *Economic Journal*, vol. 97 (conference volume), pp. 1–16.

Hall, R.E. (1973) 'Wages, income and hours of work in the US labor force', in G.G. Cain and H.W. Watts (eds) *Income Maintenance and Labor Supply*, Academic Press, pp. 102–162.

Hall, R.E. (1980) 'Employment fluctuations and wage rigidity', *Brookings Papers on Economic Activity* (1), pp. 91–123.

Hall, R.E. (1982) 'The importance of lifetime jobs in the US economy', *American Economic Review*, vol. 72, pp. 716–724.

Hall, S. *et al.* (1987) 'The UK labour market: equilibrium or disequilibrium?', *Lloyds Bank Review*, no. 165, pp. 27–39.

Hamermesh, D.S. (1986) 'The demand for labor in the long run', in O. Ashenfelter and R. Layard (eds) *Handbook of Labour Economics*, Elsevier.

Hamermesh, D.S. and Rees, A. (1984) *The Economics of Work and Pay*, 3rd edn, Harper and Row.

Hanoch, G. (1980) 'A multivariate model of labor supply: methodology and estimation', in J.P. Smith (ed.) *Female Labor Supply: Theory and Estimation*, Princeton University Press, Ch. 6.

Hart, O.D. (1983) 'Optimal labour contracts under asymmetric information: an introduction', *Review of Economic Studies*, vol. 50, no. 1, pp. 3–35.

Hashimoto, M. (1979) 'Bonus payments, on-the-job training, and lifetime employment in Japan', *Journal of Political Economy*, vol. 87, pp. 1086–1104.

Hatton, T.J. (1986) 'The analysis of unemployment in interwar Britain: a survey of research', *Economic Perspectives*, vol. 4, pp. 225–282.

Hausman, J.A. (1980) 'The effect of wages, taxes and fixed costs on women's labor force participation', *Journal of Public Economics*, vol. 14, pp. 161–194.

Hausman, J.A. (1981) 'Labor supply', in H. Aaron and J. Pechman (eds) *How Taxes Affect Economic Behaviour*, Brookings Institution.

Haveman, R.H. and Palmer, J.L. (1982) *Jobs for Disadvantaged Workers — The Economics of Employment Subsidies*, Brookings Institution.

Hazledine, T. (1978) 'New specifications for employment and hours functions', *Economica*, vol. 45, pp. 179–193.

Hazledine, T. and Watts, I. (1977) 'Short-term production functions and economic measures of capacity for UK manufacturing industries, *Oxford Bulletin of Economics and Statistics*, vol. 39, pp. 273–289.

Heckman, J.J. (1974) 'Shadow prices, market wages and labor supply', *Econometrica*, vol. 42, pp. 679–694.

Heckman, J.J. (1976a) 'The common structure of statistical models of truncation, sample selection and limited dependent variables and a simple estimator for such models', *Annals of Economic and Social Measurement*, vol. 5, pp. 475–492.

Heckman, J.J. (1976b) 'A life cycle model of earnings, learning and consumption', *Journal of Political Economy* (supplement), vol. 84, pp. 511–544.

Heckman, J.J. (1980) 'Sample selection bias as a specification error', in J.P. Smith (ed.) *Female Labor Supply: Theory and Estimation*, Princeton University Press.

Heckman, J.J. and MaCurdy, T.E. (1980) 'A life cycle model of female labor supply', *Review of Economic Studies*, vol. 47, pp. 47–74.

Heckman, J.J., Killingsworth, M.R. and MaCurdy, T.E. (1981) 'Empirical evidence on static labour supply models: a survey of recent developments', in Z. Hornstein, J. Grice and A. Webb (eds) *The Economics of the Labour Market*, HMSO.

Hicks, J.R. (1932) *The Theory of Wages*, Macmillan.

Hicks, J.R. (1970) 'Elasticities of substitution again: substitutes and complements', *Oxford Economic Papers*, vol. 22, pp. 289–296.

Hultgren, T. (1960) *Changes in Labor Cost during Cycles in Production and Business*, National Bureau of Economic Research, Occasional paper 74.

Hutt, W.H. (1939) *The Theory of Idle Resources*, Jonathan Cape.

Intriligator, M.D. (1971) *Mathematical Optimisation and Economic Theory*, Prentice-Hall.

Ireland, N.J. and Smyth, D.J. (1970) 'Specification of short-run employment models', *Review of Economic Studies*, vol. 37, pp. 281–285.

Jackman, R.A. (1986) *A Job Guarantee for the Long-Term Unemployed*, Employment Institute/Charter for Jobs, London.

Jackman, R.A. and Layard, P.R.G. (1986) 'The economic effects of a tax-based incomes policy', in D. Colander (ed.) *Incentive-Based Incomes Policies*, Ballinger.

Jackman, R.A., Layard, P.R.G. and Pissarides, C. (1985) 'On vacancies', London School of Economics, Centre for Labour Economics Discussion Paper 165.

Johansen, L. (1972) *Production Functions*, North-Holland.

Johnson, G.E. and Layard, P.R.G. (1986) 'The natural rate of unemployment: explanation and policy', in O. Ashenfelter and P.R.G. Layard (eds) *Handbook of Labor Economics*, Elsevier.

Johnson, H. and Mieszkowski, P. (1970) 'The effects of unionisation on the distribution of income: a general equilibrium approach', *Quarterly Journal of Economics*, vol. 84, pp. 539–561.

Johnston, J. (1984) *Econometric Methods*, McGraw-Hill.

Joshi, H.E., Layard, P.R.G. and Owen, S.J. (1985) 'Why are more women working in Britain?' *Journal of Labor Economics*, vol. 3, no. 1, Part 2, pp. S147–S176.

Kahn, L. (1977) 'Union impact: a reduced form approach', *Review of Economics and Statistics*, vol. 54, pp. 503–507.

Keeley, M., Robins, P.K., Spiegleman, R.G. and West, R. (1978) 'The labor supply effects and costs of alternative negative income tax programs', *Journal of Human Resources*, vol. 11, pp. 526–545.

Kehrer, K.C., McDonald, J. and Moffitt, R. (1980) *Final Report of the Gary Income Maintenance Experiment: Labor Supply*, Mathematica Policy Research.

Kiefer, N.M. and Neuman, G.R. (1979) 'An empirical job search model with a test of the constant reservation wage hypothesis', *Journal of Political Economy*, vol. 87, pp. 89–108.

Killingsworth, M.R. (1983) *Labor Supply*, Cambridge University Press.

Kindleberger, C.P. (1973) *The World in Depression*, University of California Press.

Kniesner, T.J. (1976) 'The full-time work week in the United States, 1900–1970', *Industrial and Labor Relations Review*, vol. 30, pp. 3–15.

Kosters, M. (1966) *Income and Substitution Effects in a Family Labor Supply Model*, Rand Corporation.

Kuh, E. (1965) 'Cyclical and secular labor productivity in United States manufacturing', *Review of Economics and Statistics*, vol. 47, pp. 1–12.

Lancaster, T. and Nickell, S.J. (1980) 'The analysis of re-employment probabilities for the unemployed', *Journal of the Royal Statistical Society*, Series A, vol. 143, pp. 141–165.

Layard, P.R.G. (1986) *How to Beat Unemployment*, Oxford University Press.

Layard, P.R.G. and Nickell, S.J. (1980) 'The case for subsidizing extra jobs', *Economic Journal*, vol. 90, pp. 51–73.

Layard, P.R.G. and Nickell, S.J. (1985a) 'Unemployment, real wages and aggregate demand in Europe, Japan and the US', Centre for Labour Economics, London School of Economics Discussion Paper No. 214.

Layard, P.R.G. and Nickell, S.J. (1985b) 'The causes of British unemployment', *National Institute Economic Review*, February, pp. 62–85.

Layard, P.R.G. and Nickell, S.J. (1986) *An Incomes Policy to Help the Unemployed*, Employment Institute/Charter for Jobs.

Layard, P.R.G. and Psacharopoulos, G. (1974) 'The screening hypothesis and the returns to education', *Journal of Political Economy*, vol. 82, pp. 985–998.

Layard, P.R.G., Metcalf, D. and Nickell, S. (1978) 'The effect of collective bargaining on relative and absolute wages', *British Journal of Industrial Relations*, vol. 16, pp. 287–302.

Lazear, E.P. (1979) 'Why is there mandatory retirement?' *Journal of Political Economy*, vol. 87, pp. 1261–1284.

Lazear, E.P. (1983) 'A micro-economic theory of labor unions', in J. Reid (ed.) *New Approaches to Labor Unions*, Jai Press, Conneticut.

Lee, L.F. (1978) 'Unionism and wage rates: a simultaneous equations model with qualitative and limited dependent variables', *International Economic Review*, vol. 19, pp. 415–433.

Leibenstein, H. (1957) *Economic Backwardness and Economic Growth*, Wiley.

Leslie, D. and Laing, C. (1978) 'The theory and measurement of labour hoarding', *Scottish Journal of Political Economy*, vol. 25, pp. 41–56.

Leslie, D.G. and Wise, J. (1980) 'The productivity of hours in UK manufacturing and production industries', *Economic Journal*, vol. 90, pp. 74–84.

Leuthold, J.H. (1968) 'An empirical study of formula income transfers and the work decision of the poor', *Journal of Human Resources*, vol. 3, pp. 312–323.

Lewis, H.G. (1963) *Unionism and Relative Wages in the United States*, University of Chicago Press.

Lewis, H.G. (1986) 'Union relative wage effects', in O. Ashenfelter and P.R.G. Layard (eds) *Handbook of Labor Economics*, vol. 2, Elsevier.

Lillard, L. and Willis, R.J. (1978) 'Dynamic aspects of earnings mobility', *Econometrica*, vol. 46, pp. 985–1012.

Lindsay, C.M. (1976) 'A theory of government enterprise', *Journal of Political Economy*, vol. 84, (Dec.), pp. 1061–1077.

Lippman, S.A. and McCall, J.J. (1976) 'The economics of job search: a survey. Parts I and II', *Economic Inquiry*, vol. 14, pp. 155–189 and 347–368.

Lucas, R.E.B. (1977) 'Hedonic wage equations and psychic wages in the returns to schooling', *American Economic Review*, vol. 64, pp. 549–558.

Lucas, R.E. and Rapping, L. (1969) 'Real wages, employment and inflation', *Journal of Political Economy*, vol. 77, pp. 721–754.

McCall, J.J. (1970) 'Economics of information and job search', *Quarterly Journal of Economics*, vol. 84, pp. 113–126.

MaCurdy, T. and Pencavel, J. (1986) 'Testing between competing models of wage an employment determination in unionized market', *Journal of Political Economy*, vol. 94, pp. 53–39.

McDonald, I.M. and Solow, R.M. (1981) 'Wage bargaining and employment', *American Economic Review*, vol. 71, pp. 896–908.

MacKay, D.I. (1970) 'Wages and labour turnover', in D. Robinson (ed.) *Local Labour Markets and Wage Structure*, Gower Press.

Maddala, G. (1977) *Econometrics*, McGraw-Hill.

Maddison, A. (1980) 'Measuring labour slack' *Employment Gazette*, (July), HMSO.

Main, B.G.M. (1982) 'The length of a job in Great Britain', *Economica*, vol. 49, pp. 325–333.

Maki, D. and Spindler, Z.A. (1975) 'The effect of unemployment compensation on the rate of unemployment in Great Britain', *Oxford Economic Papers*, vol. 29, pp. 128–140.

Malinvaud, E. (1977) *The Theory of Unemployment Reconsidered*, Basil Blackwell.

Malinvaud, E. (1984) *Mass Unemployment*, Basil Blackwell.

Marris, R. (1964) *The Economic Theory of 'Managerial' Capitalism*, Macmillan.

Marshall, A. (1920) *Principles of Economics*, 8th edn, Macmillan.

Medoff, M.H. (1978) 'On estimating the relationship between discrimination and market structure: a comment', *Southern Economic Journal*, vol. 46, pp. 1227–1234.

Melino, A. (1982) 'Testing for sample selection bias', *Review of Economic Studies*, vol. XLIX, pp. 151–153.

Metcalf, C. (1974) 'Predicting the effects of permanent programs from a limited duration experiment', *Journal of Human Resources*, vol. 9, pp. 530–555.

Metcalf, D., Nickell, S.J. and Fioros, N.L. (1982) 'Still searching for an explanation of unemployment in interwar Britain', *Journal of Political Economy*, vol. 90, no. 2, pp. 386–399.

Mincer, J. (1974) *Schooling Experience and Earnings*, NBER.

Minford, P. (1985) *Unemployment, Cause and Cure*, 2nd edn, Blackwell.

Mitchell, O.S. and Fields, G.S. (1984) 'The economics of retirement behaviour', *Journal of Labor Economics*, vol. 2, no. 1, pp. 84–105.

Moffitt, R. and Kehrer, K.C. (1981) 'The effect of tax and transfer programs on labour supply: the evidence from the income maintenance experiment', in R.G. Ehrenberg (ed.) *Research in Labour Economics*, vol. 4, JAI Press, pp. 103–150.

Morishima, M. (1969) *The Theory of Economic Growth*, Clarendon Press.

Moylan, S., Millar, J. and Davies, B. (1982) 'Unemployment — the year after', *Employment Gazette*, August, pp. 334–340.

Mulvey, C. (1976) 'Collective bargaining and relative earnings in UK manufacturing in 1973', *Economica*, vol. 43, pp. 419–427.

Nadiri, M. (1968) 'The effect of relative prices and capacity in the US manufacturing sector', *Review of Economic Studies*, vol. 35, pp. 273–288.

Narendranathan, W., Nickell, S. and Stern, J. (1985) 'Unemployment benefits revisited', *Economic Journal*, vol. 95, pp. 307–329.

Nash, J.J. (1950) 'The bargaining problem', *Econometrica*, vol. 18, pp. 155–162.

Nerlove, M. (1967) 'Notes on the production and derived demand relations included in macro-econometric models', *International Economic Review*, vol. 8, pp. 223–242.

Neumann, G. and Rissman, E.R. (1984) 'Where have all the union members gone?' *Journal of Labor Economics*, vol. 2, pp. 175–192.

Nickell, S.J. (1977) 'Trade unions and the position of women in the wage structure', *British Journal of Industrial Relations*, vol. 15, pp. 192–210.

Nickell, S. (1979) 'Education and lifetime patterns of unemployment', *Journal of Political Economy*, vol. 87, pp. S117–S131.

Nickell, S. (1984) 'An investigation of the determinants of manufacturing employment in the United Kingdom', *Review of Economic Studies*, vol. 51, pp. 529–557.

Nickell, S.J. (1986) 'Dynamic models of labour demand', in O. Ashenfelter and R. Layard (eds) *Handbook of Labor Economics*, Elsevier.

Nickell, S.J. and Andrews, M. (1983) 'Unions, real wages and employment in Britain 1951–79', *Oxford Economic Papers*, vol. 35, pp. 507–530.

Oi, W.Y. (1962) 'Labor as a quasi-fixed factor', *Journal of Political Economy*, vol. 70, pp. 538–555.

Okun, A.M. (1981) *Prices and Quantities: A Macroeconomic Analysis*, Brookings Institution.

Oster, S.M. (1975) 'Industry differences in the level of discrimination against women', *Quarterly Journal of Economics*, vol. 79, pp. 215–229.

Osterman, P. (1975) 'An empirical study of labor market segmentation', *Industrial and Labor Relations Review*, vol. 28, pp. 508–523.

Oswald, A.J. (1982) 'The microeconomic theory of the trade union', *Economic Journal*, vol. 92, pp. 576–595.

Palmer, J. and Pechman, J.A. (eds) (1978) *Welfare in Rural Areas: The North Carolina–Iowa Income Maintenance Experiment*, Brookings Institution.

Parsons, D.O. (1972) 'Specific human capital: an application to quit rates and lay-off rates', *Journal of Political Economy*, vol. 80, pp.1120–1143.

Parsons, D. (1977) 'Models of labor turnover: a theoretical and empirical survey', in R. Ehrenberg (ed.) *Research in Labor Economics*, vol. 1, Jai Press.

Pencavel, J.H. (1974) 'Relative wages and trade unions in the United Kingdom', *Economica*, vol. 41, pp. 194–210.

Pencavel, J. (1977) 'The distributional and efficiency effects of trade unions in Britain', *British Journal of Industrial Relations*, vol. 15, no. 2, pp. 137–156.

Perloff, J.M. and Wachter, M.L. (1979) 'The new jobs tax credit: an evaluation of the 1977–78 wage subsidy program', *American Economic Review*, Papers and Proceedings, May, pp. 173–179.

Phelps, E.S. (ed.) (1972) *Microeconomic Foundations of Employment and Inflation Theory*, Norton.

Pindyck, R.S. and Rotemberg, J. (1983) 'Dynamic factor demands and the effects of energy price shocks', *American Economic Review*, vol. 75, pp. 1066–1079.

Pissarides, C.A. (1976) *Labour Market Adjustment*, Cambridge University Press.

Pissarides, C.A. (1982) 'From school to university: the demand for post-compulsory education in Britain', *Economic Journal*, vol. 92, pp. 654–667.

Pissarides, C.A. (1985) 'Job search and the functioning of the labour market', in D. Carline *et al.* (eds) *Labour Economics*, Longman.

Psacharopoulos, G. (1972) 'Rates of return to investment in education around the world', *Comparative Education Review*, vol. 16, pp. 54–67.

Psacharopoulos, G. (1981) 'Returns to education: an updated international comparison', *Comparative Education*, vol. 17, pp. 321–341.

Psacharopoulos, G. and Layard, P.R.G. (1979) 'Human capital and earnings: British evidence and a critique', *Review of Economic Studies*, vol. 46, pp. 485–503.

Rau, N. (1985) 'The microeconomic theory of the trade union: a comment', *Economic Journal*, vol. 95, pp. 480–482.

Reder, M.W. (1951) *Labor in a Growing Economy*, John Wiley.

Reder, M.W. (1962) 'Inter-industry wage differentials', in National Bureau of Economic Research, *Aspects of Labor Economics*, NBER.

Rees, A. (1963) 'The effects of unions on resource allocation', *Journal of Law and Economics*, vol. 6, pp. 69–78.

Reid, F. (1981) 'Control and decontrol of wages in the UK', *American Economic Review*, vol. 71, pp. 108–120.

Riley, J. (1979) 'Testing the educational screening hypothesis', *Journal of Political Economy*, vol. 87, pp. 227–252.

Robins, P.K., Spiegleman, R.G., Weiner, S. and Bell, J.G. (eds) (1980) *A Guaranteed Annual Income: Evidence from a Social Experiment*, Academic Press.

Rosen, S. (1968) 'Short run employment variation on class I railroads in the US 1947–1963', *Econometrica*, vol. 36, pp. 511–529.

Rosen, S. (1976) 'A theory of life earnings', *Journal of Political Economy*, (Supplement) pp. 543–568.

Rosen, S. (1985) 'Implicit contracts: a survey', *Journal of Economic Literature*, vol. 23, pp. 1144–1175.

Rosen, S. and Quandt, R. (1978) 'Estimation of a disequilibrium aggregate labor market', *Review of Economics and Statistics*, vol. 60, pp. 511–529.

Rothschild, M. (1974) 'Searching for the lowest price when the distribution of prices is unknown', *Journal of Political Economy*, vol. 82, pp. 689–711.

Rottenberg, S. (1956) 'The baseball players labor market', *Journal of Political Economy*, June, pp. 242–258.

Routh, G. (1980) *Occupation and Pay in Great Britain 1906–79*, Macmillan.

Rumberger, R.W. and Carnoy, M. (1975) 'Segmentation in the US labour market: its effects on the mobility and earnings of whites and blacks', *Cambridge Journal of Economics*, vol. 4, pp. 117–132.

Sargent, T. (1978) 'Estimation of dynamic labor demand schedules under rational expectations', *Journal of Political Economy*, vol. 86, pp. 1009–1044.

Sato, R. (1967) 'A two-level CES production function', *Review of Economic Studies*, vol. 34, pp. 201–218.

Sato, R. and Koizumi, T. (1973) 'On the elasticities of substitution and complementarity', *Oxford Economic Papers*, vol. 25, pp. 44–56.

Schultze, C.L. (1985) 'Microeconomic efficiency and nominal wage stickiness', *American Economic Review*, vol. 75, pp. 1–15.

Sen, A. (1973) *On Economic Inequality*, Clarendon Press, Ch. 2.

Shapiro, C. and Stiglitz, J.E. (1984) 'Equilibrium unemployment as a worker discipline device', *American Economic Review*; vol. 74/3, pp. 433–444.

Sheflin, N., Troy, L. and Koeller, C.T. (1981) 'Structural stability in models of American trade union growth', *Quarterly Journal of Economics*, vol. 96, pp. 77–88.

Shepherd, W.G. and Levin, S.G. (1973) 'Managerial discrimination in large firms', *Review of Economics and Statistics*, vol. 55, pp. 412–422.

Shorey, J. (1976) 'An inter-industry analysis of strike frequency', *Economica*, vol. 43, pp. 349–365.

Smee, C. and Stern, J. (1976) 'The unemployed in a period of high unemployment: some notes on characteristics and benefit status', DHSS mimeo.

Smith, J.P. (ed) (1980) *Female Labor Supply: Theory and Estimation*, Princeton University Press.

Smith, J.P. and Ward, M.P. (1985) 'Time series growth in the female labor force', *Journal of Labor Economics*, vol. 3, no. 1, Part 2, pp. 559–590.

Solow, R.M. (1962) 'Substitution and fixed proportions in the theory of capital', *Review of Economic Studies*, vol. 29, pp. 207–218.

Solow, R.M. (1979) 'Alternative approaches to macroeconomic theory: a partial view', *Canadian Journal of Economics*, vol. 12, no. 3, pp. 339–354.

Solow, R.M. (1980) 'On theories of unemployment', *American Economic Review*, vol. 70, pp. 1–11.

Spence, M. (1973) 'Job market signaling', *Quarterly Journal of Economics*, vol. 87, pp. 354–374.

Stern, J. (1979) 'Who bears the burden of unemployment?' Ch. 4 in W. Beckerman (ed.) *Slow Growth in Britain*, Clarendon Press.

Stern, N. (1984) 'On the specification of labour supply functions' in R. Blundell and I. Walker (eds) (1986) *Unemployment, Search and Labour Supply*, Cambridge University Press, Ch. 9.

Stewart, M.B. (1983a) 'Racial discrimination and occupational attainment in Britain', *Economic Journal*, vol. 93, pp. 521–541.

www.nber.org

Stewart, M.B. (1983b) 'Relative earnings and individual union membership in the United Kingdom', *Economica*, vol. 50, pp. 111–125.

Stigler, G.J. (1962) 'Information in the labor market', *Journal of Political Economy*, vol. 70, pp. 94–105.

Stiglitz, J.E. (1984) 'Theories of wage rigidity', Working Paper No. 1442, National Bureau of Economic Research, Cambridge, Mass. HB 3CCNAT

Summers, L.H. (1986) 'Why is the unemployment rate so very high near full employment?', *Brookings Papers on Economic Activity*, 2:86, pp. 338–396.

Symons, J. (1982) 'Relative prices and the demand for labour in British manufacturing', Centre for Labour Economics, Discussion Paper No. 137.

Symons, J. and Layard, P.R.G. (1984) 'Neoclassical demand for labour functions in six OECD countries', *Economic Journal*, vol. 94, pp. 788–799.

Taubman, P. (1976) 'The determinants of earnings: genetics, family and other environments: a study of male twins', *American Economic Review*, vol. 66, pp. 858–870.

Taussig, F.W. (1929) *Principles of Economics*, 3rd edn, Macmillan.

Taylor, J.B. (1983) 'Rational expectations and the divisible handshake', Ch. 3 in J. Tobin (ed.) *Macroeconomics, Prices and Quantities*, Basil Blackwell.

Tobin, J. (ed.) (1983) *Macroeconomics, Prices and Quantities, Essays in Memory of Arthur M. Okun*, Basil Blackwell (US Publisher: Brookings Institution).

Todaro, M.P. (1969) 'A model of labor migration and urban unemployment in less developed countries', *American Economic Review*, vol. 59, pp. 138–148.

Ulman, L. (1955) 'Marshall and Friedman on union strength', *Review of Economics and Statistics*, vol. 37, pp. 384–401.

Viscusi, W.K. (1980) 'Sex difference in workers quitting', *Review of Economics and Statistics*, vol. 62, pp. 388–398.

Wadhwani, S.B. (1985) 'Wage inflation in the United Kingdom', *Economica*, vol. 52, no. 206 (May), pp. 195–207.

Wallich, H. and Weintraub, S. (1971) 'A tax-based incomes policy', *Journal of Economic Issues*, vol. 5, pp. 1–19.

Wallis, K.F. (ed.) (1984) *Models of the UK Economy*, Oxford University Press.

Weiss, Y. (1972) 'On the optimal lifetime pattern of labour supply', *Economic Journal*, vol. 82, pp. 1293–1315.

Weiss, A. (1980) 'Job queues and layoffs in labour markets with flexible wages', *Journal of Political Economy*, vol. 88, pp. 526–538.

Welch, F. (1979) 'Effects of cohort size on earnings: the baby boom's babies financial bust', *Journal of Political Economy*, vol. 87, no. 5 (2), pp. S65–S98.

Williamson, J.H. (1966) 'Profit, growth and sales maximisation', *Economica*, vol. 33 pp. 1–16.

Willis, R.J. (1986) 'Wage determinants: a survey and reinterpretations of human capital earnings functions', in O. Ashenfelter and R. Layard (eds.) *Handbook of Labor Economics*, vol. 1, Elsevier.

Zeuthen, F. (1930) *Problems of Monopoly and Economic Welfare*, Routledge and Kegan Paul.

Central Statistical Office, *Social Trends*, HMSO.

Department of Employment and Productivity (1971) *British Labour Statistics. Historical Abstract 1886–1968*, HMSO.

Department of Employment (annual) *New Earnings Survey*, HMSO.

Department of Employment, *Employment Gazette*, HMSO.

ILO (1985) *Bulletin of Labour Statistics*, Geneva, ILO (57).

National Board for Prices and Incomes (1970) *House of Work, Overtime and Shift-working*, Report No. 161, HMSO.

OECD (1982) *Marginal Employment Subsidies*, OECD, Paris.

OECD (1983) *Employment Outlook*, OECD, Paris.
OECD (1985a) *Economic Outlook*, vol. 37 (June), OECD, Paris.
OECD (1985b) *Employment Outlook*, OECD, Paris.
OECD (1985c) *Labour Force Statistics 1963–1983*, OECD, Paris.
OECD (1986) *Employment Outlook*, OECD, Paris.
OECD (1987) *Employment Outlook*, OECD, Paris.
US Department of Commerce (1984) (Bureau of the Census) *Statistical Abstract of the United States*, 1985.
US Department of Labor (1985) *Employment and Earnings* (January).

Index

Wallis, K., 79
Ward, M.P., 51, 52, 77, 78
Watts, H.W., 43, 78
Watts, I., 120
Weintraub, S., 276
Weiss, A., 233
Weiss, Y., 22
Welch, F., 150

Williamson, O. 95
Willis, R., 150, 151
Wise, J., 119, 120
work sharing, 282–3, 292–3

Zabalza, A., 49, 50
Zeuthen, F., 192